THE END OF THE
ROAD

One Man's Journey Into and Outside of Himself

U.R. MCFARLAND

Cover Design by Alix Locke

Interior design by Booknook.biz

TABLE OF CONTENTS

INTRODUCTION/FOREWORD

You are encouraged to utilize this amusing work as a "how to" or "how not to" book.

For you novice travelers out there seeking a bit of an edge, this book could be your ultimate guide.

For the hoards of you who yearn for adventure but remain hesitant after contemplating potential expenditures anticipated, explore your way through the publication simply to unearth just how far you can go, live well, live comfortably, and live happily ever after on what was once labeled "a shoestring budget."

For those of you who have it but want to keep it for future exploits, you'll be exclaiming, "Why didn't I think of that?" Or, "Hey, I can definitely do that. It'll be fun!"

Some specific "how to's" explored/field tested in the upcoming format deal with highlights such as: begging with dignity and purpose, photographic equipment, pros and cons of traveling alone, vehicular choices, food storage/cooking/refrigeration, personal hygiene products, discretional bathing incentives, portable laundromat, free camping locations, avoiding run-ins with carnivores via handmade deterrents, banking challenges in foreign countries, direction seeking do's and don'ts, profiting from the power of prayer, keeping a promise, avoiding negative confrontations with locals, gravitating toward nirvana, getting the ultimate bang for your buck, coming to grips with reality, embracing mankind, and so on.

As you are about to discover, your author never once entertained the slightest thought of writing a book regarding a journey he took from Western Maryland (USA) northwest to Yellowknife, Northwest Territories (Canada), a distance covering 10,060 miles, most of which occurred on intentionally selected scenic routes over the course of a month in 2016.

A year or so prior to the yearnings to make this excursion, Mr. McFarland shared with me that he had acquired a large photo of Sitting Bull staring directly into the camera that shot him causing his perpetual stare to penetrate clean through any and all viewers forevermore. His gaze remained on the author from the wall to the right as these lines were being written. Could he have been the inspiring push setting U.R. on this journey? He did not know but he hoped so. Powerful good men in life remain powerful good men in death.

This 2016 passage brought forth a book of amusement, luck, direct challenges, philosophy, enlightenment, mystery, guilt, tragedy, depression, elation, hope, and encouragement. The author initially kept a daily journal which much to his enjoyment and surprise metamorphed into this work. At the onset, three throw-away cameras were purchased, each capable of 27 shots. The author calculated that he might use two but surely no more than three. When all was said and done, twelve or so of these throw-aways at 27 shots per clip had snapped away. I personally find myself agreeing with his conclusion that all in all, one can only applaud the attempt of the throw-away to help bring this story to life for you.

First and foremost, U.R. confessed to me that he simply wanted to satisfy a bucket list craving to make a pilgrimage following scenic highways hugging our Great Lakes, trails Lewis and Clark's Corps of Discovery traversed during the infancy of the 1800's, our great West, up the Canadian Rockies, and targeting Yellowknife as our final destination as she lies at the end of a road. Then, south and east again for the trip home.

Other than Lewis and Clark's path along the Missouri River, Yellowknife, Wild Bill, Custer, Sitting Bull, and Wounded Knee, no other specific targeted objectives were planned. All other destinations reached simply popped up in or along the path or mysteriously pulled the author to them.

That old saying, "It's not the destination but the journey taking you there" holds the true enchantment of travel and proved accurate once again on this sojourn.

The natural beauty of the countryside passing all around on this trip was only surpassed by the creatures and folks who seemed to emerge daily to thrill, enchant, cradle, and perplex. These lives encountered were the true stars of this panoramic masterpiece found surrounding us each day.

Don't let references to "us/we/our/etc." fool you. I can attest that this drive was made solely alone by U.R. but it soon became apparent that one is never really alone even in our triumphs and our calamities.

The path taken is laid out clearly in the text. So clearly, in fact, one could retrace U.R.'s course. Your author had spent many years in Alaska. He was once approached by some folks back East requesting the best routes for them to take to Alaska. They were told, "Go up to the Great Lakes, take a left, and keep on going."

Another theme you'll find running, bouncing, and oftentimes crash-landing into the prose regards sheer luck - how much we all have - sometimes without appreciating it or even realizing it. See if you can find any that even escaped notice by the author. You may also conclude via these passages that luck just may be a mysterious gift granted solely to you from an entity who loves you without reservation.

Be on the lookout for passages in this book addressing: those elusive Columbia Falls, paranoia, the Grand Dame of camping, the paranormal, hints and observations regarding hygiene, possibly the coldest bath in recorded history, encounters with those living alternative lifestyles, a hypodermic needle, a bear who practiced safe pedestrian etiquette, the author's struggles/frustrations with technology, the pro's and con's of aging, unanticipated contact with Native Americans, a very brave boy with a bloody nose, the plight of America's aborigines, enchantresses, a shaman or two, an inspirational thalidomide baby, the Wall of Death, an embarrassed bison, dining with Sitting Bull, Custer's last view, the pizza girl of Sheridan, Wyoming, a lucky penny for Wild Bill, vicious dogs, an admitted fabricator, trench mouth, the Hay River water girl, a Nigerian/Muslim/Jamaican Voodoo priest, the ostrich deli boy of Yellowknife, flying bulldogs, the Tloc Moi free trip for two, the Manning 500, Head-Smashed-In Buffalo Jump, the cemetery of Nye, restrooming with the Russian Mafia, casting a giant shadow in the Bighorn Mountains, a prostitute, philosophical religious reflections, mesmerizings, an almost bear attack or two, the demonic winds of Shelby, Montana, an elk who took out an 18-wheeler, forbidden love affairs, at least one ghost, scary heights, scary lows, winged creatures intent on eating you, an audio mirage, some of the greatest people on the face of the Earth, a few of the not so greatest people on Earth, captivating photos of breathtaking vistas, and the like.

If one of your passions borders (no pun intended) on travel, if another of your passions is to laugh, and if you're a person who can put the needs of others primary to your own, this book was written for you.

You'll also find an ulterior motive for this project which will be revealed to you near the end.

U.R. shared with me that it was his fondest hope that you will receive many chuckles reading this publication, some awakening or reassuring insight, be inspired to take your very own path to the end of a road, and, just maybe, be moved to sacrifice a portion of your thoughts, your time, and/or your affluence to the less fortunate. There's a lot uv'em out there.

U.R. and I have been close for years / decades. I knew he had it in him but never once did I expect to be moved in the directions this magical work took me. I was either crying, howling, or scratching my head throughout it's reading.

This book also made me realize just how much we are all the same and just how much we are all different.

And alas, he caught me; as I couldn't wait to read what was up around the next bend. I'm also plotting my very own journey now. Hope I'll run into you somewhere out there too.

Proctor Muley

Another of Your Personal Representatives
at the
Society for a Free Roaming Mind Set.

DAY #1, 7/1/2016

Started from Oldtown, Maryland to Sandusky, Ohio
Drove from 11 AM to 9 PM.
Starting Mileage: 33,676
Miles This Day: 354

I took Route 68 to Morgantown, West Virginia, Route 79 to Wheeling, West Virginia, and took Route 250 out of Wheeling to a Walmart near Sandusky, Ohio conveniently located on Route 250. After Cadiz, Ohio it was a beautiful drive all the way to Sandusky.

DAY #2, 7/2/2016

Used Walmart lavatory, bought apples from Walmart, had a quick breakfast of dry cereal and dehydrated bananas I had made for the trip, was back on the road at 9 AM. Drove to three or four state parks seeking shelter for the night, all full due to the 4th of July weekend. Number 5 had a vacancy. I needed to buy a state pass for $31. It was good all year but I was only staying all night. Beyond the pass, I would have to fork out an additional $10 — possibly $5 for senior citizen benefit. Do the math. That much to sleep in my van, no shower, and a hope that I wouldn't be at the end of a line of 40+/- people needing to use the restroom in the AM. I opted for Walmart again.

It has been a long day. I pretty much hugged Route 23 North in Michigan, skirted around Bay City, and hugged the coast of Lake Huron up to Alpena. On the way I had to stop for two female turkeys, with broods too many to count, crossing the highway cautiously. All appeared to be in good spirits. With the help of a friendly gas station attendant, I found my Walmart Astoria that had been eluding me for quite some time. Lake Huron was beautiful and I'd recommend Route 23 to one and all.

Ending Mileage: 34,475
Miles This Day: 471

DAY #3, 7/3/2016

Had my morning meeting at the Walmart lavatory, bought hotdogs and ice. It's the least I can do, they're putting me up for the night…I met a Lion named Dana as I was leaving. He had just set up a table at the front doors and was selling tickets for a rubber ducky race to benefit local kids sports and whatnot. Dana was a personable guy and as it turned out, a good salesman too. I told him my goal was to reach Yellowknife, Northwest Territories, Canada, and take in as much scenery and history as I could going out and coming back. He shared that he also liked to travel, that at present his forte was bird watching, and that his last trip was in Montana watching birds for three weeks without a shower. As it had been a few days since soap or water had touched my body, I figured this fact may have prompted Dana's ever so discreet pointers. He indicated that on long bird watching trips where bathing is not within easy access, he and others like him enroll the services of baby wipes. He said always go from north to south on these and don't mix up the order — face, ears, neck, torso, etc., always leaving the buttocks and private parts for last. I queried him to see if my private parts would start smelling like my face. He eluded an answer and whipped back that after 21 days in Montana using the above method, he felt he might have an organic bear deterrent. Dana also encouraged me to utilize Walmart facilities along my way as often as possible. They've got food, bathrooms, security, etc. Everything but showers.

I broke off the conversation as other local people were lining up to sign up for the rubber duck contest. This gave me time to return to Walmart and pick up some much needed baby wipes. As there was a lull in Dana's patrons on my second exit of Walmart this morning, we struck up further conversation. He told me the most he could go on trips such as I was taking was three weeks — not because of his bathing routine but because he missed his wife and kids so much. Without an ounce of bravado, he let me know that he was a graduate of Michigan State targeting a degree in zoology / entomology. He also wrestled in college. He ended up in flight school at Pensacola, Florida. Dana was a Vietnam-era helicopter pilot while en route to a 21 year career in the Navy. Somehow, he also found time to graduate from the Naval War College. Somewhere in the admirable list of accomplishments, he shared that one of his favorite memories was getting to meet astronaut Alan Shepard, Jr. All that, and there he sat selling rubber duckies. I did not feel pressure but was honored to buy a rubber ducky sponsorship from the latest hero that I have met. Dana may have had a little inherited push to join the Navy as his father, Gordon, was a 20 year submariner climbing to the esteemed rank of "Chief of the Boat" on two different submarines during WWII in the Pacific Theatre and another after war's end. Dana shared that he was 13 years old before he realized that his dad's name was not "Chief" as that was how everyone addressed him. Dana did not conceal the pride he justly had for his father but being an observer, it wasn't much of a leap to feel the pride Gordon must have had for his son likewise.

28th Alpena Optimist Club
Rubber Duckie Race Raffle
Monday, July 4, 2016 - 1:00 - 3:00 p.m.
601 River St - Island Park - Alpena, MI 49707

$5.00 Ticket Winning Numbered Duck
$1,000.00 cash - First Prize

$5.00 Donation $5.00 Donation

Need not be present
to win 1st place.
Must be 18 years old.   Lic. No. R36107

The Alpena
OPTIMISTS SERVICE PROJECTS
A Partial List of our Activities:

Sponsor Youth Hockey
Sponsor Youth Baseball
Punt, Pass, Kick
Optimist Kiddie Park
Spring Break Fun Day
Kids Fishing Day
Brown Trout Festival
College Scholarships
Childhood Cancer Fund
Youth Oratorical Contest
McRae Park Ice Rink

N⁰ 219

DONATION

The reason I initially figured Dana for a Lion was because back home, the Lion's Club sponsors the rubber ducky contest. As I was parting, he yelled to me that there was a good place between Rogers City and Cheboygan for a bath along the coast in Lake Huron. I must have left an impact on him, too…I sure hope so. Turns out, Dana was not a Lion but an Alpena Optimist Club member. He's still a Lion in my book. Dana and I corresponded and talked by phone after much of this was penned to paper. I requested and received his permission to share with you some of his paraphrases and quotes: 1) I'm a bug in a big forest. 2) Showing up is 90%. 3) Diplomacy failed in the first place so why does anybody think it will work in a war? And, 4) History is the mass movement of individual people led by someone that accidentally got to be the head of the parade. And there he sat selling rubber duckies.

Back to Route 23 heading northwest. For some reason, I couldn't find that place for bathing that Dana told me about. I was feeling a little desperate and a whole lot dirty. I drove by a lake that had an empty dirt parking lot almost like a turn around for school buses. As school was out, I was in, not cold but chilly enough to wake me up. I felt like a new man. This lake was called Long Lake. Although I could see some scattered cabins a great distance from my unsecluded bathing pool, I only saw one boat out fishing so far away, I couldn't tell you how many souls were on board. I was determined now to do more bathing in the future if practicable. I also decided to wear my bathing suit so as not to offend any locals. Unfortunately for me, in my haste when packing I picked the bathing suit (green/black/blue with ball net) whose elastic around the waist had given up. Thank God for that strong drawstring. It would have to serve me throughout the trip. The bath boosted my spirits more than anticipated. That, or I had been dirtier than anticipated.

Feeling the strain of driving so many miles on those first two days, I thought it best not to make this an endurance trip but to travel casually but still putting some miles behind me each day. By the way, all soap used on this trip was biodegradable. I continued on Route 23 hugging a most beautiful blue Lake Huron. I stopped and had lunch - some soup (survival) heated over my two burner Coleman propane stove and made coffee as well utilizing a tea strainer that trapped almost all of my coffee grains. I helped two guys launch their fishing boat. As soon as they spotted my Maryland tags their curiosity took hold and I told them my bucket list goals. They gave me a neutral "good luck." I don't think it was sarcasm but it may have been close. I fed some seagulls there to their quacking delight — sociopaths!

On my way to Mackinaw City, I saw more turkeys crossing the road, and more than once had to stop while a band of Canadian geese waddled across the road. These were adults and they should have known better, but I guess they owned that strip of land before we did. I didn't care, I enjoyed their march. Maybe they were trying to get motorists to slow down as many, many folks seemed to be in a hurry. Remember, it was the 4th of July weekend and these folks hadn't seen as much warm weather as I had already seen in Maryland. Route 23 along the northwest stretch of Lake Huron looked a bit like the land of the rich and famous — big estates/Mercedes/Jaguars/expensive boats (more power to them if they worked for it and got it honestly).

PHOTO #1

PHOTO #2

I crossed the very beautiful, very long, and very high Mackinaw Bridge. It cost me $4 to get off the bridge. I wondered if you didn't have the $4, would they make you back up across it again? The first exit off Mackinaw Bridge was Route 2 and I took it. One of my big goals for this trip was to travel on scenic highways. They're the ones lined with dots on your maps. I'm sure glad I stuck to this goal. Because I did so, I saw more beauty, less traffic, less stress. Sure, it may have taken me a little longer to navigate but what can you see doing 80 mph hurrying past Chicago?

PHOTO #3

Route 2 was absolutely breathtaking with plenty of convenient pull overs for picnics and photos. Note: take more film than you think you will need. You'll need it. I kind of did a controlled and safe ubie after passing a sign that said, "Dried Fish for Sale." It was like a mom and pop's store for people who like fish eating and catching. There were giant teethy stuffed fish adorning all the wall space. It was like a fish taxidermist museum. I must have been mesmerized as I didn't think to take photos. I also regret not getting a photo of my hero, Dana, this morning. If you're still out there Dana, send me a photo. Did I win?

Back to the dried fish. They had all kinds. Two bikers there who I was tempted to offer some of my baby wipes to preferred the dried whitefish. I had that in the past and it's good. I've had dried salmon which they also offered. I had not ever tried dried lake trout, so my selection of that ended up with me being $6 shorter but high on my 3/4 lb of lake trout. My original plan was to make about three meals out of this which I could have but as it was dry but somewhat greasy, and giving off a smell that a bear would die for, I opted to eat all of the evidence in one fell swoop which I did at a picnic ground overlooking Lake Michigan to my south. It was very rich but I didn't care. I reminded myself that this was not mere gluttony but precautionary as I was and had been in bear country for some time now (actually since leaving home). One of my other plans to decrease the likelihood of having a bear in camp was to not eat where I slept. Then I thought, when was the last time you saw a bear attack at Walmart?

Continued on Route 2 to Manistique then up Route 94 to Munising. Having a National Parks pass for life that cost me $10-$15 while fishing in Canaveral National Seashore, Florida a few years back was a great investment - thank you Uncle Sam for that gift to seniors. So, I started targeting National Parks as I got in free and only had to pay 50% of whatever the fee was — usually $10+/-, costing me $5+/-. I found Hiawatha National Forest on my map to the south of Munising on Route H13. Drove what seemed like a good ways to get there only to find they were full up. I met the "host camper." These are people who strike a deal with Uncle Sam to manage the site for a while for free camping privileges. He was kind, friendly, and apologetic. I gave him my best look of hopeless wanderer and he allowed me to park in an overflow parking lot for free for the night. I told him how much he made my day and this seemed to make his day. I selected a flat spot that was adjacent to the toilets and free good water. It was called Pete's Lake and I woke up to find 3-4 other hopeless wanderers he had allowed to stay in the overflow parking lot. But I got the best spot. There's a phrase I hate, "If you snooze you lose" but I was snoozing and winning. Thank God for gregarious campers who don't mind a few wood ticks in their underwear now and again.

By the way, Pete's Lake was beautiful, small, natural, clear, etc. I could see ancient logs laying on the bottom. They had a wooden fishing pier that I and my Parodi cigar had to ourselves listening to my first Loon's lonely call. No mosquitos present. They had also attempted a garden of natural and ancient flowers and fauna on one bank near the walkway. I took a photo of them and it turned out fuzzy. I also took a photo of one of those ancient logs under the water but it turned out too dark. Again, this whole area including Hiawatha National Forest is well worth seeing. I kept scanning the forest for Hiawatha but he eluded me. Take some time and look at all the locales with Native American names and then take some time to look for some Native Americans. What happened to them?

Ending Mileage: 34,722
Miles This Day: 247

DAY #4, 7/4/2016

Backtracked from Pete's Lake back up to Munising. Saw Munising Falls, great area for time sharing. I took a handful of photos at the Falls and not one of them turned out to do true justice to this serene locale. Before Bruce Crossing and Champion, I found Higley's Saloon or what was left of it. Boy, if those walls could talk you'd probably need an interpreter.

PHOTO #1 - HIGLEY'S SALOON

Camped in National Forest (Chequamegan), $12.00. Later I learned that as a senior I would only have had to pay $6.00 - spread the wealth! I was exhausted getting there. I was trying to read the instruction board when up pulled some hard looking people on four wheelers. Never judge a book by it's cover...they offered to help as I was a novice at these parks. They told me to take the forms, find my spot, fill forms out, put the money and form into a lockbox provided, and take the perforated end with information to campsite and attach to clip provided. I asked them "How much?" They told me $12.00 I thanked them, they gunned their engines and rode off into the dust filled setting sun but only after the older, obviously alpha male, stopped his four wheeler in front of me and wished me, sincerely, a happy 4th of July. Up until that time I had forgotten it was the 4th of July. They had also paid me a complement as I was to find out later. By telling me $12.00, they were assuming that I wasn't a senior citizen. I get that a lot. I don't think it's due to my physical appearance. Possibly it's due to my immaturity — I think I've never really grown up. It's a sobering thought to know that I will be 70 on the next go round. Anyway, $6.00 was a small price to pay for the complement and to meet hard looking folks who were, in reality, softies and I'm the better for it. I never saw them again at the campsite but I did hear a lot of firecrackers later toward evening from the far side of the lake.

Had a good supper of dehydrated soup and beef jerky, a beer to celebrate the 4th, and another Parodi cigar (manufactured in Scranton, Pennsylvania - hard as rocks, strong, and I like them). I brought a jug of tequila along also but elected not to use it for fear of having too good of a time. My father got drunk once in his life that I am aware of when he was probably in his 50's at a convention. I asked, "Dad, did you have a good time?" His answer came quick, "Yes, and that's why I'm not going to do it anymore." I queried my teetotaling mom about it. All she would say was, "He fell into the band." Now there's a function I wish I would have attended with them.

The campsite had a nice steel fire pit and grill. I'd never used one like that before but it worked well. I had some difficulty cleaning pots and pans but had brought the right assortment of things you get to take home with you when you've had to stay in a hospital. I brought my own urinal for night use made from a liquid fabric softener plastic bottle with a large, secure, non-leaking lid. A leak could put a damper on any trip. (No pun intended.)

I learned this day that my Stanley thermos would keep coffee very well for 12-24 hours. Thank you to my almost in-laws (girlfriend's family) for getting me this thermos so many years ago for Christmas. This was the first time I actually used it. A thoughtful gift that fit just right, not like the luggage bags former girlfriend's mothers seemed to prefer for me at Christmastime.

As I drifted off to sleep, I couldn't help to be thankful for what this country allows us to do and the opportunities we have to better our position in life if we so chose. I also thought of my Uncle Albert. The Beatles had a song mentioning "Uncle Albert." My dad's father paid a doctor $100.00 to cut Uncle Albert's trigger finger off as a result of too many baseball injuries to that digit, we have the receipt somewhere. He was one of my dad's best friends growing up as dad lived on the hill and mom and Uncle Albert were raised down in the valley. He was my mother's favorite brother. She had all brothers after losing an older sister to one of those ancient maladies that took loved ones away too frequently in the past. Mom never knew her sister and I've never seen a photo of her, nor do I know of any existing. She also lost another brother she barely remembered named Robert. Robert died on the operating table having his appendix removed. Mom's mom was going through Uncle Robert's record collection a few weeks after the funeral and found his handwritten goodbye note to everyone in case he should die on the operating table. Several members of that same family including my grandmother knew beforehand that they were going to die. And then it would happen. If my mother knew, she never told us.

Back to Uncle Albert's trigger finger. Even though he had no trigger finger, he was still drafted into WWII and was killed by Germans while acting as a forward observer for a mortar team. People used to wonder why I would tear up when the Beatles would sing "We're so sorry Uncle Albert..." There's a person I'm looking forward to meeting in the future. But, I don't know when— not yet anyway. But it shouldn't be too long... old age is like leftovers — I'll make the best of what is left!

While I thought of Uncle Albert, Mom, Dad, and the rest of the family, thoughts of Lewis and Clark zoomed in to remind me that I would soon be traveling across land and water that they had traversed in 1803+/-. I must keep reminding myself also what a lucky guy I am to even attempt what I am trying to do.

I chuckled with contentment just before sleep scurried away with me while being lullabied by the loon of this lake near Washburn, Wisconsin on Route 13 heading north. As he had sung me to sleep last night, he/she woke me this morning just as daylight was gobbling up the night. It was like having chickens on a farm, but a touch more wilder on the lake, now sweating up mist that visited the entire campground as if it were silently looking for someone to tell them the good news that the sun was just approaching the lake in it's silent majesty.

Ending Mileage: 35,004
Miles This Day: 282

DAY #5, 7/5/2016

Started the day off with a bang after breakfast of hard boiled egg on multigrain with cup of coffee (warm). Gas in Washburn was $2.89 for super and $2.29 for regular. I know this as I mistakenly pumped the super first as the manifesto on the pump was arranged in a confusing manner, with the price for the cheaper being above the pump for the most expensive — capitalism at it's finest or just a human error. I think not on the latter... Possibly due to the deception at the pump, I added injury to insult by driving off with my locking gas cap on top of the van with the door to the gas tank spout hanging wide open. Did the elderly lady tailgating me notice this and flash her lights or beep her horn to warn or stop me? No! But she was able to swerve and run over my gas cap when it fell off in downtown Washburn. Realizing what had transpired, I did another controlled ubie in hopes of finding my gas cap and I did, back there and over there, and over there. I picked up the pieces for fear of a littering fine, knowing bloody well that this was solely my fault and not hers. But why did she swerve and nail it so precisely as if she was an old hand at this? (No pun intended.) So, this was the "bang" I mentioned above. Fortunately, I had the foresight to bring the yellow gas cap that came with the van when I purchased it and it has a device that hooks it to the gas tank port. I guess the salesman had heard that I have an extensive history of laying objects on the top of the car and driving off (i.e., two wallets, a check for $175.00 made out to the US Chamber of Commerce later found at an 18-wheeler pull over on Summit Mountain going east from Uniontown, Pennsylvania stuck in the grass overnight in a rainstorm. The briefcase it was in was not quite as lucky nor was the two years of work contained in the ex-briefcase). I will say this for Ford Escorts — you can drive them across downtown Uniontown, Pennsylvania, through several lights in a rainstorm and still drive halfway up Summit Mountain ladened with a briefcase on its top before inertia and gravity outfox that old Escort. I didn't hear or see a thing. When I got home I couldn't find my briefcase. Do you think there are still witches out there still putting spells on people like that? I hope so. Because I'd hate to write it off to the brain taking periodic vacations.

PHOTO #1 - SKELETON OF OLD FISHING BOAT "THE CORNUCOPIA"

Shell of old fishing boat near Cornucopia, Wisconsin. They had three laid out there side by side like old men sleeping. No matter what angle or distance I tried, I couldn't capture all three. So, I settled on the one I thought had the most character. That's Lake Superior there sitting behind the boat. For those of you who didn't purchase the color photo option for this book, feel free to color Lake Superior a bright, sunny day blue or encourage your younger offspring to attempt it. Note: I, personally, would closely monitor their efforts. No doubt, the original crew are no longer with us but I'll bet they are still out there fishing Superior especially on good soft days. By the way, the name of the boat was The Cornucopia and she's still pointed in the right direction to take that crew out.

A hundred feet or more from The Cornucopia sat the Cindy Marie, a hand built fishing boat still plying the waters of Superior. It was like Cindy Marie was a daughter or granddaughter of The Cornucopia carrying on the tradition.

PHOTO #2 - CINDY MARIE

I did another controlled ubie near the outskirts of Portwing to make sure what I thought I saw was what I saw. I was correct. It was an event notice still strung up in the pines along side of the empty parking lot of the Port Bar. It read, "Port Bar Annual Testicle Festival." Although my camera didn't pick up the dates, it read in white letters against a yellow background "Sat. June 18th, 2016." Just my luck, a penny short and a few days late. As earlier mentioned, there was not one vehicle in the bar's parking lot. It was plenty late enough in the day for the regulars (sounds better than alcoholics) to be there wetting their whistles and let it be known that they could quit anytime they felt like it! I think it was around 10 AM. Not a soul...had something happened here on the 4th? I didn't see any telltale police tape...is it only open for the Testicle Festival? Or did they just have enough of it with these testicles? I couldn't find out. I guess the only way to find out is to return here on June 18th, 2017. It should be pretty interesting as long as nothing gets out of hand...

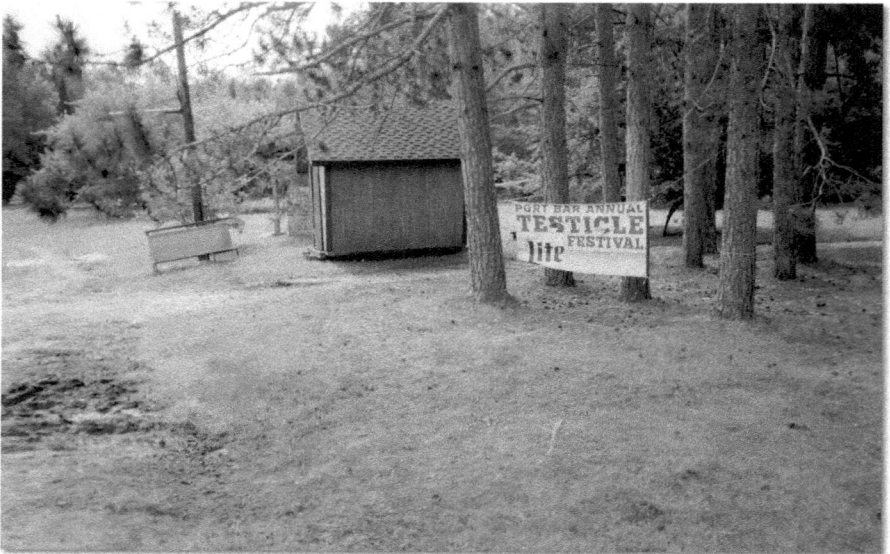

PHOTO #3

I continued on Route 13 and as I'd be running out of Big Lakes soon, I decided a bath was called for. The previous in Long Lake had rejuvenated me so well, I figured Lake Superior would only best that to some higher degree. I found an older picnic area with a sandy/dirt road running along beside and up on a bluff above a beautiful cove. I saw other folks swimming and splashing about and positioned my bath at a distance from them that they would be clueless to my true objective. There was a nice root-encrusted, winding path down to the beach that was more small stones than sand. The water was very clear. I had put the old bathing suit on, discreetly of course, up at the van on the bluff actually mooning Lake Superior as I now came to realize but I had not thought to bring my snorkels and goggles down to check out the bottom that I could see from the beach. Let's say I regretted that at the present. Well, that wasn't my mission anyway, so down the steep bank toward the clear blue of Lake Superior. I was able to stop my descent but only when I was up above my waist in that clear blue water. Is there a name for water just before it turns to ice? I immediately realized why Gordon Lightfoot said, "She never gives up her dead." There's got to be a Native American word for cold but I'll bet it's a lot more than four letters. Shrinkage was immediate upon contact. I feared shrinkage could turn into disappearance. Remember, I was only in up over my waist. I had another 4-5 feet to go to cover my 6 foot 5 inch frame. I jokes. I'm only 5 feet 10 inches. I grudgingly crawled back up the beach. The little pebbles didn't help. It was as if they wanted me to stay semi-submerged until the cold took me and some fishermen would maybe find me a few weeks later in their net, saying, "What the hell is that? It looks like a 5 foot 10 inch glob of snot. We still might be able to salvage that black, green, and blue bathing suit though."

I managed to secure my biodegradable soap (Ivory). I had called the 800 number provided prior to this trip and actually talked to a human being after punching in 20+/- codes directed by a talking machine telling me what to punch next. Some higher up executive in management wanted to feel important one day and introduced the talking machine to his friend in accounting. They agreed, after getting permission from the board, to present this concept to the board who did the math and approved the talking machine. Which, in turn, took the place of the ten folks they used to pay a decent wage with benefits package to for answering inquiries such as mine in person. With the help of the talking machine, they now have one girl whose territory is everything east of the Mississippi to respond to my inquiry. By the way, she works out of her home somewhere in New Jersey and just got a formal email from accounting that she can only work 32 hours per week and that her insurance and retirement packages would be subject to change soon. People will soon be saying, "Gee, what happened to the tax base?" I don't know. Maybe there's an 800 number we can call.

Anyway, this nice sounding, youngish lady assured me that Ivory soap was completely biodegradable and I can assure you that it floated in Lake Superior, against all odds. The bath in Superior was actually refreshing after I got done screaming and could now feel my fingers and toes, or at least most of them. To my relief, shrinkage had indeed taken its toll, but nothing beyond that.

As I dried off on the inclining pebble beach, I noticed that all of the other bathers/swimmers had packed it in and I had pebble beach for as far as the eye could see to myself. I really didn't get to enjoy this respite from humanity for as long as I would have liked. I could hear Superior's little waves lapping at the beach now as the wind had died down. As soon as I realized this absence of wind, I made haste for the van with my accompanying black, green, and blue suit, my Ivory soap, and my striped oversized towel, given to me by a psychologist friend for my retirement. (Note: for retirement - not as therapy. On the other hand maybe I should call Bill to make sure.) Realizing that I had left my bug spray locked in the van in clear view on the passenger's seat, I raced back up that root infested path. Relief turned to dismay once I got there, all the while trying to knock the very aggressive bloodsucking critters off with my oversized towel. (Thanks Bill - for whatever reason.) The above dismay came once I realized I had left my locked car's keys on the pebble beach for fear of losing them in the clear blue Superior. Down that root infested path I went, swinging and swatting that oversized striped towel (thanks again Bill and April - his wife's name is April - another psychologist they told me I was working with), at what seemed like a horde of bloodsuckers now sucking out my last potential pint to donate to the Red Cross. I wonder what the Red Cross' position is on mosquitos, formally speaking of course. We finally made it down to the keys and back to the van. I did not commit an error here describing it as "we" as the horde went with me both ways. I guess you could say they had my blood up...but they probably like it. It's probably part of the beginner's manual for adolescent mosquitos. *Step #2, try to get their blood up. It will be closer to the surface for those of you who have shorter stingers.*

I had my first optical illusion of this trip that I am aware of. I was still driving and scratching on Route 13 somewhere past the Testicle Bar (can you imagine what's going through a person's mind who was having a mental lapse while reading through the first description of the above when they get to this last line?) and Wentworth, Wisconsin. I had to come to a sliding stop at the base of a rolling hill. Both sides of the highway for at least three to four miles were lined four feet deep with these gorgeous yellow flowers — great contrast between them and the greens of the surrounding hillocks. However, at the bottom of the hill I almost slid past a flag girl, which I'll grant you is 100% better than sliding into a flag girl. Yes, she had her stop sign but her yellow/green bibs and helmet blended in perfectly with roadside flowers described above. Still panting with fright as to what could have transpired with regards to my slide, I rolled the passenger side window down long enough to warn her that she was blending in. She gave me a vacant stare with no verbal reply. I wound the window back up in case some of those mosquitos at the pebble beach had hitched a ride. She eventually reversed her sign from stop to slow without so much as a nod, let alone a thank you.

I pondered her reaction for a long time. Surely Wisconsin doesn't hire deaf flag people, no offense to them. Maybe the "Slow" on her sign was like a dual message to motorists, like, "Look out for me, I'm slow." Maybe 15 minutes after my slide there she exclaimed, "Holy shit, that guy in the van could have slid into me!" Either way, I was on my way to Minnesota by the time the thought had struck her. I forgot to mention another important factor. She looked to be maybe 19 or 20 with blond hair. Just possibly, I may have been the only living witness to her first blond moment. Don't you love it when you speak to someone and they become lost for words. Maybe somewhere in 8th grade social studies, they may spend some weeks studying a course titled "Positive Techniques Utilizing Conversational Challenges." For miles after that I figured I'd find a place with the yellow flowers four feet deep on both sides of the highway to shoot a photo for you, but I never did. It was like someone sprinkled fairy dust on both sides of the highway for three to four miles and it sprung up into these yellow flowers just in that one area.

PHOTO #4 - HOMESTEAD

Old Finnish homestead house built at the turn of the century towards Brule. I was impressed with its simplicity and sturdiness. Had it not been sturdy I probably wouldn't have taken the photo.

Another controlled ubie and walla - a windmill on top of these rolling hills near Brule, built in earliest 1900's. Hats off to the folks who restored and maintain the above.

There was a heavyset lady on a riding lawn mower just feet from the little parking lot for the homestead and windmill. I passed her at least twice while checking out the above. She never spoke, waved, or

PHOTO #5 - WINDMILL

PHOTO #6 - MISSISSIPPI RIVER

acknowledged my presence. I was going to ask her if she had a daughter who was a flag girl. Maybe the women in this region are mail order mutes from Finland. That's worth investigating but I wanted to get onto Minnesota— something was gnawing at me to get there and it wasn't mosquitoes.

I took a sashay west of Duluth, took Route 2 northwest til it met Route 200 and headed west. Feeling a great urge to urinate, I crossed a little muddy stream that had a restroom facility in a cozy little cottonwood cove. I left a liquid donation in the restroom, came out and had a second urge to stretch my legs. I dicked around the stream bank which wasn't overly photo worthy. However, I came upon a small plaque notifying me that I had just crossed the Mississippi River. I almost fell over and took a photo. I felt that if George Washington could throw a silver dollar across the Potomac, surely

U.R. McFarland could throw a silver nickel across the Mississippi, and did so successfully.

No ubie required here. Entering Akeley, Minnesota, I drove upon a giant Paul Bunyan, complete with kids and their mother who were vacationing from Wisconsin. I asked the kids to climb up again so as to give you some perspective to Paul's size and a couple of them did for me. This nameless lady and kids had acknowledged my presence and I was back in business again with the human race. Paul was well maintained or fairly new to the area. It was fun for me to watch the positive relationship this lady had with her brood. I got really good vibes here. I couldn't linger as I had set my sights on getting to Fargo, North Dakota today.

PHOTO #7 - PAUL BUNYAN

Before leaving Minnesota I succumbed to one of my many weaknesses — buffet. And in this case, an Asian restaurant buffet tucked in a little corner of a big strip mall. Not realizing that my diet for the last few days had caused my stomach to shrink, my mind was deceived into thinking I could easily wolf down the usual cup of sweet and sour soup, followed by the usual three plate special, followed by a fourth plate of dessert. I usually always just order water as I don't want to appear a glutton. Remember that Saturday night show before or after "Gunsmoke" called "Have Gun Will Travel?" Well, this little antidote could be titled "Have Asian in Minnesota,

Will Deposit In North Dakota." I got lost or turned around in my panic. The highway was much too busy with no forested land to run into, but from past experience I knew I had very little time if any to make my move (no pun intended). There was nothing but field after field of wheat and other things I couldn't identify. I could find no gas stations, Tastee Freezes, nothing. I looked far down the highway for the next ramp. I was going to take it and let things fly as they will (pun intended). I took it and saw a parking lot full of cars. Instinctively I felt this could be my salvation. Did I say salvation? It ended up being a church. On a Tuesday? What could they all be doing there on a Tuesday? They don't have weddings on Tuesdays. I concluded that it had to be the end game on a funeral. Far too many cars for Bible study. No matter my own condition, I wasn't going to ruin a perfectly good funeral by busting in there. I thought of going between the cars in the parking lot but that's probably the eleventh commandment. I couldn't go in the car. It would certainly end my trip and then that long ride home with the windows all down even if it rained. At this point I was praying and once again, God came through for me. He told me to race back towards the highway. This time I noticed a farm lane used only by farm equipment. I never used my van as farm equipment but will attest that I did so this evening. About a 100 feet down the farm lane I noticed three what appeared to be compost piles equivalent to the size of my van. You've heard that God works in mysterious ways. There's four compost piles there now. I almost felt like leaving that farmer a thank you note but given the circumstances I felt that I'd done enough for him that day, in an anonymous way of course.

Afterwards, I got to thinking that my feelings must have been akin to a sperm donor on a certain level. By now, somewhere, someone's having a slice of bread ignorant of the fact of who helped it taste so sweet. From one came many comes to mind. Joy comes to some through outright adversity of others. Remember me when I'm gone. I'm glad I could help. Without intentional blasphemy, I am reminded of the last supper, "Eat this bread as it is part of my body." I'm taking a break now to give God some time to contemplate my fate.

God spared me once again and I am truly thankful.

I was back on the road in no time and up came the rest stop that I had given up on. I got rid of the rest of my Chinese buffet there, pitying those who arrived just as I was leaving. It wouldn't surprise me if they walked in there, turned and ran out calling 911. I didn't stick around to find out or to give them time to report my license number to the state police.

With that all behind me (intended pun) I hit Route 29 South for Fargo, North Dakota. I'm not saying where those four compost piles were. I don't want some irate reader to report me. I don't know the statute of limitations on such goings on but I figure they could still charge me with trespassing, littering, and leaving the scene of a terrible accident, with a count of public indecency pending which of the Bible Belt I was in. I'm still in a quandary about that church parking lot on a Tuesday night.

Back to Route 29. Speed limit is 80 mph. This helped in my potential get away/escape if indeed there was one occurring. I had been looking forward to seeing Fargo because I had bought an apartment building once owned by the family of one of the stars in the movie Fargo - he was the sales manager. He was also raised in my hometown of Cumberland, Maryland. Hello Mr. Famous Actor and hello Cumberland. He is a great actor. One might say a legend in his own time with a medley of intriguing caricatures that only he could own, gifting his spellbound audiences in wonderment and appreciation for his craft, skills, and talents. He can play the guy you love, the guy you loathe, and the one you're not so sure of. I'm positive in his circle, he's considered an actor's actor. I no longer own the building but the sale of it helped pay for this trip. Thank you to his brother, Fred Macy, whom I bought the property from.

I saw two dead porcupines on the highway today. I wish they

were just pining (thank you Monty Python) but I don't think they were. Well, it's been one long and one noteworthy day. It's taken me several pages just to give you the highlights.

By the way, I zipped through Fargo without giving her fair scrutiny. I blame this on my hesitation to spend much time in population centers and a lust for what awaits around the next bend or at the end of that long straightaway. I often ponder what I may have missed with regards to this preference for getting from Point A to Point B. But, then again, I'll never know, will I? God, I wish I would have bought that crystal ball that time. I was so tired after traversing through three states today, I forgot to note where I holed up for the night. It had to be somewhere south of Fargo on Route 29. It will have to remain a mystery but if you're a betting person, put your money on another Walmart.

Ending Mileage: 35,560
Miles This Day: 556

DAY #6, 7/6/2016

After yesterday's excitement, I couldn't wait to see what today would bring. A roadside historic site noting nearby monument to Sacajawea and Sitting Bull caught my eye. It was up and down rolling hills/grassland - nearly treeless. It was very quiet. I drove farther than I thought it would be and virtually stumbled upon it as there was no sign along the road. The lane in was pitted with deep holes/ruts and an occasional busted beer bottle. Sacajawea's marker was a tall pointed cement/hard stone thing about 8-10 feet high with her name on it. I took a photo but it did not turn out. She has always been somewhat elusive to historians, especially her life post Lewis and Clark. Now,

PHOTO #1 - SITTING BULL

she remains elusive even to my camera. Nature joined with my throwaway camera in the shot I captured of Sitting Bull - "Local Man Claims to have Captured Sitting Bull!"

This monument does him justice and the setting let the viewer see the magnitude of the blue sky and heavens blanketing this man's country. He was killed for this grass. A plaque there reads that he was killed at Fort Yates in North Dakota just north of the line separating the Dakotas. However, in 1953 his remains were brought to this site. You can only see the solemnity and respect that this great man deserves when you review the photo. I can attest that 50+/- yards from this monument was an overflowing dumpster complete with overflowing dumpster stuff — you got the picture. I was going to raise hell but there was no one around, no park superintendent, nada. I quickly snapped my second photo of this day — two horses loped up as if they were guarding the gravesite.

These horses made fitting superintendents for him now. Note the countryside behind the horses. He was willing to die and did so for that land. Can you blame him? Years ago, I wrote a piece that said, "Jesus has come back many times and they've killed him every time." I think that men like Sitting Bull, Abraham Lincoln, Gandhi, Martin Luther King, etc., were in fact Jesus or Jesus-like figures and look what we did to them. What's that saying, "History has a way of repeating itself." I told Sitting Bull that I was sorry. That dumpster and rutted unkept road got my blood up, this time without the mosquitos and I thought I could get to Fort Yates to vent my anger.

PHOTO #2 - TWO HORSES

By the way, I had dropped down into South Dakota on Route 29 and took Route 12 west out to Mobridge, South Dakota. My original plan had been to take this route and come up to Sitting Bull's burial site near Fort Yates. If you look closely at your map of South Dakota you'll find Sitting Bull's grave near Mobridge, South Dakota, which is where I stumbled upon it this morning and got the photos of the monument and the horses. If you take 63 North off of Route 12 you'll soon be in North Dakota. 63 turns into Route 6 and Route 24 that took me to Fort Yates. If you look on your map, you will see Sitting Bull's burial site. "The rock was rolled away and the body was no longer in the tomb" comes to mind.

I ended up at Sitting Bull College in Fort Yates trying to find some sort of visitor center. I pulled over to ask three Native American kids, about ages 7-10, where the visitor center was. Their heads down to their shoulders were instantly inside my passenger section which was full to capacity but still giving me a good safe view out that window. They politely asked if I had some water. I gave them a half quart jug. They seemed appreciative but asked for nothing else. They appeared healthy/hardy/happy but not real clean. I suppose it was like looking into a mirror regarding those three depictions. They pointed up a hill to the Visitor Center which looked much like the other handful of red brick buildings that made up the small campus. I saw no one who looked like students of a college walking around. But, school/college would have been out save for summer school.

I made my way to the Visitor Center. It was OK but not overly impressive. There was a white lady there doing beadwork. The person running the Visitor Center greeted me with warmth and kindness. I addressed my dismay of what I'd found at the Sitting Bull gravesite near Mobridge, South Dakota. Her demeanor changed a little. She informed me that she too was appalled, as she knew that site all too well. She went on to tell me that it was in private hands and they're not keeping it up. She also educated me that Sitting Bull was not killed at Fort Yates but 30 miles west of Mobridge very close to where he was born and that his true burial site is here in Fort Yates. With some flare to the nostrils she looked me in the eye. Actually, she looked down into my eyes as she had a perfectly proportioned body but somewhat larger than my own and taller, too. I'm 6'2". Well, maybe I'm just 5'10". She had to be 6'1" or 2". Anyway, she lamented in a warning me kind of way that, "History was written by the winners." I assured her that I was well aware of that, that I had taught history, and had always struggled with what whites had propagated on the Native American. The nostrils de-flared. I told her looking up into her dark, less defensive eyes that I had also many times in the past made my feelings bare on the subject in that I wished the Native Americans would have won because I think it would be a better world now if they had. The white woman making the beads for the first time spoke by saying, "I like that." My new Amazonian Sioux friend pointed out the window to Sitting Bull's burial site. I had the urge to reach up and give her a hug but I didn't want to push my luck. I think I scored two points here by showing no fear and treating these interesting ladies as equals. I did pick up on a good personality observation. The Sioux were kind and friendly, but don't piss them off. They also have great memories which Custer must have forgotten. Note: there were white men who fought on the Native American side back east. They painted their faces black and wore interesting garb. I learned this at the Fur Rendezvous at Fort Frederick, Maryland. The two I saw that day alone along a forest path on first sighting embellished the term "menacing" and for quite sometime afterwards.

Ten minutes later I was at the burial site of Sitting Bull (Tatanka Iyotake). It was a picnic area reasonably maintained. I prepared lunch at the table nearest the stone and marker designating his resting place. The cement platform it rests upon could use a little paint. There were weathered cut off old logs surrounding it that possibly supported a chain fence that once surrounded it. I was glad to see no chain. I think that Tatanka Iyotake would not have wanted any chains around him. There were white prairie flowers all about the grave site. There was a cove of a large lake behind him possibly manmade. Many visitors had left stones and coins at the base of the marker/headstone. I left a piece of wood and some sage plant I found nearby, as well as some salt. I didn't know if he liked pepper or had ever even tried it. So, I held off on the pepper. I said a prayer for him to be in heaven or the happy hunting ground - same place, different name. I told him that I was sorry again. God and Sitting Bull know where he finally ended up with regards to body parts. I'm hoping his spirit still hunts and walks the land with the people he so loved.

Long after this journey's end, my brother, John, game me a great National Geographic book entitled, "The Indian Wars" by Anton Treuer. On page 45, I found this quote from Sitting Bull. Did he want me to find it? I surely hope so. "The warrior, for us, is one who sacrifices himself for the good of others. His task is to take care of the elderly, the defenseless, those who cannot provide for themselves, and above all, the children, the future of humanity." Long before this journey was conceived, I purchased a splendid photo of Sitting Bull, framed it in wood, and gave it a place of honor in my home. He looks to me everyday. Was he the silent wind pushing me to make this journey? I surely hope so.

PHOTO #3

I had lunch there with Sitting Bull. Two raw hotdogs on multi-grain bread with ketchup, a pack of crackers (jalapeño) and a cup of cold coffee. I think in Sitting Bull's day that would have been a meal fit for royalty out here. If you look at the photo, you can see a water tower in the background that supplies water to part of the reservation that sits up there on a prominent point. I was saying my good-byes when I noticed three young adult Sioux males in street clothes walking toward the reservation. One split off from the group. The other two stood there for a few seconds and walked on.

I was full of trepidation at the point of intimidation. My mind told me, "Beware, this so and so's gonna want money and booze." I was wrong on all counts, especially the "so and so." As he drew closer, I tried to appear confident, strong, and fearless. This was the first male Sioux I think that I ever met and he looked both wiry and wily. Had this been 200 years ago I would have been petrified with fear for my top knot. I think I saw too many John Wayne movies as a kid — the ongoing indoctrination/brainwashing of white America to help justify Manifest Destiny. When we do it, we call it Manifest Destiny. When other countries do it, we call it genocide or Holocaust.

He barely scanned me and immediately told me his name was Eagle. I called him Mr. Eagle and he seemed to like that. He indicated he was amazed that I had come so far from Maryland to see Sitting Bull's final resting place. I told him about my bucket list and the goal of reaching Yellowknife, Northwest Territories, Canada. He exclaimed, "Boy, that's way up there." He then asked if I had said a prayer for Sitting Bull and I told him I had. He seemed pleased with this. He then told me that Sitting Bull was not a war chief but a medicine man. I said kinda like a preacher. He was tickled with that. He appeared proud to share his knowledge of these things but not arrogant. He told me he was not related to Sitting Bull but was a direct descendant of "Gall" who played a major role in Custer's demise at the Little Bighorn and I found out later had been mentored by Sitting Bull.

Without asking me for a thing, he told me he liked my boat (kayak). He wished me a safe journey and I wished him likewise. We shook hands and bumped knuckles twice. I took a few minutes to clean up my lunch site and to pack everything back in its designated place in the van. I looked back up towards that water tower to check Mr. Eagle's progress and Bingo! He was gone - the old vanishing act again. I was simply amazed. How do they do it? Look at that photo again. There's not a tree or a bush for Mr. Eagle to conceal in. I want to learn how to do that. Maybe it's a gift just to the Native American.

One of my major goals on this bucket list was to follow as much of Lewis and Clark's route as possible/as practicable. I picked up their trail not far out of Bismarck, North Dakota. I found those parts of their trail were designated as Route 1804 or Route 1806 in honor of the years of their super human trek.

Remember, I picked up the trail outside of Bismarck but they had already floated down the Ohio River from Pittsburgh, Pennsylvania, to St. Louis, Missouri, and upstream on that river for hundreds of miles before they ever even reached near to Bismarck. I shouldn't have to emphasize upstream too much. Their keel boat carried 30,000 pounds of supplies and hard/soft wear for the trip. Don't forget to take into account the weight of boat and the men who manned her. Also be aware that in those days there were no dams on the Missouri, making her run even faster than she does today. I can assure you that even with the numerous dams impeding her natural flow today, the areas I visited let me know how powerful her current remains. These were tough people. I don't know how they did it. These would be great guys to have on our Olympic team.

I saw a brown sign with a fish and boat on a landing decal in white print/paint. I was to see many more of these welcomed signs on my journey ahead. All I wanted to do was to touch base for the first time with the "Mighty Mo" as the Missouri is oftentimes and affectionately called. Further down the lane I came upon another sign that told me I was on land of the Wilton Sportsman's Club - Don Stickel Boat Landing and Campsite. Now it was getting interesting. Was I going to be able to break the bond that had developed with Walmart? I wasn't sure I wanted to. I remained in bear county and had consumed not only the Lewis and Clark journals but every book, movie, and documentary I could get my hands on long before the concept of making this magnificent journey of my own was conceived. Every book, every documentary talked about them running into bears that had no respect for them or the multitude of bullets needed to bring one down. I was heading for Canada - can't take a gun there. I had a vast assortment of knives, the biggest being a Ka-Bar, a small hatchet, and a large short-handled heavy axe. With none of which did I want to interact with a bear. I got a feeling that after a few more maulings or folks being drug off into the forest and eaten on for a few days, Canada may repeal some of their current firearms positions. I also had a foghorn-like device that I figured if used would indeed hurt the bear's ears, thus infuriating him/her to a higher level. Last but not least, I had a can of pressurized bear spray. Whatever you do, don't read the fine print that comes with the bear spray or bear foghorn directions. In so many words, it says these products may not have the desired effect on your bear. Reading this did not jack my confidence of the pricey deterrents up to the level I wanted it at. I also brought along some homemade deterrents as extra precaution. I will describe them later because I can't wait to get on with this. Rambling over the countryside has caused me to ramble on and on with my pen. If you're getting bored or sleepy just lay this down and resume reading it later when you have nothing better to do. I will assure you that it does get better at least in my mind's eye - but just possibly, I could be a tad prejudiced.

Back to the Sportsman's Club. Driving beyond the previous signs mentioned, I came upon campsites with cement picnic tables on cement slabs with galvanized roofs or rooves — not sure — Webster couldn't help me on that one either. So, take your pick. Remember, I'm in charge of the writing but you're in charge of the reading. There he goes rambling on and on again.

Back to the Sportsman's Club II. Not only were there more than adequate camping sites, I also located a lone brick outhouse which will be described here as sufficient but you could tell which ever club member's turn it was to clean up the place enjoyed cleaning the campsite areas much more than he enjoyed cleaning the outhouse. I wouldn't stoop to reporting him for this omission. Remember, the 4th of July weekend was just back a few days ago and maybe they had a crowd. Whether they had a crowd or not, someone or maybe some folks had way too much of what looked to be at my first and last glance way too much chili.

At present, I was the only camper present. I wanted to stay here as it was such a lovely spot overlooking the Mighty Mo as the campsite sat high on top of a level bluff above the river. Was I trespassing? Could I get arrested? Could I be accosted by angry Sportsclub members? If that was the case, I was hoping that it wouldn't be by the last one who used the brick outhouse. I was also pretty worn out from yesterday's 556 miles. Another great thing about this site was an abundance of rough firewood left for me by my predecessors. A truck cruised by slowly and went down one side of a loop that took you to the boat launching area. I heard voices (real ones this time). I needed to know if I was welcomed here and who and how much I needed to remit. I couldn't see the boat launching area or its accompanying steel fishing pier that was built to bob and weave with the current from my desired cement picnic table, but soon learned that it was directly below me hidden by a slight knoll rising slightly at the edge of the bluff. How easy it would be to conceal your position from someone in this rugged landscape. Let's say if you were a native, a bear, or an irate Sportsmans Club member who recently had used the toilette facilities.

Anyway - I clambered down over the bluff because I felt too tired to take the loop. Much to my chagrin, I learned quick just how costly this could be through this low lying, thick and sticky brush that covers the hill from the top of my bluff down to the road across from the boat launch. Halfway down I wished I hadn't worn my shorts and the thought immediately grasped me, "Hey dumbass, you're in rattlesnake county." Fortunately, he/she wasn't there or took pity on this dumbass easterner. What was there was a big smiling guy who had a look on his face that reeked of "wait til I tell the guys about this dumbass easterner I met running through snakey brush with shorts on down the hill above the boat launch."

He was really quite nice once he realized I was no major threat to the loved ones he was determined to protect from the dumbass easterner (by now you can finish the rest - you've heard it enough times). Gasping, I asked him if he was a member of this club and he confirmed that. I asked if they allowed non-members to camp here and he said yes. I asked if I could pay him as I'd found no drop box to leave payment in, etc. He told me that there was no charge and went on to tell me that most of the other Sportsman's Clubs along the Missouri charge likewise. Of course, they frown on you messing the place up or burning the place down. I let him know that he'd made my day and to thank fellow members for their gift and generosity.

I spent the next few minutes watching he and his wife watching their three or three and a half year old son giving a mimic fishing demonstration with a stick and a string. What a scene. I was told by my mother that when I was a toddler, my babysitter was a string on a stick that I caught thousands of invisible fish with in a tiny fair-weather brook running along our yard. Ponder, ponder. The sun just starting its slow drop in the west making the gray top of the Missouri River look somewhere beyond an orangish pink.

I didn't get that photo other than with my mind where it will have a permanent place on the banks of my memory. The little boy had no clue that I was even there. It was just him, his stick and string, and all those fish he was catching. I thanked my nameless friend again and headed back to my camp through those bushes, but this time I was listening ahead for any hissing or rattling.

So now, I was camping on a site that Lewis and Clark could have selected for their own in 1804. What a great feeling. I noticed it was starting to stay light a little longer now and suddenly realized that it should be. I'm further north now. I should have more light than I want by the time I get high up in Canada. I'm so very fortunate to get to do this and all I have to do is drive my van.

The river is very wide here with a multitude of visible sandbars. I saw another guy in a small motor boat trying to get to the boat launch but had to swing his boat way up river and coast down to the boat launch due to the sandbars. He looked like this wasn't his first rodeo and he had that boat in and then in behind his truck and away before I could offer assistance that he no doubt didn't need, and would have no doubt waived off.

I forgot to note that I'd seen a lot of buffalos today back on Route 12, but heavy traffic at the time prevented getting a photo or doing a ubie. There must have been 75-100 of them in a tight packed herd close to the highway. I saw two more smashed porcupines again today (bad average for them the last few days), possibly a dead antelope, and one live whitetail buck still in velvet.

Traffic had dwindled to very little once I got on Route 1804 earlier today much to my satisfaction. I guess folks out here take Lewis and Clark for granted like we take George Washington's exploits for granted back home. I'd like to personally impede the progress of taking things, places, and historic souls for granted across the globe. We can learn so much from their deeds, good and otherwise. I drove past Mt. McKinley in Alaska going to work and could make it out on clear days but soon started taking it for granted and in doing so made her just another bump on the horizon. I mentally kick myself in the butt for that every time the thought rolls back around in my brain pan.

One thing I was happy to notice on Route 1804, almost all vehicles approaching contained waving drivers. I guess we all shared the bond of wanderlust. After a while, you just can't wait to see what's up around the next bend. I think I've had it since childhood — thanks Dad and Mom for those Sunday drives.

Had a great supper of crackers, dried vegetables, soup, and an apple. I cooked over the steel enclosed pit provided by my unknown, except for one, members of the Wilton Sportsman's Club. I will and did send them a thank you card — seriously. I saluted them via two beers and a cigar, recalling that it was a pint of grog per day for Lewis and Clark's men.

Before climbing into my bed in the van, I stopped and sat in the front seat to jot down some preliminary notes to describe today's discoveries. Didn't Jefferson (President Thomas - USA) name Lewis and Clark's expedition "The Corps of Discovery"? I don't know if they would have selected me or not but am sure that I would have been one of the responders to their advertisement.

The reason I was sitting in the car to note down some thoughts was that a storm was brewing. I wonder who used those words first to describe the build up of a storm — perfect choice of expression! It had begun with the help of the wind to blow under the roof over my picnic table. Thoughtfully, I checked out how clean the water was coming off that roof and once satisfied, I positioned what pots/pans/etc., I had not already in use to catch some delicious rainwater - they don't make it any fresher than that.

Tired now and only about 9:30 PM, I crawled back into the back of the van after dousing my fire even though this brewing storm was really starting to percolate with heavy enough winds to rock the van. Rain coming down in torrents, and my favorite of all, cracking lightning that blasted as if a bully knowing there would be no challengers and lighting up the sky and land for further than the eye could see, and then that on again/off again silent darkness trying to hide from the next resounding boom and flash. I think it's God's shock and awe. I always loved each and every thunderstorm I've ever been a part of.

Speaking of thunder/lightning storms, let's whisk you away from Route 1804 for a few minutes. Being there and driving it is a lot more thrilling than reading about it through the recollections of an old fart. I'd say he was about 11, making me 10. He being my late but great cousin, Harold Appel. What a character study. I always called him Haroldie. One hot/sticky summer day at Cumberland's Constitution Park pool, we were presented a dilemma. Should we take the 25 cents the guy offered us to run around the perimeter on the cement walkway surrounding the outside of the pool and get soaking wet winding up his car windows in the parking lot across the street, or should we stay dry and penniless up in the concession stand overlooking the pool, affectionately called "The Casino" back then? We took one look at each other and thought it over for about a half a second and took off running. It wasn't raining cats and dogs but it was close. Halfway there running side by side/step for step, we saw a bolt of lightning shoot up into the heavens and then shoot back down on us. Of course, this occurred faster than the time we parlayed our decision to get rich just for winding up windows, for back then a quarter made you rich at the Casino (concession stand) as it only cost five cents for any one of the two pinball machines which we were hot to trot on. I recall that we both woke up on our backs in the rain. Our cheap tennis shoes laying near us had been knocked off and laid back there steaming. There was a crack in the cement from the lightning strike. I also recall that each of us woke up laughing because we were so happy to still be alive. If you think this was fiction, ask any one of the hundred or so other patrons who witnessed it from the Casino. The guy never did give us the quarter. Maybe, just maybe that's why I'm like I am or like I'm not. Come to think about it, Haroldie changed a little after that, too.

I sure hope this is not boring you. But, now, you know why I love thunderstorms. Let me get you back to Route 1804 on the Mighty Mo.

*Forgot to write mileage down — carried over to next day totals.

DAY #7, 7/7/2016

I got up at 6:20 AM. The sun was already low in the sky. "Come on boys, we're burning daylight." Thank you John Wayne. By the way, if you think John Wayne wasn't that popular, Haroldie's older brother's name is John Wayne Appel and he is still with us. I still call him Johnny. Anyway, I felt very rested. When you go to bed at 9 PM or thereabouts, you have no trouble getting up early. There's a lot to be said for not having a TV that controls our sleep patterns.

That nitrogen blasting storm had long since moved on. For those of you who hate and/or fear storms, you should now take into consideration that without them you don't eat. Lightning bolts blast nitrogen into our dirt, making it possible for food/plants/trees/life to grow. So, find a reason to quit fearing them and start loving them. I always like to confront bigots (of any color). Do you really hate that person or do you really fear that person? There he goes again — getting off the subject.

Back to 6:20 AM on 7/7/2016. I climbed down out of the back door of the van as this was my only open access in or out. I had that thing stuffed to the gills. I had estimated the trip to Yellowknife would be about 5,000 miles one way. Being a fond believer that a scout is always prepared, I packed everything I could possibly think of needing. It is better to have and not need than to need and not have. There were a few places on my map up in the Northwest Territories that I would be traversing that had gaps between civilization that I estimated looked like 100-150 miles. That's a long walk if you forgot the tire puncture kit, and then again, there's that long walk back.

Back once again to 6:20 AM. The storm had transformed the land and riverscape. All of those sandbars were under river water now, running with a velocity and roar that certainly went unnoticed last evening. Nature is ever changing. She is never boring. Why do we label so many things "she" like ships and other contraptions that carry us through perilous places and times? Is it a throw back to our mothers? Why do dying men call out for their mothers and not their fathers? Three cheers for all the moms out there and those who are no longer out there. I know mine is gone but I can still feel her protecting, guiding, and caring for me. Thanks Mom. God gives us all an angel at birth and we don't always realize it until he takes her back. I often feel Dad there, too. Why do we all think at some time that Dad is so stupid, only to learn (oftentimes too late) that you were blessed to live with a man of wisdom and courage far beyond your own. I guess time has been standing still at 6:20 AM again. Oh, how the mind doth wander…

The Mighty Mo appeared to be about 1/2 mile wide this morning and like I said coming on in strength. Remember above when I wrote how the storm transformed the river and the land? I didn't realize how much until I would hear a distant clanging thud of a sound that upon inspection told me was debris floating swiftly down "Mo" and interacting with the steel fishing pier next to, but downstream, of the boat launch. Regardless of all hazards, the cool crisp air around me signaled it was time for another bath whether I wanted one or not. Even though always donning my bathing suit (quick trivia question: what color was it?) I preferred early morning dips to avoid the maddening crowd.

PHOTO #1 - MAN-LAID BOULDERS ON THE MISSOURI RIVER

I took a photo near my bathing site which was a little back water below the launch and pier - kind of a slow swirling eddy. The water was chilling but not to the bone. I bathed quickly but meticulously. Well, as meticulously as one could with that ball mesh always hindering progress. What can I say? It served its purpose. How would you feel if that was your only purpose in life? The photo shows man-laid boulders along the east bank of Mighty Mo. For the life of me, I don't remember what looks like a parking lot, cars, and a small boat just entering or exiting. I estimated the speed of the river to be under 30 knots. I dried off quickly in the brisk morning air. Like I said, last night's storm was long gone but you could still smell it coming off of the land - maybe it was the smell of nitrogen. I'm considering having a quiz at the end of this narrative so read on carefully and concentrate.

That reminds me, I'm going to give you poor devils who've ever had a kidney stone or more some helpful information. One teaspoon of lemon concentrate per day has helped me as I have passed or laid many a kidney stone in my time. It's like an exclusive club. I tell those who haven't, "You haven't lived til you pass a kidney stone." I could go on and on here but would rather refer you to your own medical references. You know they say that the study of medicine is a practice. Well, I never felt I was practicing when I was passing a kidney stone. I felt I had a real handle on it. Haven't had one for four years now but recall all previous more than well.

I worked with two ladies who had both children and at least one kidney stone. When asked which they preferred, with no degree of hesitation, both proclaimed they would rather give birth again than to have another kidney stone. I didn't take off and leave you. The reason behind this last unrelated segment was due to an unexpected bolt of pain just coursing through my lower back — thank goodness it did not linger.

I wiped dry as best I could while carrying on that ongoing battle with the ball mesh. I grabbed my Ivory and washrag, wrapping the striped towel (oversized) about my neck. I had already pitched camp and drove the van down around the loop to the launch area making sure she (there "she" is again) was in park with the emergency brake on so as not to watch her bobbing down the Mighty Mo on her way to St. Louis while I sat there in the water struggling with that cumbersome mesh.

You saw the man-laid rocks/boulders in the photo. Picture me gingerly trying to make my way back to terra firma across them when what to my amazement stuck between boulders, river, and sand was a bone with teeth. I snatched quick (like the lightening bolts of last night). Well, maybe not that quick, but those few who know me know I wouldn't have wasted any time in my procurement of such an artifact. Lo and behold, Mighty Mo gave me sort of a present. The jawbone with teeth of a small or young horse, donkey, or burrow. I could only conjure up what event took place to cause it's demise or where it occurred. This piece was part of a whole that died somewhere up the Missouri from here. How far? Don't know.

Remember many words back, I mentioned that a scout is always prepared? It was at this instance that I realized I had forgotten to pack my radio carbon dating kit, damn! Forgive me for making jest of some poor beast that dies so that I could have a memento of my trip. We used to call them acid trips. Looking back on it, it sure cost less for gas....

I pray that this beast had a good life with plenty of grass, grain, and water and died swiftly not knowing what hit him. I'll keep it with all due reverence. Maybe you'll be able to see it under plexiglass at the Ron McFarland Museum in Oldtown, Maryland - admission $9.00, nursing infants admitted free.

People say things like, "Oh, he was only a cat or a dog or a groundhog..." I guarantee you that on a scale of ten, that cat, dog, or groundhog loved his life as much as you love yours and did less damage to his fellows than you have done to yourn.

Feeling greatly refreshed and absolutely inspired by the jawbone, got to thinking maybe an elk, a bison, or a cow - don't know. Teeth are too big for a whitetail. Maybe a Native American pony…

The next goal on my map was Fort Mandan area. There was a fort Lewis and Clark built to spend their first winter in and an Interpretive Center. I wasn't going to pay for an interpreter, so I had high hopes that the curators there spoke at least some English.

PH⊙T⊙ #2

On my way there and not too far north of Bismarck, North Dakota, I snapped another photo of the Mighty Mo looking north. Note all of the wildflowers along the road. That was another perk in driving the scenic routes, as I noted the larger/faster routes had little if any natural fauna that make me feel as good as a warm blanket on a cold night when it was there. It all gave each little winding road its own distinct personality. These seemed like happy roads. The others were just cold gray marauders. I challenge all states to sow wild native flowers in the median strips between the dual lanes to warm them up and make them happier.

With a dirty laundry bag getting heavier, I decided to kill two birds with one stone. I would now utilize my homemade traveling laundromat. It's a simple device made up of one five gallon bucket and one sturdy, tight-fitting lid. You could do it without the lid but you're going to hate yourself in the morning. So, we've decided to go with the tight-fitting, sturdy lid.

Step #1: Remove the lid.

Step #2: Add 1/2 cup of biodegradable laundry detergent.

Step #3: Add 2-3 gallons of water.

Step #4: Place dirty clothing into the bucket. In this case, 3-4 pairs of shorts, no underwear (that's another story in itself and more information than you need or want to know, at least at this time), 2-3 pairs of socks, and 3 short-sleeved shirts.

Step #5: Clean excess soap and water dribbling down over sides of bucket because you have used too much water and/or detergent in this, your first rolling laundromat since the 60's.

Step #6: Secure lid snuggly.

Step #7: Make sure you followed Step #6 to the letter. Who wants to look in their rearview mirror and see soap suds climbing the back walls of your vehicle?

Step #8: Completely enclose your rolling laundromat with large plastic bag (color of your choosing). Secure with twist ties at the top.

Step #9: Place your laundromat anywhere in your vehicle in an area that you feel confident will support her (there's that "her" again) additional weight without allowing her (ditto) to tip over. Suggested area: within sight of rearview mirror.

The ups and downs of the road combined with gravity and iner-tia should indeed provide for well-cleaned clothing. The longer you leave them in, the cleaner they will become. Sounds like a good motto for a new product — but wait, there's more! Keeping an eye in the rearview mirror, north by God we headed.

I must give some credit here to a deceased ex-friend of mine for this concept, knowing all the while he would have been inclined to take full credit for himself without disclosing that he found similar instructions in "The Mother Earth's Newsletter" popular in the 60's with many a hippie that I initially despised but joined ranks with after plying their goods. Do you think that Richard Nixon would have different outcomes had he tried a little mescaline? Let's just say Bob shared the rolling laundromat concept with me decades ago on a trip we made to Alaska. Blame it on the 60's.

Let's keep going on to the Interpretive Center. I had another optical illusion that could have ended up very painful.

I came to a "T" in the road at that end of Route 1804. On the map it looks like Route 83. I needed to take a left here and with no traffic coming from my right, and with proper turn signal on pulled out to the left. Almost immediately, I noticed the car and then the 18-wheeler approaching my front beginning to swerve. I was desperately peering ahead trying to see the animal or what was making them swerve with such erratic abandonment. Then to my right I noticed traffic going in the same direction as myself. Then it hit me. The erratic swerving was to miss me. I had turned left up the wrong way on a two lane highway (speed limit at least 70 mph). Another hasty but well-timed ubie and I was at least heading in the designated direction thinking, "Have I given cause to adding these shorts to my rolling laundromat?" By the way, those swervers mentioned above flashed no lights, made no gestures, but did have somewhat startled expressions on their faces. Glad no one was texting…what happened or my poor guilt ridden excuse goes like this: they were resurfacing the two lanes I should have pulled on to, making them lower than my horizontal view and with no traffic coming from the right I pulled out on what initially appeared as a single lane highway. Thank you again God for watching out for me and all those innocents I would have taken with me. Once I regained some semblance of sanity, I couldn't help chuckling that it was certainly a John Candy/Steve Martin moment. If you haven't seen "Trains, Planes, and Automobiles" starring the above two guys — see it! It's an extended laugh for 2+ hours. Thanks John and Steve.

PHOTO #3 - STATUES OF LEWIS AND CLARK STANDING WITH A NATIVE AMERICAN - NOTE WHO HAS THE WEAPONS

I made it to the Interpretive Center in one piece. The lady greeters were very kind, spoke English, but wanted $7.50 to check the place out. Seeing me balk, they said in unison that the price included a walking tour of Fort Mandan (where Lewis and Clark cooped up that first winter). Not showing my hand, I bundled (thanks "Pickers"). I asked if they could throw in a shave with that price. They giggled and were more than accommodating. The elder of the two, looking up at my cap, said, "I'll never tell."

The reason I mentioned the cap was because the logo of a major TV network is in vivid colors against the dark blue of the cap. I have intentionally utilized this same cap for leverage many times since I bought it for a dollar at a Goodwill store in Florida. It works like a charm. Beyond displaying it, I never used it to exploit. When asked if I work or worked for this TV network, I always tell the truth even about where I bought it. Most folks never ask. But, once they notice the cap, they seem to stand with better postures, smile more, and sneak peaks over my shoulder looking for the cameraman. I pride myself on not taking full advantage of this simple cap as it would be so easy to do based on the vanities, desires and aspirations that most of us are stuck with. Oh, to have such a cap when I was sexually active, pre-Bonnie of course — we don't want to piss off the proofreader now do we.

PHOTO #4

I had a great shave and assured all of my fellow visitors to the bathroom that I had received official permission to do so. There were no complaints or questions especially after they spotted the hat. I didn't stare but caught glances in my mirror of guys standing at the urinals. They had such good postures but most of them kept looking over their shoulders for that camera. Wouldn't it be fun if you could make a sound like a camera running in any public restroom, not just those serving places with great historical significance?

The Native American sitting crosslegged though slightly anorexic was so lifelike that I had to snap this photo. Many artifacts in this center were those sent back to Jefferson (President Thomas - USA) for show and tell. The painted buffalo hide behind him was mesmerizing.

All of my years of studying history and I continue to learn new stuff. I, like most others, pictured the members of the Corps of Discovery fighting their way up the river in their buckskins and coonskin caps. In reality, they were handpicked soldiers and wore uniforms like the heavy wool one in Photo #5. I was impressed with the hat. That's black bear fur on the crown with a whitetail deer's favorite tail on the left side. I wonder if they borrowed this idea for the hat from the British Army. I would imagine that the uniforms alone impressed the Native Americans, probably the women more than the men. It is a known fact that most of the Corps spent many a fine night with the Mandan hosts' women. I've never read how many of the Mandan women bore light-skinned babies. Captain Clark is believed to have fathered at least one. I imagine the enlistment ratios increased dramatically once this kind of news reached St. Louis.

I had been aware of the air gun they took along but not aware that it had to be pumped 1,500 times before firing. I thought that's a lot of pumping for one shot. But then, myself and the group I was part of learned that it was somehow a repeating rifle. I'd love to see the blueprints on that one. It was said that the Native Americans were very impressed with this gun as well as the long/large pikes (spears) Lewis had especially made for this trip with impressing them being his objective. I've also read that Lewis' large black Newfoundland dog was thought by the Native Americans to be a God. I'll bet he ate well. Lewis' statue holds one of the pikes in Photo #3.

With our little green wrist bands we were then given a tour of Fort Mandan, a short walk from the Interpretive Center. Our tour guide was a young, sweet Park Warden who couldn't have been out of college very long before she landed this job, which was obviously something she had her heart set on for some time. She was a real

PHOTO #5

pro considering her age, etc. She knew her material and presented it as well as anyone I've ever seen in similar circumstances. We learned a lot from her. Forty-five men wintered at this Fort. They got there just prior to winter's onset, built the Fort using 3,000+/- trees, and nestled in. Temperatures that winter dipped to 60 degrees below zero. Remember, these guys had no access to winter garb that we take for granted. It was from here that they sent the big boat loaded with their findings, etc., even a live prairie dog, back to President Jefferson (Thomas, USA). It is here where they built/prepared smaller vessels capable of continuing their journey up the Mo. It is here they hired Charbonneau and allowed him to bring his wives (yea, there was more than one) including 16+/- year old Sacagawea who more than once saved not only their journals but probably their butts as well.

Say what you want about Charbonneau but he was keeping a lot of people reasonably happy throughout this time.

The more than friendly Mandan village itself lay across the Mighty Mo from Fort Mandan. It is believed population of that village was approximately 5,000 with a leap in population occurring approximately nine months after the arrival of the Corps of Discovery. It was a beautiful location for the Center and the Fort, especially this time of year with flowers galore, abundance of different greens, and sliced down the middle by the beautiful Mighty Mo with a slight whispering breeze cutting down through the cottonwoods.

PHO⊙O #6

Please refer to your maps on page North Dakota. Route 1804 kinda joins Route 83 North to Garrison and does a 90 degree left to White Shield then north toward Raub and mysteriously becomes Route 37 North, and then west to Sanish where she miraculously becomes herself again all the way out to Williston, North Dakota. I found no prospects for free camping there. It was here that I veered from my original plotted course after noticing on my map the Little Missouri National Grassland. Remember the word "national." This meant that with my lifetime National Parks pass I could get in free with 50% off for seniors. I'm not as dumb as I look!

Without hesitation all of us headed south. I'm still traveling alone. I just threw that last part about "all of us" in to see if you were paying attention. It would be to your advantage now for me to repeat that I'm seriously considering giving you a test at the end of this trip. So, pay attention! You will not be given any warning with regards to quizzes. I'll bet you'll pay closer attention now from here on out!

PHOTO #7

South it was, then on Route 85 to Theodore Roosevelt National Park North Unit within the boundaries of Little Missouri National Grassland. I would have been very pleased to lock in a site at either one of the two campsites listed — Squaw Creek or Tulip Campground. I thought Squaw Creek sounded more romantic of the two so I set my sights on her. On the way there, I took today's seventh photo at a pullover but did the grand site little justice. The topography is my mind's stereotypical expectation of the West. The highway takes a slow right beyond the pullover and if you have a magnifying glass you can locate the bridge in the right upper center that crosses the Squaw Creek. As you can tell, another article I forgot to pack was my Sony 12,000ZT 200M lens. Take my word. There's a beautiful bridge in this photo. Think of it as like a Find Waldo puzzle. What do you expect, this book was cheap! Next time, try the hardback. If you're really confused, see Photos #8 and #9.

You're probably saying to yourself or to all those friends you're encouraging to buy this book, "Why didn't he just show the one larger of the two photos?" Look closer. Look at the background. These are two different buffalo. They should have a warning on these throwaway cameras - warning, objects may appear further away than they actually are....these photos do show the always changing diversity of the land in this region — far western central North Dakota. I love the eroded hills behind the standing buffalo. These photos were taken less than 1/2 mile apart. I came around a bend and standing buffalo had been rolling in a dry woller. I either startled him or he was very embarrassed as he rolled up onto his feet before I could grab my camera while he was rolling. Never saw one roll in person like that. Some day people will have chips probably near their eyes that will take instant photos of exactly what their eyes are seeing. I don't know how the trigger device will be activated. Maybe like a wink, a tug on your left ear lobe, or the index finger on your right hand firmly but gently jabbed up your right nostril just short of the first knuckle. Don't laugh. It is your trigger finger. Any-

PHOTO #8 - LONE BISON SITTING DOWN

way, I probably won't live to see it but many of you current skeptics will be saying, "God, this guy was like Nostradamus."

PHOTO #9 - LONE BISON STANDING UP

Anyway the landscapes are worth seeing both photos and for your first time you get to see the by now infamous stripped oversized towel. Should this grand book that started out as a brief journal become infamous, don't be surprised to see this notorious towel at auction on eBay. Just think, what would you give for it right now. Think it over. Give me a call. I'm flexible. Maybe you could bundle or I could throw in my light and dark blue washrag. He who hesitates is lost. Where do you think the people are now who bought IBM early? Think about it. I'm listed and home a lot.

Squaw Creek was very nice. No showers, but clean toilettes, and well-spaced water pumps. I didn't think it initially, but a few days later after this water had sat in it's containers it started tasting a bit what I'd suspect slightly alkaline water would taste like. It became soft, slightly oily, and a toss up between slightly bitter and slightly salty. I exchanged it as soon as I could but lived to tell the story.

PH⊙T⊙ #10 - A-LINER MANUFACTURED IN PITTSBURGH, PA

It was great to meet the kind and helpful host camper. My TV-lo-go'd hat had what appeared to be an adverse effect on him. He seemed reluctant to give me his last name but was forthright in tell-ing me that he was a school bus driver from Houston and has vol-unteered as the host camper here for the last few years for about two months each summer. He told me hosts get all free camping privileges plus $10/day in pay. He indicated that he waived his pay and told the park service to put his pay towards other needed park stuff. He had cut firewood at his site in small piles that you could procure for a small donation. I don't know if the donations ended up in other needed park stuff coffers or not.

His camper was a metal foldable a-frame that weighed less than 2,000 pounds which he hauled here from Houston behind his four cylinder Subaru which he checked could haul over 2,000 pounds. He was gracious enough to show me the interior. One large bed left side of door, one small bed right side of door, sink, collapsible shower, kitchen area in center with impressive head room. Now I'm 6'4" well 5'10" and I had room to spare. After camping in my van for a week, his place was like a palace. I never did see the Subaru. I hope it wasn't in the shop with transmission problems or something, but I doubt it.

When I snapped the photo of the A-liner I encouraged him to get into the photo but he declined. I forgot I still had my TV network hat on. Now I did and still think he was as honest as the day was long, but I still don't know his last name and have no photo of him. One of my hobbies is being an amateur, unlicensed detective but I'm not going to call Houston Board of Education and ask them if they have a driver with his first name. He told me there's only 700 school bus drivers in Houston. I do have a cousin, Steve, in Houston though. I wonder if he knows any school bus drivers?

The campsites were offset from the road on maybe 45 degree angles and although close it felt like you had plenty of room and privacy. This time, I had my choice of three or four. Things had died down since the 4th. This evening I met my neighbor campers. He was a guy from Minnesota and his wife was from Czechoslovakia. She had a major Czech accent but was very nice. I told her that a friend of mine named Drake had traveled throughout Europe and he told me the Czech people were the nicest. Actually, Drake told me the Czech chicks were the hottest. See how I can clean up my act when I have to? It's not that easy you know. She had a twing in her accent that made her sound like the women in the movie "Fargo." She and the teenage boy and girl talked a lot in Czech. They spoke much louder and faster when they talked in Czech than they did when discoursing in English as if they wanted other campers around to know they were Czech. Or just maybe, Czech is a louder/faster language than English.

In bed this night at 9 PM — I wish those Czech campers would talk in English now.

Ending Mileage: 36,175
Mileage For Last Two Days: 615

DAY #8, 7/8/2016

Arose at 6 AM. Saw the host and asked him about Teddy Roosevelt National Park South Unit. We were in North Unit. He said go back to Route 85 and south for about 80 miles, but it was worth it. It would be even taking me farther south than my initially planned itinerary. I considered that Teddy Rosevelt's ranch was out there somewhere near and I'd like very much to romp on the same ground that Teddy did - Bully! He came out here soon after the deaths of his wife and mother. I'm pretty sure they died on the same day. Talk about needing a little time off to get away from it all. Poor bastard.

Before making my decision about the southern route, I met the "Grand Dame" so to speak of my camping neighbors. She was the mother of Greg, married to the Czech girl/lady. The "Grand Dame" told me Greg of Minnesota's Czech wife could speak six languages. I wanted to ask her how fast and how loud but I held my peace. The "Grand Dame" and I call her that as she came off regal with a quiet grace, charm, and elegance without flaunting it. Though camping, she appeared to be floating in a dress that was more suited to be in the wardrobe of an Elizabethan play than to have just spent a peaceful night, hopefully, in a green tent along the Squaw River. This lady was a real class act or her social worker had confided with Greg that it would do her good to have a three day pass away from the asylum. I jokes. I really felt this lady showed signs of well-traveled, well-educated, etc. I enjoyed her brief company.

I told her it was a disgrace that we Americans were one of the few inhabitants of this planet who can't speak more than one language. She shared that she had walked in Spain last year and was amazed how advanced they were (i.e., recycling facilities everywhere, even in the smallest of towns).

I spouted that we Americans were so brainwashed that we are superior as Americans and can fix all the wrongs of the world and that our brainwashed attitudes give us a mentality that we should feel sorry for the poor backward people (i.e., Spain, etc.) Whether she agreed or not, she was displaying some positive nodding.

I think both of us realized that if we kept on this same line, we would be storming the Bastille soon. Fortunately, Greg joined us and I learned that he had spent time in Alaska as a marine biologist (no, he did not look like George Costanza). He said his main job there was in trying to restore fisheries. I asked him if he felt he had been successful and much to my fisherman's delight, his answer was in the affirmative.

I asked him if he felt that man was still or capable of depleting fish populations around the world? Then came the hammer. He said that depletion by man fishing was far less of a problem than man's pollution and he cited dead coral reefs around the world as like a ticking bomb. It was difficult after the above but we parted on a friendly note as they were returning to Minnesota and I needed another day to rest up here on the Squaw.

As I had come so many miles in so few a days that I felt that the road had beaten me up. Again I reminded myself that this was not an endurance race but a glide through beauty and history. Why ruin it by hurrying? It could be my last hoorah.

After they packed up and got in their vehicle to leave, I made sure they saw me waving goodbye to them and to my delight, I saw hands and arms waving back at me. My mind drifted back to the "Grand Dame." What a catch she must have been for Greg's father all those years ago. I got the feeling that he was gone, over to the other side. I got such great warmth, kindness, and vibes from her. Oh! To have had her for a sister! I'm sure she was closer to 80 than to 70 but so regal. I felt like I was in the presence of royalty. The great thing about this royalty thing is, she treated me like an equal, not a subject.

Remember my portable laundromat description thousands of words back. It was time to see how it worked out. They had bounced around in the five gallon bucket for a day or so and had a soak cycle all night. To my delight the lid had done its job and there were no leaks. It was at this time that I wished I could have developed a rinse/spin cycle in my bucket. In this case, the user of this reasonably thought out device must take on the role of the rinse cycle and then the spin cycle — keep in mind to follow that very order. With plenty of water the rinse cycle was relatively easy. I just held the bucket under the water pump. It took approximately 5+/- buckets of fresh water to run out the soapy water until it was near on clear. The spin cycle was a tad more difficult. All of the cleaned clothes had to be tightly twisted by hand to ring out excess and there was a lot of excess. It took some time. Looking on the wrung out clothes now laying over my picnic table made one ponder if the newly administered wrinkles would be permanent or temporary. Did I leave out the mini toilette plunger I had brought along to act as a manual activator through out the above cycles save for the spin cycle? And, if you're wondering, I sterilized it with bleach at home prior to the trip. "A scout is always prepared."

At this point, I was feeling somewhat triumphant, but was faced with yet another pressing issue. I couldn't fit my clothes dryer in the van. I needed a clothes drying line but wanted to be discreet so as not to make fellow campers think that I was destitute or cheap. The last laundromat I'd seen was in Minnesota and I didn't want to waste my money in a laundromat anyway. "Anyway" is usually del- egated to the first word in many of my sentence structures. I think this is the first time it ended up on the very end.

Hint hint — don't forget about the test and quizzes. It could be "open book" test or quizzes. But, do you really want to drive yourself completely mad trying to dig up little known facts like this? Get real! But, I do encourage you to read on but only while concentrating as best you can. Only you know your limitations. Right now could be a good time to set this book down and call some friends and let them know just how much you are enjoying this intriguing adventure and encourage them to pick up their own copy. You know you'd be doing them a great favor and they'll always remember who turned them on to this never dull, exciting, action packed masterpiece. Go ahead, do it now. You owe it to yourself. What do you have to lose? This can wait til you get back.

If you're back now, this would be an excellent time for me to let you know that if you can show proof of 5-10 friends who bought this book after being inspired by you to do so, I will personally send you an autographed copy. Of course, your only expense will be shipping and handling. The hardcover is just slightly more than the paperback version but you don't need to remind any of your 5-10 friends of this. But wait, there's more! If you succeed in convincing more than 10 of your friends to buy this book, I will personally send you an autographed hardbound copy. They'll love you even more for what you've done for them. I'm going out on a limb here but I'd go as far as saying that they'll even start inviting you to those private parties you didn't even know they were having. Anyway, I don't mean to toot my own horn or appear self serving but we need to get this book out to the masses. I'm counting on you.

Back to the drying cycle - Pop Quiz!
Where are the rinsed (by hand) clothing laying now?
Answer: ˙ǝlqɐʇ ɔᴉuɔᴉd ǝɥʇ uO

Don't expect so much help on the next quiz. So, stay on your toes! (Who the hell came up with that expression? And, what the hell does it have to do with scoring well on quizzes? Don't know and don't even want to go there - just part of a stream of consciousness or near consciousness.)

As stated hundreds of words and prior to your first quiz, I needed to dry those clothes. Initially, I was going to use rope (not to hang myself - I hadn't been at that juncture since Day #2 or #3). Bathing really helps and can offset any number of suicidal thoughts. Cleanliness is next to Godliness. Filthiness is next to a rope. So, if you're about to be at the end of your rope, take a bath. I recall a couple who visited our mental health facility. You could still smell them in the offices they visited 2-3 days after they had left and we sprayed those offices down thoroughly with Lysol as soon as they were gone. Some people have a power all their own.

Anyway, I decided to use my spare cinch/tie down for my clothes line. Now this sounds simple enough, doesn't it? And it worked very well. With help from my Walmart collapsible step stool (not the cheap one from the hardware section but the stronger one I had exchanged for the broken cheap one). The stronger one was in the household section. Sounds to me that the boys in stocking had some sort of mix up in codes or were laying bets on how many of the cheap ones would come back in many more pieces than they had at purchase time. Such was the case with mine. The cheap one said it would hold 250 pounds. My good friend Bobbie must have weighed 251 pounds at the time of breakage. I can still see the look on Bobbie's face as his 251 pounds went down through that collapsible (you got that right) step stool, splintering it into several smaller pieces that conveniently fit into a plastic Walmart bag for its return trip.

I will refer to this Bobbie should he be a part of this text in the future as "Living Bobbie." There was a previous ex-friend "Bobbie" mentioned thousands of words back that had initial inspiration regarding the portable laundromat. Should he return in any future text, I will refer to him as "Dead Bobbie" as is the case. And knowing Dead Bobbie (past tense) he would probably be somewhat amused. Hint hint — great nearly useless trivia for your next quiz. Note Living Bobbie had shown me how to cinch down my kayak on top of the van. Dead Bobbie was, shall we say, "out of sorts" at the time....

Now, I don't want you to start having any anxiety or worse still, the dreaded panic attack regarding this testing and quiz business. Ask any of my former students. I was firm but fair. Better still, I was just fair. Sure, I had some discipline problems, but remember, I got mostly C's in undergraduate work and like everyone else in the 60's did not run across any instructors who prepared any of us to become instructors. I'm proud to say, I failed no one in almost 10 years as an educator (in title only). I don't think you light up a kid's future prospects by failing him/her.

Anyway, back to my clothesline. Did I remember to tell you that I was no way aware of the stronger collapsible step stool Walmart was offering in households. I returned the cheaper one's pieces to the customer service department. The lady there said I could get my money back or try another one while staring oddly at my stomach. It was the only game in town. I may just have to give another one a try so I could reach the top of the kayak now strapped down tightly to the top of the van. To end this quandary, I enlisted the aid of my significant, Bonnie — 32 years and still a challenge…we marched back to the very spot we had first locked eyes on the first collapsible (you got that right) step stool in hardware. There they lay askew as if some dissatisfied or disfigured customer had walked by and simply kicked the lot of them. Blessed Bonnie (nickname - Precious) bent over as her back was not hurting as bad as mine (that day) and said those magic words, "Hey, wait a minute." Her keen eyes had noted one way in the back that didn't look like all of the others. It was different. It was stronger. I think it said it could support more than 251 pounds. The clerk we approached became immediately defensive and said, "That one belongs up in households." Right away I became suspicious that he may have been the stocker who did the switchermarue (don't bother - it's not in the dictionary) to give himself the edge on this week's company pool about how many of the cheap ones would be coming back in pieces. He just had that look about him…there's another phrase whose origins greatly interest people like myself. Note to Precious….please take the word "challenge" above as a compliment. I also want to thank the beastly brute that threw the stronger one onto the weaker ones' pile because you were too frigging lazy to return it to its rightful place up in house-holds. So, you saved yourself about $5. Did the one you ended up with break yet? Give it time. But I do owe you some remote degree of thanks. Your obvious slothfulness enabled Precious to find the stool I used throughout my trip and it's still not broken yet. So there you have it. God works in mysterious ways. I still want to have Living Bobbie to take it for a test drive.

I pity you the reader now cause I'm almost getting lost in the dust of my wordiness. My Dad used to cal me "Windy." I told you earlier that he was a lot more astute than I gave him credit for.

Let me take us both back now to that clothesline novel. I had to stand on stool #2 to reach the tree limb high enough to hold my wrinkled wet clothes on the line. I did the same process on a second tree limb across the way from the first. For you novices or you lifelong spoiled bastards first kept by your mommy and now kept by the woman you ought to treat better, utilizing two limbs like this working in unison works better than the use of just one as the novice who initially uses just one limb for his clothesline will oftentimes note a distinct sagging.

Finally it's up. I'll bet you're relieved, too. So we might move on with more interesting material such as bear attacks, snake bites, bomb threats at Walmarts, etc. Oddly enough there was a guy out West while I was camping at the Squaw (Precious, please note it says "at the Squaw" not "with the Squaw" — you can never be too careful) who was mauled, killed, and partially eaten (I hope for his sake in that order) while biking in a remote region. Did you ever have a dog go nuts and chase you on your bike because something in the sight or sound of the bike's wheel spokes triggered an attack? If I wrote a manual for bikers in remote areas, I think my first rule would be - don't go where there are bears. No offense to that poor guy, but some people have the attitude that it won't happen to me — well it happens to someone! It has to happen or thousands of news-people would be out of work.

I keep veering from the clothesline story. I guess cause it's a bit boring for me, too. Don't you feel better now. You've just been made aware that you're not alone. I knew a bond would start to develop. Who would have thought that it would take a clothesline story and a biker eaten by a bear to bring it about? I now utilized the wooden clothespins I had brought along for just such a purpose — a scout is always prepared. However, once I got all the wrinkled wet clothes pinned up on the orange cinch tie down clothesline, it began to rain. Actually, it only rained briefly for a few minutes. I like to refer to this type of rain as a "dry rain" just to see the different levels of puzzlement on listeners' faces. I also find it useful in finding out who's listening and who's not. If you get an "a ha" from the listener after you say, "It was kind of a dry rain" you know that he was not listening or should be pronounced brain deficient if not brain dead. These are the folks who do not fare well on quizzes.

Pop Quiz #2! Fill in the blank: A scout is always _____.
Answer: pǝɹɐdǝɹd

I can see now with how you're scoring on these first two quizzes, your mind's going to have to run a little faster if you're going to keep up with me. Now, now, don't be fretting so. Remember I'm the writer. I have two distinct advantages over you. I have the answers and I know when the pop quizzes are coming. Just keep trying harder - never give up!

If some of your friends had this book, you could ask them to help you. A good time to ask would be at that first party they invite you to. And look around, there may be a lot more people you could tell about this book at the party. They could help you, too and then more parties. You see how this thing could just snowball? And it's all because of you. You never dreamt this could all happen to you. You never saw yourself as a leader or even better a catharsis for change in your own time. We're talking living legend stuff here. Now just don't give up! You want that signed hardbound copy don't you? I've got so much confidence in you right now.

Back to the wet/wrinkled clothes on the orange cinch tie down line. While putting up this line I had noticed an official Park Warden vehicle cruising by slow two or maybe three times. I even gave the lone Park Warden a wave on one of the times, with renewed confidence as my collapsible step stool had remained in one piece.

The dry rain ran off somewhere to the east and the dear sun came back for a quiet but bright visit. The quiet only being interrupted by the dry rain dripping from my wet/wrinkled clothing. Accomplishment had just set in when the Warden came by on his third or maybe fourth lap. This time he stopped, no doubt to admire my clothesline. This, as it turned out, was not the case.

As the dry rain had put a damper (no pun intended) on my drying cycle, Ranger Tim put a damper on my clothesline. Ranger Tim was a young Ranger... 25ish, originally from Idaho and he missed those mountains. As he was carrying a 40 Glock on his side holster, I gave him my undivided attention. Ranger Tim was courteous, professional, respectful of our age difference and polite. You could tell, he was well-trained and this training coupled with obvious good upbringing, manners, etc. won my respect immediately. With an apologetic quiver in his voice, he informed me that "they" (apparently his higher ups and not necessarily him) frowned on attaching anything (i.e., clotheslines) to trees not just here but in all the National Parks throughout the land. That I could understand. What I couldn't understand was why he waited til I got the thing up before approaching me about it. These were just thoughts of mine at the time. Remember - he had the gun. I had a can opener. I jokes. I never once felt threatened by him and never once did his demeanor reflect aggressive authoritarianism. It was more like he was apologizing and hated to do it because, frankly, I think he admired my clothesline. It must be terrible to have to enforce laws you don't agree with. That's why I think he drove around so many times. I think he was just hoping the clothesline would just go away.

I told him that I should have known but I didn't. I've found in the past when dealing with law enforcement that immediate admission of guilt with a sprinkling of stupidity or oblivity of the laws often-times receives a warm welcome from the enforcer. For all that young Warden knew when he walked into my camp, I could have been an axe murderer just luring him in with my clothesline.

So much for my ingenuity. I told him I was just pleased I was able to get it up as I was not all that familiar with the simple cinch and S-hook tie down that everyone but me is familiar with. So much for my academic education again. That college boy's got no common sense! Don't they love to say that. I guess it makes them feel better about their own choices versus vocational endeavors.

Anyway, after the Ranger asked where I'd washed my clothes cause he couldn't think of any laundromats between here and the one in Minnesota, I filled him in on my portable laundromat and told him it worked great except for the spin and rinse and of course the drying adaptations. It was at this time that he came clean (pun intended) and he shared that when he and his wife first moved out here from Idaho (again - that look of homesickness) this place was more likened to a barren desert than his beautiful mountains in Idaho. I told him how much I had cherished a week in Idaho and the people I met there many years back. He continued that he and the little woman (I've seen some pretty and good sized women out West. He must have got one of the little ones) had no washer/dryer in the trailer (a long thing that makes you go crazy) they had to live in and that they had to wash all their clothes in the bathtub and wring them out by hand. I spouted off as that is a big part of my nature, that I bet his wrists and arms got strong. "Spouted off" is another play on words I wish we had time to explore here now but I'll just bet you're hoping I can just move on.

To make a long story even longer, I worry constantly about my reader's attention spans as I understand that with the advent of technology, computers, texting, Facebook, instant gratification, etc., that attention spans have shortened considerably in just a brief period of time. No wonder some of you are doing poorly on the quizzes. Have you ever been telling a really funny or interesting story and the people you thought were listening intently begin a totally unrelated conversation on another subject? There you have it! Proof is in the pudding - yet another one of those sayings that warrants further in depth study. But, since one of my goals is to finish this work before I die, maybe I should return to the original theme if I could remember what it was.

This info reminded me that Minnesota's "Grand Dame" whom I was talking to scores of paragraphs back was also anti-technology. I remember sharing with the "Grand Dame" that when Steve What's-His-Name died I thought they were going to carve his head out at Mt. Rushmore. My own feelings were more mixed due to what I perceived as a potential downside to ever increasing / encroaching technology. I fear for the loss of jobs, criminal invasion of privacy, free enterprise being held for ransom, crippling of our military infrastructure, and so on. Picture if you will an ingenious hacker with no scruples, moral fiber, conscience, etc. Don't expect a person or Country with the above traits to have your best interest at heart. Way back at the onset of the Industrial Revolution most everyone thought it to be a positive direction for mankind to head only to realize later that it may have cost us the planet.

Anyway, Ranger Tim did allow me to continue using my clothesline but only if I hooked the tie downs on to the elevated fire pit, across and looped around the picnic table with the far end extending to and attached to my kayak atop the van. Now, I will ask for your input. Picture the nice straight line of my original clothesline between the two trees, and in your minds eye picture what appeared to be haphazard with absolutely no aesthetic or artistic merit generated from my second clothesline described above, which one held greater natural like beauty? I had even looped dirty tee shirts around the branches so as not to disturb the bark on my initial line. It didn't matter all that much as they had already dried pretty good while I was discoursing with Ranger Tim. When the Ranger was driving around so many times before his friendly chastisement of my initial line, I think he was torn between who gives a shit, performing his duty, and hoping I wouldn't come at him with a homemade battle axe.

I also learned from him that campers are not allowed to cut any firewood, dead standing or otherwise. I'm so glad he didn't pick up the newspapers and state maps of Idaho and Montana that I had been studying earlier in the day as I had my four foot Swiss Army saw hidden under them that had been my intention of procuring firewood with prior to his arrival in camp. At one point he had both his hands on the maps oblivious to what lie below.

He was a good guy and I liked him. I would hope that he gets reassigned to his beloved mountains in Idaho. I did tell him how we miss those little mountains in Western Maryland when we "snow-bird" to flat-as-a-pancake Florida in our winters now. He said, "Ah yes, those little Appalachians." Feigning indignation and hurt feelings, I fired back, "Oh yea, but they used to be as tall as the mountains out here." He saw through my attempt at humor and we had a hardy laugh together. I took the all but dry clothes down and reset the second line per his instruction.

From the road it must have appeared much like photos I've seen from the Dust Bowl in the thirties and those poor souls seeking to out distance that dust by heading west with everything and everyone they owned.

The host walked by but didn't stop after Ranger Tim had gone. I got the feeling he was doing a follow up regarding the Ranger's instruction to me.

I felt reasonably well rested and decided to explore some of this northern unit of Teddy Roosevelt National Park. Immediately upon exiting the entrance to my Squaw Creek camping area, I noticed

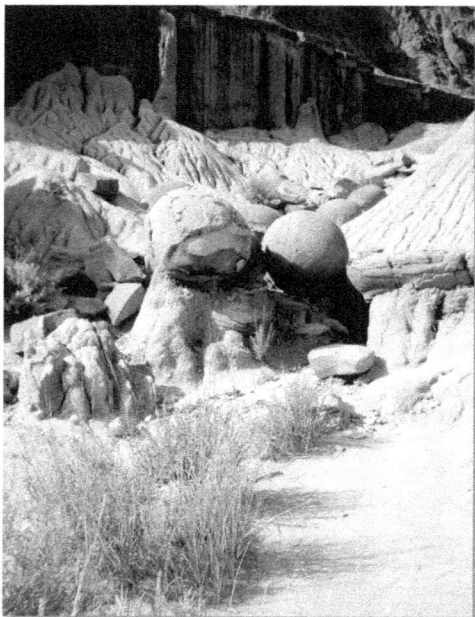

PHOTO #1 - ROCK CANNON BALLS

some unusual formations just across the two lane narrow highway that meanders through the park. Be careful gawking because everyone else is, too. They call them cannon balls but they are stones. Very spherical with different sizes from pretty big to a little bigger down to a little smaller. Some were partially buried/partially sticking out of the constantly eroding hillsides. They had some scientific explanation for them being some strange mineral deposits, but that didn't satisfy me because one of my other hobbies just happens to be unlicensed, way short of a degree, amateur archeologist. Sure I'll agree that they were strange mineral deposits but no one explained to me how they got that shape and there were hundreds or more of them just in this one small area. As I've said oftentimes before, "Your guess is as bad as mine."

Finally you get to see what the author looks like and thinks like (Photo #2). These eroded little enclaves were just around the corner from where I shot the mysterious rock cannon balls. It was a scorcher of a day with temps in the very high 80's. You've got five numbers to work with here as high 80's would be from 85 to 89. Had I said low 80's you'd be working with 80 to 84. Anyway, I'm just trying to use a writer's ploy to help you to interact. It really could have been in the low 90's though… Hint hint. Good news for you. I never quiz or test people on dates or numbers - there's so many of them, and with leap year throwing everything off, why even bother?

Regardless of the temp, my perch inside the enclave was the coolest seat in town. I found the mosquito repellent unnecessary. But, a scout is always _____. This is not a test, I'm leaving it blank for you to fill out to help you again with your interaction and of course your self esteem, which should be improving if you printed in the correct word. If you used cursive, we're going to have to target that interaction even further down the line than I had initially expected. Hint, hint. To see if your printed response was correct, you may feel free to turn back to review answer to Pop Quiz #2. Now, if you've done this with my prodding or better still, if you went back and checked the proper answer prior to my prodding, your interaction is definitely improving. Now don't get a swelled head about this. We both know there's a lot of room for improvement simply by looking at your responses to Pop Quizzes #1 and #2. I do want to see continued improvement, and I commend your efforts. Stay with it. You've got some potential. Granted at this time, it appears limited. Just seeing your mentor sitting on a chair smoking a cigar inside of a small enclave has no doubt been of inspiration to you.

PHOTO #2 - HAPPY OLD GUY IN CHAIR WITH CIGAR AND BUG SPRAY

Are my legs that thin? Must be the camera angle. By now, with this slight improvement regarding your interaction, you've probably wondered 'how did he snap that great photo with just a throw away camera from Walmart? Is he truly a mystic or a conjuror of sorts?' Truth is, I wasn't in there for five minutes. Remember, I said this was very near the highway. Like I said, I was only in there for five minutes. Astute students would have already caught this by studying the length of my cigar. Now, see what I mean about you having a long way to go yet.

Anyway, a rental car slid to a stop with Indians pointing and yelling in Bombayoise. Hearing this language, I knew it wasn't our beloved Native Americans but the real ones, the ones Columbus was really trying to find. Poor guy. He was only off by a continent and two oceans. No wonder he died broke. Anyway, these Indians poured up the path in front of me. I could hear them coming/jabbering like pissed off bees. I didn't want to frighten any one of them. So, I called out to them trying to put a little Bombayoise accent into my English dialect. No problem, they already knew I was there. The nice Indian girl who agreed to snap my photo told me they all thought I was a statue carved in the eroded mountain. I felt as much pride when she told me that as when I first learned how to whistle. I directed them to the big balls around the corner, again putting a little Bombayoise twist into my chosen language. I could have lied but this was all entirely true. I snuck out of there while they were all jabbering up a storm back at the big balls and drove quietly from the parking area. With all those strange 10-armed gods and goddesses they mystify with over there in India, I wanted to give them something to ponder like was he a real man or a persona from the Bugavadgea taking the form of a real man? What can I say? When you live alone and travel alone, this is how you get... these Indians may have taken this to heart as I told the girl who snapped my photo that I was communing with the spirits.

PH⊙T⊙ #3

I drove around the park for about an hour. It was extremely hot. Thank God for a good wind.

See the unusual mesa (I think that's what it's called, Webster thinks so too). This mesa kind of points down to the Little Missouri River. My camera did no justice regarding the steepness of most of these mesas. It was way too hot or a good walk would have been out to the front along the flattish-like top. All of these rivers in this region were more sand than water (almost). This photo was taken from inside a pavilion built of all native rock and stone by the CCC (Civilian Conservation Corps) started by Teddy's cousin, Franklin, in the 30's during the Great Depression. Good job boys - well done - well built. I never saw any Marlboro men anywhere, but roadside signs designated this area as a major cattle driving region.

This photo shows the abundance and varieties of formations that cover most all of this park. Do you think that an Indian or desperado could hide out there?

PH⊙T⊙ #4

I had to take a brief but necessary break just now. I'm writing this at my picnic table back at camp. A bird scored a bullseye on my ear, shoulder of my hard-earned recently clean shirt and map of Montana that I had been studying and plotting a course on. Think about it, it only took me a day's drive, lots of hand rinsing and help from a Ranger to produce this formerly clean and slightly wrinkled shirt. What's that saying, "gone in an instant." Somewhere out there in the cottonwoods the other birds are giving him high fives with their wings. Maybe it's payback from the spirits I was communing with earlier. Anyway, I hope he's happy with his fifteen minutes of bird fame.

The park is starting to fill up. I guess because it's Friday, I think. What's great about travel - the extended kind - is that you lose track of time. Once way back in Oregon, I discovered it was Thursday when I thought it was Friday the whole day. So, I got to have two Fridays in a row once upon a time in Oregon. It was mystical. The hashish didn't hurt either.

Let it be known that the author has not used any form of illegal drug for over two decades now. This is your brain on drugs. This is your brain not on drugs. There's not much difference is there.

In the late 60's I was traveling across Texas. At that time in Texas they were locking people up longer for personal drug use than for murder. Now ain't that a bitch! What kind of a mindset does it take to go along with it and justify that it's for the good of society in general? Whose society and whose general? Talk about your cruel and unusual punishment. I wonder how the people who made the laws and the people who carried them out will justify it when they're standing before the pearly gates. I'll bet there will be a lot of apologetic stuttering with some alligator tears followed by, "I was only following orders." Wasn't that Eichmann's defense strategy?

There he goes again. Off on another tangent. Should we try to stop him now or just wait til he puts the straight jacket on himself? Makes you wonder about the origin of the phrase "going straight."

I see lots of popup tents on backs of trucks and a tent next to me on top of the roof of a Land Rover. Hope it's not dented.

I find people eager to talk if I start the conversation. An older couple 50 feet to my rear won't even look in my direction even though I know damn well they know I'm here. Maybe they're talked out, constipated, antisocial, had a cruel neighbor 20 years ago who didn't, but told them he saw a couple on America's Most Wanted that looked surprisingly like them, maybe they're still paranoid about the potential for axe murderers still lurking about in our national parks driving Dodge vans with red kayaks on the top, ad infinitum.

I found a substitute dishwasher or should I say utensil washer by accident today. I finished off the rest of the soup I'd made many sentences back at that Sportsman's Club along the Missouri River. I had a handful of spoons/knives/forks (used but not yet washed). As I did not want to give these unclean utensils the opportunity to give me "trench mouth" — see origin in medical manual— a blistering death of upper layers of skin on feet - (trench foot) due to prolonged periods of being wet and skin on/in mouth and gums (trench mouth) due to eating from dirty utensils, dishes, etc. Key word here is dirty. I suffered from the latter especially so in college. Thought my entire head would eventually rot off. Surmised, initially, come to think of it, it could have been a negative side effect of the quickie I got or gave with the drunk sophomore girl Friday morning after Biology 102. Built up my nerve and with my tail between my legs approached the team doctor ever so discreetly. He had been the team doctor for 35+/- years so "ever so" might work with him but "discreetly" was out of the question. After looking at my mouth and enjoying gagging me numerous times with his tongue depressor, he began his insistent quest for lurid details of just what occurred that caused my procrastinated need to seek his learned opinion. He looked up to the ceiling and then down to the floor as highlights of the drunk sophomore rolled from my blistered tongue. After my divulgence, he was still, deathly still, for what seemed like too long, spun around on his backless circular shorter chair than mine and as quick as lightning was right back in front of me, peering at me over the heavy black rimmed glasses that seemed to continually slide down his shiny reddish large nose. From behind three days of whiskers came a grunt, followed by a gasp for air as if it were his last, I heard him say in that raspy voice, "Well Mr. McFarland, I think you'll find your malady and cure on Page 1,037." He thrust a heavy, large book into my lap, spun around on that short round chair in a flash and vanished through a small brown wooden door I hadn't noticed before. To my delight when considering optional outcomes, I learned that I had a simple case of trench mouth and the cure was peroxide rinse times one or two, and it was gone like the drunk sophomore and the good doctor through that little brown door. I could swear that I heard a female giggling on the other side of that little brown door while I was studying medicine at college.

Note: I found later that any remarks regardless of causal effects regarding trench mouth should not be brought up on a first date. Wait at least a few dates. Once she gets to know you, I'm sure she'll be a lot more understanding.

I know you're scratching your head but there definitely was a link here between trench mouth and cleaning utensils. Think about it.

Anyway, I had been putting all of my dirty utensils in a tall plastic container for safe keeping and bear proofing. I had recalled on an earlier piss outing to the lavatory here at Squaw Creek, I had noticed hot and cold running water, brown paper towels, and a push up soap dispenser — you do the numbers. Yea, I put the dirty utensils into the plastic former large peanut butter jar that had my soup in for a day or so in my cooler, hit the soap dispenser maybe four times into the jar, tightened the cap firmly and utilized my hand and arm as an agitator device and within a very few seconds and before any other campers had gathered to spectate, I was already in rinse mode. Thank you Squaw Creek! Note: I never had any bouts of trench mouth on this whole trip. I thought I did once. To be on the safe side I prescribed a gargle with peroxide that I'd packed for the trip, but only had to take one dosing. An ounce of prevention is worth a pound of cure. A scout is always _____.

I'm not telling you this time.

It's been a long day and noting that perhaps some fellow campers somehow resisted the urge to communicate with me this evening caused me to ponder if it could be time for yet another bath already. In theory the baby wipes were a great idea but in practice one can never be completely sure when traveling alone. It was time for the portable shower to do its magic. I had already learned that ice cold water inside the portable shower plastic holding tank could be warmed up to a reasonably lukewarm/comfortable temperature. You could just lay it in the sun on a rock or hood of a car, etc.

The only place I had to hang it was from the same tree branch that had earlier concerned Ranger Tim. So as not to draw attention to myself, I got my still intact plastic folding stool and sat on it under my very slow cascading shower head, which could be turned on and off at will with a trigger mechanism at the base of the holding tank. I had positioned myself, the shower, the stool, and my vehicle so as to give as much ample cover as not to make the older American's Most Wanted couple, or the recluse from West Virginia who had recently arrived and set his camp across the street from mine, upset. I had ample privacy and the only open area was the campsite just past mine left empty by the Grand Dame's troop earlier today.

About midway through my most comfortable, refreshing, and possibly much needed shower, I peered through the biodegradable soap dribbling down over my face and again as luck and timing would have it, waved to my two new fellow campers who had just chosen the site formerly occupied by the Grand Dame. I waved while still seated and pointed to my green, black, and blue bathing suit to assure to them that this was not a nude camping area. A quick return wave from them and they started their ritual unpacking in what appeared through the biodegradable soap suds to be in great haste. I found out later from them that much to there relief they saw my bathing suit later, but only after I had stood up. So my initial pointing down towards my bathing suit had not had the desired effect that I was trying to project and hence, their hasty unpacking. They were on their 14th day out and heading home to Minnesota - no Fargo accents here either. As we were heading in opposite directions, they gave some good cues regarding great but free potential campsites to come up later in my path.

Ending Mileage: 36,175
Miles Last Two Days: 615

DAY #9, 7/9/2016

Did you ever think we'd get out of Day 8? Me neither. There had been a lightning storm in the middle of the night. They need it around here. I found myself praying for rain for most of the places I passed through out West as it was obvious that they had come up short lately. I was unaware that we were having somewhat of a drought back home at the same time until Precious told me later.

While shaving this morning in the restroom and talking to a guy at the other sink who was giving himself a spot bath (it looked like he was an old hand at this) a little boy of 8-9 with big glasses came in. As I was finished shaving, I offered him my sink. It was then that I noticed he had blood on his hands. Could this be the axe murderer in disguise? Not funny! I asked him if he'd cut himself as he was displaying no alarm that most kids his age would if they had blood on their hands. He nonchalantly responded with two words, "Bloody nose," giving us the impression that this happens frequently. With my clean sink partner at my side showing as much concern as I was, we both asked something on the lines of, "Did you bump it?" in unison. Again, with that casual matter-of-fact nonchalance, he replied, "I get them a lot while I'm sleeping." After assurance from him that his parents had him to a doctor regarding this and wishing him an end to those nosebleeds, my sink partner and I left this brave bookworm looking kid at the left sink as he appeared to have a handle on everything. I still said a prayer or two for him after leaving. I thought about this brave kid a lot on this trip and still do today. He'll be one of my heroes for as long as I have memory.

I decided to take the host's suggestion and drove down and through the southern unit of Teddy Roosevelt National Park and I was glad I did. I never did find Teddy's old ranch house that he lived in, in his cowboy days. I think he intentionally chose this isolation to help him get over the great loss of his wife and mother. A good reason to come back some time.

I stopped at one of the many pullovers and decided it was a good place to pee as no one was around. So, I followed a trail that led me out of sight of the parking pullover as I'm such a discrete guy. While peeing, I heard voices coming my way from the same direction I had come from. I thought to myself, I should have seen any hikers when I was parking the car as it was pretty much barren. It sounded like a girl and a guy or two girls. I'm sure I heard them twice. I was surprised to find no one there or any where when I went back to the van. This was the first time I'd heard voices since 1978, in Alaska.

This story is well worth mentioning as it is true and should serve to intrigue you. I am pulling off Route 94 with a gorgeous view of Hump Lake near a place called "Home on the Range." I kid you not. Somewhere close to the South Dakota/Montana border. It's so small and underpopulated you'll not find it in your atlas but it's there cause I saw a sturdy metal official looking sign. Back to the voice. I was cross country skiing near Bethel, Alaska one weekend. I made concentric circles back then to keep from getting lost and knowing I'd likely connect back up with Bethel if I kept my wits about me. Best shape I was ever in. I cross country skied to school where I worked every day and then did cross country skiing on the weekends, allowing me to spend some more quality time away from my wife.

I was out further than I'd gone all winter but maintaining my arch path to ensure a safe return home before dark. I'm not sure of how far I was out. I'd guess I was somewhere between almost too far and not far enough. Anyway, I heard a distinct female voice, I couldn't make out words but I'd have to say it was like a soft wailing or cooing. It seemed to be coming from the top of a rolling knoll facing me down in a narrow valley. Note: Bethel is surrounded by rolling, treeless hills of tundra making for great CC skiing. Although it took me away from the planned route of my arch, I seemed to be mesmerized by the sound. There was a breeze blowing ever so slightly. It wasn't blowing hard enough to drown out the sound or be the source of the sound. I hadn't seen anyone all day since losing sight of the village and that was the usual case. I did see some ptarmigan earlier but spooked them to flight before I could draw my 22 Ruger pistol for a shot. Ptarmigan are delicious. The higher I made my way up the hill the louder the wailing or cooing became so I knew I was closing the gap. I was also concerned that it could have been someone injured. I had seen a girl fly past me almost this far out about a month back with her sled and 6-8 dogs. Could it be her? It definitely was a sound that only a female could make. If only I could hear some words.

Suddenly at the crest of the hill there she was. No, I didn't see her but she was still there cooing. I'd come upon an Eskimo coffin alone on that hill. Yupik Eskimos bury their people above ground in wooden coffins with their favorite metal tea cup nailed to the top of the coffin above the occupant's head. The cooing or wailing stopped abruptly when I reached the coffin. I can qualify the truth of this story as the hair on the back of my neck just raised up as it had done on the day of the event. I guarantee you, I was back home in the village before dark.

Looking back, I don't think the coos or the wailing were directed at me. I think she was reaching out to a loved one or just maybe a young lost child.

I made inquiries all over Bethel but no one knew of her. I think no one in the village believed my story. No one would go back there with me and I'd become reluctant. But, if you go southwest of Bethel, Alaska maybe for 2-3 miles, you might hear a cooing.

So I'd like to think the voices I heard back in the park today came from the spirits of Indian maidens who had sought my company but couldn't quite cross from their realm to mine. I never felt anything evil or frightening from any of these contacts but I assure you, they were real. Why are people so afraid of ghosts? They're living proof of life after death.

Back to Montana. Today I saw what I think were free-roaming ponies/horses, wild and free, too far away for a photo but plenty close enough to see and admire. They were stout and healthy. What a great symbol of our West - wild and free.

I also saw a lone cow (Black Angus) on the very top of a steep hillock. He appeared to be watching cars going by with intense curiosity or maybe he was wondering, "How am I going to turn around on this steep hillock without falling down?" Do cows think like that? If you should find out, please let me know.

I stopped at a rest stop for lunch near the junction of the Rosebud and Yellowstone Rivers. A sign there read that 40,000 buffalo were killed where you're looking in 1860, and that Clark of Lewis and Clark went back down this river on his return home trip in 1806. This would have been 40 years plus an additional century before I was born and much of this country remains the same now as when Clark looked on it. I'm so glad, especially for the parks that were saved and declared off limits to the greedy hand of man. Did I say we were all so lucky to live in this country? Had men like Teddy Roosevelt not thought to save it, there'd be a used car lot or a pawn shop beside Old Faithful now.

Temperature had reached 95 degrees - then another brief midday thunderstorm. I guess if we didn't get thunderstorms something would melt or crack. Open book quiz! What does lightning add to our soil? Multiple choice:

A. Chromosomes
B. Zombies
C. Nitrogen
D. Water
E. None of the Above
Answer: ↄ

I hope you got this correct without peeking.

Had a fine supper of the rest of my now moldy bread and the rest of my getting iffy steak I'd brought frozen from home. If it's good enough for Joan of Arc, it's good enough for me. Note: Joan had visions while leading her French Army against the somebody elses. They later learned that Joan and her army were snacking on moldy bread - hence the visions. But better still, "I've got a tapeworm and it's good enough for him" — Moe of the Three Stooges, 1930's.

When living with Eskimos (Yupik) near the Bering Sea in 1975, a tiny bit of moisture had made its way into their dried salmon. The mold looked much like blue cheese but it wasn't. If they ate it, I would eat it - it was one of my rules of engagement back then. I never once got or felt ill after eating it and like many of my Yupik friends, started to prefer the salmon with a little side order of mold. I guess they had seen my initial reluctance to eat the mold on my first outing. In reassuring and convincing voices, they encouraged, "Ron…Penicillin…." I loved those people and still do, and always will.

With confidence in my own metabolism versus mold, I had my supper at a wayside historical marker letting me know that Chief Joseph and the Nez Perce had passed through this rugged area in their flight from Uncle Sam just trying to get to Canada. I recall that they were just 30 +/- miles from Canada when Uncle Sam caught up with them. Their major transgression was that the land they had called home for many moons was a valuable piece of property Uncle Sam now calls Oregon, Washington, and Idaho.

Lewis and Clark owed the Nez Perce a slight bit of gratitude. The Nez Perce did not kill the party but befriended them and saved them from near starvation. But like I said, these Native Americans were hoarding a valuable piece of land that we had a right to…. what would you say to people today if they just walked into your house and claimed it, the food in your freezer, and oh yea, they want your car, too.

I fell asleep at a campground named Aspen while thinking of the Nez Perce and my first sighting of snowcapped Rockies in the distance today. They helped the temperature to drop back down to 68 degrees at 8 PM. Once again, my stomach won yet another battle against fungi and microbes and I dozed off looking forward to what tomorrow would bring.

Ending Mileage: 36,728
Miles This Day: 553

DAY #10, 7/10/2016

In three months, I'll be 70. That's kind of a disturbing thought to wake up to at 6 AM after a good night's sleep. Not too much we can do about time, just roll with it and hope you end up in all the good places.

Consumed a light breakfast - Cheerios and a fruit bar. Boiled more coffee in my tea percolator (I've always been a rebel). Fire taught me another good lesson. I wasn't paying no mind to the boiling coffee and it boiled over my Coleman stove. This will be a good test of how much you can abuse a Coleman stove without rendering it useless. It cleaned up good and easy and seems no worse for what I'd put it through.

I filled up my five gallon portable shower again last evening but was disheartened and pissed to see that the load-bearing handle you carry with and hang it from when in use was splitting all over the main seam. Obviously an engineering error as I never exceeded the five gallons. The lakes and streams around here are fed by the melting white stuff I spotted on the backbones of the Rockies yesterday. I really need my shower to work and I'm heading north into colder streams and lakes.

I took the time to sew that busting seam in a light drizzle with overlapping 20 pound test fishing line. It wasn't pretty but it held and will have to do. "Function before form" - Frank Lloyd Wright. It's the little things like that that can make a great trip go south — no pun intended. I'd love to have the engineer who designed it right here/right now. I'd have some words with him, if I could speak Chinese. Is there anything not made in China now? Our leaders remain baffled as to how the Chinese are a dominant economy now. How do you spell Duh?

I remained on Route 94 to Forsyth, Montana and took off northwest on the dotted Highway 12. It was good to get off that big ole 94 and to get back on a designated scenic highway that I could cruise at my leisure. I cruised past places with romantic sounding names like Ingomar and Delphia and Lavina as well as tiny towns with tough sounding names like Musselshell and Roundup and Two Dot. I also learned that I'd been skirting the Yellowstone River for miles again without even realizing it. It's not just the Indians and animals that can choose to sneak up on you. The whole West has a way of sneaking up on you in a surprising and for me, a delightful way. I couldn't wait to see what was up around the next bend and she never let me down.

Made it to Lewis and Clark National Forest close to Neihart south of Great Falls and only had to leave Uncle Sam $5 to stay for the night. It was misty and chilly but the camp provided a clean john. I wonder why we call bathrooms "johns" and assign that same nomenclature to a guy with a prostitute. Either way you need to be careful lest you get shit on…I've never been with one. That, or she didn't charge me (pre-Precious, of course).

The camp also provided a good working hand pump and you didn't have to chill the water. To my surprise I found no garbage can. I couldn't figure it out, there was more than sufficient signs about not throwing garbage into the "john" and about how difficult it was to clean out of the "john" once dispensed there. I could only assume one of three possibilities: 1) the guy who cleans them was proactive in the areas of job security, 2) some other local wanted and needed that job, or 3) the guy who cleans them had an ex-girlfriend with an axe to grind.

This campsite was situated in a narrow valley surrounded by rugged steep hills/mountains, I wasn't sure. As from the valley floor, you couldn't see the tops of these hills/mountains, vegetation was thick and it just looked like a bear could walk into camp from any one of the four not-so-beaten paths leading in or out of the dense forest. You can tell a well-worn path. None of these fit that bill. As you're well aware by now, a scout is always prepared. I had saved empty, well-cleaned plastic peanut butter jars. I had six of these filled with smells bears don't like - three with mothballs and three with bleach. They transported safely in a mini-cooler I had brought along just for them. All one had to do was to remove the lids and place them in alternating equally spaced places under the van to allow them to emit their aromas and still stay dry if this rain kept up (you'd think we'd say kept down, not kept up). Things would be a little different if yours truly would have been there when they made up the English language. Do you suppose they made up ten or so words a session and then called it a day? I'm going to leave this train of thought. I don't want you to become more confused than you already may be.

Anyway, some of you did better on that last quiz, hint, hint. I'm not above putting recipes or certain ingredients on tests, continue concentrating. I'm also wondering how much time you've devoted to increasing our membership in this book club. I know you've got a lot to think about and if you're not on disability or welfare, have a lot of work to do. But surely, you could set aside a little time each day in our quest to get more friends, family, fellow workers, etc., to buy this book.

Keep in mind, I'm not doing this for my own gratification. I'm doing this for you. Think how proud you'll be at our convention, when you're singled out and praised for selling more of this book than anyone else did in your town or your entire state for that matter. It doesn't matter to me. Someone's going to win this thing. It might as well be you.

I know you can't wait to read on but you've earned a break. Take some well-earned time off and call or email a handful of those friends, family members, or fellow workers. Think how proud they'll be of you when you stand up to that applause at the convention. And, I'll be there — the first to shake your hand. What a moment!

You can come back after you've made that handful of contacts. Start with the ones who like you the most. If there aren't enough of those, start with the ones who owe you money. Just never get discouraged. You'll get the hang of it. After all, "Einstein" didn't invent the light bulb on his first try. Try to reflect confidence and most of all enthusiasm. If you're feeling reluctant, pretend they're in their underwear. See, this can be more fun than you imagined.

Back to the bear deterrent. I think I may have also disclosed earlier that the atomic bomb of deterrents may well be used urine, the older the better. Sprinkle gingerly around the vehicle. Don't be reluctant to splash some over the tires. Animals do the same thing. You are just marking your territory, telling the bear I'm here but you need to stay out as I also have a back up can of bear spray.

Disclaimer: In the event that you utilize previous mentioned ingredients and the bear or bears continue to find you of interest, it is the expressed wish of this author that suggested ingredients in the previous paragraph do not reflect any degree of perfection in any scenario requiring utilization of said deterrents where bears or any other carnivores are of concern. We can only attest that the author has had a degree of success, so far, when personally employing said ingredients and their dispersal. The author also feels that you may want to enlist the old tried and true trapper's motto with regards to unexpected carnivores showing up in camp, "I don't have to outrun the bear, I just have to outrun one other person in camp." The author has no sound statistics on the recent correlation of more elderly in-laws being invited on camping trips. It definitely warrants further study. End of Disclaimer.

Peeing completely around the trunk or trunks of trees close to camp <u>could</u> also be a deterrent. It would be wise to inspect your surroundings prior to application of this <u>potential</u> deterrent in the event that fellow neighboring campers have arrived without your knowledge. Male campers seem to have a distinct advantage over female campers with application but don't let me discourage you girls. Except for one older gentleman in a white camper truck down at the far end of this campground, I was it. Maybe there's a reason for this particular campsite being not so popular. I sure wasn't going to ask the older gentleman in the white camper after seeing him peeking around the john, spotting me laying down a little fresh <u>potential</u> bear deterrent around a tree, and galloping off like he did back to his camper without even so much as a wave. Sometimes you just start to contemplate, are bears or old guys in white campers more of a threat? I had no old galloping guy in a white camper truck deterrent, so I just kept an eye out (great saying, but not as great as "keep your eyes peeled." Who thought this stuff up? It's in English.)

As reflected earlier, it had rained off and on everywhere I'd been in the last few days. Everything was saturated. I could not find any dry kindling. I used the chemical laced fire starter rectangles that I had bought numerous years ago— possibly too numerous. They did accept the flame from my lighter — I could rub sticks together but that's silly if you have a lighter. They did fire up the way they are advertised to do. However, they would not ignite even the wettest of wood products per their somewhat now limited guarantee. I suppose I could call the manufacturer if my cellphone worked in this dead zone, but I doubt if they would send help out in this rain.

I turned in not too long after late dusk. As the rain clouds had hidden the stars and with no moon out, it got as near to 100% dark as it gets on this planet. This is the only one I'm familiar with so far.

I wasn't even asleep yet when I heard it. A low guttural growl. My blood boiled immediately. Then a second growl and a third. It was raining too hard to hear it walking around my van wondering if it should eat the whole thing and it's contents here in the murky darkness.

I fumbled for my bear spray and Ka-Bar. I wasn't sure if I had the bear spray or mosquito repellent. There it was again, that same rumbling growl but this time it sounded closer. I was in panic mode. I guess you wouldn't be!

It was way too dark in that valley to see his silhouette. Let's take a quick break. You see that "his" in front of "silhouette." I can only speculate why but more times than not in my distant and current memory when something was about to eat me, I always referred to the eater as "him." Do you catch yourself doing that, too? It could just as easily be a big hungry female bruin who would be just as adept at getting the job done. In fact, you'd have about 50% odds if you had time to place a bet. But who thinks of gambling at a time like this?

Bears are astute learners and know how to break into vehicles. I was trying to gasp for air as quietly as possible just waiting for a window to be ripped from my car. Should I let him take me quickly or fight with all that was in me, swinging and plunging that Ka-Bar while squirting him right in the face with the bear spray or the mosquito repellent?

I really didn't want to hurt the bear but overriding that was my wholehearted belief at the time that I didn't want to be eaten just yet and not in this fashion.

When one is this frightened, adrenaline puts all your senses on high alert — this was Death Con 3. I'd like to give credit here. I heard Death Con 3 in a movie but can't remember which one - must have been during the Cold War. Anyway, let me know if you meet someone who's about to be eaten by a bear who's concerned about plagiarism.

I hadn't heard the growl for what seemed like incalculable time. Did time stand still like you hear about? Don't know. Did my life flash before my eyes? Nope. It was too dark. How quickly they forget. Besides the rain pelting the kayak, roof of my van, and the ground all there about, I heard nothing. Had he lost interest? Had something frightened him away? I doubt that. When you're the biggest badass in the valley you can fear no evil for thy claws and thy jaws they comfort thee or something like that.

I didn't budge. I find it odd how we all squint our eyes attempting to peer through the darkness even though we have a lifetime of unsuccessful attempts. An ounce of optimism would have helped here but I couldn't find any. I knew that once they hone in on prey (you know it's spelled differently but it sounds exactly like pray).... This respite in growling did give me time to pray - and I thought, what better time? And so I did. I figured I'd already rocked God the wrong way by making past promises of being a better person, etc. If he'd just get me out of another bind like so many times in the past. So, this time I just prayed, "Please God make the bear go away." Just then a little voice said, "Dummy, how could you hear him growling in all that storm outside?" I thought, God, You've got a solid point there. It was exactly at this time that the muffled guttural growl returned. My God, why have Thou forsaken me? He hadn't. I felt it this time. It was my own stomach growling. Oh what a relief it is...... There never had been a bear. God works in mysterious ways.

I've never had a prayer that wasn't answered. Sometimes the answer was "no." But it was the right answer. I tell everyone that I am not a Bible thumper but God knows me on a first name basis. Remember, you're never alone even if you think it's just you and a bear.

DAY #11, 7/11/2016

I got up a little later this morning. Nothing had disturbed any of my six peanut butter jars. Had a smashed hard boiled egg between a smashed piece of bread, dried bananas, and cup of java. The old guy in the white camper truck was already gone. Maybe a bear scared him away. He didn't stop for coffee.

Still making my way towards Great Falls, Montana on Route 12 and then onto Route 89 North, I noticed a small stream on my right with a rough cut area parallel to the stream but not too rough for the van and I to cautiously check out. I saw no "No Trespassing" signs there. As a matter of fact, the further west and north you travel the less signs of ownership there are. For days I would travel seeing fences that went forever. About every mile, there would be an old used black tire draped over or tied to one of the fence posts with white paint reading "No Hunting" but very, very few "No Trespassing" signs between the Mississippi River and all of Montana. It must be an eastern phenomena. The past distinctions between our North and our South have faded and blended but I've felt and seen the distinction that remains solid between our East and our West. And I'm glad it's still there. Keeps life more interesting. Go West young man!

Anyway, as the van and I crept down closer to the little stream, I realized the rough cut area was really the result of spring washout from the melting snow on those gorgeous mountaintops of the Rockies. Turns out, it was the Belt River that has a tremendous, meandering watershed all over these parts. It was crystal clear and probably home to numerous wonderful trout. They're my favorite fish to fish for. They are beautiful and tasty. But more than that, they need clean, fresh, cool water. When you find them, especially native trout, you've found clean, sustainable water that the hand of civilization hasn't ruined. It brings me sheer joy just to know they are there.

Many years ago on a hot July day in West Virginia, some friends and I decided to cool off in a large pool on the North Branch of the Potomac River just west of Petersburg and short of the Smoke Hole Caverns. It's still there. We grabbed snorkels, goggles and fins and jumped off the big rock you can see from the highway. We saw fish all over from suckers, carp, catfish, and fallfish to a very large resident bass under the limbs of a submerged tree that had to have taken decades to wash downstream to its current residence. That bass would get as excited as hell just watching folks plunging in off of that big rock that I'm sure folks of every age have done for ages. I watched him watching the jumpers. A penny for his bass thoughts. It appeared to be a real treat for him.

Upstream in this West Virginia version of pristine wilderness was the gold for me. I finned my way up to the upper end of the pool where oxygenated bubbles scrambled in with fast moving riffles succumbing to gravity. There was the gold! Eureka - four rainbow trout, one golden trout, and two brown trout so intent on catching and eating all the aquatic insects that make for a great trout smorgasbord being carried there with a push from the riffles. They had no clue that I was right behind them. Three more feet and I could touch them. They were just feeding at their leisure like a thin hungry girl at an all-you-can eat. There was no scarcity of foodstuff for them here. They had rich pickens - sounds like a country western singer to me. I remained with them until I was a series of white wrinkles.

All the while, my fishing pole, bait, and fishing license were up in my car. The thought had never entered my mind that I could easily have caught them all. It was one of those pristine moments, dreamlike, but genuine. That is the type of scene I'd like to flash before my eyes when my time comes.

Now, Belt River was calling me. She was saying things like, "Come on in. You need a bath. I have been waiting for you. I am here for you." I was drawn to her like a (I was going to print like a pig to rotting fruit but somehow the romance seemed to fade from the prose). So let's say like a butterfly to an apple blossom - ah, much better.

I parked the van at the edge of the Belt to cloak my actions from the highway. You never know what kind of reaction to expect from passersby, especially when you have your hand down inside your trunks soaping up. I took a photo of the pool I intended to bath in while still sitting in the van.

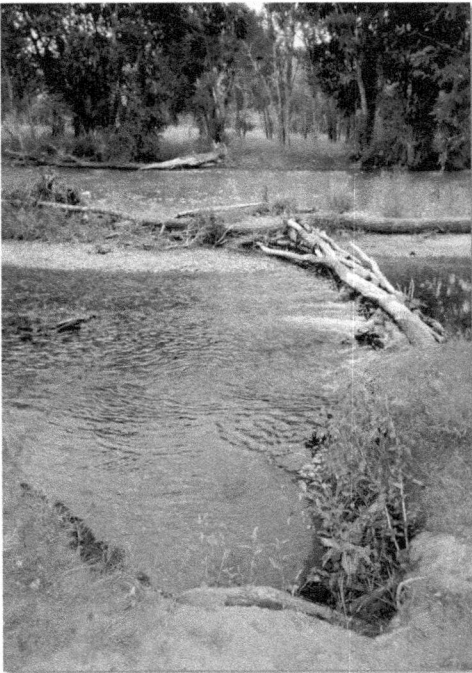

PHOTO #1 - NATURAL BATHING POOL, BELT RIVER MONTANA

I quickly assembled soap (biodegradable), towel, bathing tenners, washrag, and hastily changed into my black, green, and blue bathing trunks. If you look closely at the photo there is even a strong and much alive root exposed that serves a dual purpose as your step leading you down into the pool. It is not known if thoughtful Montanians or nature herself dug this bathtub size pool out of the bank. Nature's tub was about two feet deep and gave my 6'4" (OK, 5'10") frame plenty of room. Too bad they don't make biodegradable bubble bath. I would imagine passersby would possibly respond in a negative fashion though.

So, I stepped on that root step and proclaimed the hell with gradual emersion, I'm going in. Now, I know why they report that many a cowboy was reluctant to soap up. I yelled obscenities at the Belt River for she had conned me. Prior to this bath, I had labels for different levels of water temperatures. Labels ran from cool but cozy, to two-screams-and-you're-used-to-it. That wasn't the case here in the pristine Belt River on this hot sunny day in Montana just east of the Rocky Mountains.

Cold isn't a cold enough word. Bring the beer and the milk and the eggs over here boys to the Belt River. You don't need a refrigerator. They'll keep real good.

Remember the former two-screams-and-get-used-to-it label. Well, the Belt River label goes like this: one prolonged and projected piercing scream broken up briefly with short frantic gasping followed by another prolonged and projected piercing scream and so on. Had I had a companion to time it, we could have submitted it to Guinness World Book of Records for the shortest bath and rinse ever recorded in the Western Hemisphere.

As I hastily dried off once the blood in my veins thinned enough to move again, I looked up at those white capped Rockies to the west and could almost hear them cracking up. Think about it, even a beautiful white capped mountain can become desperate for entertainment. You're welcome.

You know, when you're screaming and gasping like that with cars passing by just 30-40 feet away doing 80 mph, it's oftentimes difficult to remain discreet. Nonchalant won't work either. So never mind their laughter or catcalling, dry off, get back into the van and haul ass. Turn the heater on if you have to. Remember, you're free and you're clean. I wonder if that phrase would have worked on women in the 70's (pre-Precious of course). Hi baby. I'm free and I'm clean. I'll just bet it would have worked in Montana.

The next lunch was raw hotdog x2 on two pieces of multigrain bread (mold removed) with ketchup. Also downed a cup of dried vegetables that had been rehydrated in a styrofoam cup while bouncing up highway 89 towards Great Falls.

PHOTO #2 - NOT SO GREAT FALLS AT GREAT FALLS

I was expecting like Niagara Falls but they weren't. Actually there was a series of falls. I think three or four that Lewis and Clark had to portage. I think it cost them a month or at least a very long time (something they didn't have a lot of as they were still east of the true Rockies and winter was creeping up on them). Like Lewis and Clark (I'm assuming this — I've never actually talked to either one of them) I too wanted to get out of Dodge, or in this case, Great Falls.

I continued following Route 89. This could be construed as mis-leading. I was actually riding on top of Route 89 inside of a van. Yet another mind-altering play on words. Frankly, I was feeling a bit on the tight side and had grown melancholic with thoughts of forking out another five spot or more just to sleep and shit in one of our great National Parks. So, I set my sights on making sleeping arrangements in Kalispell, Montana. Rule of thumb when traveling. If you're not sure your targeted destination has a Walmart, refer to the index section near the end in your Road Atlas. It has states/cities/provinces and whatever they call these same things in Mexico all in alphabetical order. They also list the populations of each city. Any city having a population of say 5,000 or greater will have a Walmart - 'nough said? You got it? My Atlas shared with me that Kalispell had 14,223 people in it at this time of my passing. Not my death, just my passing through Kalispell. So, I was a shoe in for locating accommodations tonight. Unless you have dyslexia, you can follow these simple suggestions found throughout this entire narrative and travel with confidence.

Speaking of dyslexia, I worked with a reasonably nice lady once who had it. We had hundreds of clients whose charts were kept in metal file cabinets in, you guessed it already, alphabetical order. Need I say more? She later became an office manager. In that same office, we had the nicest and most competent of many of the sec-retaries we chewed up there. She was very intelligent and thought-ful but had a remarkable habit of filing any form, paper, financial record, fact sheet, etc., that's title started with the word "The" under "T". Think about it. Those of you who laughed immediately are doing well. Those of you who hesitated before laughing, or those of you who are still trying to figure it out, and worse but not the least, those of you who never got it but laughed to make us think you did, can feel free to pick up the application for work before you leave. It's over there in the file cabinet under "T."

Route 89's entire length was as beautiful as her waters were cold. She connected with Route 2 near Browning, a fascinating town that I felt had seen better days due to the influx of white people followed by the influx of alcohol to ply the once noble Native American with, followed by the worst that capitalism has to offer — taking advantage of the weakness of others to fill the pockets of a greedy minority. It was just the vibe I got. I may have missed the speculation target by a mile but this is what I picked up on there. Maybe there were evil spirits about. Don't know. Didn't stay long enough to find out.

I'd been to Glacier National Park way back traveling to Alaska with Dead Bob and then again about 1990 or 1991 with Precious who overlooked telling me that she had a fear of heights. I don't know what would have possessed her to tell me before plans were finalized to go to some of the highest mountains in North America. Maybe she just forgot or I forgot she told me. I won't elaborate but I can assure you that she remembered quite loudly while I was trying to drive her over "The Highway to the Sun." It's funny to me what people will hold back sometimes. She really loves Florida though.

As I'd already been through Glacier National Park approximately 1 1/2 times, I decided before leaving Maryland that I would skirt her southern boundary on Route 2 and end up entering good old Canada on the west central side of the Rockies on Route 93. This entire ride was as lovely as Route 89 had been.

I was still targeting that Walmart in Kalispell though for my nightly repose. But, I was getting pretty tired as I pulled into Columbia Falls, a quaint, clean looking small town of 3,645 souls per my Atlas index which you know by now if you've been paying attention….Pop Quiz time!

A town with a population of 3,645 is not likely to have:

A. Fish
B. A bistro
C. Large women
D. A Walmart
E. A dentist with dyslexia
Answer: D

No peeking! Do you feel that these pop quizzes are helpful? Circle your answer:

Yes
No

They say that periodic testing can serve to boost one's self esteem and give one the self confidence and inspiration to achieve goals such as selling of books to family, friends, people in the workplace, and now even on Facebook. Keep your hand on the rudder and your eye on the goal. With your newly found confidence, I have all the faith in the world that I'll be personally shaking your hand and patting you personally on the back for your astounding number of family, friends, people in the workplace, and now even folks on Facebook who will be admiring you, inviting you to parties, luncheons, the club, to meet their single sibling, etc. Just imagine it, and all because you took it upon yourself to promote our book. Yea, that wasn't a typo. I'm considering far greater things for you than you can possibly imagine.

Still hoping that Walmart had anticipated a population surge in Columbia Falls and had planted another Walmart there. I searched, but in vain. I did come across a Super 1 Food Store. They are popping up at numerous locations west of the Mississippi. I think they are taking on that juggernaut Walmart. I found them very clean and well-staffed (eager to help) but prices are towering above Walmart. Message to management: if you're going to take on the juggernaut, you'll need to bring those prices down. But what do I know about competition strategies between marketing outlets? My expertise in this area only covers areas such as parking, lighting, bathroom facilities, and the like.

I soon learned that Super 1's competitive strategy does include all areas of my humble expertise. I would stake a claim on a secluded but well lit area of the parking lot rendering quick and easy access to restrooms for my morning rest.

I had time to check out the Falls but could not find them or any signposts to lead my way there. Surely to God, it couldn't be that hard to find the falls in a place called Columbia Falls.

I gave up and asked a guy who looked like a local. But no luck, he was Canadian and had just arrived here and wanted to see the falls also. We promised to look each other up when we met with success.

Determined more than ever now, I stopped at the Montana Coffee Trader's Shop. I asked the cashier there while paying for a coffee that I would have for breakfast in the morning. She sighed and paused as if she had grown tired of telling tourists how to find the falls. In an apologetic tone she lamented that there were no falls, that there never were any falls. The only people this would have made happy was Lewis and Clark.

Turns out it was a sharp newspaper editor's ploy to lure in more population to buy his newspaper. His success rate, so far, had not exceeded 3,645. The town was named after a logging company called Columbia Falls. So, for all intents and purposes, they could have named the town Treeburg or Loggington. I must agree that Columbia Falls sounds much more inviting and I for one would go there.

In fact this was actually my second search for these elusive falls. I mentioned hundreds of words back that Precious and I had vacationed to Glacier Park in 1990 or 1991. As she had some problems with heights, we agreed to drive from our timeshare on Flathead Lake up to Columbia Falls as the map said nothing of major altitudes with regards to the drive there. Armed with this information and assurances from me and then further review of the atlas coupled with 40 more minutes of reassurances from me, she agreed to consider going. Finally after seeing me tie the noose around my neck and securing the other end to our third floor balcony, she reluctantly agreed, if I allowed her to take a blindfold and not yell at her anymore.

The compromise completed, we set out to see Columbia Falls. I recall it was an overcast rainy day, the kind you'll have around falls. As we were approaching the town of Columbia Falls, we happened upon a makeshift sign that read, "Columbia Falls - Closed for Repairs." As God and Bonnie (Precious) are my witnesses, I made her take the blindfold off just to read the sign. I shit you not. Gull-ibility getting the best of us, we accepted the makeshift sign as gos-pel, put there we figured by a good samaritan who saved us the time it would have taken us to drive the last stretch to the falls. I'd love to meet the person who made the sign. If you're out there, please feel free to contact me. There may be a discount on a book purchase in it for you.

My bad. I forgot to mention, I had stopped earlier today at a roadside historical marker near Lake Francis. It was the site where Lewis and 3 +/- other of his men had killed two Blackfeet for steal-ing horses and guns. The Blackfeet had duped Lewis and his men by pretending to be friendly and helpful so that they could steal horses/guns. Lake Francis was a disappointment for me but not as much so as it was for the two Blackfeet. The marker didn't say but I remember reading somewhere that they were young boys trying to make a name for themselves. Their names were not mentioned on the marker. So, they really missed their objective - fame.

Again, this is a great example of the clash of two different cul-tures resulting in disaster. Had the two boys pulled it off, they would have been received as brave heroes that night in their home camp. However, the culture that killed them saw them as mere thieves.

So, remember, the next time you come across a culture different from your own, it might be wise to study and learn their ways and values. It very seldom makes a hit with any peoples if you kill some of their kids. No one has ever solved the mystery behind the death of Lewis many years later on the Natchez Trace (Tennessee). Offi-cial records say probably suicide. If this was true, Lewis shot himself twice. Just maybe, and I know this is somewhat of a stretch, just maybe it was Blackfeet.

Back in Columbia Falls, I kept an eye out in an effort to improve and/or boost US/Canadian relations by looking for the Canadian guy who had also been looking for those elusive falls. I couldn't find him. Those Canadians are extra hard to find when you're not in

Canada. I hoped that Columbia Falls wasn't his main target of a two week vacation. I looked a while longer for a man weeping but I never found him. If you read this and you're still out there searching for the falls, feel free to contact me. You deserve a free book. I can't waive the handling and service charge of $15.99 but the book is free to you for the asking.

Turned in at Hotel Super 1 around 10 PM and there was still light in the sky.

Ending Mileage: 37,322
Miles Last Two Days: 594

DAY #12, 7/12/2016

Woke up to a brisk and misty morning. This would have been my Dad's 94th birthday. After a brief stop in the restroom at Super 1 and purchase of some fresh bread, I headed up Route 93 still in the Rocky Mountains of the great state of Montana but within reach of Canada's great province of British Columbia. Am I really here or is all this a dream?

I had a quick brunch along a charming little lake at a picnic site that was vacant except for what had formerly been a nice rawhide jacket with fake lamb's wool interior. It was a bit soaked and a bit dirty. No telling if it had been there for two hours or two weeks. Makes you wonder about the former owner. Could this have been a benevolent gift for someone who needed a nice lightweight coat? Was it negligent forgetfulness? Was it the end result of a drunken stupor? The list of possibilities is endless. But, I know you're as anxious to cross that border as I am.

With that in mind, I packed up and started backing out from my picnic area when I heard a sickening crunch sound and knew what it was immediately. I'll give you five seconds to guess what the crunch was.................Close, but no cigar. I forgot to reattach my back bungee to the rear one attached to the kayak. It was crushed but not broken and hadn't punctured my tires. I've been informed that many of you had guessed that the crunch was indicative of a flat tire which was a good guess, but no cigar.

I hope I'm not expecting too much from you all. Did you catch that "you all" which indicated more than one reader which is the result of a positive, proactive sales campaign which I'm confident that all of you readers are eager to compete in. Remember, competition is the first step to fame and recognition. Do you want to be remembered? Do you want to be popular? The shear attempt of selling this book could get you that far. The world is your stage. Ask others who have had success selling this book to family, friends, people in the workplace, Facebooks, or just through emails what it could hold in store for you. I don't want to make you feel pressured so I'll move on towards Canada. Are you coming along or not?

Closer inspection of the crushed bungee revealed that yes, it was crushed and yes, the end of the head had broken off. And yes, I had pulled a stupid. After a brief rant with a good deal of ominous cursing, I thought it best to punish the one responsible. The punishment should fit the crime and memory of the punishment may help in making better choices in the future. The punishment would consist of repairing the crushed bungee instead of discarding it and using one of the identical spares that the prepared scout had thought to bring. Remember, bungees don't grow on trees and who knows what lies ahead up that dark and lonely highway to the north. With assistance from my trusty vice grip (one of many of differing sizes the prepared scout had brought) and my large short-handled "J.B." axe hammered and bent it to work and to my utter amazement, it did. God looks after fools and those who run over bungee straps.

Are you wondering what the "J.B." stands for regarding the "J.B."

axe? I'll tell you. It's large, maybe a five pound head, hand-forged with the initials "J.B." forged into the steel. I found it buried in the sand in my hand dug, sand basement under my old log house (one of few still standing as of 1984) in downtown Fairbanks, Alaska. Now what's so significant about the "J.B."? My father's initials were J.B. and I've already told you today would have been my father's birthday. I really feel he is just one of many guardian angels who have helped me all along this path I call my life for as long as I can remember.

Think about all the scrapes and jams you have mysteriously escaped from that you couldn't have escaped from, figured out, or fixed on your own. Something or someone came to your rescue. Today was my Dad's turn. What better day than on his birthday. Thanks again my earthly father.

I'm not positive but it could go something like this: you get into a bind with no obvious light at the end of your tunnel. With desperation, you pray to God. As God just might have bigger fish to fry besides you today, He calls in the troops for you. The troops are a whole host of guardian angels assigned to you because you've been known to do, say, or participate in such bizarre crap that could easily end up in or lead you closer to your demise.

For some folks, I think you only need a couple of these guardians. But I must thank God for the host that were assigned to me. They must really be dedicated because God knows they've had and got their work cut out for them. Remember, I'm not a Bible thumper but this is some of what I believe.

Back to Route 93. Got to Eureka. Mailed postcards to neighbors Dennis and Sandy Cowgill, Oldtown Volunteer Fire Department friends, nephew Nathan and wife Mere, Dianna via Oldtown Post Office, and Live Bobbie. Wish I could send postcards to my parents like I always used to. Never underestimate the power of the postcard. I sent one from Alaska to my Uncle Leo and Aunt Georgie. Every time I saw them for years after that, they always rejoiced about that postcard. What's it take to write a postcard? About ten minutes tops of your time and these folks remembered it for decades and it brought a joy to them.

Canada at last — made the border crossing at Roosville. I thought I'd be one of few vehicles there. But, as you can see in the photo I was very wrong and there were that many cars behind me when I snapped this photo. Did I look like a tourist?

PHOTO #1 - BORDER CROSSING, ROOSVILLE, CANADA

It pays to be honest. But it pays more to be dishonest, maybe. You don't notice it but they have cameras looking under your car. They are pros and have heard every lie, exaggeration, desaggeration (I made that word up a long time ago), con job, etc., in the book. Years ago while crossing the border back into the States, my lovely first bride and I thought it best to our advantage and to avoid possible incarceration that we thoroughly vacuum out the interior of our vehicle. Over a mile from and not in view of the crossing, we found a car wash. We spent the best part of an hour vacuuming and vacuuming again and again to make sure we missed nothing. Back up at the crossing, the Border Patrol guy gave us the usual questions, and smiled and then said, "You sure did a good job with your vacuuming." I didn't fall out of the car but it felt like I was going to.

Back to the present and being honest, the Canadian Border Patrol guy checked my passport, driver's license, registration, insurance, etc. He asked if I had any firearms and I told him I wished I could. Could you stand another story at this time? I sure hope so.

Dead Bob was entering Canada with another friend. To be kind, I'll just describe the other friend as a borderline moron but a high school graduate. Although Dead Bob should have but didn't coach the moronic friend prior to advancing to the crossing, he soon learned the error of his ways. When the Border Patrol guy got to the part about "Do you have any weapons?", moronic friend blurted out, "Oh, yea, we've got plenty." This slowed their day down considerably.

Sensing that my "wish I could…." statement about firearms may have sent a "red flag" to my Border Patrol guy, I had to think quick on my feet which was extremely difficult while still sitting down. I told him I did have bear spray and a foghorn. They have cameras sending real time photo images to the monitor that my Border Patrol guy was scanning showing him the entire interior of my van. There it was in open sight, my small four ounce can of mace. I knew he had seen it. Like I said, "honesty is the best policy." Already knowing that he had already picked it up on his monitor I reported, "Oh yea, I have this small four ounce can of mace for self protection." He gave me a look that registered, "Why didn't you keep your big mouth shut honest fellow?" And said, "We'll have to confiscate your mace sir." I'm not as dumb as I look. So, with all due respect and politeness, I asked why he was confiscating this small four ounce can of mace and not my family sized can of bear spray? He said because the bear spray was for defense against bears and the mace was for defense against people. I told him my plan was to take the small can of mace on short hikes and the big bear spray on longer outings. I could sense he had a good sense of humor (as most Canadians do) but in his position, he was trained not to display it. He did slip up a little before telling me to pull my vehicle over to one of four cement enclosed holding zones (my term - I don't know what they call them). He told me with a signal of glee in his eye designed to catch my eye that I might be able to slow down a baby bear with my four ounce can of mace.

I parked the van as told and assume they really gave it the once over as I made my way through locked doors which opened via some unknown push button from inside. There looked to be four to five other fellow detainees displaying different degrees of stress. I did not have a long wait before I was verbally summoned to approach a young girl in Border Patrol outfit behind a partition similar to a bank teller's station back in the States except for the bulletproof glass.

She was already well aware of the purpose for my visit. We had already non-verbally settled on the rules for our upcoming interchange. I wouldn't try to wile her with my charm and she wouldn't give or take any shit. She was more neutral than a robot. No warmth, strictly business. I was thinking, she couldn't be Canadian. She wanted to see my passport and driver's license. This would be the second display of these two documents and I was less than ten feet into Canada. Once satisfied that I was myself and had not exchanged identities with another person in the last ten feet, she completed three to four pages, one of which would become my receipt. I signed where she indicated.

I handed the four ounce can of mace to her through some porthole device that she controlled. I was glad she gave me a receipt and asked her if I could use the receipt on my return trip to retrieve my mace. She told me I could not and that they destroy any and all confiscated items every evening. Now that's a job I'd like to have, especially if I owned a thrift shop in Canada.

I remarked that this was such a waste and asked if I might donate the mace to some needy person in Canada. She said, "Your mace will be destroyed this evening, sir." Not an ounce of humor rose from her cold, cold heart. Surely, she couldn't be Canadian. I could sense that winning an argument or getting a rise out of her had long since vanished possibly decades before today. My best choice was to retreat and did so on my own terms with dignity and an air of, "you can't humiliate me, lady." I met with success in this choice until I reached the push button door which I now remembered she controlled. I stood in front of the door for a good long two seconds before she would release me from her hold. No way is she Canadian.

I crossed paths with a second Canadian a'hole not long after my intercourse (right!) with the girl at the border crossing. You can't miss her. She's the one with a four ounce can of mace in her pocket. While trying to forget about making her day, I came upon a truck pulling a trailer with Alberta (Canada) license. He was doing about 25 mph or about 32 km/hr in Canadianese in a 70 km/hr zone.

I figured he was just gawking as the scenery was fantastic. When we came to a legal passing zone I put on my left blinker and as I pulled along side of him, he floored it. I had to floor my van in dangerous fashion and still did not make it in front of him until I was in a no passing zone. Thank you lady up ahead who pulled off the road seeing us coming at her. Canadians are really good at this as I was to witness such driving skills throughout this trip.

I was very shaken up. I pulled over at a large gravel parking lot that had portopotties. I'm not sure about the spelling on that - Webster wouldn't help. I guess the people who write dictionaries feel it's below their dignity. Anyway, the anal pore who just gunned it pulled in behind me.

I thought I was ready for whatever was coming next. I'd take a beating to get in one good punch. I felt he deserved my attention. Rolling my window down, I heard indiscernible yelling with very few pauses for breath taking between expletives. The foul sounding, raucous verbalities were not being directed at myself but towards this guy who was beating a hasty retreat to the portopotty (I'll spell it differently each time - one of them is bound to be right).

At this point, I didn't know if I should thank the female passenger or feel sorry for the guy who made me wait even longer as I still had a morbid curiosity of what he and or I might be up against. All the while, he was in the portapottie, her tirades continued unceasingly and even grew louder as if she was firing her verbal broadsides through the green door he possibly had sought safety behind. Wasn't there a song about a green door? I was watching all this unfold from my rearview mirror. I decided discretion was the better part of valor when I saw her scoot across the seat to the drivers side and continued blasting salvos through that green door at him at a deadlier distance.

Note: please be aware that of all the times I've spent crisscrossing Canada, 99.9% of the Canadians were kind, polite, helpful, sharing, caring people who were damn good drivers. Don't allow the above descriptions to cloud your assessment. They are as a whole and individually a fine peoples. Those above could possibly have been transplants or aliens.

That's the Bull River down there below the elderly guardrail. I thought the contrasting colors were extraordinary. But, my real photo target was the little cloud

PHOTO #2 - BULL RIVER

that just hung in there far below the promontory of the mountain behind it. The cloud appeared lost or as if it were awaiting someone or something coming down the river. It just hung there suspended in time. Had time stopped? Don't know.

Not far up on Route 93, I happened on to Fort Steele. It was huge as were the snow capped mountains making a semi-circle around the Fort. The other end of the Fort property butted up against a large bend in the Bull River which completed the other half of the semi-circle. Views everywhere you looked. I also snapped a shot of several Clydesdales that are just one of many attractions at Fort Steele. Fort Steele held some particular significance to me as Bonnie's (Precious) mother's maiden name was Steele and that family held significant history back home in Cumberland, MD (i.e., Steeles Tavern - specializing in wines, liquors, cigars, and boat rentals on the Potomac River way back. Precious doesn't want me mentioning anything about moonshine beer, so I won't.)

PHOTO #3

PHOTO #4 - CLYDESDALES AT FORT STEELE

Fort Steele was restored with original buildings, etc. used by Mounties and as a trapping/mining hub way back, completely enclosed in that walled fortress. The parking lot was near full and my guess was well over 100 vehicles. I was so tempted to take the tour which would have consumed the better part of a day. I talked myself out of taking the tour in hopes that Precious might join me there in some distant vacation. I won't tell her about the mountains surrounding the place.

Wondering if I'd made the right choice in not taking the tour at Fort Steele, I proceeded on my trek north. I stopped for a snack at Skookumchuck - yea, that's the correct spelling. Feel free to challenge by checking your atlas.

Constant driving not interrupted frequently can become monotonous and dangerous. So, I know my frequent stops to take photos, or read historic roadside signs, snacking, or just to marvel on the shear captivating beauty that this planet throws at us was a boon to my sanity, enjoyment, and safety.

This lunch snack also made me feel better about not taking the tour back at Fort Steele. I smelled something foul while having my snack at Skookumchuck. I think I discovered the Athabaskan translation of Skookumchuck - it means, "white man stinks."

Later this same day, I crossed the Columbia River splitting part of the very clean and vibrant city of Invermere. I'm not sure if this was the headwaters of our Columbia River or not. It may be but I think it's just too much of a stretch. Refer to your maps. You will not be tested on this. But stay alert, nevertheless. The Columbia River in Invermere rolls out into the Kootenai River. There were more kayaks here than I could count. I could count that high but remember, I was trying to drive as safely as possible without taking out any Canadians.

It was at Invermere that I was given a firsthand look at Canadian banking institutions. As you know, it is still July 12, 2016, making this not only my father's birthday but a Tuesday as well. I tried to find a bank but could not. Banks in Canada don't have the same appearance as easy to find banks in the U.S. I saw three college aged girls sitting on a bench possibly awaiting a bus. As the light there hadn't turned green yet, I yelled over to them for directions to a bank. All three tried to help me at once. However, all three were rattling off names of streets to a person from far away who had just pulled into town three to four minutes ago. All three talked Canadian and I could tell right away that these were true born and bred Canadians, no transplants or aliens here. When the light turned I thanked them graciously as if I had heard and understood their directions.

I parked the van in the heart of the downtown. What a lovely little town. Like most all of Canada - sparkling clean, no litter, no banks. That's not exactly true, they had three to four banks. I just couldn't find them. I wanted to exchange my greenbacks for the Queen's currency. It was getting later in the afternoon - maybe 3ish. I asked a couple for directions who turned out to be locals. I was within a block that housed three banks. The first one was closed on

Mondays and Tuesdays. The second one had an ATM that had a long line out into the street. As I have elected never to use an ATM in the U.S. I was damn well sure I wasn't going to end that run here in Canada. I hit pay dirt at the third bank that was open til 4 PM. I made it in the door at 10 til 4. There was a line of different internationals seeming to be as eager as I was to see how the world money market would treat them this day.

There were four teller windows, only two of which were telling. One of the tellers closest to my line was counting the day's take and never once looked up from her assigned duties. She looked native. The other open teller was a Hindu sounding man without a turban who was jovial and talkative much too long to all those patrons who had beat me through the doors. Did he not know that they close at 4? Did he not know how much I needed to pee?

It was about this time that a nice girl looking to have both native Canadian and Asian genes approached our line and as nice and genuine as could be, told myself and my fellow line members that we would have just a short wait. Did she know that they close at 4? Did she not know how much I needed to pee?

In desperation, I caught her attention and pointed to the native teller who never looked up in my futile attempt to suggest that opening up another teller line could be helpful, as the clock and my kidneys ticked on. She responded by smiling to me and shaking her head up and down the way we gesture in the U.S. when we use that movement to mean "yes." Apparently, the up and down motion of the head in Canada means something all together different. How ironic, I just had to pause briefly to take a pee while transcribing this for you. I don't know about you, but for me the pause sure made this story more poignant. If you have to go now, take a break. This story will be here upon your return.....................etc.

It was about this time that a very well-dressed lady came out from a side door that I had hoped would lead to a restroom. It wouldn't matter. Banks seldom if ever have restrooms available to the public and if you ask me to verify it, I'll shake my head up and down in U.S. English. Anyway, this third lady, who looked to be 100% WASP Canadian, locked the front doors. It was 4 PM. She knew it was 4? She did not know how much I needed to pee. I could hold my silence no longer. I asked her through grit teeth if they had a restroom I could use. She said she was sorry, meaning her answer was a qualified "no" but there were public washrooms outside just around the corner, but that my wait shouldn't be much longer. I thanked her anyway while listening to the one working Hindu teller droning on and on to a customer who was now just two in front of me as our line had moved itself over in front of his station while somehow having the cunning instinct that the native teller, who never looked up from her work, was not going to be of any significant help to any of us.

Finally I was second in line but became somewhat dismayed when the patron in front of me told the Hindu teller that she just wanted to open up an account. Now it had become a bladder holding marathon. I wasn't sure I could do it but what choice do you have in a locked bank in a foreign country after 4 PM?

At last it became my turn. If that Hindu so much as reached for a sign saying his window was closed, I would become very instrumental in his next incarnation. He wasn't curt, but just short of it for me. He assisted in my transaction very swiftly with little if any eye contact and no unrelated verbiage that he had displayed with the female customers who had proceeded me. I concluded that his reaction to me had a causal factor of one of three things:

1. He could smell me.
2. I wasn't a female he could possibly score with in his sick and twisted fantasies. Note: I have my own but consider them normal.
3. He thought I was of a lower caste than he. Explanation: they have a caste system in India. Depending on what rung of

that caste system ladder you are born into designates who you can shit on and those who can shit on you from a caste above yours. Those on the lowest rung are known as "the untouchables" and as you can figure, has nothing to do with Elliott Ness.

That bastard saw me as an untouchable! "Shookumchuck!" I need a bath. But first, if those locked doors will permit exit, I'm going to scurry around the corner to the public washroom entrance. I raced there and made it only happy in the knowledge that the $300.00 American I handed the Hindu had been slid back to me, without touching me, in the form of $380.00 in the Queen's currency. Was the wait worth $80? My urologist would probably say no.

Heading north from Invermere you'll find the Kootenai Valley. On a scale of 10, it is much like the Shenandoah Valley but about five to eight times higher, wider, wilder, and with beauty loaded in all directions. Much to my ecstatic surprise, Radium Hot Springs popped up. I had already learned of a lot in town where campers could stay for free. I learned this from a probable college student working her summer in the tourist information building. She was reluctant to tell me as her job was to steer tourists to local/provincial/and the Queen's lodging facilities. As I had noticed differently colored nails on her digits, I told her that I liked her nails. This worked as her attitude changed and under a hushed breath less her counterparts would overhear, she gave me excellent directions to the free lot.

I was now free to while away the rest of my day in search of leisure and to overcome "Shookumchuck." I found both at the Radium Hot Springs. The bathhouses are actually not in town but above the town in the Queen's Kootenay National Park. Note: Kootenay is spelled with a "y" on the end in Canada but in the U.S. it is spelled with an "i" on the end. Don't know why. Maybe it's a misprint on my atlas. Either way, we're stuck with it.

If you find yourself within striking distance of these bathhouses, give them a try. For $6.20 Canadian you have your choice of three Olympic size pools of varying degrees and a very, very, hot, hot tub. Don't be self-conscious. If you look around you'll find people older, grayer, fatter, and more self-conscious than yourself. Once submerged, you'll feel right at home. You should supply your own towel and bathing suit. They provide the soap. You're only required to take one quick shower to enter. I felt the need for two prior to taking the plunge and helped myself to an optional one prior to leaving.

There were plenty of people there but it wasn't crowded. You could always find your own private place in the well-built easy-to-access pools. Views from the open air pools ranged from stupendous to marvelous, as you could lie back from any spot and look up into the Canadian Rockies that appear to be looming just above you and far into the clouds.

I met some very memorable characters there, especially once inside the tighter confines of the hot, hot tub. I needed a good cooking so I stayed in the hot, hot tub for going on an hour. It was smaller and less room than the pools provided, but never once do I think I imposed on anyone's space and no one imposed on mine. Good thing I took the two baths before entry.

There was an older Canadian woman who I think thought I was hitting on her. We had a good discussion about police versus shooters in Dallas. She had very concrete views bordering on my own views about the right to bear arms. I made sure she was aware that most all of the shooters they read or hear about in American are on the lunatic fringe and not at all representative of the average non-violent gun owners and hunters in the U.S.

There was a guy speaking broken English with a Russian sounding accent. I got great vibes from him. We were heading in opposite directions, so we told each other points of interest to look for. He was an average looking guy with a pretty wife and two kids, a boy and a girl who were too cute for words. He laughed heartily after everything I said. I'm not sure if he comprehended it all.

I also met a guy who looked like a young James Bond with a beard and his, I think, half Indian (Athabaskan) girlfriend or wife. He turned out to be a farmer from Saskatchewan that loved to hunt. Once he or I said "hunting" the conversation was on. He liked to hunt elk and deer. He thought we had elk in Maryland. I told him about some of my most memorable hunts and favorite rifles and he told me about his. We both realized that Canada and U.S. hunters have similar problems with poachers. I think if we would have talked hunting for another 15 minutes, I would have received an invite. But alas, the girlfriend or wife pulled him from the hot tub and somewhere out into the pool.

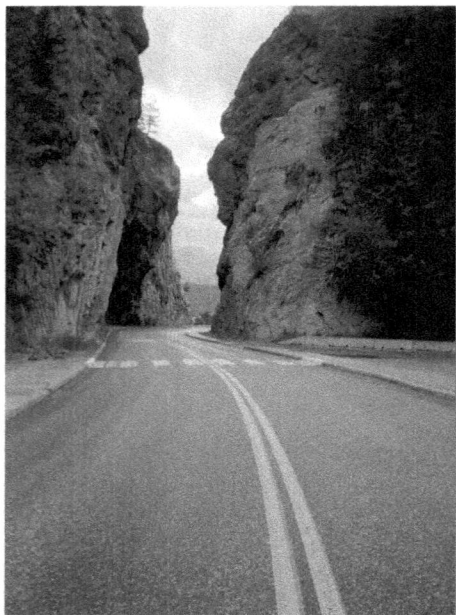

PHOTO #5 - HOLE IN CLIFFS GOING ON HIGHWAY JUST SOUTH OF RADIUM HOT SPRINGS

I kept thinking, $6.20 for three baths and all this, too!

I would later take a photo going back down the mountain of a man and his wife I'd also met in the hot tub. He and his wife had journeyed from Holland to see his Canadian sister he hadn't seen in 30 years. He had tears in his eyes when he told me this. I took a photo with his camera of the three of them standing along the cut you see in my own photo while returning to my place of rest. What a day. What a day! Happy birthday Dad. Thanks again for those Sunday drives!

Ending Mileage: 37,621
Miles This Day: 299

There was still plenty of room in the free camper's lot. I found a spot where any approaching vehicle headlights would not be able to find me and wake me up. I was refreshed — thank you Radium Hot Springs — but dog tired.

I crawled into the rear of the van, set my fan up for circulation and some white noise and settled in. There was still some light in the sky as the scouts for dreams started sneaking into my brain and I was very responsive to intercepting whatever was following behind them.

What the?? I heard a distant voice that definitely was not male. I thought I must have had a dream just plunge into my brainpan, but for the life of me I had no visuals accompanying this dream. I started fading away again surrendering to any dream that wanted to delight, harass, or freak me out. But there it was again, that distant, muffled female voice. I knew it wasn't a dream now as she had my complete attention.

Did I say it was pitch dark outside? Well, it was pitch dark outside. I did the squint into the darkness thing with my eyes again knowing it wasn't going to work any better than it did on scores of other attempts in the past. We (meaning us humans) don't ever want to give up on that one. It must be like Charlie Manson's mother telling her friends that, "He had just fallen in with the wrong crowd."

I got to the point where I figured the female I'd heard outside would be knocking on one of my windows soon. I hoped she wasn't drunk, I hoped it wasn't a setup by a newly formed Canadian mafia, I hoped it wasn't the girl who took my mace back at the border crossing, etc. So much goes through your mind at a time like this. God forbid, the one yelling through the green door!

Things seemed to take a turn for the worse when she called something out and it sounded like she was in the front seat. Oh please, not another dead Eskimo spirit. I was prone with my head behind the back of the two front seats wishing that, "Scotty could beam me up," but chances of that happening were slim. I don't think I was paralyzed with fear but I was on my way there. The thought occurred to me that it might be a good time to end the trip and get sized up for a straight jacket. They have socialized medicine in Canada. I was hoping it would cover any prescription psychotropics, a small room with grills on the window, and three squares per day.

And there! She spoke to me again but this time it was different. I heard what she said. She was my newly purchased, just for this trip, cell phone telling me that her battery was low. Next time I'm going to get one with a male voice. Like I said, it was pitch dark and I remembered putting the cell phone in it's case and then inside one of my duffle bags up on the front seat floor on the passenger side — hence the muffled voice.

I was relieved that it wasn't a drunk, a setup, the control freak back at the border, etc. and that much of my sanity was still intact. I figured she would give me this warning a few times and then shut off. Keep in mind the closest thing I have to technology back home is my microwave. I wanted to draw the line somewhere. I have no computer, no email, no Facebook, etc. Don't laugh. They can't find me.

I had a computer at the job that I retired from and could do cartwheels with it. But, when I saw computers taking people's jobs away I saw the writing on the wall. Have fun with them until the grid goes down or when our enemies learn how to jam our weapons systems — both great and small — good luck to us all.

I'm getting on my soap box again so I'll jump off for now but don't be surprised if you come upon more ranting and raving later on in this work. Remember, I just roll with it and spit it out in ink on this paper. You can call me "Windy" if you like.

She would ring me up every few minutes just about the time I would be drifting off with the same message. I started yelling back at her to let her know I'd heard her message 15 +/- times by now. See how technology can lure you in? I'm yelling back to a chip as if it was flesh and blood. Cursing didn't shut her up either. If anything had run the battery down, she had. I could only imagine what my fellow free campers were contemplating if/when they heard the banter in that van from Maryland. All I wanted was to go to sleep, but technology wasn't going to let that happen.

Getting in and out of the van wasn't like walking through a revolving door. Did I say it was pitch black? Did I say my keys (technological) to open the back trunk door were up in the console? Did I say she kept calling?

Her big mouth did her in. (Have you heard that anywhere before?) I reached for the last sound of her voice and made contact with the duffle bag and ripped it back over top of the seat. No drowsiness now. You could say I was pretty well near wide awake (another neat phrase).

If it was possible, I would have strangled her if I could have gotten away with it and not broken a commandment. With these three strikes against me, I had to just content myself with waiting for her next call to pinpoint her location. Which I did, spread her open and turned her off with help from her still powerful light source.

Now at least I could get back to dreamland, which I wasted no further time in getting to.

I'm not sure if I told you this was the first cellphone I'd purchased since my old kerosene one. I thought I had shut the damned thing off. It was starting to remind me of one of my marriages. But I promised Precious we wouldn't cross those waters in this book.

Anyway, loud and clear and seemingly full of power she continued to contact me. No choice, ripped the duffle bag she had hid in back over the seat, found her, spread her open, and used her still powerful light source to locate the push button keys up in the console so I could escort her outside and then get some much needed rest. I hit the button whose technology opened the back/trunk door. I slid half to three quarters out and realized it was misting out - not raining. I said misting but providing enough liquid to ruin a perfectly good cell phone, my only link to Precious. I crawled back into the van with a death grip on the phone. She wouldn't shut up. It was like Edgar Allen Poe's 'Telltale Heart' or something.

I knew where my stash of plastic bags were and secured four of them around her to ensure she would remain dry. I left her in the space between windshield and hood and scurried back into the van feeling secure that she was safe and I could at last succumb to my fatigue in slumberland. Sleep, sleep, wonderful sleep at last.......
zzz......zzz........zzz.

Son of a bitch! It was her again. I had only succeeded in partial success. She was vibrating against the metal hood or window like a child locked out of the house in the night. Yea, it was time for the straight jacket again. After one or two "why me, God's" our lonesome somewhat sleepy free camper arose or more accurately slid out of the back of the van, grabbed that wench in the plastic bags and ran her up a steep grass hill behind the van and abandoned her. She finally shut up sometime before daylight. It would have been a great time for some poor homeless person to hear her calling out in the misting dark before daylight. He'd be saying, "But Officer, I swear I heard a woman calling out and some guy was giving her a hard time."

DAY #13, 7/13/2016

Sometime after daylight I retrieved her. She was dry but silent. Was she broken? I had gotten the silent treatment many times before. Precious has almost perfected it into an art form.

Next time you're out and about, try to find a payphone. She was my only link to the outside world. I had no choice. I plugged her back into the juice from my van. I can assure you that the four plastic bags were on standby.

I found myself in the midst of downtown Radium Hot Springs in the mist and fog. Here was a well-kept older park nestled in with residential housing. There was not a soul on the streets. I watched a guy and his younger female helper cutting grass on the park's baseball field in the fog and mist. He must have had an obligation to a contract to fulfill as they both appeared soaking wet. I assumed they were independent contractors. The only thing I heard him say as they loaded weed wackers, etc. back into his truck was, "There, that oughta satisfy them."

I needed fresh water and he showed me the way to a spigot near one of the park's picnic tables. He spotted my Maryland tags and told me I was a long way from home. Being aware of this, I told him about my Yellowknife destination goal. He just shook his head and got back into his truck. I offered him a cold cup of coffee but he declined and off they went to their next contractual obligation. They both should be getting over their pneumonia by now. The mist continued floating down and the temperature was only in the low 60's Fahrenheit. I witnessed different reactions from folks when I related my bucket list goals to them. It ranged from complete surprise to envy with a tad of "Margaret, keep the children away from this guy."

I found a restroom in the same park but it was locked. I would have to seek another alternative facility. Might as well have breakfast and enjoy it. It consisted of a cupful of dried Cheerios, a snack bar, a small handful of dried bananas, and a cold cup of coffee. Who cares if it's hot or cold? My main objective was in getting the buzz.

While enjoying my breakfast, I felt a light bump on the van. Now, what could that be? I looked back in the mist and there was a big eyed curly haired baby/fawn mule deer. It didn't appear desperate. I'd seen a lone female the evening before. I hope they hooked up. The fawn vanished behind a house before I could get my camera. Another miracle happened as I was driving away from the park slowly hoping to spot the fawn in the mist — a guy exited the locked restroom. He'd left it clean for me, and for that I was grateful. You could say, I left a part of me in Radium Hot Springs.

I had paid $8.30 Canadian to travel through Kootenay National Park just to go to the bathhouses above the town on Route 93 North.

The pass was good for two days. I was slightly disappointed having to pay this until I got into the park above the bathhouses yesterday.

I was tempted to hit the bathhouses again but I was still nearly clean from yesterday's cook and showers. I pressed on in the direction of Banff and Lake Louise. I took five photos in pretty much rapid succession as all of their beauty, even on a misty day, was overwhelming.

Photo #1 - Looking down on a bend of the Kootenay River through pine trees hugging the edge of Route 93.

Photo #2 - Folks just heading out on a float trip down the Kootenay. Folks going downstream backwards is a strong indicator that they are most likely beginners.

Photo #3 - Looking across Boreal Forest to two mountain knobs encrusted in mist.

Photo #4 - Looking across Boreal Forest at two mountain ranges with mist/snow vying for supremacy up an unseen valley. Highway is horizontal in the foreground.

Photo #5 - More mountains, more Boreal Forest, more snow and baby glaciers.

PHOTO #1

PHOTO #2

PHOTO #3

PH⊙T⊙ #4

PH⊙T⊙ #5

Note the dense traffic. There's a camper coming way down the highway if you look closely. I was elated that traffic was not heavy. Again, beware of gawking because the vehicle coming at you is gawking also.

Traffic will probably be more dense in the not too distant future once book sales sky rocket thanks to you dedicated readers who can't help but share the joy this book is bringing to you not only on a personal but on an esthetic level you never dreamt could come from reading such a low-priced travel classic. I would even encourage those people who are unable to travel for some reason or another to read this book. If sales keep accelerating as expected, there's works in the way for a braille series. Never underestimate any avenue for potential sales. Remember, it is not necessary for you to finish reading this book before you leap into your sales quest. I am so looking forward to personally shaking your hand at the convention. Depending on your productivity, you may also find yourself sitting at my very table at one of our free succulent brunches we're planning for our top achievers. Yes, you can bring that new special someone you met while selling this book. If he or she can't make it, plan on bringing one of your parents. At this time, not knowing the magnitude of sales impact, we must limit you to only one guest. The law does not allow us to pay for your guest unless he or she has sold a minimum of seven of these books or greater. Don't let your guest outsell you, as you'll want to impress them with your own sales conquests. I told you this thing was going to grow and grow and grow for you. So, what are some of you waiting for? Does the thought of infamy scare you?

In shocking contrast with the beauty noted in photos 1-5, I came across a stretch of highway where both sides as far as the eye could see was burned out. I drove through this sad desolate area with such remorse. Too many trees gone to count. God only knows how many critters the fire took, crippled, or left homeless. I know I drove for at least 10-15 miles through blackened ash, nothing living visible.

It could have been from a lightening strike, careless campfire, one flipped cigarette tossed from a vehicle. I've seen idiots flip lit cigarettes from vehicles. Maybe people are wising up. I cannot recall seeing one flipped cigarette on this whole trip. If I were king, there would be stricter laws. Caught throwing a lit cigarette out of a moving vehicle:

- 1st Offense Penalty: Holding cell — 10 days — no cigarettes.
- 2nd Offense Penalty: Holding Cell — 100 days — no cigarettes — with chain smoking cellmate who is allowed to smoke outside the window of your cell door.
- 3rd Offense Penalty: Same as above plus cellmate must cut one of your digits off in order for the cellmate to obtain cigarettes. We didn't increase the number of days so as not to appear cruel.
- 4th Offense Penalty: Same as above but cellmate must also set your hair on fire while you are sleeping in order to obtain cigarettes.
- 5th Offense Penalty: If you've come this far, penalties, to date, have had no impact on you. You are hereby remanded to the custody of this author and subject to his sole disposition of diet, activities, socialization, and punishments. May God give your soul a break. Special considerations could be rendered to you should you sell greater than seven of these books while in custody of the author.

One of the major goals of this lengthy outing was to visit Lake Louise and paddle in her cool emerald blue waters. She's one of the most renown waters on the planet. You've no doubt seen her in numerous advertisements and wrote her off as a composite or a fake as her beauty is hard to accept unless you're right there with her. I've seen her in the past maybe five or six times where she lays, and have never seen any site that matches hers. I even bought a kayak just for this trip with the plan to give her her maiden voyage in Lake

Louise. This being said, I held to plan and continued on Route 93 north/west towards Lake Louise dead center through the Canadian Rockies.

Although it was a Wednesday, the closer I got to Lake Louise, the heavier traffic became. Something told me, don't say it's so…. had she become too popular? Past sightings of her had happened later in August and once before winter had left in March. This was mid-July. So, note this on your travel calendar. Do not go to Lake Louise in July.

People were fighting for parking rights along the road going to her at least three miles out. There were people in the woods trying to hike that last three miles just to get a glimpse of her. It was as if Monica what's-her-name was in town. (I jokes.) People and cars everywhere on a narrow winding road.

A lady had tried to wedge her twenty-foot Mercedes into an eighteen-foot space and was standing outside the car looking indigent as if it were the space or the Mercedes' fault. The front of the Mercedes had now caused two lanes of exhausted, frustrated drivers to funnel into the remaining lane and two thirds. Do you think there was some horn blowing? Do you think there was obscenities being yelled? Do you think middle fingers were getting more exercise than they usually do? Do you think there were fender benders and near misses? Do you think the indignant lady got back into the car and moved it? Answer to previous question: No!

Never being known as a quitter, I felt that this might be a good opportunity for me to find out how it feels to be a quitter and at first opportunity did a ubie and headed away from the beautiful and serene Lake Louise. I still had to pick my way past the Mercedes and it's indignant owner. I said nothing to her as I passed through the funnel at 5 mph tops. I would have said something but what would I have accomplished? I could have offered assistance in moving her car but would no doubt have been rammed by those still trapped behind me.

Once I made my way out, it all seemed like comedic surrealism. Mel Brooks couldn't have done it any funnier. I love Canadians but there's one word they are reluctant to post out on the highway before you enter Lake Louise in July - "Full."

I forgot to mention, there were pre-teen kids in green shirts with green flags, possibly just a volunteer church group, who although they were too young to drive were directing traffic. Maybe, maybe, I was in a new Mel Brooks movie or was given a free preview of what part of hell was like. I tried my best to laugh it off but it was difficult. I escaped from Lake Louise back out on Route 93 still heading north/west with my virgin kayak. I was kind of in shock and dismay was setting in, not even getting to lay eyes on her. I had caught a raw deal.

This despondency soon lifted while coming out of a bend in the highway. For a second, I thought it was a wreck or animal sighting due to the handful of vehicles stopping ahead and pulling off to the left.

PHOTO #6 - BOW LAKE TAKEN FROM PARKING LOT ROUTE 93

There she was. Lake Bow. I found a new love. She wasn't as big as Lake Louise. Hell, she's not even listed on my map. I soon forgot about Louise. Bow was just as serene, just as majestic, just as blue. I was back on Cloud Nine (don't know the origins for Cloud Nine). If you know, contact me or one of our many sales associates. For assistance in joining our sales team feel free to contact me 24/7.

No crowds, no traffic jams, drive up restrooms, well spaced picnic grounds. Bow had it all. I had lunch with her. She was quiet but had an air about her that was nearly irresistible. I cannot imagine early voyagers, trappers, natives traversing a trail 200 years ago coming upon her not saying, "This is the place. We are staying here. This will be our home."

I lingered with "Bow" for an extended lunch. I was joined by one of her children. A large gray colored bird with black wings and tail. She scoped me out while perching in a medium-sized blue spruce. Once she saw I was no threat, she landed at the far end of my picnic table. I had found love twice in this spot in a span of ten minutes.

PHOTO #7 - VIEW OF GRASSY BEACH WHERE FICK-LED BIRD HAD BATHED. NOTE: REFLECTIONS OF MOUNTAINS IN LAKE.

We chatted a bit — she in Birdineze while cocking her head rapidly back and forth. I cocked my head back and forth trying to project non-aggressive curiosity and friendship in as non-threatening manner as I could muster. Keep in mind, I haven't had that many conversations with birds, with the vast minority being in Canada.

She seemed receptive to continuing our discussion. I could sense she was losing much of her shyness and becoming quite coy. Either this bird was a real pro or there was some chemistry going on between us. Her cadence softened, her head cocking was visibly slower as we moved closer. Her dark, soft, subtle eyes moved from my own down to the table. She made a quick lunge for my lunch. I cocked my head rapidly back and forth to reassure her that she could do no wrong in my book (no pun intended) and that I would gladly share my lunch and my heart with her.

She moved closer again somewhat cautiously but with the air of a woman who knew she'd be eating out of my hand in no time. And that's how we spent lunch. Her gray feathers were almost fur like as she came in very close to peck and eat pieces of my pumpkin spice Flex Bar. I knew we had a future when instead of eating the crumbs from the pumpkin spice Flex Bar now littering the top of the picnic table, she opted to eat them out of my hand. Trust is one of the backbones to true love.

I suggest you try this. It's very easy once the trust barrier is overcome. Most creatures, large and small, will respond in similar fashion. Please do not attempt this same strategy with larger carnivores or the majority of reptiles as results may vary. I wanted to get her photo but she became fickled. I think she had just done that grey curly hair on the grassy beach before my arrival and it had turned out curlier than she preferred. So no photos of this lady today other than the ones snapped in my head that will last a lifetime.

This photo was taken at my picnic site on Bow Lake where two hearts met and throbbed as one for a brief moment in time. Alas, satisfied that I had satisfied her and knowing that our love was one that friends and family could never fully understand, we both agreed to part ways. We cocked our heads back and forth. She waited for me outside the restroom. We both knew this thing we had couldn't last. She flew along the side of the van up the gravel lane to the parking lot. I cocked my head back and forth one last time and pulled out on Route 93 again without so much as a peak for a beak in the rearview mirror. I tried to forget about her. Parting was the best thing for both of us.

PH⊙T⊙ #8

PH⊙T⊙ #9

This photo is the north/west end of Bow Lake. You can see the glacier that feeds the blue waters down to her. Have a drink. She's clean. Note: the reflections. The mountain is solid granite, by the way.

I had numerous opportunities to photo more breathtaking vistas, but every time I'd pull over the mist graduated to rain. One seldom looks behind you on a journey of this sort. But, a scenic overlook caught my attention. As I peered back down at the road already covered snapping a photo of Highway 93 looking south - incredible.

I came upon two or three active glaciers that have not succumbed to global warming, yet. The immensity is hard to comprehend. My throw away camera did its best capturing two out of three. Canadians are more apt to call them ice fields than glaciers. You could walk out and upon these glaciers but I got cold feet.

Something continued to pull me up the highway.

PHOTO #10

PHOTO #11

PH⊙T⊙ #12

We have an interesting formation near home in West Virginia called Saddle Mountain. I couldn't pass up a shot of this saddle with accompanying waterfall not too far from the town of Jasper, British Columbia. Jasper is a bustling, clean, small town of less than 5,000 folks. It's a renown jumping on / jumping off terminal for the scenic Canadian railway. The town is surrounded by rugged, rolling, snow-capped mountains silently beckoning to all travelers, "Come to me.....Come and see the majesty of creation and time. I'm here and I will wait for you...."

Snapped a quick photo of a totem pole in Jasper. Note all the traffic. The train station was near here. Notice the white bunny cloud. He looks like he's trying to get to those beckoning mountains. I hadn't noticed him when I took the shot.

Jasper was so laid back

PH⊙T⊙ #13

and picturesque, it seemed like a great place for postcards. I made an inquiry with some of the locals who told me to try the drugstore just a few blocks from where I'd parked near the totem pole. A few blocks turned out to be a major trek for the old man across much of the south end of the city. The drugstore didn't carry them but a corner touristy-like shop did. I think it's another example of technology destroying jobs. I find it increasingly difficult to find postcards everywhere I go, not just in Canada.

I stopped at a local bar/pub and grill. I had not had much red meat so far on this trip discounting my beef jerky. One of the daily specials was a very large Angus burger with any frills you wanted them to smother it in. I got the works and a soda. I would like to have had a beer but I was the designated driver. I shared some fun banter with the bartender who also doubled as waitress. Stop what you're thinking right now! Not being sure just how effective my last bath had been, I sat alone in a semi-isolated area, people watching while writing postcards to Precious and friends left behind. I had some pangs of loneliness here but enjoyed the barkeep and numer-

PHOTO #14

ous chattering excited patrons, all better dressed than yours truly. My guess was they were waiting to board or reboard the scenic railway. The burger was great and that with all of the toppings plus chips filled me substantially for $10-$12 +/- Canadian. Never heard an "Aye" all day.

Leaving Route 93 and hopping a ride onto Route 16 North/East towards Hinton and sober as a judge (another quaint but I'm sure not always true saying) you'll come upon this massive granite behemoth seemingly blocking your passage as if to say, "Are you sure you want to leave Jasper so soon?"

Found sleeping quarters in the Freson Bros. Hilton. Actually it was the Freson Bros. Market. Open 24 hours a day. Clean bathroom. I had pulled into Hinton pretty late although there was plenty of light left in the sky somewhat blocked by the rain and mist battle that continued to rage for yet most of another day.

I had asked a girl at a gas station for directions to free lodging for the night. It was she who turned me on to the Freson Bros. Market. I almost asked her if they had child labor laws in Canada as she was the lone gas station attendant and she looked to be no more than 15 years of age. I didn't ask as she already looked petrified of me and I didn't want to finish her off. I thanked her as kind and politely as I could and her petrification appeared to turn to relief. Maybe she thought I was going to rob her. Who knows? Sleeping at the Freson Bros. parking lot was very similar to sleeping at Walmart and I did an exceptional job of it.

DAY #14, 7/14/2016

Having scouted the restroom at Freson Bros. last evening, I was content that in this morning mist I would find clean, well-stocked, and spacious nook to perform my morning ceremony. What I didn't know but was to soon find out, the lights in the toilette (French) was on a timer and my complete ceremony lasted longer than the lighting, causing yours truly to finish up in the depths of darkness. Good thing I have a feel for these things.

One feels isolated and alone when traveling by ones self, especially so in a foreign country. When the lights go out in the restroom, I can assure you that these feelings are compounded. This was one of the few times in my life that I wished someone else would join me during my morning ritual and let me see the light. No one came in but we lived to tell the tale. As I was away from Canada's national parks I must note that prices for gas were considerably lower. Here in Hinton, it was about $5.00 Canadian for a Canadian gallon, which is about 5 litres. They sell it by the litre. While leaving the park yesterday, fear of running out of gas caused me to purchase it for $7-8 Canadian. Beware! You have been warned!

PHOTO #1 - WALMART PARKING LOT, HINTON, ALBERTA

I absolutely felt like a traitor while driving out of Hinton when I passed by a Walmart. I did another ubie in case some of you readers think that I would stoop to exaggerate or even lie about the popularity of free camping at Walmart and snapped this photo. Now mind you, it is 8 AM and many free campers have already left. Count the large campers still left probably having Canadian bacon and eggs. Now count the other vehicles that are or could be holding sleepers. Now, do you believe me? And do you skeptics believe me about the rain?

Say what you want about Walmart and most of these other big chains. They're a Godsend for campers who don't have or are more intelligent than to spend $30 or more a night to have the same if not as clean amenities by utilizing free resources. Love ya Walmart. Love ya Freson Bros. Love ya Super 1.

Please allow me to digress slightly. Now, where I found lodging at Freson Bros last night, there was a majority of 18-wheelers free camping, a handful of travel trailers, two capped trucks, my van and one other.

That poor nomad in the other van (white Econo Van) slept in his front seat all night slumped over the steering wheel. Maybe he'd shot himself for not thinking of putting a bed in the back of his van. Or maybe he had everything he owned and possibly properties of others crammed into the back. Who knows. I wasn't about to find out which possibility fit cause if he wasn't dead, he was sleeping quite comfortably be it slumped over the steering wheel. What could I have done either way? The worst part scenario if I had overcome apathy and checked on him would have been to awaken him after he finally fell asleep in that position twenty minutes before I woke up at 6:30 AM. Live and let _____.

Insertion: The Cherokees have only one commandment that covers all ten of ours — "do no harm."

I think I already related to you that the track phone I purchased for this trip could not be used in Canada. If I haven't told you, take my word on it. I don't want to bore you with another story that just goes on and on and on. Let's return to this story. But before we do, I'd like to address the fact that one of the most overused words in this entire story is "I"....sorry about that. It just goes with the territory (no pun intended) when you're traveling alone. Sure, I could fabricate an interesting companion, a pet, etc. I haven't had any imaginary friends since I was five years old. So, you'll have to put up with it. Besides, the van's filled to the gills (neat saying) and there's no room for any sized companion unless it was one you could keep in a small jar. Besides, I enjoy doing things alone. You only have to make one person happy and you only have to ensure the general well-being of one person. I've never felt real comfortable in a pack.

I stopped at a pullover called Kelly's Bath hoping for a free shower. The name was deceiving, but for the first time in way too many miles I came upon a working public telephone. I was able to reach Precious via a collect call. It felt strange to use a phone again and great to hear her voice.

She continues to worry about me due to my traveling so far and alone. This had been a running theme so far on this journey. I told her that I was worried about her worrying to the point I was afraid it could distract my driving. This seemed to work and subsequent collect calls later proved that she did not dwell on worrying, at least not to me. Anyway, she had done further research regarding my track phone. No, it would not work in Canada, but yes, I could still use it to call 911 while in Canada - maybe. I recharged the phone on a great outlet that came with the van, hoping 911 would work, hoping that my phone wouldn't call out to me all night long like she did back in Radium Hot Springs, and hoping this would help offset some of Precious' concerns.

It's great on a long journey like this one to know you have someone who loves you back home. It gave me a boost. I've made other sojourns in the past without having a special someone waiting at home and the trip was not the same with regards to it's positives and negatives. Bonnie's (Precious') niece was having the worst luck finding the right guy for her. I went out on a limb for her and asked her how she thought Precious and I got together 32+ years ago. This beautiful creature had no clue. So, I told her, "prayer." I hope this hint worked for her as she is now a happily married mother of one, so far.

I hadn't realized this morning, but it had become much cooler than it had been on the entire trip so far. I expected the van's thermometer to go up after noticing it read 51 degrees Fahrenheit around 9 AM but by 10 AM, it had dipped to 49 degrees. Oh yea, I'm still heading north by northwest on Route 40 out of Hinton. Another reminder that I was heading north came as I passed a roadside 'Beware/Caribou Crossing' sign. Not only are you warned with the words but a large yellow wooden caribou attached to the sign. I wanted to get a photo of the sign because it was so distinct and large but the rain was coming in intermittent torrents and it was not safe to pull over. Later, I wished I had because these signs continued along this highway for 16-20 +/- miles, but I could not find an intact one. The poor caribou would be missing an antler or a leg or an entire head. The only one that was completely intact was the very first one I'd come upon. Now ain't that something. What's the chances? Oh yea, Highway 40 is also known as Big Horn Highway. I've heard some of the locals refer to it as Who Can Get Drunk and Shoot the Caribou Sign Highway.

I never saw any big horn sheep or caribou on this trip, so far, but will let you know if I do as it is such a thrill to see them even at great distances. They are majestic tenfold to me. They're also good to eat. I prefer mine completely dead and fried. (Not funny but it probably got a chuckle out of you.) Caribou is as lean as meat can be and still be meat. It is white like a white pork chop. If anyone brags about getting one, he has an ego problem. I found them as difficult to kill as shooting cows in a pasture once you get the wind right. Maybe I shouldn't criticize the other hunter for bragging, but killing any creature great or small should be done with the utmost reverence. He loved his life as much as you love yours. And by God, you better eat him, every speck! You owe it to him. He gave his life to lengthen yours.

Thoughts of Precious consumed a lot of my time on this trip - mostly positive thoughts. I knew she would still worry about me even though she had become less verbal about it. I worried about her, too, mostly her health and safety. She stood as much or maybe more of a chance of having an accident back in Maryland as I did up here in Alberta. Should she regress to letting me know how much she is worried about me making the trip, I will tell her the time to worry about me is when I don't feel like making such trips.

I remember my Dad's passion for playing golf. He started going south in Maryland winters to play golf in the Carolinas with his cronies. When he no longer felt like going, I knew he was close to his end and he was gone in a year or two after that.

PHOTO #2 - SUMMITVIEW SCHOOL

I stopped in Grande Cache looking for a Dodge dealership for an oil change. None there. I came upon Summitview School and had to take this photo. I agree with their slogan:

Persist
Until
Success
Happens

But whomever came up with the team's chosen name of "Death Racers" is a person I'd like to meet - maybe not race with - just meet. Go Death Racers! Apparently this team plays for keeps.

The road (Route 40) to Grande Prairie was uneventful or I fell asleep. The last time I drove through Grande Prairie, it wasn't much more than a small crossroad whistle stop. That would have been in the winter of '84. Now she was metropolitan, modern, fast paced city of over 37,000 souls. What made her boom, I don't know, but boom she did. I guess thirty-two years can change a place.

About the third mall I drove past, advertisements for "Express Oil Change" caught my attention. I figured these guys could secure my warranty just as good and probably cheaper than a dealership. I was ushered into a bay before you can say, "How much?" All of the employees were Indigenous Peoples except for one young token white guy. Maybe his uncle was on the board. I interrupted two Indigenous males who appeared to be on break and asked if their prices were better than the local dealers. One of them immediately addressed my concerns and assured me that I would pay much more at a dealership. That being said, I was reasonably sure that I wasn't going to be scalped (pun intended). I think that Native Americans would sense the humor in this on a scale akin to the rest of us late comers.

It would do us all some good to study how the British/Canadians treated their Native Canadians in comparison to how we treated our

Native Americans. It wouldn't be wrong to say the native Canadians had less of an axe to grind than did American natives.

I lived with Aleuts for a brief period of time during which time I concluded that the Aleuts hated a white man as soon as he stepped off the plane because of what the Russians had done to them way back. I have never gotten the vibes of being hated by any native peoples I've encountered outside of the U.S. of A. We need to fix that embarrassment. Were these people who did that to them really Americans?

The young white male was assigned to change my oil. I wanted to watch so I could do it myself after the warranty runs out. I told him that I was not "looking over his knuckles" (Americaneze for scrutinizing his work) but simply wanted to learn how. He said, "No problem, it's nice to have someone to talk to." I hope that he was just being nice and not having a problem being the sole minority. He may have been perfecting his skills as a dry joker. (Origin of phrase dry joker is unknown to this author — your guess is as bad as mine.)

The bill for my oil change was (are you sitting down?) $77.24 Canadian. While still in shock, I approached a local red-haired patron also getting his oil changed. He had a commercial medium-sized truck. He told me that his vehicle requires synthetic oil and two oil filters per oil change 3-4 times per year at an average cost of $400.00 a throw. I told him he could drive to the States in a day or so and probably save money. He laughed heartily thinking that I was joking. I kept the receipt for my warranty and you skeptics can request a free copy. Please show proof of purchase of this book and send $9.00 for shipping and handling - cash only.

Route 2 will take you out of Grande Prairie north/northeast towards Peace River (aren't these romantic sounding names?) I once resided on "B" street in LaVale, Maryland. Nice house, pool, and neighbors, but not overly romantic or original. The street I live on now is called Opessa Street, after a Native American named King Opessa. I feel that it's much more romantic and original and I've lived here almost 30 years compared to the 1+/- year on B Street. There's a lot to be said in a name.

The neighbors have asked the author not to pinpoint his location for fear of an onslaught of autograph hounds, sales people, book publishers, and the like who would absolutely disrupt the solitude we all crave and share out here in Western Maryland.

Driving on Route 2 was charting unknown waters in Alberta. The author had never been this far north in Alberta. And if you have caught the addicting wanderlust bug, the author can't read your mind but knows what you're thinking and feeling, it's like groupies following The Grateful Dead. You don't know what's coming up around the next bend but you're anticipating another mind-blowing landscape, surprise sighting of a furry creature, or a unique encounter with other humanoids who share your passion for the road. It's all out there waiting for you. All you have to do is get to the concert.

Quiz time. I'll bet you were hoping I forgot. I'm in good spirits. Sales are rocketing. I'll take it easy on you with another multiple choice:

Slang phrase meaning to scrutinize another's work:
A. To Be Or Not To Be
B. Your Grandmother's Underwear
C. Scrutiny on the Bounty
D. None of the Above
E. Looking Over the Knuckles
F. Both D and E
Answer: Ⅎ

Well, how did you do? No one said this one was an open book test. But, no one said it wasn't. If you took the initiative by searching for the proper response in the preceding pages, you will not be chastised. But, stay alert to future enjoyable reading that might just contain hidden instructions that only the stealthiest reader will detect.

I really feel you're getting a better handle on this and some of your test scores are starting to prove me right. If you can improve in this area, would someone tell me just why a few of you seem to be slipping in your sales totals? A good salesperson is a salesperson 24/7. It's in their blood. The leaders' records speak for themselves. Say to yourself, if that leader can wrack up 15 or more sales per week with family, friends, neighbors, in the workplace, on Facebook, or even eBay then I know I've got what it takes to match or even surpass his meager sales. Hell, you could do it standing on your head. Look at him. What does he have that you don't have? Think of how proud that special someone's going to be of you. Think of the rewards that are in store for you! It'll look good on your resume.

Just a second— telephone...sorry, now where was I? Oh yes, your rise to infamy. As you are considered a part of that vast network I call my family, I feel close enough to be candid with you about that last phone call. Please don't tell any of the other sales associates about it. It's our secret. It was the publisher. We may be setting some records. I, for one, want your name to be on the top of that sales ladder.

It never fails to amaze me how previously unknown people such as yourself are catapulted to star quality lives once they set a goal in book sales and achieve it.

I'm sorry I get so excited about your upcoming claim to fame that I end up taking up your sales time. Why don't you take a break from reading here, have a cup of strong java, and return to your list of potential sales contacts, OK? While you're enjoying doing that, I'll just trudge along back to the narrative up Route 2 towards Peace River. Somebody's got to do it. We all have a cross to bear.

On your way towards Peace River, you're bound to go through Dunvegan and cross over the bridge spanning the vast, and on this day, rain swollen, Peace River. I took a photo after crossing it once making the north bank. As you can see from this photo, the bridge is massive and I'm glad about that. As if it weren't, crossing the Peace would be considerably more difficult.

PHOTO #3 - BRIDGE OVER PEACE RIVER, DUNVEGAN

There was a quiet little park on the north bank with well-spaced picnic areas, restrooms, hand pumps with good water that I took advantage of regarding all the above. We take so much for granted. Look at Photo #3 once more. The sun is winning its battle with the clouds and rain that have been my companions for some time. Like visiting guests who get up early and leave before you're even out of bed so as not to wake you, the rain took its departure.

Look at Photo #4 - see the blue sky? It took awhile before I realized the sun had won another battle and chased the clouds and rain away. I hardly missed them, though the mist has always been an enchantress for me and always will be. I'm always looking for Robin and Maid Marion in it. Found them once but that was an all together different trip.

Please refer to the wooden church in Photo #4 beside the pine

PHOTO #4 - CATHOLIC CHURCH

tree. In the event that I have yet to clarify something for you, photos are numbered starting with the #1 (oh really!) on the day the photo was taken unless I got screwed up. There will be some readers who will actually go back to see if they can locate any such screw ups on my part. I had students like that in the past. You know people like that also. I'm sure you do. They get their rocks off finding fault. They are a sorry lot of losers who need a hobby or better still a friend. You can reach out to them as a friend and let them try everything in their power to bring you down (misery loves company) which given time they usually find success with. They must be miserable. When I come across one, I can't help but think "all those abortions out there and this SOB made it."

Let's get back to the church. Maybe we should really hurry. Did I tell you it's a Catholic Church built in 1800? That's a ways back. If those walls could talk, you'd better know Latin. I especially liked the little wooden fence. I guess that was for keeping midget hostiles out.

Anyway, there was a plaque and likeness of a priest who had spent 15+ years there converting midget hostiles (I made that last part up). It was said that this priest never slept in a bed. He slept on the floor atop his buffalo robe under his blankets. He selected three pieces of wood for a pillow each night which he used to start up fires again the next morning. If you look closely at the likeness of him, it appears that he has a kinked neck. (I made that last part up too, just to make you laugh — Catholic readers have my permission to laugh as well and should there be any blame to be had, place it on my shoulders.)

I kinda snuck up behind a girl in period dress taking down the Canadian maple leaf flag in front of a fur trading post in the same park and dating back to 1800. That's a long time to date, you'd think she'd be married by now! (I made this joke up in memory of Henny Youngman - it sounded like one of his.) If you're 70-80 years old you probably remember him (i.e., take my wife…. Please…) Thank you Henny.

PHOTO #5 - GIRL/FLAG, FUR TRADING POST

Arrival close to closing time does not have its advantages except in bars and bank robberies. I asked her for a quick peek inside which she allowed me. I wish I would have requested a peek instead of a quick peek as she had taken me literally. She opened the door, gave me that ever so quick peek and slammed the door snuggly. She was polite and courteous but obviously had bigger plans than hanging around a fur trading post.

It jumpstarted me trying to remember when I'd had that last bath, had it been that long? Were my baby wipes going stale? I don't know. I wasn't hitting on her, but it cost you the photo I wanted so much to take for you in there. I caught a glimpse of some furs, some traps, some barrels and some other stuff, I think. What I don't go through for you. The van snuck a lean into this same photo. She was tired, but full of fairly new oil and feeling on top of the world or on the way there at least.

Our next stop came at the Peace River Airport. The sun's been out bright and sweet since Grande Prairie for the most part. The airport was clean and lively with plenty of vehicles in the parking lot. The bathrooms were not crowded but with enough activity to warrant not taking a spot bath, though I doubt anybody would have cared. I have my dignity. Yea, I might stink but I have my dignity!

For miles and miles around Peace River as far as the eye could see yellow fields of something planted by the hand of man dominated the landscape. It was quite beautiful and that much more so after days of rain and mist. I'm not a farmer. I ventured a guess. My guess was milo, and that guess would prove wrong later in this story. The photo was taken at the highest point around, which was the pull off the highway into the airport parking lot. Again, my little throw away camera did its best but was not up to task to capture miles and miles of yellow, magnificent yellow. My mind caught it for safekeeping in the recesses. I caught myself humming, "follow the yellow brick road…"

Yes, Dorothy, there is a Walmart and a Freson Bros. in Peace River. Secure in the knowledge bed and breakfast was a done deal, I cruised the streets of Peace River after crossing said river. It was 1/2 to 1 mile wide here, high and muddy. I'm guessing muddy because of all the drizzle of late.

PHOTO #6 - FIELDS OF YELLOW

An Indigenous male of 20 or so pumped gas for me in downtown Peace River (population 6,240 souls). Before I realized it, he was there pumping gas for me with a big grin on his face. I suppose he wanted to show me that all Indigenous Peoples, not just those in the lower 48, had built in stealth. I gave a big grin right back at him, silently complimenting him on his stealth. This guy could also read minds, or at least people. Before I could ask, he told me that Freson Bros. Market was open 24/7 but he wasn't sure about Walmart. That may not seem to matter much to you but a free camper prefers all night illumination in parking lots for safety and security reasons. Think about it.

He also needed to vent. As out of the blue, he spoke of the recent death of his 80 year old grandmother who had succumbed to cancer. "She had beat it twice, but it won the third time." He also said he had words with her during the third time. She told him she was tired of fighting and just wanted to be with her deceased husband. I told him that they are really living happily ever after now. This gesture of understanding and compassion brought his grin back and his grin made my day.

The temperature is 73 degrees Fahrenheit in the Freson Bros. parking lot and "Granny's Getting Tired" (Marlon Brando in 'The Missouri Breaks'). Could find no working phones to call Precious. It's 9:20 PM Canada time. Sounds like a good name for a beer. I should get a patent. Do you think anyone in Canada would drink it? I must be pretty wired. Besides my two cups of cold coffee, I had a small Coke with my chicken today. Chicken you say? Yea, a Walmart rotisserie - what else? Freson Bros. don't sell them or either ran out before I got there. I did buy a blue rubber frog with yellow and black markings on its back and large brown eyes as a thank you gesture to Freson Bros., along with some Cokes, etc.

Ice has been a major expenditure. The Cabela's Coleman cooler I bought for this trip specifically as it was advertised to keep ice up to four days, keeps it for an average of two days (block ice included). Well, it did say up to four days. I supposed 0-4 = up to 4. So, the number 2 falls within that realm. So, no false advertising there. Maybe it's defective. Don't know. Does anybody have a shipping box that will hold a 50 qt. cooler?

That additional small Coke is keeping me up tonight. I'm grateful for the privilege and insist that whatever conclusions you may have, I think this is a great lifestyle. Here I lay in this comfortable homemade bed with almost memory foam. I'm reminded of a years-gone-by trip made from my back door in Fairbanks, Alaska, to my parent's back door in Cumberland, Maryland (4,999 miles). That trip was foolishly made in five days and four nights of driving (Datsun pickup, 4 cylinder, 5 speed, extended cab, full of my stuff, but no bed). I recall crawling under the truck in complete exhaustion and sleeping in the middle of the day, in the middle of a shopping mall parking lot in one of the Great Lakes states. No one woke me or checked on me. They had to see me or hear me snoring. I also speak a running gibberineze in my sleep. Maybe it was reverse or counter karma for the guy I wouldn't disturb from his sleep or death this morning back in Hinton. Why the rush to get back home so quick? There were five males per every female in Alaska at the time and she was either married, or 300 pounds, or playing hard to get, or a combination of most of the above. I was starting to eye up the cat and his name was Smokey. Prospects and ratios back in the lower 48 were far better. I had something to get to. Was it worth risking life and limbs of others let alone by own? Nope. But you see, I was younger and far more stupid then.

DAY #15, 7/15/2016

Slept well but not as well as previous. It was still light out last night well past 10 PM with daylight erupting somewhere close to 4 AM.

I'll bet you're saying to yourself, "The author is no longer recording mileage at the end of the day." Your assumption/discovery is on the money. When your internal clock is being bombarded with different time zones and the sun lingers in the night sky way later than it had been a few days ago and restlessly bounds up from nowhere much earlier in the AM, etc., etc., you have a tendency to ere on time/distance/space/etc. This is a forgone conclusion to be expected on extended travel especially when traveling alone. I'm positive that many of you travelers have experienced the same phenomena. It is called "screwing up the mileage" as a result of forgetting to log it in at the end of the day. Be it forgetfulness, fatigue, mind dead, etc., expect it to occur especially with free camper types. Looking at it another way is to see it/accept it/embrace it as a gift. You can throw your watch away now.

We are all prisoners of time. Try this for a day. Take your watch off and count how many times you look at your empty wrist that day. If this is your first maiden voyage of time and space traveling without your watch, you can also expect something akin to withdrawal symptoms for that chronicler of time we need to free ourselves from. Without knowing what time it is, we may all live a little longer or at least think we did. Isn't it amazing that many retirees get a gold watch at a time when they might benefit more if they threw all their timepieces away?

It could be economically beneficial, too. Sorry I didn't get you a birthday present - I don't have a watch. I was crawling out of a bar in Alaska way back. It was mid summer so there was no complete darkness. I asked two guys coming across the porch to the bar what time it was. They told me 4:15. I enquired if it was AM or PM as I had lost my watch. This may have been an attempt to get my attention from the Great Spirit, that I did not take full advantage of as after looking upon that empty wrist about a hundred times a day, I purchased another watch. That was over 30 years ago. Wonder where I'd be, what I'd be doing, who I'd be with had I recognized the loss of a watch as a divine message of good advice and not bought another?

Anyway, please accept my humble apology had you been enjoying the mileage updates up to the 12th. I can assure you that the total will be chronicled for you once, if ever, we reach the conclusion of this journey.

I bought a twelve pack of baby Pepsi from the Freson Bros. to show my thanks for their hospitality. It was here that I met a friendly cashier (I knew she was Canadian right away). She asked the standard questions (i.e., where from, where to?) She told me that she and her husband had planned a motorcycle trip from here to Yellowknife some years back, but bailed out as their daughter was too young at the time. She has somehow managed to get older since then.

My new friend cashier told me that it should be 80-90 degrees Fahrenheit this time of year and the 4-5 days of rain was not the norm. I asked her how to get back to Route 35. She said to return to Route 2, head southeast, go through two satellites. I said, "Two satellites?" She cleared her throat and said two sets of lights and make a right. Her demeanor reflected some slight embarrassment regarding "the satellites." I attempted to steer her away from any embarrassment by telling her she was speaking Canadian English. She laughed and said it was "Canadianeze"which I'm sure I had referred to earlier somewhere back in this text. And all you readers thought I was just kidding or made it up, didn't you.

She also told me the road to Yellowknife from here wasn't too bad, pending weather. I asked her what all the yellow stuff was in the fields around here. It wasn't milo. It is canola for making canola oil. I told her they must have the market cornered as I've never noticed it before and that I thought it was so beautiful. She said in a good year, the yellow blooms can last up to two weeks.

She also told me that if I return this same way, I could do some free camping in their driveway. I told you I met a friend, but she was just your typical, run of the mill Canadian. It's hard to get used to. We could learn so much from them. They are givers, not takers. If you look at your road atlas you will find that I had no choice but to return this way as there's only one road north from Peace River towards Yellow Knife - the exciting and magnificent Highway 35. I recommend it to all travelers. I also recommend Freson Bros. Market and parking lot.

Speaking of Canadian friends, while traveling near Prince George in British Columbia way back a lifetime ago with Dead Bob, we came up on a Canadian family unknown to us prior to that. Dead Bob and I had been sleeping in the bed of his Ford Courier truck amidst our haphazardly packed stuff. They had us to their home for drugs and supper and gave us free lodging for the night. As we approached the Ford Courier the next morning, it had been fitted out with a cap. Our host had put it on while we slept in that morning. He would accept nothing in return beyond our thanks. He said it was a spare of his and that we would probably come back that way sometime in the future. Like I said, it's hard to get used to.

The author took his next bath in an unknown stream crossed over by Highway 35. Color was brownish due to rains, but not too cold. We only registered some minor screaming but buku degrees better than Montana facilities, possibly due to no glaciers in sight. The bathing area was down a rut-filled, bumpy road that I hoped wouldn't tear my oil pan off. While bathing with support from a large rock in mid-stream, I could hear an occasional vehicle passing over head on the bridge above. I heard a slight ruckus in the thick cover that lined the stream below me. I was glad I took the family sized bear spray can with me for comfort. I also carried a small cowbell and a plastic pop bottle with about 6-8 spikes enclosed which served as a great warning device. I rang the cowbell, shook the spike filled pop bottle, and yelled out "hey bear" to signal the bear that I was a formidable opponent should he or she be sizing me up for lunch. If it was a bear, he/she probably didn't realize that I wasn't a formidable opponent, but I was the last one there that was going to make him/her aware of this. Thus concluded a leisurely bathing experience, followed by a quick dry off while ringing the bell and shaking the bottle of nails. You'd be surprised how fast you can dry off up there off of Highway 35.

Never saw him/her, didn't want to, and didn't linger. Could have been a Hoary Marmot, a squirrel, or an endless list of non-life threatening creatures. But, I've always found it better to ere on the side of caution versus lunch along the river bank. In case you're wondering, what the hell is a Hoary Marmot, they are called ground hogs up north and out west Hoary Marmots. It probably helps them with their self esteem issues.

Speaking of lunch, several miles north at the tiny town of High Level I spotted a Subway. Hoping they offered the $3 for a 6" daily special like many Subways do back in the States, I hastened on in. I'm not positive, but I'm guessing the owners were Pakistani. The lady taking my order was very nice and polite but they have to be. The young man actually making my sub was like a mini version of the "Soup Nazi" from Seinfeld, not friendly and a notch or two below neutral bordering on a low grade level of disdain. I watched him making my sub like a hawk to ensure he added no ingredients that I hadn't ordered. For some reason, he seemed to peer back to see if I was watching once he wrapped my sub up and I was reasonably sure that he could not contaminate it, I asked if they had the $3 special on 6 inchers which I would have ordered to go following my current 12" order for $6 (do the math). At this time, through grit teeth, the "Soup Nazi" persona seemed to re-emerge and he growled, "Only 12 inchers for $6." Maybe math is different in Pakistan. I elected not to purchase any carry out for fear that he would make it away from my scrutiny. He slammed the 12 incher I had ordered on the counter and I countered by slamming my money back to him on the counter. I stared him down like a matador with the bull. Neither of us blinked. I had given him $7 Canadian but told him to keep the change as I wanted nothing to do with anything that had touched his bare hands. He had worn the mandatory plastic gloves while making my sandwich, but plastic gloves can be cunningly compromised by an evil mind with bad intent.

I chose to eat outside on benches provided by the establishment and took a seat where I could watch him work his merriment. When leaving to go outside I was approached by the kind/polite lady who had taken my order. She thanked me, told me to have a nice day, and to come back again. Grammatically, her entire statement came out as if she was asking a question. Somehow, no matter how much I delved into my memory banks, I could recall no commercials on TV for Subway that represented any like scenario.

I had ordered a 12" Italian sub even though they only had white flat bread. My preference being the health conscious wheat flat bread was compromised by an overwhelming desire for a gut bomb not made by my own hand. Damn the possible intrigue, full steam ahead!

A hands on inspection was in order as I could see him watching me watching him through the shop window. Although, it would be so easy to conceal, I could find no unwanted foreign matter in the multitude of fixins I had politely ordered. However, the meat had the appearance of "mystery meat" which looked like a conglomerate of God knows what put into a blender and left to harden in the sun for an undisclosed amount of time.

Like I said, I was in the mood for a gut bomb and my mood was about to be satiated regardless of the outcome. To make a long story short - I ate the damned thing in one fell swoop. I never got sick, but suffered from tremendous gas for almost two days. The moral of this story goes like this: anyone can buy a franchise from Subway, sometimes you can tell a book by its cover, and maybe they have a caste system in Pakistan.

To be honest, I'm not sure these people were from Pakistan. I used to go on a party boat fishing trip every year in the Chesapeake Bay with friends from Virginia with WASP origins. We were joined there on several trips by an Indian from India who owned a convenience store in Virginia. I never met a better fellow. He would give you the shirt off his back and didn't suck up to you or look down his nose at you. He would make a good manager for that Subway up in High Level or better still, an owner.

Most of the way from Peace River to here in High Level, the highway's path was surrounded by big/poor farms owned by Moravians. Don't know much about them other than it appears they have very active sex lives as is disclosed by counting the number of kids. You don't have to ask couples how long they've been married. The formula is simple. If they have eight kids, you can bet they've been married about eight years, maybe seven. Eight years would equal 96 months and 96 months divided by nine months would equal 10.66 kids if you wanted to push it. There are averages involved and I just don't want to get into logarithms or heavier math as I feel the invention/acceptance of the "0" was helpful, it was also confusing. I wasn't tutored in elements of mathematics in college but bugged the instructor so much, he gave me a "D" if I would agree never to take another of his classes.

Anyway, the size of the farms warranted the necessity of large families and I'm sure the male Moravians weren't above using this for leverage if their female counterparts had a headache tonight. Am I displaying jealousy or just simple envy? Being Moravian is a hard life but the perks are good.

There was a Moravian couple in the Subway with more kids than I could discretely count. I fumbled through some more math. If my 12" Italian cost over $6 Canadian, the Moravian meal must have run $108+/- Canadian as there was mom, dad, and about too many jabbering, mostly blonde, kids filling up there. I could only hope they didn't have the "mystery meat." Another reason for my decision to eat outside was because it must have been about 120 degrees Fahrenheit inside the Subway. I should guess it helped the Pakistanis to toast the flatbread quicker or reminded them of their homeland or something. But you know, given the temperature, one would assume that the place would smell like curry-laced human BO or Moravian sweat glands, but it didn't. Either everyone there had had a recent bath or my sinusitis had saved me once again by numbing my olfactory sensors. Whatever it was, I am thankful.

Who am I to talk. A few days ago back in Jasper, a cashier displayed outright distaste possibly for the odor I was omitting and it hadn't been that many days since my baths at Radium Hot Springs, or had it been? I filled the tank at the High Level Esso station and quick stop. Though I thought they were Thais, it was owned by Filipinos. They were very nice. There seemed to be more of them than they needed to run the place. I shouldn't judge. I didn't take gas station/quick stop 101 in college.

Pop Quiz Time!

How many children does a Moravian couple living near High Level, Alberta have on average in a calendar year?
A. More than you can count
B. 10.66
C. 1.3
D. Blonde twins
E. None of the above
Answer: Ɔ

Most of you did very well on this quiz, or were exceedingly close with the answer you had chosen incorrectly. We could also conclude that the average person pays more attention if they're reading something that has to do with carnal fantasies.

Keep in mind, you do not have to answer all pop quizzes correctly to score high on this manuscript. The same is true for those of you who have made that commitment to be a successful spoke in that big sales wheel we call our family. You don't have to sell this book to everyone you come into contact with. You just have to make every attempt to do so.

Every successful salesperson knows that he or she is not going to score a touchdown every play. It's the occasional touchdown that wins the game all the way up to the Super Bowl. Yes, we have decided that any and all sales people who successfully surpass 100 sales of this book will receive a free, very large, silver-plated ring with your own initials, number of sales, and the year emblazoned on the flat large rectangular top representing our book. Shipping and handling will be a mere $11.99 which can be broken down into three easy payments pending your personal preference.

Remember, I still want you with me sitting at that front banquet table at our soon to be announced convention. Frankly, we can't set a date yet as we can't determine the size of the hall or convention center that will be needed to accommodate all of our winning sales associates. Just make sure you are there. I've been hashing it over with our accountants to explore the possibility of booking free passage for, let's just say for now, our top 10 or even more. Think what it will do for your resume. Remember, the sky's the ceiling.

Back to the Filipino Esso. The nice Filipino lady (I know for sure she was Filipino as I had taken the liberty to ask her what her nationality was and I doubted she would lie to a guy wearing my TV network cap). She also told me I had about 700 kilometers to go before I would reach Yellowknife. You've come a long way baby but you got a long way to go.

While exiting the restroom, I was approached by a Filipino who shook my hand and knuckle bumped me. He said his name was Matt. I assume he was part of the family running the Filipino Esso Quick Stop. He said he had been to D.C. and had noticed my Maryland tags. (Clarification: the country is spelled Philippines. The people are spelled Filipinos. It's got to be confusing, even to them.) I told Matt that Maryland had given D.C. to George Washington. Matt thought this was funnier than I did. He did a medium howl.

Matt shared that he, too, travels far and wide and would travel more if it wasn't so expensive. I gave him a free lecture on time shares. He seemed very interested in this and would definitely look into the possibilities for him and his family.

I told him where I live in Western Maryland and told him I'd "leave the light on for him" and he was welcome anytime. He knuckle bumped me again and disappeared into the day looking back at me wearing a wide grin kind of like the Asian bar owner in 'Good Morning Vietnam.'

Matt wasn't gay, he wasn't a narc, he wasn't setting me up, etc. There was only one other conclusion. Matt was a nice guy. It's hard to get used to. You guy readers out there, think of what your suspicions would have run too if a guy approached you at a restroom in the States. Like I said, it's hard to get used to up here.

Back on the road again north of High Level on good ole Route 35. This region seemed to have more horses than people. I think the Moravians have the big/poor looking farms in order to feed the horses. I wonder how they feed all those horses through the winters up here as I'm sure the winters here are long and nasty. And a horse eats about a barnful of hay a week.

Oh God! I hope they don't eat the horses or sell them as mystery meat to Subway. If I should meet a Moravian later, I'm going to ask him if horse meat gives you gas.

The U.S. is one of the few countries that does not eat horse meat or at least we think we are. We don't eat carp either and everyone else does. I boiled up a carp once to feed my cats with. While keeping an eye on it as it boiled, I noticed the aroma was great and the meat of the carp was as white as snow. I tried a chunk. Not bad and it didn't kill me.

I have a friend who will remain nameless who told me on the phone that he and his family have eaten horses for years and they prefer it over beef and pork. He urged me to try some if given the chance. I've never been to his home…

We have this thing that tells us that some animals are so majestic, we just can't eat them. I don't know how I justify eating other creatures who, to me, are just as majestic as a horse. I must hide or elope from this present train of thought less I become a vegetarian. I think they're called vegans now but I wasn't sure of the spelling.

With lots of horses, you get lots of flies. I will take the liberty to warn you should you travel through these parts in warm weather - count on it. They are big and relentless. Their sole purpose in life seems to be to get away with as much of your epidermal layer as they can gnaw off.

I've been attacked by triangular shaped deer flies on Assateague Island on Maryland's far eastern shore. They were similar but took smaller chunks. They are another reason I live in Western Maryland. I've been attacked by black flies in different parts of Canada and Alaska. They weren't similar and took even smaller chunks. But this was my maiden voyage with these monsters. They look to be about half the size of a full grown horsefly, but one soon finds their one and only true weakness. They are slow. Thank God. But that's your only advantage.

It does take approximately four strikes with a rolled up newspaper or magazine to finish them off. Your first shot seems to stun or confuse them but it takes another two to three reasonably solid coupe de graces to put them out of your misery.

Be ever so careful when defending yourself against a pack of these while driving as they can become a life threatening distraction. Pull off the road. You'll kill more of them. They have a kamikaze like philosophy. Yea, they attack in force, gambling that at least one of them will get you. The Canadians have a phrase for it when they see you doing battle with them. They say, "There goes another crazy Yank who didn't know what our flies had in store for him."

Later on in this story I plan to buy the first fly swatter I can find, as it would only serve to delight these unwanted guests should I break out a window slugging them with a rolled up newspaper or magazine. Maybe that's part of their evil strategy. I wonder what they are called. I know what I call them, but I will spare you from hearing it.

The co-runner lady who runs the Northwest Territories Welcome Center with her husband told me these treacherous flies were attracted by the heat. She's thinking higher Fahrenheit. I was thinking more on the lines of body heat.

Speaking of heat, it went from a comfortable 66 degrees Fahrenheit this morning to a muggy 84 degrees Fahrenheit this early evening when I crossed the 60th parallel making my new residence in the Northwest Territories and waving a fond temporary farewell to Alberta the Magnificent.

There was a husband/wife team who ran the Welcome Center. Their job was to check folks in to the campsite located on the grounds and to answer any questions travelers might come up with (no pun intended). When I saw other campers cranking out a lot of

PHOTO #1 - NORTHWEST TERRITORIES WELCOME SIGN

queen's Canadian for a single night, my urge to explore free camping alternatives kicked in to high gear. I approached the male counterpart.

In the space of a very few minutes, I had heard the story of their lengthy marriage and places their own wanderlust had carried them to, plus numerous gravel pits with bathing lakes, the best he felt being Mile 66. He also highly recommended free camping behind what he called the Government Building at Enterprise, further north on Highway 1 as Highway 35 in Alberta mysteriously becomes Highway 1 once it crosses the territorial line for some reason. I never asked why for two reasons. The first I thought was maybe it was better off unquestioned. The second was the fact that I couldn't get a question into him. I soon realized why when I saw a sign stating "Free Coffee" with an arrow pointing to two large percolators running as hard as he could push them.

Knowing that I was oftentimes heavy winded myself, it felt good to allow someone else to carry that mantel for me just this once. He told me they never winter up here anymore and as soon as the first signs that the short summer is about to be pushed out of the way by the long, long winter, he and she close things down here and head for Baja, Mexico as fast as their travel trailer could carry them.

He asked me if I wanted a cup of coffee and shared, without me asking, that he drank the stuff all day long (keep in mind the further north you go this time of year, the longer the days become due to the Earth's tilt towards the sun which I wish we wouldn't take for granted so much). Think about it for a second. It's a pretty big affair. Think about it if you ever eat or drink. I thanked him but told him I'd already met my coffee quota for the day which was a measly two cups. He appeared to take this as an admission of weakness on my part and bellowed that it was nothing for him to drink 4-5 pots in a given day. I fed his ego a bit by telling him that was remarkable. I could see his better half shaking her head. I felt I should not feed the flames of his caffeine any further. I returned to my vehicle and retrieved my thermos bottle that held about four heavy cups when filled.

I do not know what if any conversation they had in my brief absence, but upon my re-entry he spotted my thermos, put an arm on my shoulder, marched me to one of his percolators and filled her up with some blend of very dark, high-grade octane coffee.

I've seen very similar scenarios in bars with alcoholics being pleased when you show signs of joining them, but this was my first known experience with a caffeinated intoxicated person. I still liked him and found his antics amusing. I never felt threatened by him. But God help the person who stumbles into there if he runs out of coffee.

We seemed to bond quite a bit better when I shared with them that I had lived in Alaska for 9 +/- years. It's akin to people who have had kidney stones bonding for only they know what real pain is all about. Until you've lived through a winter in the far north your imagination is a sorry substitute that will never get it right. Not that winters up there are a scourge. They are simply long, challenging, and a bit trying at -70 degrees Fahrenheit. I like to tell friends that -70 degrees Fahrenheit was cold but didn't feel nearly as cold as -56 degrees Fahrenheit with the wind blowing. It's a dry cold. It was nothing to go out all day (remember in winter, the days are shorter due to the Earth's tilt) cross country skiing at -20 to -40 degrees Fahrenheit. Remember, you would be dressed for it with no exposed skin. You could remain quite comfortable. In fact one of your primary objectives was to not let yourself get sweaty. Freezing sweat will kill you at those temperatures.

She and "Caffeine Charley" (I never did get his name but I think this nomenclature befits him without condemning him) bid me a fine Canadian farewell and wished me luck on the remainder of my trip. Before I left, she told me that Yellowknife would be packed to the gills this weekend due to some music festival there and that there probably would be no room at the Inn. She hadn't heard my

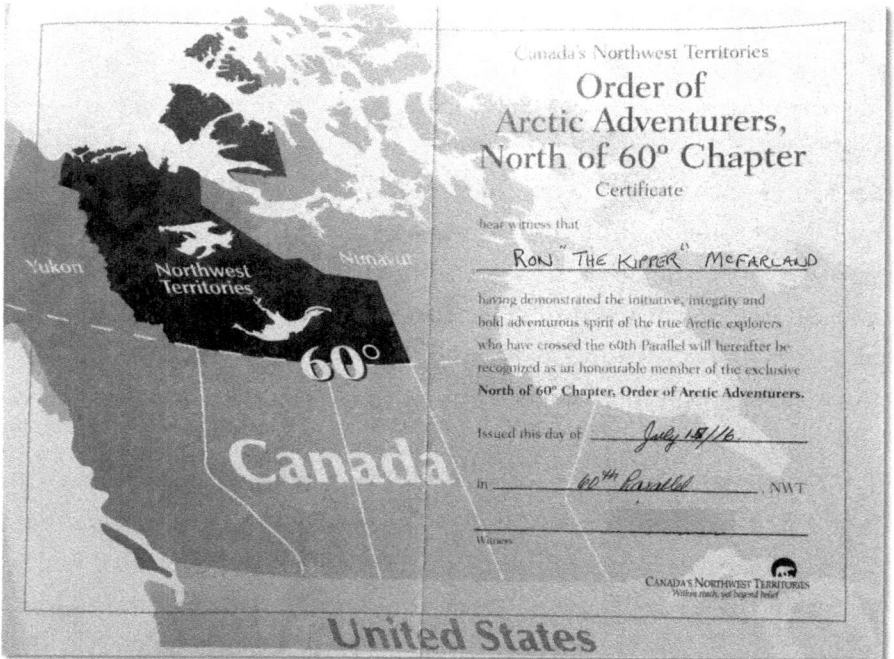

free campers conversation with "Caffeine Charley." She also gave me the Order of Arctic Adventurers, North of 60 degrees Chapter Certificate, which is awarded to travelers who have crossed the 60th parallel on the globe heading north. I am proud of it and will cherish it and I hope a copy will take, so it can be an integral part of this journey's description.

Drove to the gravel pit on Mile 66 recommended by Caffeine Charley. It was spacious, maybe a square mile in size. There was another vehicle at the far end. I went to the opposite far end so as not to interrupt this guy's sleep, shooting up, and/or sex life. I found it a courtesy of the road that I appreciated when I had first choice free camping at a gravel pit. There are gravel pits all over the north country. They need gravel to build the road. Over time, you end up with a large deep hole that used to have a lot of gravel in it. Over time, you end up with a large hole full of water (clear) where gravel once lived. Over time, fish end up finding their way into the pit. Time is an interesting companion. Don't ask me how. They don't stock them. It's one of those great gifts given to us from the one who takes care of us. Usually up north, the gravel pit fish I have caught were delicious Arctic Grayling. It's interesting, there's gravel pits full of fish that came from nowhere or somewhere all along interstate 95 on the East Coast of the USA.

It was high time I took yet another bath as it felt like my clothes, especially the shorts, were starting to stick to me. It probably was a good day and place to utilize my portable laundromat even though I knew the rinse/spin cycle was not working well. But first, a toast to crossing the 60th parallel. The toast would be one beer and one Parodi King Cigar manufactured in Scranton, PA. I found a great place on a little knoll of sand and small rocks to perch with my back to the lake and sun giving me a full view of most of the gravel lot leading to the edge of the gravel pit. Here, I could enjoy the warmth of the sun's rays bouncing across the top of the water, drink my beer and smoke my Parodi King slowly to savor the moment and still keep an eye out for any potential four legged creature whose idea of savoring the moment was to have yours truly for an evening snack.

I was vigilant and thanked God again for this place, giving me a life that allowed me to do this, and keeping me, my vehicle, friends, family, and Precious safe and sound. Does God have a thankless job? First of all, He probably sees it more like a hobby than a job. But, I fear that where too many of us are concerned, God does have a thankless job. Let's not do that to Him. I think He's earned more "at-a boys" than we give Him. So get with the program.

I was somewhere close to my second drag on the cigar and my third gulp of beer with the sun bouncing across the water filled pit and messaging my back with a soft warm hand, when the breeze I hadn't appreciated died down and up they came. Those damned big flies had found me on their radar and another kamikaze attack was launched. I blew smoke at them. It deterred them, but, they were well-trained. They just altered their route of attack away from the Parodi King screen of defense and plunged in to me with a determination that, had I not been their target, would have been admirable. Afterthought: if their planes could fly in reverse, would we call them Kazikamis?

We were forced to surrender the field and retreated to the van. We, being the beer, the Parodi, and myself. This negated all plans for bathing or

PHOTO #2 - ALEXANDRIA FALLS

laundry. Victory wasn't truly or totally theirs as the three of us sat behind the wheel with the driver's side window cracked blowing Parodi King smoke out the crack. They were slow to give up their attack but landed on different parts of the van, probably to come up with an alternative attack plan. Some of them reluctantly started flying off in the direction of my unknown free camping partner at the opposite end of the lot. High fives were given all around and I made myself a promise to send a thank you card to Scranton, PA's Parodi plant. We can now combat any attack by these blood suckers by simply never leaving the vehicle. Victory is sweet.

I stopped for a quick meal inside the van near Alexandria Falls just south of a whistle stop named Enterprise still on the fly filled but beautiful Route 1. The wind picked up and the flies died down. It's another gift from the one who takes care of us. Say 'thank you.'

PHOTO #3 - ALEXANDRIA FALLS

It gave me time to hike the short trail for a view and three quick snap shots of the falls. That's the Hay River flowing over them. There were two other falls nearby but the wind was dying down. It was decided to travel to Enterprise, fill the tank, and secure respite for the night.

I met a guy and his young daughter at the only gas station in Enterprise. We did the usual where are you heading? Where are you coming from? He said he lived in Yellowknife and he was on a camping trip with his daughter. I told him that I was told there was a big music festival this coming weekend. He said, "Yes, and that is why we are camping."

PH⊙T⊙ #4 - ALEXANDRIA FALLS

He noticed that I was attempting to scrape off some of the upper layers of dead/smashed flies from my headlights. He quipped that they were worse last year. How bad where they Johnny? "So bad they were clogging up vents in radiators causing vehicles to over-heat" came his reply.

I didn't realize it til later but I'd made it to the government build-ing suggested for free camping by Caffeine Charley earlier today. It sat across the highway from the only gas station in town that for the life of me escapes me. But was something like Edna's gas station or Edith's - not sure - I forgot to get a receipt. I'm sure it was a short female name (short meaning number of letters - God forbid I would insult a woman of lesser stature). Remember guys, short women make you appear taller.

By now it was after 11 PM and the sky still held plenty of light. I had a midnight snack of dry veggies and watered down oatmeal. The "Government Building" turned out to be a police or Mountie station that looked abandoned but well maintained. There was a large SWAT-like truck facing my selected sleeping quarters with lettering identifying it as a "Police Tactical Force Vehicle." I felt a duel sense of security coupled with a sense of "I hope my van doesn't get impounded with me in it." It didn't matter, I was too tired to go on. My last challenge for this evening was to wait for the wind to pick up, run around to the rear of the van, pop the tailgate up, and dive in without taking any hell flies with me. Somehow, it was successful. Maybe they were all full.

DAY #16, 7/16/2016

Had to backtrack to Alexandria Falls, 4km south, this morning for morning dumping. Only other option was over a hillside bank near "Police Tactical Force Vehicle" and I felt that it could disrupt my concentration with resulting constipation. I know, more information than you needed or wanted to know....

I didn't know what lay ahead for me but I can tell you that behind me laid very rough outhouses at the falls. You could say they were functional but needed a little work. Now I can't read your mind but I know what you're probably thinking. "Why didn't he go yesterday evening when he was at the falls?" Well, let me just rebut that thought right now, smart ass (loaded with puns). I've always been, always will be, and prefer to be a morning person. Life is full of mysterious rhythms. Some people develop sleep patterns. Try it. It works.

PHOTO #1 - MOOSE/CARIBOU HORNS

Second stop in Enterprise. This morning was for breakfast of cereal, pumpkin flax bar outside of the community center. Every time I eat a pumpkin flax bar, I wonder how the bird I fell for back at Bow Lake a few days ago is doing.

Business in Enterprise with moose (4) and caribou (2) antlers adorning the outside front of the business. I don't know about moose, but I have shot a caribou. If you find yourself around any-one bragging about shooting a caribou, you tell that person that you heard it from me that it was only about one notch up from shooting cattle in a field - just get the wind right, get ahead of them, and let them come to you. I think I repeated myself from an earlier passage. I think I repeated myself from an earlier passage....

You'll find that one of the greatest fears up here in the north land is running out of gas (the petrol kind) when you find yourself in the middle of the middle of nowhere and realize that you only have 1/4 to 1/2 tank of gas and you pass a former gas station quick stop and learn that it has not been in operation since gas was 19 cents per litre, a cold chill kind of invades your psyche. So, it was with great relief and pleasure to find the one and only gas station at Enterprise last evening even though petrol was going for $1.19 per litre at present. Now I know why Mrs. Caffeine Charlie told me to make sure I "top her off" at Enterprise.

The following occurred prior to breakfast this morning: now, keep in mind, I'm nearing the gas station with the female's name in Enterprise but I'm still south of it on Highway 1 due to my morning deposit back at Alexandria Falls. I saw emergency blinkers from a vehicle up ahead. Up here, you always stop to see if you can be of assistance to anyone sporting emergency blinker lights. These lights belonged to an older camper truck. Pulling up slowly and surveying with caution, I came upon a man and woman about my age standing outside the truck spitting hell flies. Yea, the hell flies arose this morning sometime before 7:30. I stopped but kept the motor running and offered my limited assistance.

These folks look to be WASPs. The lady came over and said they had run out of gas. Besides a few swats at the kamikaze's, she looked none the worse for wear and not the least bit stressed. The man appeared to have had one too many this misty morning or possibly a recent stroke. He was a man of few words. In fact, he was a man that said nothing. I actually hoped he was drunk and not stroked out, but it was a toss up.

I told her that I had room enough to haul one of them to the gas station in Enterprise which was about 2-3 kms north. She said it was OK and that her son was walking to get gas.

I had passed him walking south away from the gas station in Enterprise and he had no gas can. Maybe they lived close but I noticed they had Alberta tags and we were well into the Northwest Territories.

Unbelievable! She wasn't drunk and I hesitate to call them stupid or challenged. Let's just give them the benefit of the doubt and call them fearless. By the way, did I tell you that it was extremely flat up here? So, if they intended to drift to Enterprise for gas, well, that was just another bad choice they made today. I wonder how their day went yesterday? I will remember the expression on her face for a long time. It was as if she was conveying "Doesn't everyone run out of gas on a regular basis up here like we do?"

Not feeling sure if I could handle the big rowdy music crowd camped out in Yellowknife for the weekend and feeling the need for a few days break from the road, I decided to explore Hay River and drove north on Route 2 and soon found myself eye-to-eye with a gorgeous Anglo-Sax girl of 15-18 years of age who was running the Chamber of Commerce in Hay River. Now, Precious, none of that. She was young enough to be my granddaughter and we both knew it. Without me asking or her being so accustomed to being asked, she said, "They're called 'bull dogs' up here." It didn't take me long to figure that she was referring to the kamikaze hell flies I may have mentioned a few times since initial contact was made some miles back. Nough said! The Canadians had hit the mark better than I had! 'Bull dogs' was a fit and proper descriptive narrative for these hordes. But remember, the Canadians have had a lot more time than I've had to come up with this perfect nickname. And, you can tell that they hate them on a far different level than some traveling tourist who only had to live with them for what really amounted to a brief period of time. She also taught me that they are of the family of deer flies much like the ones we are familiar with back in the states, just 3-5 pounds heavier (I jokes). I told her we called them Chihuahua's back home. But, I had made that up. She was bright. She knew.

She did tell me that for some reason, they were not as bad in Yellowknife once she knew my destination. Maybe she told me that to get rid of me. Don't know. Don't think so, but wouldn't blame her as I still had not resolved the lost opportunity for a bath yesterday and

I doubted that I didn't smell any better today than I had yesterday.

She did her job as a Chamber of Commerce hostess and told me about a commercial camping site right on Great Slave Lake. It hadn't dawned on me how close we had to be to the Great Slave. I was so elated I bought three bracelets from her that had been made by a native lady from this area.

PHOTO #2 - GREAT SLAVE LAKE

Terrible is not a terrible enough word to describe the jarring, bumpy, washboard road that led to the campsite. On the way there, I caught my first glimpse of Great Slave Lake and took a photo. That's it way out there sitting above the slough running into it. A sign near where I shot the photo reported that the lake had been 5+/- times bigger just after the ice age had lifted off some 10,000+/- years back. They discovered this after locating sand dunes bucu miles inland from the lake shore we know today.

There was a rainbow at the end of the worst 3-4 miles of road I've ever experienced. I was actually debating about not pressing or bouncing on for fear of compromising the van's frame or oil pan. I was glad that I did. The rainbow's name was Frazier and he was the owner of "2 Seasons Campground" on the far southwestern end of Great Slave. There were campers large and small and a few tenters all claiming their little piece of heaven right up to the edge within a few meters of the Great Slave. Couldn't blame them. Had I gotten there first, I would have staked a claim edging right up nearest to the lazy rolling waves that appeared to be licking at the driftwood laden beach. No luck for me getting a site on the beach. Frazier informed me that those chosen and taken sites are mostly full timers many of whom are still of working age and choose to live a semi-nomadic life in the warm season.

Frazier also told me they only have two seasons up here - very cold, and less cold, although it was currently balmy. It wouldn't be much of a stretch to figure out how Frazier came up with the name for the campground.

PHOTO #3 - YURT WITH SHOWER ROOM TO LEFT

Frazier looked to be in his mid 40s. He offered me a ride around the campground. It was a pretty significant piece of property running along the lake for almost a kilometer and back into the bush for a few hundred meters with campsites throughout. Note my intermittent usage of the metric system. Not knowing that I was a fond believer in the free camping ethic, Frazier offered to put me up in one of his yurts. His first offer was $150 Canadians per night. When he saw the color leaving my face, he brought it down to $100. When I confessed to him that I was sleeping in my van, he offered me any one of the small but well-spaced campsites back in the bush. He also said he had a hot shower room which he would throw in for a total of $10 Canadian per day. The hot shower pretty much solidified the deal. Somehow I felt that Frazier sensed it would as we chatted in his truck.

He shared that he had been in the car parts and maintenance business three years back when he started clearing out the brush to make the "2 Seasons Campground." Four years ago, he had made a fortune in his prior endeavors mentioned above. But after paying employees, overhead, and taxes, he had to take out a $50,000 loan to make ends meet and this was the path that led him into the campground business.

I earnestly praised him for his recovery and the work in progress that he has already accomplished with this campground. I did not want to play hardball with Frazier as he had treated me so kind, but I had hopes of maybe finding a campsite right on the Slave. I assured him his offer was good and that I was planning to drive up to Fort Resolution via Highways 5 and 6 this very day. He told me it's a great drive but they are working on the road and there's not much in Fort Resolution. As Fort Resolution is the end of the road heading northeast from Hay River, Frazier knew I'd be returning this way and said that when I did, his offer would stand and I could leave the money at his house if I couldn't find him. How prophetic! I never did see Frazier once I left his truck but I did thank him again before hopping out.

Frazier was a man of his word. A few miles out of Hay River on the road to Fort Resolution, I linked up with the construction that devoured most of Route 5 for about 35 miles. This was no rinky dink operation. These folks meant business. These were big excavation equipment. The kind with tires bigger than your vehicle. I was amused to see how many of the large/gigantic trucks, graders, earth-graders, steam rollers, etc., were being driven by women. In this case mostly all native women. The majority of the flag people, engineers, etc., looked to be native also. I only spotted one or two white guys working there and they looked out of place. I had no intention of being sexist regarding the women above. I was delighted to see and highly respected to see any woman taking on a job so taxing and important. I saw two climbing down from equipment that had to be over two stories tall, who could at any other time and place been models in a glamour magazine.

It wasn't like traveling through construction sites in the States. It went something like this. You would come up upon a flag person. All but one were Indigenous females. You had to be observant as sometimes it looked like they were waving you on but they were merely slugging it out with the bulldogs. I felt sorry for them. I found no bulldog spray, and mosquito repellent won't even slow them down. If you could invent some spray or ointment to run the bulldogs off, you could quit your day job.

When the flag person did wave you on, it was like running the gauntlet. You were responsible for getting through the maze of heavy equipment that didn't stop to let you pass. If you were lucky, you'd steer on to a side of the worked road bed for maybe 100-200 yards (or meters) before you'd find yourself dodging or playing chicken with a piece of equipment that would make your van and contents flatter than a pancake if you weren't on your 'A' game. Average speed was "slow."

It wasn't like they were intentionally trying to harm you. It was more like they had a timeline and had fallen behind because of the recent rains. And, no matter where you are in the summer up here, old man winter is always closing in on you. There were two stretches where my van was not sliding but more like sailing through milkshake like mud that appeared to have a pulse.

Per Frazier's earlier suggestion, I stopped at Little Buffalo Creek Campground. This provincial campground hugged the Little Buffalo Creek. The creek was a long, dark, silent, meandering beauty, maybe 50 feet wide with a well-built boat ramp coming off the parking lot. Frazier had told me that this creek was full of pike and walleyes and it looked it. There was about 15 campsites but not one of them was occupied. I figured there was only one or two reasons for this. Number 1 was the condition of the road and number 2 was the bulldogs.

It was eerie quiet except for an occasional onslaught of bulldogs when the wind died down. There was a sign near the outhouse that read, "Make sure to sign in at the Office." Unfortunately, there was no office. Across the highway there was a well-used lane. Could this be the office? No. I did find 3-4 rough, older but maintained cabins with people's names on the front, like "Frank and Jenny's Cabin." This would have been ideal had I been able to rouse someone up. Yelling didn't work. Blowing the horn didn't either. It was like a ghost town. I would have considered renting a cabin. Not a soul in the campground, not a soul at the cabins.

My mind started conjuring up scenes of alien abductions or roving bands of bruins who had found their own kind of smorgasbord here on the banks of the Little Buffalo Creek. The hair started standing up on the back of my neck. Other than road work vehicles, I hadn't passed any other vehicles that looked to be tourist or free campers. I got the hell out of there and continued on towards Fort Resolution feeling very alone.

The last ten or so miles or kilometers going into Fort Resolution on Highway 6 were paved and a pleasure to drive on when compared to hardships that Highway 5 had thrown up in my path.

Fort Resolution was somewhat of a disappointment. No romantic campsites, just a rundown weather beaten bunch of fixer uppers at best with a lot of folks around who looked like they really didn't want to be there but were stuck there.

PHOTO #4 - LARGE BOULDER, GREAT SLAVE LAKE, FORT RESOLUTION

I drove through town and snapped a photo of a large boulder, one of many lining the beach. There was a small gap between the boulders and I watched two native moms, six kids, and one native dad frolicking in the surf. A scene no doubt occurring on thousands of beaches all around the globe at this very moment. But here it was in Fort Resolution. I tested the waters with my hands and decided that maybe the people frolicking above were not frolicking but in shock from the frigid waters grip. When it's that cold, "grip" is a good descriptive choice as it grips so hard, it feels like it's crushing your skin. Anyone who's experienced "the grip" knows what I'm talking about.

I got one hand wet in the Bering Sea during early winter many years back trying to ice fish through a crack. No matter what I did, including getting my wet glove off, drying my hand, slamming it into my coat pocket, holding it against my body, etc., couldn't break the grip. It hurt as if my hand was caught in a tightening vice even after I got home inside my little toasty cabin. Running cool water over it seemed to ease the grip. It didn't feel cold. The only sensation I felt was extreme pain. God forbid that anyone should fall full body into cold like that, but they do it quite frequently up north but I assure you, not by choice.

I made my way to the one, and I presume only, general store that for all intents and purposes served as the social oasis for the village. The locals were not friendly, but not unfriendly either. They basically ignored me. I passed many folks as I made my way up the front steps of the store. No one spoke to me. This is highly unusual especially in a Canadian native village. It's a sign that something has recently occurred that has consumed the usual happy/friendly/devil-may-care attitude that one can usually expect based on past experiences.

I did not feel at ease like I usually do in such surroundings. I cruised through the narrow aisles of the tiny store. Every available space had something for sale. I got a tin of corn beef for under $7 Canadian which was the best buy I had encountered. It was very crowded inside the store. There must have been 20 some folks packed into 20 some square feet of space or so.

Still, no one spoke to me. I smiled and nodded but no luck striking up any conversation. They were talking among themselves but mostly about things like, how long to put the Hot Pockets in the microwave and such.

And then I spotted her, a 40ish looking pale, thin, white woman who looked overly dressed. The lake was cold but the air temperature was a pleasing 70 degrees Fahrenheit. Anyway, I assumed this would be my first chance to converse with anyone here and get the lowdown on Fort Resolution. Much to my surprise, this woman went out of her way to avoid any eye contact with me, did not speak, or even acknowledge my presence. Was she crazy, abused, the new school marm, all of the above, etc.? Don't know and after witnessing her level of enthusiasm for communication, did not want to venture there. It kind of looked like a bad case of lingering cabin fever. That or someone had a gun to her back. At this point my desire to possibly find a cabin along the Great Slave had begun to waiver.

I was finally addressed by a heavy set, reasonably friendly Indigenous lady sitting behind a makeshift counter. I paid her for the corned beef and asked her where I could mail a postcard to Precious from. She said, "You're standing in the Post Office" as she pointed to a pile of stuff of all shapes and sizes in a corner of the tiny store. She said just lay it over there on top of that pile and it will get out.

The post office was a room about the size of a large box built into the corner. I really didn't think that a person could fit into the post office, but who am I to say. I'm just a free camper hoping to pass by unscathed. I wasn't sure if Bonnie (Precious) would ever receive this postcard, but it could serve as proof of my last known whereabouts.

While exiting the general store/post office, I came upon a guy who appeared to be running the show along with the lady storekeeper. With all due respect, he appeared to be the seed of an Indigenous local and an India Indian and he was very nice. Had I run into him first, I may have lengthened my stay there. But it was the luck of the draw and I had come up empty on my first draw. With full knowledge of the road that laid ahead of me back down to Hay River, I said a confused and cautious bon voyage to Fort Resolution. By the way, Precious did not receive the postcard. Before I left, the nice fellow saw my kayak and told me that Great Slave Lake is brown looking now due to all the recent rains and too choppy for kayaking. He added that had I been there last week, I would have found her blue and calm with a mirror-like surface. What had I said earlier about the luck of the draw?

My way back was similar to my way up, only backwards. The

road workers had had enough for the day and except for an occasional flag person, the highway was mine. I recall passing just two vehicles coming in the opposite direction on the challenging Route 5. Yea, I slid back through the same mud I had slid up on. I kept telling myself that it would be easier this time as I was heading south and with help from the shape of the globe and gravity I was actually sliding downhill. The road crews must have been working on the shoulders as all 40,000 or so ruts made for an interesting obstacle course once again, especially where the soupy mud had attempted to conceal 10,000 or so of them. It would be a great place for the bulldogs to get a bath, do some bulldog socializing, and bed down for the brief night while awaiting the arrival of those tasty flag girls in the morning. I was very concerned that I would get stuck in the muck and have to spend the night with a family of bulldogs. By family, I'm guessing two over protective parents and maybe 5,000 or so siblings. I still wanted to give Little Buffalo River camp a second chance. So, I stopped there again. Still desolate and free of humankind. Still, very much eerily silent. Hurriedly, I examined the provincial outhouse and found it rough, smelly, but adequate.

Finally, another human being. It was a bearded gentleman who looked to be in his high 40s. One eye was closed and the other one was trying to. I'm not sure if this was a medical issue or brought on by liquid spirits. This Anglo-Saxon was driving a red truck with well-made, but homemade, dog mushing wooden cages for at least ten dogs with silhouettes (French) of laughing husky heads cut through the doors to act as breathing ports for the dogs who had stayed home or were out on a mushing trail mushing away.

He told me that he'd moved here about ten years ago from southern Ontario as it was too crowded down there for him. His daughter was the musher and had done very well on her last race. We had maneuvered our vehicles so that we could chat from each other's driver side windows without getting outside in the domain of the bulldogs. Out of curiosity, we were eyeing each other up. Me with two eyes and him with whatever he had. I'm positive it was between partially one up to two. Of course, the sun was low but shining directly into his face. So, maybe he just had an unusual squint. Don't know. Didn't ask. He proved to be a nice enough fellow.

Seeing a handful zooming into my van, I started to bitch about the bulldogs. He said, "Oh, we're used to them up here," as he swatted at them with his hat and blew smoke at them from his cigarette. And he was gone in a cloud of dust just as fast as he had blown in.

The van and I trudged, slid, and bounced our way slowly back to hard surface near the wood bison management area. I felt like a stop to pay homage to the hard surface was in order, so it was completed with a pack of crackers and some cold coffee.

A lane was also found leading from the road to a small gravel pit lake that served well as spin/rinse cycle for the portable washing machine. I encountered no leeches in this lake other than a little mud around the edge and a few mosquitos that, believe it or not, was almost a welcome relief from the bulldogs. The tiny lake was majestic in her lonely solitude. I can only feel sorry for people who don't get the opportunity or who don't take the opportunity to witness nature's brush strokes. I continue to feel so blessed and fortunate to be one with a planet that continually showers her subjects with terminal beauty. All you have to do is look. Did someone say, "seek and you shall find?"

This time of year up north, darkness was at best elusive. The sun is never far from the horizon and at time appears to ride or bounce along it. So dark may better be characterized as a dusky dim light.

There were still a handful of miles to get back to Frazier's. Cruising along, I caught movement out of my left peripheral. Was it the elusive woods buffalo? No! It was my first live bear of the trip! It was a small to moderate sized black bear trudging parallel with the road to my left on some sort of trail frequented by local furry creatures probably for milleniums.

I hastened for a shot and took one from the van window trying to match my speed with the bear's. He/she was moving about 10 mph or 8 kph without breaking a sweat. The photo shows him (I'm figuring it's a male as it was alone) on the path about 30 feet from the van. He had come out of a stand of white birch when I first caught movement, but had traveled a hundred yards or so before the photo was snapped. He knew I was there. Bears are smart. They're one of the smartest and shyest of all creatures. That's why it's so rare seeing them. I lived in Alaska for nine years and saw two. Maybe I would have seen more had I hunted them, but I find them so cute as cubs and respect their intellect so much as adults that I find I could not drop a hammer on one if it wasn't an act of self preservation.

PHOTO #5 - BLACK BEAR NEAR HAY RIVER

After snapping the above photo, I noticed a vehicle approaching from my rear. I put on my emergency flashers to alert and protect all of us players from potential harm. The female driver with a male passenger barely slowed down as she blew past between me and the bear. The bear made a beeline for the tall timbers and I figured, he was long gone but he appeared just a few seconds later. I left my flashers on as I could see another vehicle approaching from my front. I snapped another photo as the bear came down the bank towards the highway. I was sure hoping that the oncoming vehicle could see the bear and wouldn't hit it as it now appeared determined to cross the roadway. To my delight, I could see the other driver slowing way down. I told you bears are smart. The bear came down on the edge of the road, looked left, right, and then left again and loped back up into the tree line. I assumed that was it for him, and waved to the nice lady who had slowed down to a crawl upon her approach.

PHOTO #6 - BEAR

As I was the only vehicle now on the highway for as far as I could see in both directions, I turned my flashers off. At that instant out comes Mr. Black who meandered up to the edge of the road, looked left, then right, then left again and lumbered across the road in front of my van. My only regret was that I didn't keep shooting even though the smashed bugs on my windshield would have blocked so much of the view that you would have seen more bugs than bear.

I knew they were smart but this bear was calculating. Maybe he had a furry girlfriend over there or a stashed chunk of something to eat. Only he knew and he was determined to get there. I'll say it again. He knew I was there. But, he couldn't have appreciated how much I was lapping it all up. What a gift! Thank you bear. Thank you God.

The last three or so miles to Frazier's "2 Seasons Campground" made me appreciate the 5-10 miles of smooth, mudless, bumpless highway after the bear and back into Hay River. I scanned Frazier's beach but no one had relinquished their site. There were lots of seagulls - maybe they should be called lake gulls as they were thriving on Great Slave Lake? How's it go? Fool me once - you're bad. Fool me twice - I'm a seagull. It was still nice to have them around even if they were a tad off course.

I'm sure many of you are wondering. The temperature today ranged from a low of 68 degrees Fahrenheit to a high of 83 degrees Fahrenheit. I'm still wearing the same shorts I was wearing many pages back. One of the sites Frazier had shown me earlier seemed to appeal to me as it had easy access to the hot shower near the yurts, it was centrally located between a handful of well spaced outhouses, had abundant trees for attaching clotheslines to, a crude fire pit, and sat on a corner off to itself. I don't like to be so close to other campers that I can hear them snoring or doing a host of other noise emitting things people tend to do in the night even if it's just a dusky one. Looking back and pondering about what the day had brought me could only be described as "grrrreat!"

I fired down some dry vegetables and oatmeal before my crawl of faith back into my van bed knowing I'd be sleeping well, hoping to be dreaming of bears, and delighted that a hot shower was on my to do list for tomorrow. It just made me feel tingly all over or was that something else?

DAY #17, 7/17/2016

Slept well but not long enough. That tingly feeling remained with me. Checked my bedroll for anything crawling. Found nothing but some errant sand which brushed off nicely. Took my first hot shower since leaving home so many miles and memories way back there behind me. The shower was seen sitting beside and above the yurt mentioned several pages back. You may refer to it at will. The building housing the shower was an oddly shaped affair with four or so sides. It appeared like the person who built it was attempting to get the unorthodox prize at an amateur architect contest. But, it was sturdy and fit my current needs to a tee.

I intentionally went very early in the morning, maybe about 6ish. I figured most of the laboring campers took their baths in the evening and the rest of the lot would probably sleep well past 6 AM. My plan proved true. No waiting in line. The shower was mine for the taking and taking I did. I washed some parts three times just to make sure my stay in the warm/hot shower would not end so soon. The temperature of the hot water stayed the same throughout my elongated shower, but the pressure seemed to ebb and flow at will which tends to make you a little jumpy in a strange shower. I suppose that's probably another thing on Frazier's challenges list.

I had a good boss one time who told me several times, "Now Ron, we don't have problems, we have challenges." His name was Ken. After hearing him 3-4 times on different occasions spouting this same philosophy, I had to interject, "Now Ken, these challenges are becoming problematic." Never heard him repeat that one again.

The shower room was reasonably clean and spacious with more than enough lights, mirrors, shaving sink, benches, etc., to get the job done. It was like stumbling across an old long lost friend you just didn't want to let go of. It was time for a hardy breakfast. The hard boiled eggs smelled funny, but I was craving an egg. I washed them off, peeled them and washed them off again. They smelled less funny so I downed two of them with some dry bread, a cup of cold coffee, a handful of dried bananas, and a cup of powdered milk for dessert. A meal fit for a king (king of the road). Or, as I think I may have quoted to you previously, but if so, still elect to repeat myself as I so very much love this quote from Moe of the Three Stooges, "I have a tape worm and it's good enough for him." Yea, I looked it up. I made reference to the same quote pages ago. Indulge me. I'm old. But I made it almost a hundred pages without repeating myself. That has been, is, and will continue to be one of the funniest lines ever uttered by a human being. It is to me, anyway.

Quiz time! It's been awhile. You deserve a break from all this reading and laughing.

What was the pet name given to the author by his father when the author was a teen?
A. Six Pack
B. Idiot
C. Windy
D. Two of the above
E. Martin Bormann
Answer: ꓛ

I bet you're surprised by that one. My Dad was complex. How was yours?

Anyway, let's get back to the trip. We've got a long way to go. Speaking of long ways to go, I've been approached by our accountants again and they have told me that although sales of this book could warrant a call to Guinness, there are still a few of you readers who are not calling your sales quotas in. I don't want to have to get ugly (ha ha - I jokes!) Remember, we're all in this thing together! All for one! One for all!

It's been brought to my attention that some of you may be slow readers. You do not have to read the book cover to cover before plunging into your sea of sales goals. He who hesitates is lost. If you snooze, you lose.

Remember one thing - I want you in our sales family. Anyone can be a top notch sales person. The key is believing in your product and surely if you've read this far, you are a believer. When was the last time you read anything with such candor, wisdom, joyous humor, sophisticated antidotes, heart wrenching truisms, mind boggling tales, etc.? And all for such a mere pittance when held up to what you walk away with each time you delight in reading a handful of pages.

I don't mean in anyway to be self promoting. I'm basing the above on anonymous testimonies from many accomplished authors, athletes, critics, movie stars, politicians, and even numerous heads of state who understandably received much more than they gave to get their hands on and their minds around this manuscript. Some of them were slow readers, too. So, get on with it! I want you at that convention table with me and a host of the headliners mentioned above who I must keep anonymous at this time for security reasons.

Remember that ring I personally promised? Well, my accountants gave me the nod to up the ante. Are you sitting down? You have my personal guarantee. Everyone in our beloved sales family who surpasses 149 sales of this book shall receive - are you sitting down yet? I can wait. A free GOLD plated ring identical to the silver rewards ring described earlier. You know you want it. You know I want you to have it. Have you noticed how many more people seem to be taking a special interest in you since you purchased this book? Have more people been smiling at you? Have you gotten those come hither looks? What do you think you'll get when they see you with me and the other celebrities at the convention? Need I say more?

PHOTO #1 - TEEPEE CANVAS CABIN
RED OUTHOUSE, FRAZIER'S

Feeling the need for a bit of rest, it was decided to lay over at Frazier's for another day. Maybe it was the lure of the hot shower as the decision was agreed upon earlier in the day.

I took a photo of my neighbor's campsites at Frazier's this morning. No one was home at the tepee and the same was true for the canvas topped cabin in the farground. The red thing that at first glance appears to be a door on the canvas cabin is actually one of Frazier's well spaced outhouses. That will become an integral part of this journey soon. Note the sandy soil and typical bush foliage.

Frazier wasn't greedy as is obvious when you study the spacing of the sites well represented in this photo. Greed seemed to factor in too many of the commercial campgrounds that I for one would avoid. They pack the sites in so tightly that you could catch something you don't want from your neighboring camper. That was another thing I liked about Frazier.

Speaking of little red outhouses, I scurried on down to the one in the photo described above. I wiped the seat off religiously and plopped down with some literature on Hays River, feeling confident in my anticipated and expected results. I could hear my pee's gentle cascading down into the belly of the toilette as I studied the low down on Hay River. While absorbed in my reading, I felt a warm and wet like sensation enclosing my ankle area and the shorts surrounding them. Immediately, my cunning brain alerted me that something was amiss. It was at this time that I wished I had inspected Frazier's plumbing job a bit more intensely. Upon closer inspection, it became evident that this was one of the jobs not checked off on Frazier's to do list. This toilette had not yet been completed or I caught it in the midst of an incomplete refitting job. The toilette had no belly yet as I had assumed. You know what they say about assumptions. I vacated the toilette with some very wet shorts splashing through a puddle of me in as dignified a manner as I could present under the circumstances. Looking back on it, there will always be a part of me at "2 Season's Campground."

Talk about starting your day off on a high note. Actually, it could have made an improvement on the smell of the shorts as I had forgotten to include them in the last portable laundromat that I realized had its onset clear back at Peace River. Talk about proactive laundering.

This latest fiasco did serve to remind me that I had forgot to dry the clothes that had been rinsed in the lake near the bear sighting so many words ago. After a brief second shower (I only had to target from the waist down) and a quick change of shorts, a crude clothes-line was fashioned between obliging pines via a spare pair of bungee chords I was now glad I'd brought along and to my relief, no Ranger telling me I had to take it down.

While wind and time worked on drying my clothes, I strolled the beach in camp. Lots of debris but no garbage. Wood everywhere on the beach. A wood carver's paradise and no need to cut firewood. Mother Nature and God just kept stockpiling it there and there was plenty more where that came from.

I did watch an enthusiastic mother and two kids attempt to launch their kayaks into the wind swept waves. I pondered, "Is she related to the folks who ran out of gas near Enterprise or was she a mommy dearest trying to see which of her children would be taken first by the multitude of flotsam?" Some of the logs coming in were as big as telephone poles, but with jagged/sharp limbs both great and small still attached, patiently waiting to impale. I was delighted to see mom take the first major hit from the flotsam that slammed sideways into her kayak, leaving her bruised and battered, but fortunately able to regain a standing position after being dumped under and banged around. While she was floundering around trying to salvage her kayak, Dad came to the rescue of the sister and brother who looked to be no more than 8 or 9.

Was she a great mom who just liked frolicking with her adorable children or was she a product of an unknown hole in the kerosene heater when she was their age? This did serve to reinforce my decision not to leave myself or parts of or my kayak in Great Slave Lake while I was on this journey.

Whether you think this mom was a naive, degenerate, negligent, calculating, sociopath, purveyor of death or what, please refer to the photo taken along the beach of flotsam coming in near Frazier's. And you thought I was exaggerating or being overly protective. Now you, too, can share in the delight that engulfed me when mom took that first hit. The poor kids made it out unscathed, physically.

Like I mentioned earlier, the beach was full of flotsam but very little garbage (thank you Canadian citizens). Canadians must appreciate the beauty of their country better than we "yanks" do. It is hard to find garbage up there, whereas in America it seems to be readily available.

I do feel the urge to go on a tirade here about a somewhat recent observation regarding the new popularity of floss picks. You know those plastic question mark shaped dental devices with a short bridge of floss tied across the top? Ingenious invention. However, many folks must see them as biodegradable as I've actually seen a few here in "O Canada" and was overwhelmed by the numbers found back in the States. Public service announcement: plastic will outlive time. Boycott it or only use the recyclable kind.

PHOTO #2 - FLOTSAM NEAR FRAZIER'S

I can't comprehend the mindset of anyone who litters. If I'm elected there will be jobs galore for litter police. That will be their only job - to bust people who litter. Why do they do it? Are they leaving their mark or to show us where they've been? Maybe they are neat freaks keeping their cars pristine only at the expense of the Earth and her earthlings. Is an empty beer heavier than the one you carried in full? Is that styrofoam cup too heavy for you? How about that baby diaper? Don't let me let you smokers off the hook. That's our ground you're pitching that out on and God help you if I see you pitch a lit one, especially from a moving vehicle. Let's play a time game. See the discarded cigarette butt on our ground? How long do you think it will take all of its components including arsenic to reach the water table? How long do you think it will take the water to reach your spigot? Let's stop calling the cigarette a butt and start calling the person who pitched it a butt. I'll have to stop here or I may not make it back. You don't want to hear my position on people who don't stop at stop signs or people who waste food. Let's just not go there for now. But it all kind of looms on my horizons.

I saw little if any graffiti from the border crossing at Rooseville all the way up to the Northwest Territories. People up here in the

Territories seem to be more aggressive about writing who loves who on rest room walls. Let's face it. First of all, you probably have deduced that none of the roadside outhouses have any lights. Don't need them in the long days of summer, and too cold and dark for prolonged utilization in winter. Secondly, what's the chances that special someone will spot your love call written for her on a toilet wall in a men's bathroom? She'll most likely be using the women's outhouse. Do you see how your chances of telling her how you feel can diminish when applying this technique? Thirdly, though, I will hand it to you, you devil, it just doesn't get more romantic than that. In the unlikelihood that she does find it. All I can say is, "Brother, you may have just opened another can of worms." I'm not sure why the graffiti increased a tad once crossing the 60th parallel. Possibly, below here, in the Canadian National Parks, they allow graffiti but only if you use camouflage paint or ink.

My recollection of the best graffiti ever composed came free to me from an unknown author in numerous restrooms of bars in the Fairbanks, Alaska area. It was simply a small dot in an unassuming area over a urinal or near the toilet paper dispenser that simply said in small/small print, "Beam me up Scotty." At the time I found it utterly hilarious and still do. I suppose you had to be there to realize the true genius behind it. My search continued for this phantom author over the years with no luck. I went as far as to enquire from other drunken patrons, bartenders, barmaids, and the like to point this restorer of my sense of humor out to me. But, more often than not my inquiry was met with odd looks and murmurings. So, if you're reading this book and you're him (I'm assuming you're a him as your prolific humor was only produced in men's bathrooms), please contact me. I still want to meet you, to thank you, and to get an update on your life since then. I'm thinking your life story would make for another interesting book. I'd like exclusive rights as your biographer. I'll sweeten the pot. If you can prove you're really him, I guarantee you a signed copy of this book. You could sell it or give it as a great gift to someone dear to you. Pick up the phone. Give me a call.

That reminds me to help you readers of this book yet another way. You have no obligation to buy just one copy. The sky's the limit on the number of copies you can purchase. Think of all those family members, neighbors, folks at work, someone you want to impress, etc. Have I previously gone over this same concept way back many pages ago? Well, even if I did, I'm not about to delete this. Let it simply serve as a reminder to you. You may want to act quickly. We wouldn't want to put you on a waiting list. I've recently been told that in some locales, sales are outmatching available print. 'Nough said? You bet!

I'm going to continue veering from the trip again in an attempt to minimize the potential for road monotony. Believe it or not, no matter how tranquil and picturesque the journey can be after mile after mile of it, a kind of monotony can try to bombard the pleasure centers of your brain. It can add to road fatigue. I think this may have been a major factor in my decision to lay over at Frazier's for a second day. So, if it affected the author, it can rebound to the reader and neither of us wants that to happen. So, take a break from your reading now and when you come back, I'll share some more drinking in Fairbanks stories with you that although are somewhat embarrassing to me, may get a chuckle out of you. So, later...

The next time you're in Fairbanks, ask any bartender for a "Gold on the Rocks." He will no doubt scan the area quickly while exclaiming, "Oh God, he didn't come back, did he?!" You see, I made the name for that drink up back in the 70's and 80's. It's just a shot (or hopefully more) of gold tequila over ice. I must confess that this was your author's drink of choice back in those days and nights. Don't try this at home kids! A water chaser was always ordered with each drink not so much to wash it down but as an aid to economics. Back then, one shot of tequila cost $3.75 American. Hell, the liquor stores would sell you the whole fifth at the same time for $8.00. But who wants to drink alone at home when you can go to a bar and out-obnoxious everyone for just a few dollars more?

At the end of a fifth at the bar, the bartender would give me the worm as a trophy. I would run around the bar with the worm in my lips wondering why the girls were somewhat reluctant to dance with me. My proofreader and editor has urged me not to divulge this next excerpt but I have promised and owe it to my readers and victims to be as forthright and candid as I chose to be. Anyway, it was legal at the time in Alaska. I must admit that for every "Gold on the Rocks" with a water chaser an additional chaser of cannabis would conclude the cocktail. Don't try this at home kids!

It's been decades since Alaska legalized marijuana but since that time many other states have more or less legalized it. This litigation is long overdue. However, I would encourage usage to proceed only in a tea or edible format as all smoke emits coal tar and coal tar is a carcinogen (cancer enhancer). So don't smoke it! Eat it or drink it! Safe and good roughage.

Later in life as a sober substance abuse counselor, I would tell my clients that alcohol as well as nicotine are our two most tricky drugs. At the same time they are making you feel more relaxed, etc, they are attacking your central nervous system whose one of many functions is to make you feel relaxed. How do you spell, "duh?" Yea, they can and will destroy your central nervous system over time.

I got beat up at the same bar right around Christmas time. Make that two times. Not two times in a row but two Christmas's in a row in Fairbanks.

I think the first beating occurred because it appeared to my beater that I was having too good of a time. Let's face it. Alcohol is a depressant. Many folks who drink do so hoping to overcome depression. So add all of this up, introduce a guy jumping around having a grand time with a worm in his mouth and depressed people are reluctant to join in the fun or misery loves company, or something far more sinister, and the sucker punch comes out of nowhere.

194 | U.R. McFarland

Talk about hitting bottom. That well-executed sucker punch broke my artificial bridge into three pieces that catapulted up into the air only to land somewhere out on the dance floor. Knowing the time and place, flying teeth served only as a minor distraction to the folks peddling their dancing skills. They continued their pulsating rhythms, but now as dancing spectators at an amateur boxing/wrestling extravaganza put on at my expense.

It did take me a day later to realize that the same punch took out one of my authentic back teeth. Now, try to knock out a back tooth. It's beyond hard to do. He must have hit me with malice or knuckles or something.

I managed to tackle him down. He had an obvious strong punch but was no match for my weight on top of him. All I wanted to accomplish at this time was to knock his teeth out - not all - just a few to let him know I had gotten his message. Turn about is fair play. Every time I would bring my fist up for his abrupt dental enhancement, one of his friends would grab my arm.

I knew the bridge of teeth he had so courageously knocked out had been held there with sturdy posts (dental lingo for metal things that secure an artificial bridge of fake teeth - which are always overpriced, hence another tool/ploy to make the dentists rich as shit). With as much politeness as possible given the circumstance, I bent down and put a deep gouge/minor laceration on his left forehead as my right post was the only one readily available and his friends couldn't grab my post. This permanent mark I left for him would serve me in finding him at a later date without his friends.

I was thrown physically from the bar, a first for my resume, by some burly guys who were bouncers or wannabes. If all this wasn't embarrassing enough, I had to fight my way back into the bar past bouncers, my new acquaintance with the scar on his head, his anonymous stealthy friends and other patrons who thought it was a bad idea. I wasn't about to leave my teeth on that dance floor. They may not have been real but they were mine. It must have been "a guy thing." Not one of the gyrating dancers would stop until, struck this time by inspiration, they heard my exclamation, "$2,800.00 worth of teeth!" Not only did all the dancers immediately drop to all fours, but I'm proud to say that the band enthusiastically joined in on the search as well. It's funny what little it takes to inspire folks. No traces were recovered, not even the unknown back tooth.

The next morning, I figured I would continue my bridge search at the local pawn shops as the exclamation of $2,800.00 may have been a Godsend but on the other hand may have been a curse. Before departure for the pawn shops, I was approached by my still groggy roommate, Harry, who handed me a broken three piece bridge set submerged in a jar of water, turned, and headed back to his sleeping quarters without so much as a yawn.

I learned later that unbeknownst to me, Harry had been at the bar and had retrieved the bridge for me. A guy can't have too many friends. Knowing Harry, he probably secured the teeth successfully for his friend but opted out with regards to his friend's rescue. Harry was a great friend and like a brother to me. He gets a free book if he shows up at any of the signings. He was a very quiet deep thinker. How he singlehandedly almost started another Indian war somewhere up the Dalton Highway is a mystery to me, but great material potential for another book. Kudos to you, Harry. I'd love to have you show up on my doorstep again. Let's talk book and exclusive rights. Thanks for getting me into my love for Mexican food.

I recall telling you I had two Christmas fights/beatings in Fairbanks. Describing the first one above has nearly worn me out. I may serenade you with details of Christmas Battery #2 later but only share at this time that some of my attackers in #2 were WAC MPs from an Army base and a male Korean who had sold me a broken couch just a few weeks prior to that Christmas surprise for $50.00 (a great price had it not been broken).

I suppose it's not much of a stretch from being pummeled in Fairbanks to the next entry regarding the Death Walls in downtown

Hay River. I elected to venture from my new campsite at Frazier's. Trusting the mild breeze that still held an inkling of winter's coolness, as if left behind by an unknown stranger who brought it here the previous winter, to act as my drying cycle. You veterans of the north are quietly shaking your heads thinking, "This guy's been there." You folks who only dream of going there or took the summer cruiseship have no real clue (no offense). You just thought there was a little chill in the air on this balmy summer's day sailing up the passage. Mark my words. More often than not, from much of May through much of August, the inkling is hardly discernible. Maybe the unknown stranger tucked it away under the tundra or under the snow on those distant peaks. But, I assure you, he will be bringing it back somewheres in September. I was told once by an Inupiate Eskimo that the word "September" translated into "the unknown stranger is coming and you're about to freeze your hindquarters off so get ready before October." I made that last part up for my own amusement, but I'll bet you veterans still have a grin on your face.

PHOTO #3 - COMMERCIAL BOATS, HAY RIVER

I, too, realize I used an excess in wordage since entering Day 17. Please keep in mind, the daylight lingers for sure all day, but through much if not most of the night the further north one travels this time of year. Hence, a lot can happen on any given date. Plus, recall the correct answer to the last quiz.

Speaking of "balmy," after enduring yet another pass through the long, bumpy, pit-filled road between Frazier's and Hay River, I came upon a little inlet off of the Great Slave and took this photo of part of the commercial fleet who secure their livelihood from "the Slave" and then rest for a spell in this inlet between jobs and weather. Note the balmy sky and sunshine.

Not an hour later did I find myself snapping this photo of the Hays River Death Wall. (Note the change in the balmy sky.) This macabre homage runs for about 100 yards along Main Street, then for another 100 or so down a side street. I was hoping that the photos were of past athletes, politicians, birthday salutes, but doubted my hopes. I spoke briefly to a lady pumping gas down at the Shell station and she clarified that all of the photos were of folks no longer with us. She said they put all of the photos up a few times a year but don't leave them up. I told her I was glad they don't leave

PHOTO #4 - DEATH WALL

them up. I didn't know any of these past folks and was still moved to depression. It must be hard passing them everyday had they been your family. Maybe on the positive side they may be saying, "Don't do what I did or you'll end up on the wall."

I looked at many of the photos. Even the smiling faces seem to have sad eyes when you realize this person is gone from family and friends. I had to pull myself away. The more I studied their faces, the more depressed I became. I nearly ran back to the van when I came upon two little boys on the wall looking to be brothers, no more than 3-4 years old. I said a prayer for every person on that wall to be in heaven.

I sped away down the road and took the left turn into the Hay River airport - see photo. It was a small airport but had plenty of cars/trucks in the parking lot. The terminal was empty of people and locked up. It soon dawned on me that it was locked up because it was after 10 PM now.

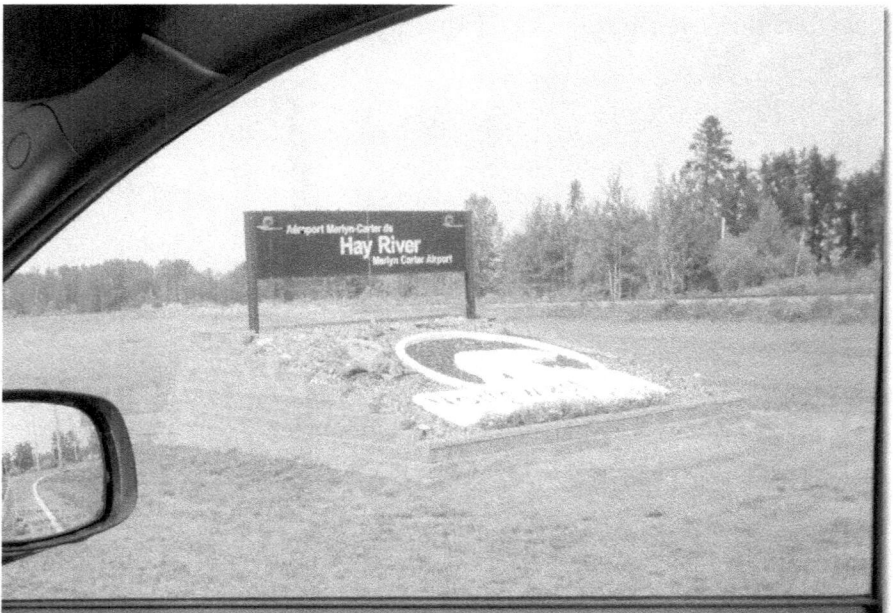

PHOTO #5 - HAY RIVER AIRPORT SIGN

A photo was snapped of some of the planes at rest. Can you see the big white and green #57 that says "Buffalo" in green against a white background? I recalled enjoyment some years not too distant when Precious and I watched a series on TV about Buffalo Airways. We enjoyed this show but it only lasted about two seasons in the lower forty-eight on our network offerings at home. For you other viewers who also liked this show, although locked up for the "night," it appears that "Buffalo" is still a viable enterprise. We could say that even though she may be off the air, she's still in the air. Kudos to owners, cast, and crew. What a brave bunch. Seeing Buffalo seemed to snap me out of the depression the death wall had lured me into.

PHOTO #6 - HAY RIVER AIRPORT, PLANES

Update: While scanning the Weather Channel recently, low and behold, up pops a series entitled "Ice Pilots N.W.T." Much to our delight, if indeed they were ever truly off the air, they are currently on and in the air where they belong. Possible reruns - don't know for sure - but glad to see them up there. God speed Buffalo Airways!

Lucky for me, the main terminal had a pay phone outside.

Although fighting a somewhat upset stomach from eating some soup that I had inadvertently burned/blackened over my Coleman earlier today, a call from the pay phone collect to Precious put that sick feeling on the back burner (no pun intended). It wasn't Coleman's fault. It was my own.

As I stood alone looking out over a closed airport, it kinda hit me once again how much I missed Precious's company and just being around her. I wanted to kick myself in the butt for taking all of her gifts to me for granted. I don't think she knew it, but tears were welling up in my eyes as we spoke. I told her that I would start my final dash for Yellowknife tomorrow and be heading home soon after that destination was reached. I reminded her that it had taken over two weeks to get this far and would probably take the same to get home.

DAY #18, 7/18/2016

60 degrees Fahrenheit at 8 AM - up, Hershey Squirt (Yupik Eskimo for bowel movement), and shower after a good night's sleep. Feeling great again. Was getting down yesterday possibly from exhaustion, bulldogs, not sleeping so well, uncooperative bowels, the wall, etc.

No wind this morning. Sneaking around quietly as the bulldogs are still asleep only to have the frigging mosquitos (large variety) put an all points bulletin out for me. They were even attacking me in the shower. They weren't as sturdy as the bulldogs, but were much quicker. Persistence levels between the two were near similar. I left a "queen" for Frazier in an envelope duct taped to his front door knob with a notation, "I figured you'd rather sleep in than BS with an old fart from Maryland." A "queen" is a Canadian $20 bill with a likeness of Queen Elizabeth (current) on the front. I ponder what goes through her mind when she sees one. What would you feel if your likeness was on a piece of currency? I gave Frazier some further written verbiage thanking him again, praising the job he's done here, and giving him an open invitation to visit me should he ever find himself in my neck of the woods, and took off.

"Took off" is a deceiving phrase. Remember, I still had to traverse the 2-3 miles back down that washed out road back to Hay River with ruts deep enough to take out your vehicle's suspension. So, "crept off" may have been a more precise description of my departure. I gunned it clear up to 4 mph once. The locals appear to be doing about 40-50 mph/60+ km on the same stretch. I suppose their philosophy is one of fly over the washboards in an effort to hit less of them. That, or they're all test drivers for some Canadian tire/suspension company.

I made it back to hard surface in Hay River in record time of 18 or so minutes. Not bad when you factor this into the 2-3 mile drive and the van was still in one piece and not making any scary sounds. Thanks be to time and local taxes, I understand that this road to/from Frazier's has been upgraded considerably since the van and I held our bouncing dances up and down it.

I stopped at the local quick stop/gas/laundromat/and popular Fried Chicken place (I couldn't believe the franchise had made it this far north). I opted out on the chicken after paying $2.10 Canadian for a small coffee.

This place was across the street from one hinge of the Wall of Death. I met or was approached by a native named Arlene in her motorized wheelchair which she maneuvered across the graveled parking lot as good as Jeff Gordon could have done. We B.S.'d a little about the weather. I told her how the wall had impacted me. She informed me that they keep all of the photos in the municipal building and then hang them back up on the wall on Canada Day (July 1st). She asked me if I'd seen the two little boys. I told her I was having problems getting them out of my thoughts. She lamented that they had drowned together in the river. I also had recalled seeing a young man in his prime with a distinctive shirt staring out from nowhere. Arlene told me this splendid example of all that's best in early youth was robbed of all of his future days by a drunk wielding a knife who sunk it home seventeen times to extinguish the seventeen year old's flame. Arlene told me that alcohol ruins everything and that she wouldn't be confined to her chair had she quit it sooner.

What a coincidence - July 1st was "one of" my wedding anniversaries. I ask my main consult if I should include this next section or not and she was lukewarm. In an effort to keep this from being a monotonous road trip, I will share the following mostly true story. The marriage that started on July 1st ended up with two divorces.

The first divorce took place in Tijuana, Mexico. We were on a six week driving/tenting trip trying to hug all the borders of the U.S. and had felt it might save our marriage by getting a divorce, but, still living together without the hindrance of a piece of paper. What did we know? We were just young hippies who should have adopted a marriage counselor the day of the wedding.

As was our custom traveling along the Texas/Mexican borders, we elected to walk across as in those times some Mexican nationals would run out in front of non-Mexican drivers and hit the lotto for your cash or your car insurance after you hit them. This was pre-Cartellion days. I think we paid a penny a piece to cross the bridge over the Rio Grande. I would have paid more, but didn't want to show my cards.

As there were large signs in English on the Mexican side stating, "Long Haired Hippie Revolutionaries Not Wanted" and as I had hair a little longer than most Mexicans, I stuffed my hair up into a cowboy hat. But, alas, the border guards were not to be fooled. This wasn't their first rodeo. They didn't really say that but might have had it all come down in more recent times. They were very quick, but I did take note that they all had different types/calibers of pistols. Government issue was not typical here.

Anyway, two of them grabbed my bride and pushed her through a green doored wooden building (green) while two other ones grabbed me by the arm and spun me down to the curb robustly while screaming "long haired hippie revolutionary!" Although, at the time, I embellished that image of myself, I remembered that they shoot a lot of revolutionaries down here and it could be to my advantage not to mess with people who killed John Wayne at the Alamo. Grasping these concepts, I put my hands on my head as a protective barrier and screamed back, "No! No! No! - Divorcia! Divorcia! Divorcia!" which was as close to Spanish as I was going to get. Their attitudes and demeanors immediately took a turn in our favor. One of them, I think it was the less sweaty of them, smiled and said, "Ah, ah, I have a cousin."

Turns out the border guard who now picked me up gingerly, but gently at the same time dusting Tijuana dust from my blue jeans did have an attorney cousin by the name of J. Renaldo Mendez. My new friend and border guard now barked a command in Spanish towards the mysterious green door and out popped my soon to be ex-wife still fully clothed yet in some degree of shock. I still admire her earnest attempt at a regal bearing in troubled times. Who knows what horrors or pleasures she would have been forced to endure there had I not known the Spanish word for divorce?

In less than 5 minutes, up pulls J. Renaldo in a 10+ year old green Cadillac somewhat dusty - the Cadillac - not J. Renaldo. J. Renaldo was somewhat portly, of medium height, with a whitish/yellowish suit and dark tie that for the record appeared to have been worn far beyond the manufacturer's recommendation regarding dry cleaning. J. Renaldo spoke much better broken English than had his cousin and the other border guards. Whether impressed by the suit or the Cadillac, we both agreed to sequester his legal services.

J. Renaldo cruised through the crowded narrow streets as if he owned the town all the while chitchatting about America and Mexico and peering more at my lovely bride than at the road.

We came to a screeching stop. Not that he was going too fast but possibly a call from the Cadillac that it was time for some new drums and/or brake pads. We had stopped in front of a small green building that housed his small green office - no secretary - nothing - spartan. There did appear to be a diploma of sorts behind J. Renaldo's desk on the wall but it was in Mexican but looked quite official. I remember it had a green background. J. Renaldo got right to the point. The divorce would cost $150.00 American and the divorce would be legal.

This was the last stop in Mexico for us. After Tijuana, there was no more Mexico. We had stopped in other Mexican towns along the Texas/Arizona borders like Juarez (dirtiest place I've ever been up to that time. Felt like washing/disinfecting my shoes once we returned to the American side). On the other hand, Nogales, Mexico (sister city to Nogales, Arizona) was so clean I'd have eaten refried beans off the sidewalk. Nogales was, some years later, destroyed by an earthquake. Go figure...

Another fond memory of our brief visit to Juarez was being propositioned by a Mexican pimp in a shoe store. He was selling his sister there at the shoe store for $20, or what he called "negotiables." She was a young, well-built Mexican beauty who I had noticed prior while she feigned shopping for shoes. Needless to say, I was taken aback but would not succumb to that level, possibly because my soon to be ex-wife was shopping for shoes in the same tiny shoe shop.

I had lost my nerve for getting the divorce at Juarez, Laredo, Nogales, and other border towns. This was it. Do or die. This had been one of my targeted objectives for taking the damned trip in the first place! With all the nerve I could muster, I asked J. Renaldo if he would take a down payment. Without hesitation he said, "Jes, $75 now and $75 when jou get home." We shook on it and I coughed up the $75. I was ecstatic to receive the original divorce form from J. Renaldo soon after I sent the balance upon returning home. It gave me a fuzzy feeling about international relations. Oh yes, the background on the divorce form is green. It currently hangs on my living room wall at home in a picture frame and looks like a diploma of sorts at a distance.

Early, some wordage back, you were told that I divorced her twice. So, I'll let you in on the rest of the story. J. Renaldo forgot to tell us or maybe he didn't know the broken English words for it. The Mexican divorce was in fact good and legal but only if no family member on either of our sides contested it.

Well, as luck would have it, her mother, who was a proactive backseat driver who didn't drive herself, found out about the divorce and proactively contested it. How, I don't know but to contest cost $0.00. I ended up going through an 18 month U.S. divorce and $500.00 to honor the contestment. She meant well and had her daughter's welfare to defend which would have been better defended had they not allowed me to marry their daughter two divorces ago. Oh well, what's a body to do?

Please don't read anything negative regarding this lovely bride or her family in this exposé. She was a beautiful, kind, and great person. We just had a terrible marriage. One more tidbit about Mexican travel back in those times before I return you to present day Canada. J. Renaldo got a phone call just after the $75 down exchanged hands and would be unable to drive us back to the border crossing. He drew us a map showing us the best routes. I can't remember the color of the paper he drew the map on. Let's just assume it was green. It wasn't all that far but the route resembled the old circus or county fairs that used to arrive in late summer. There were male "barkers" pitching us reasons why we should come inside the bars or shops who paid them for their promotional expertise. After peering into one bar and seeing a small Spanish lady on a stage with a burro, I hurried us along making sure not to make any more eye contact with any of the numerous "barkers."

We finally made it to the bridge and one more Mexican border check point and we would be back in the good old USA. Still on the

Mexican side, we were approached by a Mexican bum. Don't get my wrong. I like Mexican people. They make good friends. Most are very honest, hard working people, clean, pro family, and sincerely good people. But this bum/alcoholic approached us with a 7Up bottle. He held what appeared to be a large diamond ring. He showed us the authenticity of the massive diamond by scratching the hell out of the 7Up bottle with it. He wanted $25.00 American for the diamond. I looked at her and she looked at me. I guess she felt it was about time I had gotten her a diamond ring as I hadn't previously for moral/ethical reasons of course.

While reaching for the $25, I looked down the bridge and spotted two Mexican border guards watching us with binoculars (probably made in Mexico). End of transaction. We bolted from the diamond salesman. Those guards had a look of distainment coupled with disappointment when we crossed back into Texas. I later learned that there were other cheap stones that would scratch up a 7Up bottle. Funny thing, that's the last time I was ever in Mexico.

Let's hurry you back to Arlene on her motorized wheelchair in Hay River, Northwest Territories. As we lamented the evils of alcohol and nicotine, a sourpussed disheveled middle-aged Indigenous male brushed passed me and whispered something into Arlene's ear. Without a word, without hesitation, Arlene reached into her purse and pulled out a "queen" and gave it to him. Without a thank you, without hesitation, he plunged through the door of the Hay River Quick Stop, within sight of the sad eyes of hundreds of dead witnesses' photos clinging to the side of the wall of death just across the street from us, the living.

Arlene went on to tell me that she was a Cree Indian, and that her parents spoke Cree to each other but not to her or her siblings. The same catastrophe has happened with other native peoples like the Yupik Eskimos it was my blessing to live with for only a year. Very few of the kids can even understand their forbearer's language. Who is responsible for this travesty? I think they were trying to turn this rape of linguistics around before I left up there back in the mid 80's. It's pretty hard to learn the wisdom of grandfather or grandmother when you can't speak their language. I have a good idea who came up with this scheme and you probably do, too. Shame on those who perpetrated this concept, especially so if you knew what you were doing. Arlene was so nice. But, I had to get away - not from her, but from the penetrating stares from the eyes of the dead on the wall staring holes through us from just across the street.

On my retreat, I stopped at the Chamber of Commerce again to unload my garbage bag at their dumpster and to attempt to rinse some of the road dust and bug parts now concealing much of the front and a great deal of the rear gate as well as much of the sides of the van. Ron, why didn't you just say the van and get it over with? Can you recall my dad's pet name for me? For help, refer back a few pages.

There was a young girl, maybe 16-17, mostly white and cute as they make them in a Hay River government truck with a large water tank. She was watering the flowers. I asked her if the water coming from the hose provided to me for car rinsing was drinkable. She said that if it was coming out from the Commerce Building it was, and she checked it out for me doing her own investigation within the Commerce Building. She soon returned and assured me that it was good.

When asked, she told me that she was the water girl for all of Hay River. I complimented her on doing a great job as the numerous flowers throughout Hay River City were gorgeous. I assumed that it was a summer job for her. I topped off and filled up all my reserve water containers as I was about to take on the last stretch between here and Yellowknife and had few, if any, clues what might be in store for me on this last remaining lap. With a wave to and a wave from the Hay River water girl, I gunned the van up the road. I forgot to tell you she also told me the numerous and friendly black birds with white stripes down their wings were magpies. I should have known that but I don't remember them from Alaska when I lived there. Maybe I was too high or too drunk or too both to appreciate them then. Public service announcement to all you drunks and druggies out there: sober up! You'll appreciate the rare beauty our Earth serves up free of charge without expecting a tip.

Retracing my steps again back to Enterprise (the city, not the starship), I headed northwest on Highway 1 toward Fort Providence. I was forced to have a barricaded breakfast inside the van as the mosquitoes and bulldogs had joined forces in an obvious effort to remind me who was boss in the North. All the while I couldn't get the sweet and innocent flower girl of Hay River from my thoughts. Now, don't get jealous Precious. I was old enough to be this girl's great grandfather. Without formal verbalization, she and I had acknowledged this. I found out way prior to this trip that age does help with a certain degree of comfort factor between the sexes. I guess the young girls figure out real soon that, "Hell, I can outrun this one!"

30 miles further north, I was kicking myself in the arse verbally for not requesting to snap a photo of Arlene the Cree and the flower girl of Hay River. I'll check with the publishers to see if I should contact these ladies for a photo for this book. I supposed their mystery, beauty, and gentleness had caught me off guard and I was mesmerized yet another time on this pilgrimage. Please take that as a compliment ladies.

Traveling alone only served to emphasize our need for social contact with all creatures including those cut from our same mold. How one cherishes the slightest of friendly contact in times like these. Note to self: be kinder to strangers. It's payback time on a positive stroke.

Spotted two sandhill cranes along the highway before reaching the great MacKenzie River. If you scan your atlas, the MacKenzie is the closest thing you're going to get up here to a northwest passage as she flows northwest and dumps herself into the Beaufort Sea - see another possible "end of the road" trip there up to Inuvik. If I can't make it, will one of you readers give it a try? It's very doable. I'll go along in spirit with you.

I never felt absolutely totally alone on this trip. I always felt the presence of others, be that ancestors, guiding spirit, guardian angels, curious former locals, or whatever or whomever. Thank you for joining me and I hope you enjoyed yourself as I enjoyed your silent but reassuring company. How about helping me out with a little gas money next time? After all, I provided the vehicle, did all the driving, and gave you a free trip. Nobody likes a free-loading bastard. Come to think of it, Dead Bob may have been with me on that whole trip. He and I took many a trip together in the past and many times not in a vehicle. Free loading was one of Dead Bob's fortes but I remain fond of him, nonetheless.

Talked to a Quebecor and his wife while he was fishing near a piling on the MacKenzie. As I know about as much French as I know Mexican, I was glad he spoke excellent English (not unusual for Quebecors). He told me he only caught one small pike there and that he and his wife were on their way to Yellowknife to start a new life. I made no attempt to twist his tattooed arm for info regarding their old life. He told me there was plenty of jobs in Yellowknife in lumber, fishing, and a huge gold mine.

I topped the tank off again at Fort Providence and promised myself photos of the MacKenzie River Bridge and fishing the MacKenzie on my way back south. But, Yellowknife was calling and I had an itch to get there, and she lay less than 300 miles away - just a hop, skip, and a jump according to my odometer since leaving lovely Maryland behind 18 or so days ago.

Caught this Woods buffalo (my first) napping along the highway not far from Fort Providence. I could find no difference between these guys and the American bison other than size. I think the Woods buffalo can grow much larger than the bison. Both species look as if they could care less.

PHOTO #1 - WOOD BISON

50+ miles of the last stretch nearing Yellowknife, the road seemed trapped between mounds and mounds of solid rock oftentimes on both sides. I don't know what solid rock acreage goes for in the Territories but plenty of houses (large and small) dotted the landscape. You could say they didn't have to go too far to hit bedrock.

Small brown house on bedrock 50 or so miles south of Yellowknife. I did not get to take as many photos of these rock dwellers as I would have liked to and never saw anyone who resembled Fred Flintstone, as this section of the road was akin to an ocean storm. You would come up on a crest of the road and have a drop off of 10 feet just beyond the crest and then you'd come to another crest and so on. Folks coming in the opposite direction were fighting their own set of crests and drop offs, but not always adjacent to your own. I was tempted to take some Dramamine - no kidding. I suppose all of these ups and downs were the result of permafrost, quakes, and your guess is as bad as mine. But, it's a ride that you won't forget. It also forces you to go slow if you cherish the undercarriage, oil pan, etc., of your vehicle.

PHOTO #2 - HOUSE ON THE ROCKS

I did see one fellow who was apparently late for work, late for his girlfriend, late for a court appointment, or late for his shrink bouncing, skidding, and catapulting along in my rear view mirror. I pulled over to let him pass. I caught up with him about 15 minutes later. It seems that his car didn't want to carry him any farther without its oil pan attached. When you see someone crazy enough to knowingly destroy their sole means of mechanical travel, it makes you a bit hesitant to stop and offer assistance, so I didn't. There was plenty of other traffic on this highway who had not seen him coming in their rearview mirrors.

Eureka! I entered my grand destination somewhere close to 6:30 PM. The temperature was a comfortable 72 degrees Fahrenheit. I found out that Margot Kidder (Lois Lane fame in "Superman") was a native of Yellowknife. There's even a Lois Lane Street to honor her. No wonder she had some psychiatric challenges. You'd think they would have given her a Margot Kidder Avenue or at least a Kidder Blvd. If they did, I didn't find any. I guarantee you, had any-

PHOTO #3 - YELLOWKNIFE SIGN

one in my hometown starred in a "Superman" movie, they would have a park or something named after them. I felt the need to bond with Margot over this but she wasn't around. Will have to catch you in the next life Margot, as you unfortunately died prior to our publishing of this book. You were a grand lady and I trust remain a free spirit.

Feeling confident like an old hand, accommodations were secured at the only Walmart in town. I had reached a point where I could almost smell a Walmart, or maybe it was like a homing pigeon thing. Don't know but it worked for me.

With the previous Asian buffet experience long behind me (no pun intended), the urge to devour had built up to a crescendo. Damn the torpedoes - full steam shrimp ahead! I cruised through this beautiful town searching for any sign of buffet to no avail. Determination led me to flag down a taxi at a stop light. I figured as the driver appeared to be Asian, it upped my chances. He said, "Yes, yes, Mark's." The light changed to green and we shouted back and forth at a few miles an hour with me trying to decipher his directions given in perfectly broken English all the while trying not to sideswipe parked cars, pedestrians, etc. I was in the right turn only lane and he was in the left turn only lane. I was about to lose my best chance when the Asian passenger in the back seat wound down his window yelling, "Mark's! Mark's!" And making rapid pointing gestures in a southwesterly direction.

Well that certainly narrowed it down for me. If I could come out of my right hand turn and return to whatever street we were yelling on and find another street taking me in a southwesterly direction, I was sure I could find "Mark's." Did I say I was really hungry? The only thing that could remedy this was a good hour and a half of pure pleasure in an Asian buffet. Don't chastise me. It could be worse.

Back to my quest. As this was the first hour of driving in downtown Yellowknife I had some difficulty in getting back to the yelling street or maybe recognizing it. As I turned left on what I thought was the most logical street heading in a southwesterly direction, thoughts of what witnesses must have speculated regarding the burly, loud, desperate guy from Maryland and the Asian taxi driver and his passenger yelling back and forth only to end with the frustrated passenger throwing rapid hand gestures at the retreating Yank. If only those skeptical witnesses would have known that it was just a simple case of two helpful Asians giving it their best to help a hungry boy and his stomach.

The evening was whirling on and so were the pangs in my stomach (pangs sounds like a Far East word, doesn't it?) I started searching large and small strip malls. What's wrong with these Canadians? Enter any strip mall in the U.S. and you're sure to find an Asian buffet. Apparently our attempts at true gluttony here in the U.S. is not shared by other countries. Come to think of it, the number and ratio of bulbous folk to trim and fit folks seemed to have diminished once I left the States. There's a lesson to be learned here. But hell, all I wanted to do was to pig out.

Determination had turned to desperation. I saw an Indigenous guy walking up one of those southwesterly streets. Could he help me? He said, "I can't help you. I just asked another guy for directions myself. I'm not from here either." I should have offered him a lift but where to? I was now in what I thought was the southwestern outskirts of town. I spotted another local on foot who looked like he knew his way around. Could he help me? He said, "No, but did I have any smokes?" Thanks, but no cigar (pun intended).

Tears were welling up in my eyes. Was I going to have to have another meal of jalapeño crackers and tasteless dried vegetables? Hell no! There to my absolute delight was another cabby. This one was in a little enclave off the side of the road. I cut across two lanes of traffic to get to him. He appeared to be Nigerian and he was wearing Nigerian looking clothing, the kind a friendly Muslim might wear. He was not distraught as I slid the van into the small enclave but gave me a big white toothed grin and a thumbs up. No doubt in recognition of my astute driving skills. His first words to me were, "Where are you from, man?" If he was Nigerian, he sure sounded like he had a Jamaican accent. I didn't care. I was absorbed with visions of spring rolls, frog legs, shrimp, 4 seasons, coconut cookies, little chunks of pineapple, sweet and sour soup, and on and on and on. Could he know where "Mark's" was? He said, "Oh yes, man." He started to give me directions, shook his head a couple of times and said, "Follow me, no charge."

I felt he was reading my mind. Was this Nigerian/Jamaican my first encounter with a voodoo priest? Hunger can drive the strangest thoughts into your head. A voodoo priest at the end of the road? It could happen!

Ten minutes and several southwesterly turns later, I followed him into the parking lot of Mark's underground restaurant. I offered to buy him a meal at Mark's but he waved me off and sped away in a northeasterly direction. I could see his big smile for a block. Like they say, "you just had to be there."

I changed shirts rapidly and freshened my breath with mouth-wash. Hey, I may have been in a desperate state of near starvation but would never let my sense of social responsibility waiver. I felt like a Viking in Valhalla forgetting what it took to get here. Mark's was located down an enclosed stairwell you would enter from the parking lot. Another first - my first underground Asian buffet.

Practically skipping from the van over to the enclosed stairwell, I read the billboard as I skipped. It beckoned to me with "Mark's Restaurant," business hours (I was there with plenty of time to spare), two phone numbers to call for carry outs, etc. Neil Armstrong couldn't have been any happier on his last step down that ladder.

To make a long story end abruptly, a sign on the locked door under the dim light read, "Closed for remodeling from July 4th thru July 24th." I looked back out into the rooftop parking lot to see if anyone knew CPR.

I was alone again with my thoughts, a numbing sensation stole my spirit. Shattered, I drove in endless circles for some time, thinking, why me God? I've been a pretty good person for a good long while now. Did I miss something? Did karma kick me in the buttocks again for some sinister shit I pulled in the past? I could chuckle about it if Mark's wasn't the only game in town. I started to ponder. Is this a game that taxi drivers play with unsuspecting tourists from Maryland? That just didn't ring true - not in Canada anyway.

Found my way back to Walmart. At least, I could get one of their tasty subs or something. They weren't a Super Walmart..... Southeast of there I found another supermarket franchise called "Independent." It was a great and clean place but most prices were high (for me).

Why I did it, I'll never know. Maybe I was challenging the karma theory. I asked the normal looking guy working the deli if there might be another Chinese buffet besides Mark's. He said that he thought there was. "Thought" didn't sound like great prospects to me. At this point, I would have settled for a Chinese restaurant (drop the buffet). He then told me that he wasn't good with directions. Of all the employees to choose from in this supermarket, I chose the friends aware work release program client. No offense at all to the folks with challenges. I was also a social worker for much of my adult life. I hid my frustrations from him so as not to hurt his feelings. In spite of this, he became more nervous. He seemed to be looking around for his sponsor or whatever they call work release program coordinators here in Canada.

Sizing him up, I felt my social work licensure could be a valuable learning tool for this guy. All those seminars I was forced to attend were about to pay off. I drew him back in with, "Let's just give it a try together." He stepped towards me - a good sign. Reasonable eye contact. My demeanor projected warmth and understanding. But now it was after 8 PM and my stomach was calling up with "What Gives!?"

I told him the one street or highway coming into town that I was familiar with and could relocate. I felt it simplified our conversation as it was the only road coming into town, that being Highway 4. He, in turn, returned to his apologetic demeanor regarding his poor direction-giving abilities. I started wondering if this poor guy had a mean stepfather who burnt him with cigarettes when he was young for not giving good directions. I started feeling a bit of conscious for continuing on these lines. I started looking for his sponsor but no one stepped up.

With all the warmth, understanding, and kindness I could muster, I said in the gentlest of fashion, "If I go back to Highway 4, would that take me towards it?" He exclaimed, "Yes!" Cautiously, and then, as if his confidence or meds had finally kicked in, without coaxing, he told me, "Follow that into the town center (big buildings and stuff like that) then look for a Subway." We concurred that there as no underground subway, but a real Subway sandwich shop. He, in his newly found confidence and catapulted self image went on to direct that, "The place is Korean (close enough for me!) and it's in the same building adjacent to the Subway." Boosting his recovering ego, I praised him and told him he had given me the best directions I had received since I got to town. Unbeknownst to him, his only competition was an Asian guy in the rear seat of a taxi giving me rapid hand gestures toward the south-west.

Recalling going past a Subway today while chasing the Nigerian/Muslim/Jamaican/Voodoo priest cabbie to Mark's closed restaurant, I realized that this could be the one shining moment in this ever so trying afternoon/evening.

I praised and thanked my deli direction guy before leaving. He felt he could leave his guard down and open up to me after all we'd been through. He told me that he doesn't have a car and walks everywhere. He was pretty sure they (the Koreans) were still open the last time he walked by there. I told him I might let him feed me from the deli if they (the Koreans) were closed as his sign said open til 10 PM.

Positive feelings returned again. If the Koreans were closed, I could get a Subway special or something. I made my way there. The lackluster deli guy had given me pretty good directions plus I was starting to know my way around town a little after searching for a big part of the day for that illusive Asian buffet. Forget it! The Korean place was still operational but closed for the evening, as was the Subway shop next door. Karma/karma/voodoo/voodoo. What gives? It was only 8:30 in the evening. Back home they would have been open to at least 10 PM. But Dorothy, you're not home anymore.

I remembered a Pizza Hut across town near my Walmart suite. They turned out to be delivery/carry out only. I couldn't eat a pizza inside the van. I still had bear country to return through.

Looking starvation straight in the eye, I limped the van back to the less than motivational speaker working the deli at Independent market. He saw me coming but acted as if he hadn't. He grabbed a box of something, bent over it and stuck his head almost into the box. Had I met the ostrich deli boy of Yellowknife? Not wanting him to faint or lose it if he thought I was on a mission of revenge, I bypassed him, went to another department and found a container of potato salad and some of that fake smashed fish stuff that looks like lobster but doesn't cost like lobster — not sushi but it would have to do. I rationalized that I'd wanted fish anyway. I felt some need to approach my deli buddy on my way to the cashier. He turned away and started an impromptu conversation with a fellow deli employee who looked at him as if to say, "What brought this on?" It was obvious that he was hoping that I hadn't realized that he had recognized me. Poor devil, didn't know what a sly dog he was dealing with.

I yelled a greeting over to him and gestured for him to approach me, smiling. There was a deli locker/case between us. He was a head taller than me, and yet wobbled slowly over like a whipped puppy. I, with friendly demeanor, told him that I had found the place thanks to his good directions but that it was closed. He resorted to sorry mode about it being closed. I cut him off a little short and told him it was not his fault they were closed and praised him one last time for the great directions. He worked up a somewhat neutral "then, it's OK?" I said, "You bet! Sure is!" Note to self: include this poor guy and folks like him in your prayers. He's got such a long way to go and odds are he may never get there.

Isn't it ironic, finally reaching my targeted destination of Yellowknife and all I can write about is food. It's kind of anti-climatic, isn't it? So many journeys are. There's something to that old saying, "It's not the destination, it's the journey there." I can tell you this, Yellowknife is a small, bustling town with modern mini skyscrapers. But, it's clean and projects a small hometown feeling. Lots of water, lots of solid rock, lots of kind and helpful Canadians. I would recommend that you visit it. I would recommend that you try the buffet at Mark's restaurant. Let me know how it was, please.

Not wanting to eat in the parking lot of Independent Market and just wanting to go off by myself and eat in peace, I recalled a small park I'd passed a few times today and decided it would be a lovely setting to unwind and to savor some food that hadn't been prepared by my own hand. I do have two functional hands. Don't let these wordage choices confuse you.

I found it and pulled into the small parking lot, oddly enough catty-cornered opposite from my Voodoo priest cabbie's now unoccupied enclave. There before me was a beautiful view of one of probably thousands of arms of the Great Slave laid out just for my enjoyment. Before I could turn my engine off, a young couple pulled in quite close to my vehicle with their two dogs. A little yipper and a large golden lab. The guy had a tennis racket (try to keep that word racket in mind). I acknowledged their presence with a nod and a smile but scurried with supper in hand to the far side of this small park to one of the well spaced cement picnic tables with it's own private pavilion.

Before reaching my selected secluded table, from behind me came the sound of a tennis ball making contact with a tennis racket. Also coming from the same direction in octaves much greater than needed, were boot camp sergeant like commands to the lab, who would have responded in like fashion had he been stone deaf, about fetching, go get it, and sit at the same time the wife was shouting two octaves down, "Good Amos, good boy, good Amos." I assumed that the lab's name was Amos and not her husband's. All the while the little yipper yipped as he couldn't beat Amos to the ball, although he took four or more times as many steps to get there as Amos had.

I will note here that not one command or word of encouragement was directed to the yipper. This would be a tough call for the ASPCA but it has merit. How long would it take the little yipper to break before all of this pent up rage would surface into something ugly?

My goal of coming here was to unwind. But now, this foursome had wound me back up real tight like. I needed a mantra but couldn't conjure one up.

I hurriedly downed the potato salad taking larger and larger spoonfuls shoveling them into my mouth taking heed not to strangle. I don't mean strangling on the potato salad. I mean strangling on the foursome. Amos would have been my last choice to strangle unless the husband's real name was indeed Amos and then Amos would have been first.

What no doubt saved them from strangulation was the mosquitos who had graciously or cunningly left me alone until I popped open the lid on my potato salad. Apparently, mosquitos are attracted to potato salad, but still prefer human blood. I managed to finish the potato salad without strangling, opened the imitation lobster meat, stuffed all of it into the empty potato salad container, and retreated once again to the van. Amos and company soon followed suit and hopped into their car. Maybe mosquitos are also attracted to tennis balls.

Interjection: I know, I know, we haven't had a quiz lately. We are over due. Stay alert. Concentrate. Be on your best game. A scout is always prepared. It's coming!

PHOTO #4 - FROST CREEK REBELS FLOTILLA

Somewhere between tears and hysterical laughter, and don't tell me you haven't been there, I gazed through those tears out over the bay where the park was and there they were, the Frost Creek Rebel's houses! Remember the show on TV with the same name? They were floating/anchored out there just a couple of hundred yards straight out from the park. Seeing and possibly meeting that sturdy band of humanage was a big factor on my bucket list and another driving force that helped push me up here.

So, the moral of this story is when you think the going can't get any tougher, the sun pops out and God hits you right between the eyes with a chuckle. And far be it for me to advise you not to strangle any small or larger dogs or people as God is always with you and he does not want to be an accomplice. Good night and pleasant dreams - sleeping in Walmart parking lot, 10:45 PM, Yellowknife, Northwest Territories.

DAY #19, 7/19/2016

Woke up to a rainy/wet Walmart parking lot still happily reflecting on my luck at locating "The Frost Creek Rebels." I had slept well but nowhere near long enough. I had stayed up too late last night, some of it my own fault, much of it not.

As a thank you to my host, I bought a yellowish ball cap with a moose logo on the front. For fear of the hard boiled eggs having seen better days, the vote for breakfast at the Walmart McDonalds was unanimous with zero dissension. A cup of coffee, and an Egg McMuffin with Canadian bacon was wolfed down for $6.14. I could have gone all out and ordered hash browns for just another $2-$3. But since the only thing I like about fast food hash browns is the ketchup you drown them in, I elected to pass. While sucking down

PHOT⊙ #1 - INSIDE VISIT⊙R'S CENTER, GRIZZLY

another refill of caffeine and still yawning, I pondered with the idea that this Yellowknife Walmart hires wake up teams who drive by in the morning and blow their horns at 5:20 AM to get stragglers like me up and moving or at least had been the case on this misty morning.

Thanks to the early morning beepers, the need for a little more sleep overtook me and I climbed back into the van to try and catch just a little more shut eye. As I squirmed in, I reminded myself, as I always do since running over the bungee some days back, to make sure I refasten the bungee after re-emerging so as not to endanger another one.

If sleep did come, I missed it. Maybe too much caffeine. I squirmed back out of the van feet first on my belly as this had become my easiest route and means to exit. One couldn't help but wonder thoughts conjured up by spectators of this daily morning ritual. To them, I looked akin to a colossal breech birth. The door pops open and out slides these squirming feet followed by a rotund body. If there was a better/easier way to exit I would have done it, but most spectators were no doubt taken aback. Initially on this trip, I was a tad embarrassed by the above exit maneuvers. But, the more I thought about the reaction of spectators, I wouldn't have it any other way.

PH⊙T⊙ #2 - INSIDE VISIT⊙R'S CENTER, P⊙LAR BEAR

Still a little groggy, I drove to the Visitor's Center. It was like a beehive of activity for so early in the morning. I snapped a photo of a grizzly bear with Eskimo clothing hanging on the wall. At the top left on this photo is the hide of a wolverine. Wolverines are possibly the most respected carnivore in the north country. They're not afraid to take on a grizzly and oftentimes will run a grizzly off. They may not be very large but they are mighty. You do not want to cuddle up to one. It would probably be your last cuddle. Remember, it's not the dog in the fight but the fight in the dog.

I also took a photo of a stuffed polar bear. If you look closely, in front of his left front paw you will see my now infamous hat. I put it there to give you some perspective of this bear's size and this was not a giant one. Don't ever invite him to dinner either as you will rapidly become the main course.

Another great find at the Visitor's Center was a water cooler welcoming visitors to "fill her up" which I did in an attempt to replace the terrible tasting water from the visitor center hose at Hay River. As I was hauling my newfound fresh water back to the van, something caught my eye or better still didn't catch my eye. Where was the mended bungee chord run over some days back? It didn't take me long to realize where it was. It was somewhere between here and Walmart where I had forgot to strap it down not too long ago this morning. So much for multitasking. I had some choices to make ASAP. Should I retrace my route back to Walmart to see if I could spot it or should I dig through my fixins bag for the spare I knew I had? I opted for the latter. This trip is virtually halfway over and my negligence has only cost me one or two bungees. I reasoned that surely the chance of losing another from here on out was slim to grave. I secured my next bungee to the rear of the van. Note to self: ask the guys working the Visitor Center where I might find a bungee shop to enrich my supply of spares, just in case. A scout is always prepared. I'll promise to stop saying that if you'll promise to stop having those nasty thoughts.

Snap Quiz! I told you it was coming:

How many bungee straps has the author lost so far on this trip? Those readers unable to focus while reading may seek reference on previous pages.
A. None
B. One or two
C. Half a dozen
D. Way too many
Answer: B and D

Boy did I make that one easy for you. Take it as a reward for riding along this far with me. I'll still bet that many of you took a quick/guarded peek at the answer just to make sure. You're compulsive but compulsive is good. Compulsive people make the best book sales people and I am still counting on you. The general public who have not had access to this book, yet, await your enlightening them. Don't let them down. Think how shallow their lives are without this book. Think of the multitude of rewards in store for you simply by bringing it to them. I'm not just talking monetary or prestigious rewards. It's a reward of the heart. Those of you who have made sales over 175 books already have felt it. It's hard to describe unless you've been there. Here's a free reward for your sales efforts. The next time you're at a job interview, tell them you are compulsive - you've just got to get that job done…. The author utilized this concept to land his last two or three jobs. I poop you not! Precious told me not to cuss so much in this book.

By the way, I've received a green light to offer any one who surpasses book sales of 175 or more a gold/silver plated necklace matching the rings promised. I've intentionally sweetened the offer just for you because you alone deserve it. If you don't do it, who will? Let your compulsion show you the way. It's yours for the taking. Did I tell you that you do not have to be related to the guest you select if you make it to the convention?

I returned to the Visitor Center for more water. Less crowded this time, I got a chance to talk to the two young Canadian males working the information booth. I figured it was a summer job for college guys, but didn't ask. The youngest volunteered the origin of the name "Yellowknife." He told me that this area was first inhabited by an aboriginal peoples who called themselves "The Dene." They somehow learned to make copper tools. Some elitists would say, "Oh, these backwards people used copper tools." I challenge any and all elitists to find a rock, get copper out of it, and make a working tool. You might want to rethink "backwards." Anyway, it was so long ago, they didn't have a word for copper. The closest color to copper was yellow. Hence, Yellowknife. Pretty damned cool!

I enquired about the TV show "Frost Creek Rebels" mentioned earlier. With not the least bit of hesitation, my college summer job guy blurted out, "Totally fake!" It appeared to really stir him up as if the show had been an affront and embarrassment to all Canadians. He verified that where I had taken the photo yesterday evening was indeed the actual location for the fraudulent show. The producers had misrepresented and misled we faithful but gullible viewers that these rebels lived off the grid so far from civilization that they almost had to have air pumped in. In fact, they were as this boy assured me in very little if any danger and that emergency/medical help was but a matter of a few minutes from them at any given time of the year. He went on to add that one of the stars of the show didn't even live on a houseboat.

Talk about having a bubble busted. One of my goals on this trip was to kayak back into the wilderness in an attempt to locate the so called "Frost Creek Rebels," when in fact they were only rebels from the truth. A strong man could have hit their houseboats with a rock from the picnic table I had gulped down my potato salad from just last evening. I had the rocks, but couldn't find a strong man. I could go back to the Independent market and look up my directions man working the deli for help in finding a strong man, but drowned that thought as soon as it had surfaced.

All this way, I'm guessing 5,000 miles or so only to realize that I'd been duped by a fake TV show. I guess I would have been one of the first ones in line to buy the Huckster's Snake Oil Elixir back in the Old West. I've always been gullible when it comes to accepting or believing what my fellow man shares with me. Some would call it a weakness others would proclaim it a strength. Speaking of strength, I'd still like to find that strong man. There's a good possibility that one will read this book. I hope that he likes to travel and to throw rocks. Give me a call. I have directions and a free book for you.

Apparently, food becomes a resource for this author to offset disappointment. I found myself driving back to the Korean restaurant beside the Subway for a closer look see. On the way there, I kept an eye peeled in search of the last unstrapped down bungee. As luck would have it, I spotted one and picked it up. It wasn't mine but lifted my spirits to know that some other poor bastard had duplicated my negligence. I in turn hope he finds mine. The Korean restaurant wasn't open yet but had fading photos with prices for dinner, etc. taped to the windows. There was no buffet. Probably North Koreans. I figured South Koreans for a buffet. The only meal taped to the dusty windows that looked like it had a slight chance to fill me up was $14.95 (cheap for these parts) but considering these proprietors were probably North Koreans sent a red flag up (pun intended). I thought I'd give dining here this evening some further thought.

It's now 11 AM on an early weekday morning in Yellowknife. I had parked in a downtown parking lot of a liquor store. I needed time to weigh some options. While weighing, I couldn't help but notice a constant parade of folks entering and leaving the liquor store. Business was thriving. Maybe they had morning happy hours up here in Yellowknife. Unfortunately, none of the folks I took note of appeared all that happy. I'd venture a guess that about 80% appeared to be Indigenous folks while the remaining 20% were white or slightly off-white. It's hard to say with unknown ranges of liver damage, etc. All seemed to be in a hurry, on a mission if you like, sad.....but for the grace of God go I.

Found a boat launch on the outskirts of downtown still trying to weigh some options. Took photo of dry-docked sailboat. Note Old Towne canoe propped up in foreground. Reminded me of home. Got a green one just like it at home. Background shows yet another inlet of Great Slave, much calmer. Stomach problems this morning were not an enticement to launch the kayak yet.

PHOTO #3 - SAILBOAT

Photo #4 shows a houseboat with motorized dingies in foreground with large rock outcropping in background. These rock outcroppings, some as big as small mountains, were everywhere up here. I met a guy named Bill here who was a camera enthusiast. He gave me many tips about living up here, i.e., it's a great city to retire in. The average income ranges from $70,000 to $120,000 a year. It became increasingly difficult to consume all that Bill was sharing as I was forced to do my interpretation of St. Vitas Dance in an ill-fated attempt to dodge bulldogs who had found my bare legs again. Bill was wearing long pants. Bill did encourage me to travel up Ingram Road to where it crosses over the Yellowknife River for potential kayaking. I took Bill up on this right away. I killed two birds with one stone here. I escaped Bill's droning on and on, and hid once again in the van from the bulldogs.

PHOTO #4

On the way up to Yellowknife River, I spotted a stretch with more solid rock but these were pinkish in color. My throw away camera was not up to the challenge again, but it shows you what a good road looks like up here. And the road was great all the way up to the bridge over the Yellowknife River, which was a mere five miles from the city of Yellowknife. The river was an emerald green, gorgeous, strong and fast flowing. Many fishermen lined her banks. I watched for some time, but saw no fish being caught.

PHOTO #5 - PINK ROCKS

It was a bit too crowded for me to fish. I prefer solitude when fishing or hunting, complete solitude if possible, and this mass of humanity was far from my preference. I have no idea why I prefer complete solitude but it's always been that way. Beyond fishing and hunting, I absolutely love the company of others but in brief spurts.

I was eager to give my kayak her maiden voyage which would have also been my first kayaking experience. Common sense prevailed when I noted the high and powerful current in the Yellowknife. I didn't want to lose me or my kayak, and anyway, if I got drowned, who was going to get all my stuff back home?

I backtracked to a large lake a few miles south of Yellowknife I had recalled passing on the way up. It was called Trapper's Lake.

This would be a fitting lake to christen ourselves in. I pulled down off the road into a small parking lot that looked ideal for launching. I have no name for my kayak. We haven't spent that much time together yet.

Before I could launch, a small black car slipped hurriedly down into my launch site. It turned out to be Joe and Violet. Turns out they had been married 40 years, they lived in Fort Resolution where I'd been a day or so back. Joe said he had tried to intervene in a fight there and had gotten pummeled to the point that his doctor recommended a CAT scan in Yellowknife. I told him that I wasn't a doctor but I concurred that he should have his head examined for intervening in that fight. We both thought that was funny, me more than he, maybe. Violet just deadpanned and smiled. They offered to help me launch but I feigned I could do it.

PHOTO #6 - JOE AND VIOLET

Joe revealed his true reason for pulling down into this little alcove. My paranoia screamed inside me, "Oh no, he's going to rob me!" Wrong again! Return to the photo. He said he hates to wear dress pants and he wanted to slip on something more comfortable. I immediately succumbed to loud laughter, the kind people make instead of saying, "Thanks, I thought you were going to rob me." Why that thought even crossed my mind, I don't know. I must have forgot I was still in Canada. I went back to pretending I knew what I was doing with my kayak while Joe slipped on a pair of well worn blue jeans.

I congratulated both of them on their 40 year run together and wished Joe luck with the results of his CAT scan. I told them that I loved a woman in Maryland about as much as Joe loved Violet. We shared some more smiles and a handshake and off they sped back towards their future in Fort Resolution. Nice folks. But, now I suspect that Joe's intervention/pummeling may have been the causal factor in the cold reception I had received in Fort Resolution. The locals may have mistook me for "The Law" or a reporter from a major TV network.

Back to the launching. It seemed to take forever to get the kayak down from its perch atop the van. It took another forever to get all equipment, life jacket, fishing pole, lures, etc., ready for this maiden voyage. I used a Pixie lure and threw and retrieved many times, using different depths, speeds, angles, etc., to no avail. No pike steaks on the grill tonight. I was not overly impressed with the stability ratio of me staying dry or me getting wet. I wrote this off to this being my first attempt to test the waters with her. I had had visions of catching 4-5 foot pike or muskies from the kayak. Though she seemed to become more stable the more I plied the waters with her, I preferred having visions of 2-3 foot pike or muskies that presented less of a chance of flipping the kayak.

Though not impressed with regards to stability, I certainly admired the ease with which she covered long distances of water with just a minimal amount of light paddling from her captain.

I gave up on the fishing after an hour or so and changed from Pixies to 4 or 5 other good lures I'd packed along with similar results that I'd had using the Pixies. It was sunny and warm with breeze enough to push the kayak if I left her rest in directions I didn't want to go. Out in mid lake, there were small islands of solid dark rock that emerged from the water silent, mysterious, and beckoning. I would cruise her out to them and played amongst them with her. Their sides were too steep, wet and slippery for the captain to get out and explore unless the captain wanted an embarrassing dunking in the attempt. They were not islands but the very tops of solid rock mini mountains who were hopefully enjoying the best of two worlds above and below the surface. Note to self: bring scuba gear on the next trip up here.

It seemed to have been a long day. So, the captain left Trapper's Lake with his unnamed kayak around 3:30 PM, much satisfied with her maneuverability and more confident with her stability than previously described. It seemed like an even longer day after the captain had not succeeded winching/strapping the unnamed kayak back atop the car by 5:30 PM. It is believed that the captain had yet another, shall we say, mental lapse. They've been intermittent most of his life, but seemed to come out in force this day. The captain had earnestly watched Live Bobbie demonstrating the technique while strapping the kayak down initially back in Maryland. It is obvious now with hindsight as our reference that the captain gravely overestimated his skills in this area while at the same time making stupidity look effortless.

The captain was exhausted, nearing his wit's end, knowing that if the bulldogs, who were absent all day, should emerge, would be enough to finish him off. The captain was never a quitter but gave up at 5:35 PM. How embarrassing it was attempting to flag down a passerby. The captain's ego had busted him down to buck private. What a drop in just two hours.

It wasn't long before a smiling middle aged native lady stopped with a carload of kids. We concluded that her degree of knowledge regarding winching and strapping was on a par with the buck private's. She lamented and was apologetic to the private. The private would not hear of this and graciously thanked her for stopping. As this nice obviously verile lady was the first vehicle to pass with no others in sight in either direction on a very long stretch of road, the private entertained thoughts of the odds of having to camp here for the night, putting a For Sale sign on the kayak, and the usual host of other negative possibilities that are conjured when one finds oneself in a seemingly hopeless situation, feeling I had finally trapped myself. Maybe it was the curse of the mysterious Trapper's Lake. Why had I not even thought of snapping a photo of those solid rock peaks jutting up out of her middle? Had I been mesmerized again? Were my actions and thoughts being controlled by some demon, or worse, demons? Visions of the long toothy smile of the Voodoo cabbie catapulted uninvited into my mind's eye.

Just when the private was contemplating donning his camouflage bug suit and lying in the middle of the highway, a small black speck appeared at the very southern end of the highway. No, it wasn't a bulldog! It was a black truck that immediately bolstered the pirate's hopes. It slowed as it approached but did not stop. The private could see the driver waving and laughing as they passed. Fortunately, the private couldn't muster the strength to give him the finger. Had the strength been there, the finger would have been there.

Fortunate would be a good descriptive narrative here, but blessed is closer to the bullseye. The waving and laughing displayed by the driver had been a signal to the private that help was on the way. They must have been flying as it took them about a hundred yards to slow down enough to do a ubie and return to this haunted place where the private could have made his not so grand exit. Turns out, the driver was Hugo and riding shotgun was his friend and companion Calvin.

Calvin was a direct descendant of the Dene peoples. These hardy folks were aboriginal to this area thousands or more years before mosquito repellent. Yea, these were the guys who figured out how to make copper tools and weapons. Both of my new companions could speak perfect English, were full of warmth and humor, plus very intelligent. All of this attributes were sorely welcomed by the private in this hour of need. Though never even hearing of the Dene prior to landing in Yellowknife, the private had been captivated by the literature he had come across depicting brief accounts of their history in this region. The author was so hoping to run into some of them in person as past experiences with Indigenous folk has not only been a pleasurable but life changing memorable event that the bearer can never forget and carries away with him through all of life. Take some, give more.

What the private couldn't accomplish in two hours of struggle, they did in 10 minutes. I let them know how thankful I was, how humbled I was, and how embarrassed I was. I was feeling like the guy at the deli who gave me directions last night. Hugo would have made a great counselor. He could see or feel the depths this private had tumbled into. He picked the private up with a simple, "We have winched and strapped all of our lives and this was your first try." Hugo's counsel not only picked my spirits up but seemed to give me new found strength. We had time for some relaxing and bullshitting now. I could tell from the music left on in their truck that they love rock and roll. They especially liked ZZ Top, Led Zeppelin, and were even familiar with Edgar Winters as soon as I said "Albino." I shared that I had been lucky enough to see all in person somewhere back in my past.

I interjected yet another thank you for their help as I didn't want to keep them from their original destination that they were obviously in a hurry to get to prior to bumping into the private. Almost in unison, they told me, "This was the Dene way - to always help anyone who needs it."

As they projected no signs of wanting to get back on the road right away, I felt them out by telling them that I was a recovering hippie (very old joke). They had a lengthy chuckle as they had picked up on my jest right away. After a prolonged pause, Calvin, with a voice that, although soft, seemed to quiet the breeze and all sounds of life surrounding us, deadpanned, "Ron, I think that's something you don't recover from." What a hoot! It was now my turn for a hardy laugh that resonated across Trapper's Lake.

We then had a lengthy discussion on the pros and cons of dope and they seemed to lean toward the pro side. I only wished I could have smuggled some up here to share with them. I did feel at ease enough with these new/old friends now to share that in my hippie days, mescaline, peyote, and mushrooms were my drugs of choice. Without hesitation, Hugo asked, "Would you settle for LSD?" This was followed by three hardy laughs resonating across Trapper's Lake. Give the Taliban some peyote and the war's over...

PHOTO #7 - HUGO AND CALVIN

Unfortunately for me, they did have some destination to get to. I told them I would like to have their photo for a journal I may seek to publish regarding this trip and I assured them that they have been up there on top with the highlights. They graciously consented.

That's Hugo on the left leaning on the van and Calvin on the right pointing to the kayak.

Besides a lifetime memory and lifetime friendship, the only thing I could offer these guys were my cigars. They had told me they enjoyed smoking prior to my offer. I had three different blends ranging from Filipino cigars to Black Parodi's made in Scranton, PA. They were hesitant to take more than one each. With some coaxing, I talked them into each sampling at least all three different blends which they readily grabbed once the coaxing set in. I offered the whole stash knowing that taking it all would go against the grain in the Dene way. They said they were pleased with three and would be surprising a Filipino friend tonight with one of the Filipino cigars.

I told Calvin how happy and honored I was to meet a Dene. He said, "You got to meet two counting Hugo." This widened my newfound smile even further. My only regret as I waved in unison with them as they departed down the highway towards Yellowknife was that I was not with them heading for their destination. Had they made the offer, I would have been with them like Jack Nicholson in 'Easy Rider.' I had forgotten to tell them that just prior to that small black speck appearing at the very southern end of the highway, the private had sent a prayer to the heavens requesting someone/anyone understanding who could help. Again, another gift from God, twofold. We only spent maybe a half hour together but I will miss them for a lifetime. So, Hugo and Calvin, if you read or even hear about your starring roles in this publication, always know you have a place to stay if you like in Oldtown, MD. Come and stay as long as you like. It's your turn to visit me. I've never met any better kindred spirits.

Trapper's Lake and the author found themselves alone once again and the Trapper beckoned unto me as only a mystical lake could. She was saying, come, let me engulf and caress and cleanse your foul smelling body. She could tell that behind my ears the smell of pizza permeated the olfactory sensors.

Long ago, the author had come across a sure fired indicator that a bath is long over due. I hesitate to test you on this method as I figure you have already come across your very own special indicator that you alone are aware of and utilize on a regular basis. As stated above, you probably already have found your very own distinctive indicator but for you readers who may not have, this author is willing to bare it all with you for the sake and general well being of all mankind for millenniums to come. Here goes:

1. Use the index finger on either of your hands. Actually, any finger or even a clumsy thumb will do. It's a good idea to select the digit used from your dominant hand.
2. Wipe or stroke the posterior portion of either ear down near the rear of the lobe in a gentle but determined fashion utilizing the digit choice described in #1 with a scooping like motion. One scoop should suffice. Use two if you're not sure or if this is your initial effort.
3. Once you're confident that a successful scoop has been administered, thrust the utilized digit (refer to #1 if necessary) in a gentle but controlled ark to the nostril orifice stopping your thrust just prior to contact.
4. With the selected digital scoop securely stopped and held in its place at the nostril orifice, inhale employing both nostrils for a minimum of three seconds. Note: a ratio does fluctuate pending length of time necessary for a successful inhalation versus length of time since previous bathing experience.

The author's utilization of the above method reveals an overt smell not unlike pizza.

You can expect a similar conclusion when you employ this method. Do not expect that all of you will smell like pizza. Many who have tried this method report a diversity of fragrances akin to European cheeses, horse trailers, fermented hay, high school locker rooms in August, and more. Remember, it's not so much the smell you are after as much as the indicator you seek. The smell is simply a perk.

If you have religiously followed Steps 1-4 and have not discovered your very own distinctive smell indicator, it may be medically beneficial for you to seek professional help from an ear, nose, and throat specialist. If you have earnestly followed steps 1-4 and are hesitant or refuse to reveal your own distinctive smell indicator, I know some very good psychologists who would leap at the chance to look at your family tree and/or complete a detailed case study with you pending the limits described in your current health plan. Look for numerous other inspirational and helpful hints as you read on.

After utilizing the above fail-safe method, the author found a potential excuse for not getting an invite to Hugo and/or Calvin's digs. Time had become overdue for personal cleansing. An hour was spent and wasted searching for any and all of my Ivory soap bars that were somewhere hiding in the van. Apparently this was mental lapse day in Canada. I don't think we celebrate or designate a specific date for this in the U.S. but we should if we don't forget about doing it. Precious always scoffs at my emergencies bag but this day for me, it paid for itself as amidst its lifesaving equipment and myriad of other potential necessities, soap was found. So, Precious, let this be a lesson to you each and every time you gripe about how much room that yellow backpack filled to the gills takes up in the van. Today, it was just soap, but tomorrow it could be compasses, fire starters, needle and thread, water purifiers, car parts, and on and on and on.

There was no trouble locating the green, blue, and black bathing suit. You remember - the one that had no elastic agility around the waist area. This non-elasticity was becoming increasingly problematic as my own weight loss on this trip was challenging the drawstrings ability to take up the slack. Found where I'd last draped it after my last encounter with soap and water around the headrest of the shotgun seat.

After the near death experience taking that bath back down the highway in that glacier-fed creek (I can't remember the name) in Montana coupled with the knowledge that I was much farther north and anticipating that any dip into any water would be potentially even more life threatening in a hypothermic sense added to my reluctance to bathe more frequently. However, I told you that Trapper's Lake was mysterious. I couldn't describe her as lukewarm but her chill factor couldn't hold a candle to that Montana stream. In fact, if I hugged the edge where land bumps into water or vice versa, it was nearing upon pleasant. Not that I wanted to lounge in her watery bosom for a protracted stay, but for a pleasant period of time that one might label a quickie, I regret getting no photos of the mysterious Trapper's Lake but assure you, she's there waiting for you.

PHOTO #8 - LONE SEAGULL

I was approached by this lone seagull in the parking lot. This is not a dirty photo. Those knobs in the foreground are someone's finger knuckles who snuck into the photo. That seagull reminded me of my magpie girlfriend who joined me for lunch on Bow Lake above Lake Louise some days behind. I wonder if my fair magpie is spooning for me still, looking north hoping beyond hope that I will return to her. Though the seagull was a rare beauty, it could not undo those feelings still in my heart for my sweet mountain lake magpie. I came clean with the seagull that the best I could offer her was abiding friendship and she squawked something in seagulloneze and promptly flew off. I drove

PH☉T☉ #9 - L☉NE SEAGULL

back silently to Yellowknife alone with my thoughts but pleased that I had remained true to my mountain lake magpie.

Consideration was given to returning to the Korean restaurant for a last grand culinary extravaganza before leaving Yellowknife. Why not, I was all decked out in reasonably cleaner clothes than had been worn prior to the dip into Trapper's Lake. For fear of disappointment as the Korean restaurant was not a buffet, the author did manage to wrangle a 12-inch Korean pulled pork from Subway - close enough. For those of you who are interested, it cost $13.60 Canadian but was exceedingly good in a Korean kind of way. I thought it best to top off the half tank of gas still with me and for those of you still interested, that half tank cost me an additional $50.64 Canadian.

I called Precious from the Yellowknife airport, a busy and bustling place. I'd reached my goal and zenith getting here to Yellowknife. Road fatigue and loneliness were taking their toll. I promised Precious that I would start my journey home tomorrow.

Before turning in for another night in the Walmart Astoria, I sat in the van and wrote some postcards to friends back in the States. Intent on my writing, I failed to notice the approach or re-approach of that same gull from back at Trapper's Lake. I know it had to be the same one as it was identical. It looked at me as if to say, "You're leaving so soon and we've hardly had time to get acquainted." But alas, a promise is a promise. Don't make one unless you fully intend to keep it. Not keeping kind of kills the whole premise of promise, doesn't it?

DAY #20, 7/20/2016

Bed and sleep overtook me last night at 11 PM or thereabouts. Thanks to the latitude and tilt of our Earth, it was still broad daylight out. Slept well but arose in the same light in response to the Walmart beeper brigade at 5:30 AM or thereabouts. I completed my morning routine, and gave birth out through the tailgate. With compulsivity as my guest, I completed a second thorough search for the remaining three bars of Ivory soap tearing every piece of luggage, bags, etc., apart with the tormenting knowledge that I had recalled seeing the three neatly enclosed in a plastic bag not that long ago. Maybe the Dene can conjure up stuff they need like soap, etc, but I have my doubts. I know just from first impressions that they wouldn't or at least wouldn't conjure up all three - maybe one - but I doubt that too. I would be honored though had the Dene conjured up my Ivory soap. Remember conjuring is not stealing. And could or should they have conjured up my Ivory, I'm positive I would have found something they would have left me to reciprocate for their conjuring. I made a simple statement once to some Yupik Eskimos that I was growing tired of listening to the same old rock and roll cassettes I had brought with me from back in the lower 48. The very next morning, I found a cardboard box full of rock and roll tapes on my front porch. I never learned who to thank for that gift and don't know to this day, but have been forever grateful. But, that was their way. Oh, those primitive, backward natives?? Anyway, a donation of thanks was rendered to the Yellowknife Walmart by way of a backup 10-12 pack of Ivory soap (biodegradable). Thanks for being my home away from home. I do wish that you would consider installing showers but beggars shouldn't be choosers.

I had my most interesting and enjoyable encounter with a Walmart greeter last evening that I just can't let go by not mentioning it to you here. This greeter was many decades younger than the usual centenarian that you don't know whether to feel sorry for or question their motive for employment at Sam Walton's store. Maybe he was a greeter in waiting. Don't know, but there he was.

As was my custom, I always made an attempt to spot check (no pun intended) the condition of the rest room prior to bedtime as I, like most folks, don't like surprises in the wee hours of the morning.

I shot past him giving a polite nod and received one in turn. What met my eye in the restroom was the usual mess at the end of the day, i.e., toilette paper strewn on the floor in places you wouldn't expect. Fearful for what the morning could bring, I found sanctuary for completing #1 in #1 and then headed out after holding my breath throughout much of this inspection. Entering the exit lobby, there standing alone, was the young greeter in waiting with a big smile on his face. He knew.... He quipped, "Well, that didn't take you long." As if he'd been alerted by other Walmart greeters back on my trail to be on the lookout.

After taking a deep breath and in no way wanting to chastise him for going well beyond his training in the realm of greeter verbiage, I stopped dead in my tracks and threw one back at him hoping to catch him off guard, "Are you the manager?" This had the desired effect. He took a step back and sheepishly said, "Why, ah, no, I'm not."

Moving a step closer boundaring on his space, I blurted, "Something's got to be done in that bathroom." He queried, "Yes?" With an attempt to minimize my blurtations, I told him calmly but to the point, "My inspection had revealed that the toilettes are a mess, the soap dispenser on the left is sticking, there's not one hand towel, the blow dryer's so weak it's not worth the effort, and I was forced to dry my hands on my own shirt."

As was my intention, he picked right up on my attempt to humor him at this late hour. It was 9:45 PM. He took a deep breath and said, "I'll let them know." He was really letting me know that it was below his station in Walmart to be doing toilets, but that he could still project a level of dignity with respect to his greeter-in-waiting post.

I admired his courage, demeanor, and his delivery. He had held his own with one of the very best without flinching. I sensed that he may not really be a greeter in waiting, but that the real greeter had simply forgot to show up or stroked out at a great grandchild's wedding or something, and this management level in training person had reluctantly agreed to act as stand in greeter as long as he received his regular salary.

Seeing that he was enjoying our brief discourse as much as I was, my parting words were, "Tell them Ron said to get it straightened out." He ended our banter with "That ought to take care of it." Great short term company. Great potential growth within the company.

Finding none at Walmart, I drove around town looking for a mailbox. I had two reasons for wanting to mail two of the postcards I'd written last evening. One was I had two Canadian stamps left and at a $1.20 a piece didn't want to waste them. The other reason being I wanted proof beside photographs that I had made it to Yellowknife and assumed that they make a postal stamp over their stamps as we do in the States. There were but two obstacles in my path. Damned if I didn't drop them, they're small, in between the seat and the console. That took parking the van, a flash light, and fifteen minutes of cussing, praying and bitching before they showed back up. I swear they were giggling. They were immediately affixed to the postcards. The second obstacle was locating a mailbox. Have you ever found yourself in a foreign country having no idea of what their convenient mailboxes look like? I can tell you this much from experience that the bright red steel things resembling a mailbox are for your general garbage. The green ones are for garbage and recycling. Then there were the gray ones. I never figured out what purpose they served other than to frustrate foreigners looking to mail postcards.

Giving up on finding a mailbox, I was able to park about three blocks from the post office whose exterior looked more like a swank hotel. I had remembered its location downtown, as it was near where the Asian passenger in the cab had made rapid hand gestures to me less than a great time ago in my quest for Mark's restaurant. Having a memory can be helpful pending what it is you are remembering. That last b_ _ _ _ hit sounds like something you'd find in a fortune cookie. After all of this my mind seems to remain stained with lamentations of Asian buffet. Dorothy dear, I think it's time you head back to Kansas.

PHOTO #1 - HOUSING IN YELLOWKNIFE

Not far from the post office, I stopped to take a photo based on observations of passersby and pedestrians to give the reader some idea of what low to mid income housing looks like in Yellow-knife. Quite refreshing and unique. You'll have to take my word on the mini skyscrapers downtown. I did take photos but they're not included as the throw away camera gave me incentive to throw them away as it did them little if any accurate justice. Come to think of it, this is the first time I've pondered the origin of the nomenclature associated with a throw away camera.

There was one section of Yellowknife that I wanted to check out before heading out. It's called the Oldtown section. As my home-town is another Oldtown, the intrigue was building on me. It was quaint with lots of water, boats, and seaplanes making this area of Yellowknife obviously for the rich and famous. A handful of photos were taken but one served best to enlighten you how these folks love to or have no choice but to build on these massive rock outcroppings that make up a high percentage of the terra firma. The terra don't get much firmer than this.

PHOTO #2 - HOUSES ON TERRA FIRMA

A dockside breakfast of Cheerios, powdered milk, oatmeal, Ste-via, cinnamon, and a cup of two-day old java (cold) was ordered and I served breakfast in a small dockside parking lot across the road from the above three houses on the rock.

It was here that to my horror, I noticed a potential major disaster that needed immediate attention regarding the van. Keen eyes had led me to the plastic black shield that fits under the bumper. It was nearly loose enough to fall off. I have no idea how long this had been like this but speculation led me to believe the rough road to Fort Resolution or the road to Frazier's was the probable culprit. Fearing the worst and potential for costly repairs, I crawled under the bumper. Much to my delight, the pin (plastic black screw looking thing that holds the shield in place had somehow come loose but held on for dear life - great saying, origin unknown). Please note: you the reader have once again been present when the author's astounding mechanical knowledge had resurfaced. Anyway, popped it back in place, thanking my lucky stars, and soared off homeward bound.

This would be my first homewardly direction in about twenty days. Mixed feelings bombarded the psyche. Missing Precious, neighbors, and other comrades in arms would soon be terminated. But so, too, the vagabond life of the nomad and my favorite - the quest for what awaits around the next bend would be taking an abrupt halt. I recall similar feelings on past float trip excursions. Once you got into it coming up upon the drop car at the take out point was depressing as I would find myself not wanting it to end. I think a lot of us share a Tom Sawyer like perspective and I for one am glad for us who've contracted it.

Just south of Yellowknife, whizz past Trapper's Lake braindead or something as once again to my regret twenty more miles past, I realized that I had not stopped to take any photos of that alluring and memory-laden mystical body. This alone would be justification for returning some day in what's left of my future. If you can't remember Richard Nixon, chances are, your future will be longer than mine. So, I beseech you to go there to Trapper's Lake in my stead. She'll be there and I assure you, she's patiently awaiting to enchant and enhance you. You owe it to yourself. Maybe Hugo and Calvin will show up as icing on that primordial cake of yours.

Speaking of Hugo and Calvin, they kept making landings into my brain pan. What a thrill it would be to spend time with them again. They seemed to have captured my spirit in a most positive way. Note to self: if you get downtrodden, invoke the lift they gave to my life's outlook during that rarest and fleeting interlude beside Trapper's Lake. No, the author is not gay. He just fell in love with those guys in a guy like way on that sunny day.

PHOTO #3 - ROCK OUTCROPPINGS

Heading back down Route 4 (actually northwest of Yellowknife) and way past my lost opportunity for a photo of Trapper's Lake but not yet to the small community of Rae (you may reference your atlas but don't be overly concerned - I wouldn't test you on data of this nature), a photo was snapped at or near the entrance to mile upon mile of solid rock outcroppings that seemed to go along for the ride in their silent brooding way. It's difficult for any camera to capture miles of this perplexing geology let alone a throw away. Again, you just had to be there. Again, I encourage you to travel there and see it for yourself. In fact, I double dog dare you! (Thanks Christmas Story) and a double dog dare has to be accepted. Someday, you'll thank me. I know I had pointed out these features on the way up but they proved just as fascinating on the return trip.

Please study the above photo at your leisure. You should note what can only be described as an optical illusion. The camera would suggest to you that that part of the dashboard, steering wheel, etc. in the exposure appears to be very clean. That couldn't possibly be the case. Ask anyone familiar with the author. Even the author has remained perplexed about this and there is no rational explanation for this phenomenon. I'd sure like to hear from any number of you photographers who have read to this point in the road. Surely, you could take a brief recess from the delight and joy you're receiving from digesting these words of wisdom and contact this author with a logical explanation. I double dog dare you!

Almost everywhere you look up here, your retina is bombarded with a multitude of delightful greens. It's not monotonous but it's nice to have the greens broken up with a mass of other colored fauna, etc. One that was everywhere and ever pleasing was a wild green leafed plant reaching upwards over two feet tall with soft purple flowers caressing the main stem. Some one who never saw them rendered that they

PHOTO #4 - WILDFLOWER

must have been "fireweed." The author has never seen natural fire that exuded a purple hue. So again, the author will solicit input here from you botanists who have read this far. Take a break, give me a call. I found out later that it may also be edible. Thank you again Mother Nature.

I wasn't even going to include this photo of a fish camp near the settlement of Rae until noticing those unknown purple hued wild-flowers singing their purple song behind the camp. If you scrutinize the photo with a magnifying glass, you'll come across a blue teepee across the river.

PHOTO #5 - FISH CAMP RAE

Standing on a still in use, slightly rickety, steel bridge over another of the far reaching arms of the Great Slave, a photo attempting to capture the raw wild beauty of this region was taken. Note, the solid rock outcropping swimming mid photo left. I think that's the heart of Rae in the farground. Note the shadow of the bridge floating on top of the water. This locale was named Dehke Frank Channel. There was no explanation or origin for the name. I have a feeling that all of us would have benefited should we have met Dehke Frank.

PHOTO #6 - BRIDGE OVER THE SLAVE NEAR RAE

PHOTO #7 - MACKENZIE RIVER BRIDGE

Now heading southwest with Route 4 mysteriously turning into Route 3 even though there were no intersections, turn offs, etc, the Fort Providence pit stop flew past and I watched her for an instant in my rearview mirror. Not much had changed.

Keeping the promise to myself, I stopped at a large and handy pull off on a manmade peninsula jutting out into the Mackenzie River under the great bridge of a similar name. Guess has it that the Mackenzie might be a half mile wide here.

PHOTO #7.5 - MACKENZIE RIVER BRIDGE

Fished here for two hours, throwing numerous lures guaranteed to catch fish. The guarantee must have been a hoax, or the warranty on the guarantee had expired, but I enjoyed the attempt. The day and the water were perfect, and the bulldogs had left town. While puffing on my cigar and whipping a Pixie out as far as I could whip it, I noticed a foreign object between my crocks in the gravel. Yet another of those plastic toothpicks. Other than two guys who were leaving when I arrived, the whole peninsula belonged to me. However, some deranged shithead had successfully left his/her mark on what had been a day of perfects. I recall a lengthy harangue many pages back targeting the wisdom of littering and the subhumans who are the key players in dirtying up pristine environments for the rest of us. The good book says, "Thou shall not kill" but it doesn't say shit about mutilation….food for thought.

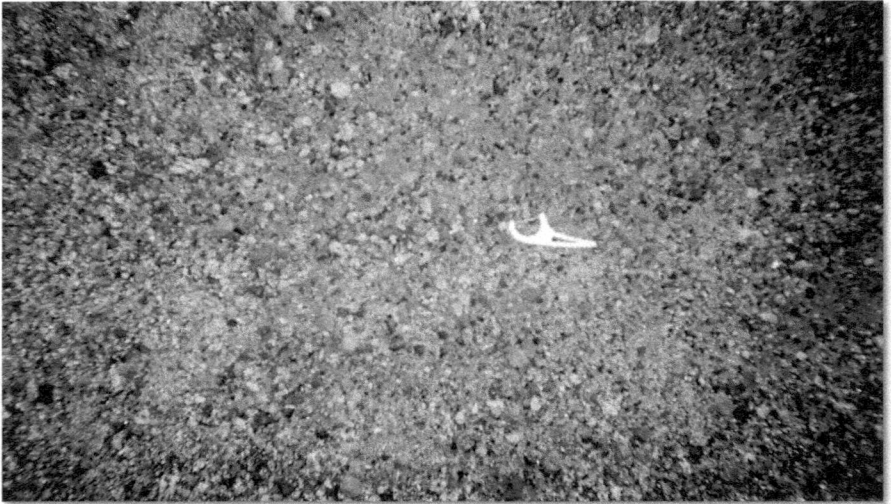

PHOTO #8 - PLASTIC TOOTHPICK

Saw two sandhill cranes near the same spot I'd spotted them at on the way up. They must have a nest nearby. It is thought they mate for life like most other creatures with feathers. Can you imagine mating for life? They must get very tired.

Just past the mating cranes, south of Enterprise, very near Alexander Falls, I took a break and caught this photo of Louisa Falls in her brown majesty. Drove to High Level, had a half priced, pre-cooked lasagna meal for just $4.50 Canadian. Couldn't pass up the lasagna, couldn't pass up the price. It was delicious but it was 10:15 PM.

Thoughts of Hugo and Calvin continued to cruise through my head off and on all day. I forgot to share with you another part of our conversation along Trapper's Lake. I told them that I was almost 70 years old and had a great girlfriend back in Maryland. They both laughed. I suppose a 70 year old with a girlfriend was humorous

PHOTO #9 - LOUISA FALLS

to them. It sounds funny to me, too. I interjected "He was my boyfriend!" From Cloris Leachman in the movie Young Franken-stein. Calvin said it was one of his favorite mov-ies. I tried another movie quote, John Candy's "It'll buff right out" from the movie Trains, Planes, and Automobiles. They knew that movie also. I told them that these were two of my favorite movies. They both indicated their fondness for comedies. It's a small world. Why can't we all get along? It would be the Dene way.

It was well past 10:30 PM before accommodations were secured in an overflow parking lot near the tourist info building. I noted no other free campers here but there was plenty of room for at least a dozen or more. Odometer readings showed that close to 500 miles were covered this day.

DAY #21, 7/21/2016

Slept very well, arose at 7:30 AM, did toiletries at the same Filipino Esso station described on the trip up. Thinking Matt, the guy I'd met there last time, worked there, I asked one of the Filipino ladies if he was around. Her countenance about faced to fear, terror, or confusion and she became as if dumbstruck. I have no clue why she responded in such a fashion. Note to self: never use the name Matt in the presence of a Filipino girl. Looking for, but never finding a deal like the lasagna meal last night, it was time to leave. I noticed a lot of photos of very happy looking couples on the wall. Remembering the photos on the Death Wall in Hay River, I was reluctant to enquire and I wasn't about to approach the Filipino girl I'd sent into shock simply by asking about Matt. I located entry forms and a crude box to drop them into. Seems it was an ongoing contest the Filipinos call Tloc Moi. One simply fills out an entry form, drop it in the box and you could win a free trip for two anywhere in the world of your choosing. Hence, all of the happy photos of couples on the wall were somewhat uplifting from those in Hay River. I filled out the entry form as I was feeling lucky. I approached the only white employee in the place to make sure I'd filled out the form appropriately which I had. I also inquired if American citizens were eligible and she confirmed this. She then informed me that she would complete my entry by stapling my gas receipt to the form. She displayed an oversize staple gun far exceeding dimensions needed to perform the act. In all honesty, I told her that I had filled the van up here last night close to 10 PM and had waived off the clerk's offer of a receipt as my targeted thoughts were somehow fixed on discounted lasagna. She put the oversized staple gun below the counter on her side, out of my sight quicker than you can say, "Bye bye trip for two." I so wanted to have a photo of Precious and me on that wall, but it was not to be. I'm sure this scenario will return to my memory bank for the rest of my life every time lasagna is on the menu. My entry blank went into the box anyway. To date there has been no notification regarding winning.

For those of you who may be skeptical of the above narrative, please review the accompanying photo of the Tloc Moi poster in the Filipino Esso station in downtown High Level, Alberta. A word to the wise — keep your gas receipts.

PHOTO #1 - TLOC MOI CONTEST

Curiosity got the best of me. Wandering if Tloc Moi means "lucky bastard" in the Philippines, I took a chance and sought interpretive assistance from another Filipino girl working there. She said in excellent English that Tloc Moi was the original name for High Level. What a slur on cultures and history. Don't you think it more romantic to see Tloc Moi on your atlas than High Level? I can't condemn Canadians for this misstep. My own hometown is called Oldtown. It originally was named Opessa's Town after a powerful and respected Native American chief. If I'm elected.... we may have a resurgence of original names. Before leaving, I told my new Filipino interpreter that I thought Tloc Moi meant lucky. We shared a mutual laugh while she pointed a bronze finger at me saying, "You funny." I'm not sure if it was a compliment but at least she hadn't gone into shock.

Route 35 was now taking the van and occupant towards Peace River in the awesomely gorgeous province of Alberta, burning up pavement between here and home. I attempted a call to Precious at an Asian restaurant. That reminds me of a pejorative term often slung unduly at those of Asian decent. If a gossack (white man) moves into a Yupik Eskimo village, he is adopted by a Yupik grandmother. Grandmother in Yupik is "gook." Mine wanted me to call her every morning on my way to work. With no phones, call meant to yell. So every morning on my way to work I would call out, "Hey Gook!" at the top of my lungs and it was culturally appropriate and greatly appreciated. To this day, I still love the sound of that word regardless of its context. (Absolutely no offense to anyone of splendid Asiatic linage.) I also love the sound of the word "lube" (no offense to anyone associated with the petroleum industry).

I inadvertently became the proud owner of an invisible dog while living with the same Yupiks. When happy, I will oftentimes bark like a dog or more often than not, answer the call of a barking dog. Dog gone it, he's crazy. Yea, I accepted it long ago. Some of my Yupik friends asked me where my dog was after three mornings of jubilant barking before leaving for work from home (former one room storage shed converted into a two room with half bath consisting of one five gallon bucket with accompanying commode seat/lid behind a thin curtain off from the couch near the entrance). Of course, you might say that everything there was near something. Talk about tiny house living popular with modern day yuppies. I liked it. I didn't love it, but I liked it. Humans left with no other options are remarkably adaptable.

On cruise control floating down Route 35, Hugo and Calvin returned to the gray matter. Some guy named Alvin Toffler, I think, wrote a book in the 70's called "Future Shock." It was part of a reading assignment for a Master's program. It was like "Future Shock" meeting my two Dene friends. Here they were modern day Indigenous Peoples who could still quote lines from a John Candy movie and recalled that Gene Wilder starred in Young Frankenstein. It's a pity that Gene died sometime during this trip or soon after.

If only we could all end up with a little speck of him to help us find humor like only he could bestow on us. What better epitaph than "beloved comedian." Although it's doubtful that I will ever see Calvin or Hugo in the flesh again, they will be fondly remembered forever. Sad but still gratifying. Note to self: live every day as if people like Calvin, Hugo, John Candy, and Gene Wilder are along for the ride.

Friends at home asked why I wanted to take a trip like this. The lasagna last evening gave me the answer. Some of you are probably saying to yourself, "Get the straight jacket. He's talking to lasagna now." That is not the case, but I'd bet if lasagna could talk it would have a heavy Italian accent. Open your mind. Let's see if I can bring you around to this. You know sometimes, even when you're not hungry, for unknown reasons, you still crave a gut bomb? I get that way about "getting out of dodge" and exploring places I've never been. On a scale of ten, it's the same kind of mind boggling sensation as craving a gut bomb. Your memories are your trophies.

Just passed over my most isolated but enjoyable bathing locations on the way up. I had referred to it previously as another no named river in Alberta. But this time, I caught the sign on the north entrance to the bridge. It's the Melkie River (origin of name unknown), but I thanked her again for knocking the dirt from me on the way up. The plan now is to find a friendly gravel pit for bathing in later this day when the wind is just right, I become aware that another bath may just be justified.

After passing two more sand hill cranes foraging near the road, we rolled into Manning. It must have been super rush hour in Manning as I was far exceeding the posted speed limit and was still holding up traffic even on tiny side streets. Possibly Manning was an Athabaskan word meaning "to floor it." I spotted a pay phone booth and risked life and limb crossing traffic to get to it only to find out the phone had been removed, possibly unofficially. Spotting a second Ma Bell conveniently attached to an exterior corner of a popular convenience store, you could say I was drawn to it. As there was a blonde WASP looking lady using it and no one else in line, I chivalrously gave her her space and sought refuge within the convenience store from Manning's bustle. My atlas had told me that Manning's population was a mere 1,293 souls, but it appeared that someone rang the bell and they all rushed out at once. It was like there was a fire, but I could see no flames or smoke. Had the road put me into some hypnotic state as I was the only one driving and now walking at a reasonable pace? Finding solace in the restroom, I emptied my bladder, but could still discern vehicles flying by outside thankful at least that I was not holding up traffic. A candy bar and two homemade cookies cost me $4 Canadian. For some reason, there were two cashiers for the one cash register. They spoke rapidly in unison while the taller counted back my change.

The blonde WASP lady had finished with the phone and had vanished into the day. There was no competition for the phone, but I doubled my pace to it hoping to blend in better with the fast moving locals. As I approached the phone, I promised myself if Precious sounded like she was talking two to three times faster than usual, I would seek professional help immediately here in Manning. That would not be necessary. I never reached Precious as the phone was dead. No operator, no response to quarters, nothing. But who had the blonde WASP been talking to so rapidly just moments ago? I'm glad I'd only seen the back of her head as this all potentially had the makings for one of those "Twilight Zone" movies.

Trying best to collect my senses, I grabbed a quick bunch of dried vegetables succulently marinated in warm water overnight in a styrofoam cup accompanied by two homemade cookies, one candy bar, and a lukewarm cup of ancient coffee. A vote was taken and it was decided that I may not stop in Manning the next time I come through here.

While weaving south through Manning traffic, realization struck me once again. I'd completely forgotten dessert. Exploring my options led to a snap decision making the selection to be gum. I followed the directions again, pushed/popped and held the wrapper up close to my mouth so as not to drop it while dodging my way through the Manning 500. I cut my upper lip on the aluminum backing. I pondered: do aluminum cuts hurt for as long as paper cuts? I'll be finding out. So long Manning. Absolutely no reason to take a second vote. Here I come Peace River!

I came upon a very old pioneer's cabin in a field not far off the road between Burwyn and Peace River. I would hope the reader can only appreciate the magnitude of the sacrifices I made simply to get you this photo. Someone had to do it, and I didn't see any volunteers jumping in.

The girl at the tourist center in Hay River was right. I had experienced a lull in bulldog attacks sometime before reaching Yellowknife. I did endure the expected onslaught of mosquito hordes, but even they had been reasonably kind to me. They reminded me of their strength, cunning, and bravado here in that waste deep field of green you can see encompassing the pioneer's cabin.

PHOTO #2 - ABANDONED CABIN

Your sacrificing author waded through that field of green to just the right spot to ensure your viewing pleasure. While I was transfixed on concentrating total effort on securing the best shot possible, Mr. and Mrs. Mosquito and their very large family lay in wait for me hidden in all that greenness plotting their unprovoked attack. Their signal to attack remained the same as always, they would wait until the hush of the slight breeze had meandered away. The breeze was cooperative from their perspective to the point one wonders if they were acting intentionally as a team in unison. One unheard mosquito command for attack and I became their buffet.

We've already touched on strength and cunning. Let's take a brief look at their bravado: they can all witness you smashing one or even many of their relatives but they keep coming seemingly even more determined. Visions of the Alamo and Pearl Harbor appeared in my mind's eye. I thought I heard some ancient distant bugle blowing retreat. I heeded it stepping high as if attempting to fly over that grassy field back to the sanctity of the van. Once there, a barrage of obscenities was verbally hurled back at them which, at best, had they known English could have only served to hurt their feelings, but it made me feel better what with the itching and all. Maybe my bloody lip from the gum wrapper had alerted them.

Further inspections of those I had brought down by smashing them on my face, ears, hands, legs. Stop! Let's just say their attack had been complete and successful. Anyway, observation assured me that these were the largest mosquitos that had heretofore fed on me. These hummers (pun intended) were super fortresses. One of the last ones to succumb to my smashing counter attack held so much of my blood and blood from previous unknown donors, we could have aided in giving someone else a transfusion. The long term effects of these vampirial like attacks can take copious avenues. The one that enveloped me was itching while traveling ten or so miles down Route 2 the wrong way before realizing it and back tracking towards Peace River again. The one redeeming occurrence of the

back tracking was the chance to slow down while passing that pioneer's cabin floating in that lush green field and throwing a final
salvo of stored up obscenities toward those blood sucking phantoms.

Having failed back in Manning, other attempts to reach Precious
from Peace River airport proved almost as futile. Public service
announcement: travelers cannot call collect to a cell phone number
if the cellphone owner does not answer. You can't leave a collect
message. The same goes for a home or ground line. The author did
attempt to scream a frustrated message over operator assistance to
Precious' home phone. Don't think it made it. Wasted lots of time
trying to reach Precious this day.

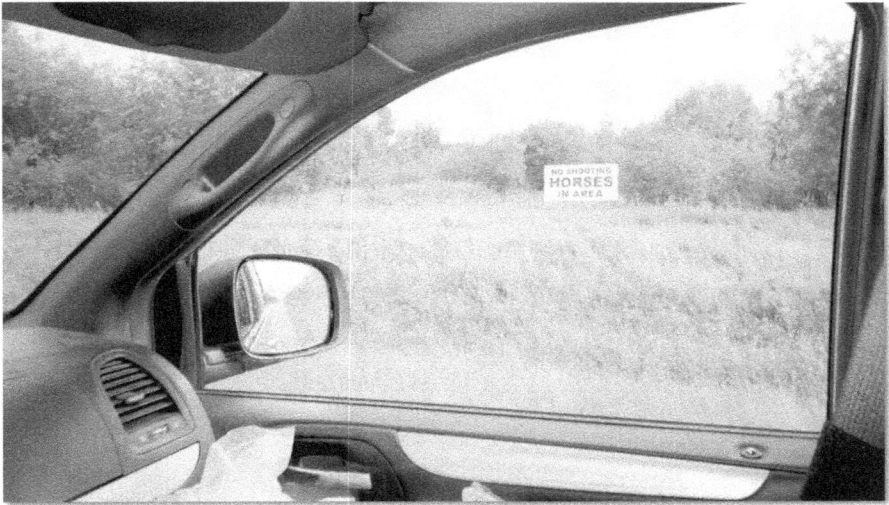

PHOTO #3

Somewhere between Peace River and Lesser Slave Lake we
passed this white sign with red letters ordering: No Shooting Horses
in Area. I guess there's some rule?? I didn't feel like sticking around
the area to investigate. I sure would like to meet the person who
belongs to the sign though. Just down the highway from the sign
was a regional jail. I'll bet no escapees venture onto the property of
the No Shooting Horses sign. Note: the author has chosen to refer

to self as "we" again as during this time, the author was carrying blood from numerous other donors as a result of the recent mosquito attacks.

PHOTO #4 - LESSER SLAVE LAKE

PHOTO #5 - LESSER SLAVE LAKE FIRE STATION

I'm inserting this photo — my first look at Lesser Slave Lake. Refer to your atlas if you haven't already. You'll find it southeast of Peace River north of Route 2. Note: the photo represents just a tiny portion of Lesser Slave. Can you detect anything on the horizon? I can't either. Now, compare the size of Lesser Slave to Great Slave to give you some concept of how vast Great Slave is. Ponder, ponder....

PHOTO #6 - BEACH/SEAGULLS TAKEN 8:15 PM, TEMP 56-73 DEGREES

The next photo is of the Slave Lake Fire Station. They had space for "Lesser" but opted out. I guess it was a guy thing. I took the photo for my sisters, bros, and buddies at Oldtown Volunteer Fire Department back home. I could find no one at the Slave Lake Station. This is not uncommon these days. Volunteer fire departments are going the way of the dinosaurs. Why, you ask? Answer: no one wants to volunteer. There are a multitude of reasons and people cling to them to justify not joining. If you can think of reason, we've already heard it. I urge you to get off your butt, turn off the computer, the phone, or the TV. Most rural voluntary fire companies are so short staffed that we oftentimes do not have enough members to make a call. So, the next time Granny's house catches on fire or your baby's choking on a chicken bone, don't condemn the fire company that you could have joined to give them enough manpower to assist you. You'll find them interesting and enjoyable people. Become one! Double dog dare you!

PHOTO #7 - SEAGULLS/WALMART

While scouting for a possible campsite on a bumpy dirt road hugging another tiny portion of Lesser Slave, a long sandy beach popped up. A photo was taken here in an attempt to capture the thousands of confused seagulls lining the beach for miles, thinking they were on the ocean. Not feeling comfortable with the quality of the rest rooms provided along the beach, the author retreated to his old mainstay back in town.

Before retiring in the free camper's section of the parking lot, the author captured a photo of thousands of free camping seagulls in fields adjacent to the free camper's designated quarters. I don't know if they were confused or just evolving. We had covered near to 400 miles this day. I could still feel the presence of others running through my veins.

DAY #22, 7/22/2016

Woke up at 6 AM. Slept very well. Another free camper had parked his free camper truck right up against my van when he had at least 40 other free places to choose from. I did not even hear him arrive. I'm surprised he stayed what with my notorious snoring and babbling in my sleep. Maybe he thought someone in the van was still up and he felt safer. Don't know. Never did see him.

Like I said, it was very early but many people were coming and leaving Walmart already. As I had eaten an abundance of fruit and roughage yesterday, I felt it best to get going early. So, I meandered into Walmart (I prefer to call it Wally World) under false pretenses, trying to look like a guy who had not just awakened in their parking lot. But they know. They all know. They probably have prearranged codes and Walmart employee slang for free campers. I may be a designated DVCWK-BO-3. That would be: Dodge Van Caravan With Kayak-Body Odor-3. Their BO code probably tops out at 6. You get my drift? (No pun intended.)

Anyway, I was politely confronted by a guy in all black, politely but firmly. He knew…. He said, "Can I help you sir?" That's Wally World employee slang for, "What the hell are you (DVCWK-BO-3) doing in my store before we open?" I told him I'd seen lots of people coming and going this morning and thought this was a Super Walmart. This was my passive aggressive response to counter his slightly authoritarian bearing and a little jab at him not being a Super Walmart manager as opposed to his current management level.

Needless to say, I figured this guy for an assistant manager or a demoted for some obscure reason, ex-manager of a Super Walmart. Anyway — I know I have overused "anyway" throughout this entire narrative. But it helps get me back on track and is an indiscreet message to you signaling I'm moving forward, probably much to your satisfaction.

Sizing me up as a worthy adversary, he politely but firmly shared with me that the comings and goings were change of shifts and/or construction workers doing some remodeling.

I could sense I'd hit some sour note with him regarding my Super Walmart reference (see above). He was about to flaunt the power of his management level position by insisting that I return to the free camper's designated area until official opening time. I also sensed that this guy had to be a transplant, maybe even from the U.S. I knew it was high time to kick out the jams and pull out all the stops if I was going to get by this guy. I had to enlist the last ace in my arsenal hole. Wincing slightly, drawing myself inside his comfort zone, while utilizing whispered short phraseology, called upon all that was good and decent in him as if we were now trusted friends, requested his permission to use his bathroom. I think the wince became the deciding factor. His response was immediate. He sat down his clipboard atop some canned peas and briskly escorted me to the Men's Washroom as it's labeled in Canada.

Following his brisk and silent exit, morning rituals were completed. It was here that I took full advantage of advice given many days back in the Great Lakes by my wrestler/helicopter pilot friend with the rubber duckies. You will remember his advocacy for utilization of baby wipes in lieu of no bathing facilities. I followed his marionette like advice on wiping regimen: face, pits, crotch, and butt to the letter. While doing so, I wished, with hindsight, that he and I would have explored just how many wipes to use per bathing incident. Only time will tell, but I did feel much cleaner than I had when I had awoken.

Before exiting the Walmart, I located my new managerial friend and thanked him again. There's no sense in kicking a guy when you've got him down. A light breakfast of powdered milk and cereal were eaten at the free camper site. As was my custom, prior to leaving the parking lot, I returned to Walmart and purchased another packet of baby wipes. Guess who was working the register?

While exiting the south end of the parking lot, I came once again upon those confused free ranging seagulls. They appeared to be the same flock I stumbled upon adjacent to the free camper's area last evening. It's difficult to tell for certain what with all the interbreeding that's so much a part of their avian lives. It's a small world. One of my favorite groups from the 70's and 80's was called "Flock of Seagulls."

To help estimate their vast numbers, I attempted to count an area of them and then multiply by the width and depth of the field, and as close as I could calculate, there was a shitload of them. I encourage the reader to study the photo, formulate your own calculations and come forth with a more accurate number if you like. You won't win anything, but it will give many of you something to do beside mooching off your worn out parents who lie to their friends about how many job offers you've recently turned down.

Come to think of it, wouldn't it be a pleasant surprise for you to buy this book for the parents who have never wavered in their willingness to support you, even though you're rapidly gaining on middle age? Hell, you can probably find enough change lying around the house or stuck in the couch while they're at work to come up with enough. Don't you think it's time for you to finally give them something back? The driveway's another valuable source for loose currency. The same can be said for under car seats. Am I asking too much of you? You might want to get hopping on it. Should I notify your student loans program your current whereabouts? Don't make me get ugly!

Returning to the seagulls, a photo was snapped. There were so many of them that only about 1/6 to 1/7 of them made it into the frame. Their demeanor was leery (again possibly due to interbreeding - a potential trait they share with some humans). Attempts were made to maneuver the van to get close enough for a better photo. However, the closer the van got, the more they fluttered away. To a keen observer, it would have taken on the appearance of some primitive dance. The whole dance, they're talking and chirping gull to each other. There's probably someone in California right now on a $30,000.00 grant wearing ear phones attempting to interpret gull talk.

PHOTO #1 - FLOCK OF SEAGULLS

Turning the engine off resulted in their feeling more secure and accepting my alien presence. They moved back in closer as if to study me or the van. Even their constant chatter seemed to slow down and came on with much less volume. Just as I was about to shoot another shot that would have given you a much greater appreciation for their reflocking uncountable numbers, here he came barreling right through the center of the flock as fast as he could safely speed his dark gray Dodge Ram through the grass amidst lifting, scattering, screaming hordes. I was amazed that he didn't take any of them out. I didn't think this was his first rodeo and their response led me to believe that although they have grown accustomed to his chosen brand of humor, they maintain a constant vigil on the look out for him. I wanted to tell them that I had nothing to do with it, but I couldn't speak a chirp of gull. I must admit that the scene just witnessed was also dance-like in appearance - just a bit faster. I must also admit that I enjoyed the Ram driver's performance once I was assured that none of these inbreds were mutilated (no reference to the guy in the truck). No doubt, his life story would be grand fodder for yet another book of intrigue, humor and an in-depth study of the black arts. Never did see him. He vanished with the same intensity that he entered the Ram onto his field of frolic. I'm positive he has left his permanent mark on the confused gulls of Lesser Slave Lake.

On the other hand, it could have been him taking a shot at his 15 minutes of fame. Maybe he saw me in Walmart this morning. Wearing my cap and then he saw me sitting in the van trying to get the best photo I could of the gulls for you and he just couldn't control himself. I've been there. I can relate.

I think I may have already addressed the subtle power the cap had on bystanders. If so, please allow me to repeat myself. Indulge me, I'm old. You can observe an abrupt change in folks attitudes and demeanors once they spot it on my noggin. Some actually look around to see if there are cameras behind me. One guy somewhere in the Dakotas kept pointing at me saying the name of the network all the while he was walking away from me rapidly, carrying a big grin on his face as if he alone had discovered something that was too hot to the touch. Too bad I did not have my camera at the ready as he and that surrealistic smile faded into the crowd. Note to self: next trip, hang an expensive looking cheap camera around my neck while wearing the magic TV cap. Better still, have someone with a shoulder mounted expensive looking, cheap movie camera position himself behind me. There would be no end to the fun! Did I tell you that I had purchased the cap in a Goodwill store in Florida for $1.00? Well, I did! Lucky me.

Later, this same day south of Red Deer on Route 2 near a whistle stop designated to be Banden there was a sign that simply said, "Rest Stop." Needing a rest, I stopped.

It was much more than a rest stop. There were numerous well-spaced campsites, fire pits, and picnic tables. A fellow camper approached me while I was cooking up some much needed fresh coffee, and one for now plus two soup meals in waiting. The fellow camper who appeared to have been lodging here for some time shared that the price for overnight camping was a more than reasonable $6.00 or $8.00 Canadian. Had there been less time left in the day and had my desire to return to Precious and home diminished, this site would have afforded me an ideal respite.

There was free water and good water coming from the same spout. I took over a gallon from the free good one. There was what appeared to be a tiny general store, more the size of a concession stand with attached restrooms. Not one to pass up a free restroom another vote was reached to take full advantage of this non-state and/or province sponsored campground. As I entered the concession stand door, there was a young Canadian guy sitting on a chair behind a counter, chuck full of all kinds of goodies from candy bars to camping necessities. I gave the young guy as fond of a greeting as I could. He had a look of utter delight on his face but seemed incapable or at best reluctant to throw a greeting back at me. His stammering or muttering was interrupted by scuffling sounds coming from the floor behind the packed counter. Up popped a medium to full figured young Canadian girl with one hand seemingly tangled in her dishwater blond hair. She gave me what could best be described as a functional, but kind greeting while catching her breath as if she'd just climbed a long high flight of stairs which I was near certain wasn't the case unless the head of the stairs emerged behind the well-stocked counter. Had I carried a dictionary in, I would have looked up all of the possible definitions of concession. At this time, I'll let your dirty mind wonder where it may. I'm not sure if there was any foul play going on or not. It would not be fair to this young, lustful couple to engage in speculation but he did reflect the ardor of a guy who will long remember this day.

Holding my "I got you" expression at bay and replacing it with my "humble understanding" expression, I sought directions to the restrooms. Untangling her hand from her hair, she pointed down a short hall and told me kindly to take a right. With my "I got you" expression battling me to surface, I thanked her and spun abruptly down that hall. Once there at the single deep to the floor level urinal I could discern some whispering interrupted with periodic giggling.

It was here at the urinal while having a grip on life that what to my wondering eyes did appear, two primitive but very inviting shower stalls. With very little hesitation, I returned to my counter mates and inquired how much for a shower. The ever-so-near-to-ladyhood girl smiled through those big soft cow like eyes of hers, still projecting the merriment of youthful exhilaration and spouted to me that the showers were free as she half sat / half laid across the mid to upper torso of her silent but seemingly delighted counterpart (pun intended).

As I had been contemplating my next shower for over 24 hours, I now knew what it was like to strike gold when you least expect it. Something akin, but not identical to the young gentleman at the counter. I briefly shared with them that aside from lakes, rivers, and gravel pits, this was the first freebie I'd come across (good choice of verbiage considering the circumstances). It seemed to miss its mark as it shot rapidly over their heads. Indulge them, they're young.

Some extended time was spent in that shower but not so much as to wear out my welcome. The shower had no hot or cold levers. It had a push button on/off device similar to starters on some vehicles that the majority of you readers are far too young to have witnessed. Pushing the button in would give you approximately ten seconds of slightly above lukewarm water. I didn't care. I pushed it many times. It would have been convenient to have a third arm, or better still, a willing shower mate. Much like you, my thoughts would return to the counter mates and conjured up youthful bliss long since out of reach for this author, but content that it still abounds out there in the present as it once did in the past.

Upon leaving, I felt an obligation to thank them once again. I honestly wanted to thank them for the shower but also felt the urge to thank them for the host of fantasies they indirectly bestowed upon my brain pan and memory banks. I held off on the latter and felt a better man for doing so.

Now, they almost responded in unison to my inquiry about the origin of this oasis. It had been the concept of a long since passed Canadian free camper who had realized a need for other such travelers, hit a jackpot somewhere, bought the land, and built it, and they came. They did not know his name as he had passed long before their time, but they were true and devoted followers of his dream. If, and better still when, there's a Free Campers Hall of Fame, this gentleman's photo should be at the top of the wall. In fact, this site would be a great location for that very Hall of Fame.

Realizing that I hadn't paid a red cent for any and all of the treats that had been freely given to me, nagging obligation arose to cough up some gratuity. I headed for an antique pop machine near the exit door. The wistful voice of the young female enchantress flowed casually against my back and up over my shoulders, "Our pop is cheaper than the ones in the machine." She knew exactly the words that would control and guide any decisions any male now or in the future should have to make. Let's just say she was extremely mature for her age and leave you male readers even more to ponder in your spare time. Don't all of you try to flock up there all at once. There's not that many campsites, and I intentionally gave up only a vague description of the location, knowing someone needed to take a stand to protect her near, but not spot on, innocence from a potential onslaught of lonely but eager suitors. As my Dad once said after successfully reading that look of desperately lonely or horny adolescence in my eyes, "Son, there's many fish in the sea and you have all the bait you need." Forgive me Dad for all the times I questioned your wisdom in the past, for I was wrong.

Anyway, mesmerized yet another time on this trip by her waif-like bleat, I accomplished a slow semi-controlled turn back in the direction of her summoning. She had for the time released her hold on her counterpart and now had a left hip resting against the side of an older style mini fridge still popular in most Econo Lodge rooms. Tempted to order a case, I came temporarily back to my senses, obligated to the true fundamentals of the free camper philosophy and aware that a large order would lose her respect, one 16 ounce for $1.25 Canadian became my selection — what else! Canada Dry ginger ale…

Feeling the desire to continue this dance with her, I continued to scan the counter. Note: there was no discernible staircase behind it. I remained somewhat under her spell while at the same time under the watchful scrutiny of her current partner who appeared somewhat more alert now when compared to our initial encounter. Bless his heart. He remained all smiles though putting my dancing trepidation's more to ease.

At last, with my counter scanning coming full circle, I admitted that I could not make up my mind sequestering their suggestions. Without missing a beat, she retorted, "You can't go wrong with banana bread." Firmly but humbly I responded, "Did you make it?" "As a matter of fact, I did" came back at me. I told her I'd take a ton….I jokes! I took a piece for $2.25. No silly, a piece of the banana bread. Your fantasies have no boundaries, do they?

There is no photo here of this couple as the author felt it best to protect their innocence. Wish I'd have taken one for myself though.

Saw a sign off of Route 2 just before Fort MacLeod that read "Head-Smashed-In Buffalo Jump." Had to check that one out even though evening had already snuck up on me, fifteen kilometers west towards the flip side of the same Canadian Rockies I had traversed in my northward trek some days ago up the western side. I'm now on the eastern side of those same ranges. Should we change "Home, home on the range...." to "Van, van on the range..."?

Sounds like all of us could use a little break right now. You amateur geographers might want to reference your atlas again. The author and van are almost directly east over those beautiful mountains from previously described Fort Steele. No matter how you slice it, those peaks are worth a peek from any and all directions. If you're planning your own trip to this region, you won't regret it. Again, I'm one of the luckiest people on the planet.

PHOTO #2 - ENTRANCE TO PARK HEAD-SMASHED-IN BUFFALO JUMP

Turns out, the "Head-Smashed-In Buffalo Jump" was a place that had occupied a sector of my mind's dream realm since hearing stories of places like this long before I could read. And now, I had stumbled upon it quite by accident. It's not on the map. Had it been dark, the sign would have snuck by. In fact, fatigue was battling with me. Fatigue strongly suggested that we seek lodging and continue south tomorrow towards Precious. Fatigue succumbed to curiosity as we did yet another ubie just to quench the curiosity.

Following a well-kept but meandering road, the pangs of curiosity were more than satiated. See photo. I did not care that I had arrived well after closing time. I seemed to have the place to myself, but was soon welcomed by mom and two of her fawns. Note the teepee behind them all being swallowed up by a marauding shadow of the silent evening. It was here that I was granted and marveled at the sound of utter silence. That's a sound I have forever cherished. Even the slight breeze appreciated it so much, she traveled through in hushed respect. I sat there for a long while just gobbling up the stillness, the teepee, the tame deer, and boundless distances of the great plain laid out dozing in the sun before me. I considered free camping here for the night but thoughts of being run off in the mid-

PHOTO #3 - DOE WITH TWO FAWNS/TEEPEE

dle of the night by a prudent civil servant convinced me to rechart my course and stay the night in Fort MacLeod with a plan to return here first thing come morning. And, who knows what might pop up in Fort MacLeod for entertainment?

While turning the van around to leave, I was surprised by yet another gift given freely to me via mother nature. Something had snuck up behind me and was studying the old fat guy sitting in the van. Turned out to be a young button buck whose curiosity stayed firm long enough for me to snap this photo of him probably debating whether to stand firm or join mom and the two fawns on the other side of the van. If you look closely, you can make out the east side of the Canadian Rockies buried at the end of the great plain way out there where it meets the sky.

PHOTO #4 - BUTTON BUCK

In contrast with the above absolute tranquility, I had recalled doing 78 mph this morning just north of Calgary and holding up traffic. That marauding shadow that had over taken the deer back in Head-Smashed-In Buffalo Jump had lumbered down the plain and overtook me in Ft. MacLeod. Though not completely dark, it was a time of heavy shadows. The town itself seemed to be yawning in anticipation of a long welcomed sleep.

It didn't take long to cruise the handful of quaint streets that were empty to the point of letting us know that the majority of inhabitants had long since set their alarms to face the challenges of tomorrow. The biggest attraction was a life-size replica of Fort MacLeod that dominated much of the downtown. I was too tired to appreciate it.

Attention travelers. I could find no Walmart hostel in this area. I was forced to strike out on my own, alone in these wilderness plains. I soon came upon a gas station/quick stop reminiscent of home except for an elongated parking lot that could have housed a small airport.

While paying for a new fresh tank of gas and too tired to mince words, I approached one of the most interesting looking specimens of mankind ever to have blessed one of my days. He was the cashier for the truck stop. He was attired in regular street clothing acceptable for our time and place. He was an India Indian sporting a pleasant healthy smile that in itself was a positive greeting of warm and immediate friendship. What stood him out from the maddening crowd was his hair. I've spent considerable time in an attempt to come up with proper appropriate adjectives to describe it for you but so far nothing has popped up to do it justice. The nearest I can come to it was something like Our Gang's Buckwheat's hair on an overdose of acid.

After he calmly assured me that I could find serene respite at the far end of his parking lot, I could only respond with a simple, "Thank you," and that I liked his hair. I asked him how old it was as it appeared like a large sprouting tree clinging precariously on top of his head with branches reaching far beyond his shoulders. He told me he had had it all of his life. Had I met him in the 70's, I'd have wanted one just like it. I doubt very much that anyone who comes into contact with him is not taken aback, but delighted in the scene before them.

I chuckled myself to sleep that night as images of him and his hair continued to drift into my thoughts. I'm so glad when those images of him return for my pure enjoyment. I would think that he has a following. Obviously, he has powers or I would have a photo of him now. My bad....

Drove 524 miles today.

DAY #23, 7/23/2016

Slept semi-well. Not peeing as often as usual during the night. Bad indicator for a potential kidney stone. You've never lived until you've passed one. It'll put an end to any good day you may be having. And if it's a particularly nasty one, it could put an end to any good week you're having. Some former fellow female employees who have had children and also a history of passing kidney stones all replied, when asked, that they would rather give birth than pass another kidney stone. There are only a few avenues for conclusion given the possibility that early people's may have experienced them. Drink lots of water each day with a shot of citrus concentrate and after that, drink a lot more. End of current public service announcement.

Awoke this morning at 6, had a fine breakfast of processed Pollock that looks like crabmeat. I presume it is good for you. Course set for return trip to Head-Smashed-In Buffalo Jump and, we're off. Just outside of Fort MacLeod, there was a doe with a buck behind her wading across the Oldman River. Unfortunately, traffic was at an uncomfortable level preventing a photo opportunity. I raced the van the rest of the way to my targeted destination with the already risen sun pushing from behind the van as if it was as eager to get there as I was.

Finally there, it was near on difficult to find a parking spot in the lot that offered well over or in the vicinity of 50 +/- spaces. Last evening I drove all the way up to the Interpretive Center that resembled Aztec or Inca like ruins built into and near the summit of the mountain mesa as a 1981 project sponsored by Unesco. Official opening by the Duke and Duchess of York occurred in July of 1987. For you scholars of British history, the Duke and Duchess of York were none other than "Lady Di" and what's his name. I, with a handful of other excited travelers, were transported to the entrance up high on the mountain face surrounded by the still silent mystic plains as far as the eye could reach that rendered one of the best parts of yesterday by a grandmother like cheerful electric bus driver whose joy for her job was obvious. It was she who carried us to the top of the mesa once parking was found at the base. It was one of the best $13 (Canadian) that I ever spent. They sport the usual gift shop, cafe, theater, etc., but also have four other easy accessed levels depicting different tools, utensils, weapons, artwork, skeletons, dwellings, etc., dating back over 9,000 years.

Head-Smashed-In Buffalo Jump Interpretive Centre

Oki, Kiitsiksiksimaatstsimohpinaan

Hello, We Welcome You

Keep in mind the method of killing buffalo by panicking the herd over unseen cliffs raising 20 meters above the abrupt stop was of necessity as this all occurred before the natives acquired horses to help them in the essential quest for red meat. It became an honored feat to participate in this process back then. Legend has it that a young brave wanted to get up close and personal to witness the short flight of the poor buffalo, but became trapped between them at the base of the cliff and got his skull crushed. Hence, the name for this location.

Maybe so, but the exhibit highlights that those flying bison who were not done in by the sudden stop, were summarily dispatched by club wielding natives proficient in wielding their 5-10 pound rock headed clubs. Dangerous, but necessary work. The natives feared that any survivors would return to the herd and warn them of the trap.

PHOTO #1 - BUFFALO JUMP

It took little effort to climb stairs to an upper trail viewpoint that leads out on to a walkway for a closeup view of the actual cliffs. One found a well-kept cement path with guardrails sporting periodic signs warning of rattlesnakes encounters should one leave the relative safety of the path.

I got a freebie guided tour catching up with tour guide and Blackfoot Indian (Donovon) while marveling at the views thrown at me free from mother nature once again. I should rename this book, "I'm Such A Lucky Guy."

Donovon reported to our small but attentive group that it was estimated that at least 100,000 buffalo were harvested at this site. He pointed out the mounds below the cliffs clearly visible in the photos were grass covered heaps of buffalo bones from animals processed immediately following dispatchings. The original drop was 20 meters but due to the accumulation of bones discarded after processing, that drop was now just 10 meters. Do the math.

Back inside, I was approached by a Blackfoot elder named Peter Strikes With a Gun. No, he didn't have a gun. That was his full name. Peter showed me large photos of a group of Blackfoot men taken in 1923. The one with his arm folded and looking defiantly away from the camera was Peter's father. I shared with Peter that my mother had been born in that same year.

PHOTO #2 - BUFFALO JUMP

Peter and I sat on a comfortable couch within sight of the photo of his dad. We shared each other's philosophies targeting world peace and why people should choose to get along. He enjoyed one of my favorite philosophies, "If we had no countries, who would we fight?" Totally forgetting that I was still in Southern Alberta, I also shared that oftentimes I wish the Native Americans would have won, as I felt their beliefs and way of life were far superior to the white man's. He responded with a hardy short laugh, bit it off, and said, "Well, that was war."

Turns out that my excellent tour guide, Donovon, was Peter's son. They consented to a photo of them standing in front of Peter's Dad's photo. They seemed pleased to grant my wish. Three fine generations of good men. A copy was promised and sent at the juncture of this writing. Peter told me that he thinks he is about 74 years

PHOTO #3 - PETER STRIKES WITH A GUN, HIS SON DONOVON AND HIS FATHER

old but cannot be sure as they do not count calendar months like we do. They count the warm seasons and the cold seasons. I thanked Peter and Donovon far more times than necessary. I recalled in their presence how I had longed all my life to visit just such a place and had stumbled upon it quite by accident yesterday. This stop over will probably be remembered as the icing on the cake to my long enjoyable journey through Canada.

After yet another "thank you," Peter said, "It was an honor." I retorted that today had been my honor to meet with them, to talk with them, and to learn from them. Peter was a very humble man, but proud to have flown to Washington D.C. as a representative of his people at an international powwow back in the 70's. He was most proud of his current responsibility. He displayed a photo of a teepee with a black buffalo painted on it dating from the 1800's. His grandfather had been "the keeper" of it and now he, Peter, is "the keeper" of it.

Lunch on the Oldman River picnic grounds, finished off the pollock I had had breakfast of earlier this morning. I had completed this culinary effort as I had grown tired of buying ice and having it melt in 1-2 days in my guaranteed up to 4 day cooler. It was here that agreement was achieved to plunge south down Route 2 and reenter the U.S., leaving great and fond memories of Canada and her peoples as specters in my rearview mirror. Did I say that I was the luckiest guy in the world?

PHOTO #4 - LAST DUCKS IN CANADA

Stopped to take quick photos of a family of ducks but most hid behind the clumps of grass jutting up inside the pond. Beyond, below the dense moisture laden clouds in the center, you can make out Chiefs Mountain making up yet another splendid portion of the great Rockies viewed from the east side this time. With dense clouds doing their best to abate, just a handful of miles from Photo #5 is a better/closer view of Chiefs Mountain. It's the rectangle to the right of the telephone pole.

PHOT⊙ #5 - CHIEFS MT.

Not long after the above shot, with depression lingering, I was soon to leave "Oh Canada" via the lackluster border crossing back into the U.S. at Carway where Canada's Route 2 merges into U.S. Route 89 in Montana.

For seemingly being in the middle of the middle of nowhere, it was a surprisingly busy place. I had a shorter wait in line than heading northward through the Roosville Crossing some odd days ago on my way north. I entertained my time waiting by mentally retracing my steps up the west side of the Rockies, the cross over, and then the southbound drive down along the east side.

Within a matter of just a few minutes, it was my turn to seek and gain permission to re-enter my home country. I recalled having to surrender my tiny can of mace to the Canadians at Roosville and felt quite comfortable that no such occurrence would repeat itself here, and it did not. However, the young man sworn in to reject or accept my re-entrance seemed overly determined to rattle my tree. Granted, I was a lone elderly (in his mind) man re-entering our country possibly appearing to need a bath, change of attire, and definitely in need of a shave, but I was not a terrorist or even anyone short of that. Did he have access to documents noting me on one of Richard Nixon's watch lists of subversives to his enriched way of life back in hippie days? Don't know, doubt it. Tricky Dickie probably had all the documents as well as a lot of lost tapes buried with him. Anyway, this guy grilled me as if he was sure that I had been up to no good in Canada. I played a respectable game with him for several more questions bordering on an insult to my character. He never backed down but backed off his futile attempt to "get my goat" possibly reading my body language that I was contemplating going over there and shaking the fecal matter out of him should his line of insinuating epitaphs continue. With a wave of his hand and verbal grunt he approved my bid to re-enter. Note to self: if elected, have our border crossing guards train with the Canadians who still get the job done, but in a much more courteous and respectful manner. Don't forget - first impressions are lasting ones. One wonders how many foreign nationals this same border guard left a lasting impression of our country with today?

PHOTO #6 - CUT BANK RIVER AND RAILROAD BRIDGE

Continued on Route 89 South past Browning. It didn't appear like they cleaned it up anymore than when I hurriedly passed through it on the way north. The town and location does have potential, but it would need a lot of cleaning up before I'd go barefoot through it.

Just southeast of Browning, we cut the cards and the winner chose east on Route 2. Just out of Cut Bank I spotted a railroad bridge linking the east and west bank of the Cut Bank River. Decided this would be a great view to enjoy some supper with. All the fixins had already been prepared by our cook. The menu consisted of: potato soup, ramen chicken noodles, beef jerky, raisins, dried veggies in water, and a toothpick. A meal fit for a king, that is, if you're in a third world country, but our troupe wasn't complaining. These fixins were found just inside the sliding door on the passenger side of the van.

The sliding door was left open to air out the van while supper was consumed. While supping, I noticed that the wind had kicked up its heels showing off for me in a loud whistling crescendo that began pelting the now rocking van with dust and debris. Just as I was enjoying this exhibition of strength, some of the smaller items stored under my elevated bed tumbled out of the van onto the ground, interrupting one heck of a good supper complete with a wild west show sponsored freely by the wind. I caught them before they rolled and tumbled too far from the van. Once secured, it was difficult but not impossible to close the sliding van door. More difficulty was realized when opening the driver's side front seat door against this same performance by the wind. It took almost everything I had to open the door, slither in quickly with the wind having the final say by slamming the door shut on my left side as if I had somehow pissed it off back somewhere on the road and it took til now to catch up with me.

I realized now that the items that I originally thought had tumbled out of the van had in all actuality been sucked out of the van. In the reasonable safety of the van, I applauded this recent display granted freely to me by the wind, but I don't know if it heard me as it was way too loud. The van was now swaying in the force of the wind with jerks and thuds as if the wind had almost transformed into an intermittent solid mass banging to get at me inside the van.

Just about the time I was going to listen to the radio for tornado warnings, the wind ran off to the east like a madman on fire would run zigzag looking for water, and the deafening sound of the wind was replaced by the deafening sound of it's cousin, the silence.

The van started up immediately as if it had slept through this entire scenario. I felt good about that as it needed a rest anyhow, and I didn't want her to become skittish every time the wind picked up. We limped cautiously into the small town of Cut Bank seemingly none the worse from our run in with the wind. Noticeably absent in the town of Cut Bank was any population out of doors. I suppose everyone had taken shelter from the wind that I had wrongly assumed had singled us out for a pounding. Had anyone been out doors in this treeless high plains landscape, they could probably apply for citizenship in the Dakotas or further east by now.

I hadn't experienced any winds like that since I lived with Eskimos in Alaska. Picture this. The kids would tie each other together with rope for safety. The older kids would hold a lidless five gallon drum under their arm. They would rapidly turn to face the wind and it would shoot the drum from them at designated targets prearranged awaiting the wind. Great game. Most became quite proficient with their accuracy in spite of their weapons of choice.

I stopped in Cut Bank for gas and coffee still enjoying the silence except for that presented to me by fellow travelers or locals who had taken respite inside from the wind. No cheerful spirits here. I reminded myself that I was no longer in Canada and that I might want to downplay the cheerfulness. I felt better as a somewhat cheerful cashier asked where I was from / headed for / etc.

It was not before I took Route 15 south at Shelby that I came to realize just what he meant when he said, "You're not leavin' now are you?" I wished he would have been a tad more persistent with attempts to have me stay a bit longer in Cut Bank.

Novicely thinking the wind had run it's course and had petered out back in Cut Bank, I hadn't noticed it barreling down behind us and then cutting across Route 15 not far out of Shelby. With such force that the van shook and then quivered and before I could pull from the roadway, one of the bungees came loose and the kayak almost slid or better put, was nearly shoved from it's moorings secured there so adeptly by my friends Hugo and Calvin back up at Trapper's Lake. No offense regarding their abilities. Nothing could have stood up to the force of the Shelby winds this day. Much to their credit, with God's help, and memory of their instructions, I was able to re-secure it under an overpass crowded with bikers who had sought refuge there from the onslaught. They all looked like they had bikers' PTSD or like folks who should have lingered for awhile longer in Cut Bank.

With a cautious eye or two on the kayak, we limped back down to Great Falls with the cruise control set on 50 mph. Oftentimes, it became necessary to brake down ever slower as for unknown reasons, the wind would up her game in near successful attempts to shove us off of Route 15. The kayak held on for dear life.

I witnessed numerous immature infant tumbleweeds careening across 15, some in front and some behind us, no doubt in a futile search for their parents whose larger wind catching frames were already tumbling ahead into Wisconsin by now. Somewhere in Wisconsin someone's saying, "Aw geez, that can't be adult tumbleweeds headin' for the house can it? Aw geez."

A range cow blew backwards in reverse across Highway 15. It would have been utterly impossible for that hooved marauder to ever be the same. There's some veterinarian up in Cut Bank or Shelby thinking, "Aw shit! I knew I should have taken that seminar on bovine PTSD last year. I wonder if I can still get it online?" Note to reader: your author took complete poetic liberty with regards to the paragraph outlined above and it was exceedingly fun.

The boy, the van, and the kayak made it to Great Falls. The wind had died down (another great phrase), it hadn't given up. It just scurried off somewhere north of Great Falls and laid hidden in the silence waiting to jump up and bully its next victims.

Possibly knocked somewhat senseless by Mariah, efforts to relocate the beloved hosts at Walmart were less than successful. Though recalling limited success with this method on previous occasions, consult was requested at a stop light. A guy and his female companion eagerly attempted to accommodate. But with several frustrated beepers behind us, we were forced to continue our directional discourse yelling back and forth from opened windows at 25 mph after the light had turned to green. While successfully keeping our vehicles from nearly sideswiping, and although his helpful attempts were intermittently broken up, I discerned that he, followed by a corresponding repeat from his companion, had yelled, "Go back to the light we had first met at and take a left." Visions of John Candy in "Trains, Planes, and Automobiles" surfaced again with strangers yelling from their car to tell him he was going the wrong way. Thanks again John!

Anyway, the very next right was taken after appropriate hand gestures, shrugs, and winks were thrown to my latest directioneers to sincerely thank them for their helpful roadside assistance, manners, kindness, etc. It appeared that the both of them were operating from previous experience with this same scenario. Whether it was from the rendering or receiving end will remain a mystery. A second right returned us to the starting gate followed by the left and there she loomed in all her compassionate warmth, understanding glory, and ready to grant all needs, the Lady Walmart. The guy and his delicate better half were spot on with their directional inputs. There should be an appropriate noun or at least a short phrase to designate and give honor and praise to folks who can successfully pull this off at 25 mph. Kudos to you all! My hat is off to you! Directioneers is a scant start up for the work you do.

Entering the Grand Lady, I connected with an electronics guy for help in re-setting my phone that had appeared dead since her long night on that wet hill near Radium Hot Springs on our first night in the lovely Alberta. The first thing out of his mouth was, "This is your lucky day!" I replied that, "I wish you would have driven here with me from Shelby." I did not go into a long explanation or even a short one for that matter. "Hit some wind, did you?" was his retort. How did he know?

Wanting to get as far as I could from the wind, I just stared at the phone in as polite of a fashion as I could muster. He caught on immediately and said, "You weren't holding the power switch down long enough. You have to hold it down for three seconds." With actions accompanying his words - Walla! Ping, and my phone was up and running as if to welcome me back into the States. I thanked him graciously and complimented him with, "I guess this was my lucky day, after all." Come to think of it, I have them quite frequently. I should be less morose.

We had traversed 350 miles this day. Not bad when factoring in the wind. Oh yea, I almost forgot. Remember when I was relashing the kayak up south of Shelby, I forgot to submit for your contemplation, it nearly ripped my shirt off and succeeded in lifting it over my head. Wish I would have had someone take a photo of that, but I couldn't see anyone. But now you've got the picture.

I called Precious back in Cumberland on my re-established phone while enjoying the relative peace and quiet inside the van, except for the comings and goings in Lady Walmart's parking lot. Compared to the screeching, howling wind, it was a much welcomed interlude. I talked her ear off for over 12 minutes. She did squeeze in that predictions indicated that Cumberland would see 100 degrees Fahrenheit for the next three or more days. She heard, "Well, I'm not hurrying home now as it was a mere 83 degrees Fahrenheit out here and slightly windy."

Looks like my head will be slightly higher than my feet tonight what with the configurations in pavement at Walmart of Great Falls. Seems like more and more folks are utilizing this travel mecca as there was much jockeying for position between travel coaches from million dollar campers towing their Range Rovers, to a little lop-sided pop up that two young brothers just climbed into after passing close by my van with what looked like a loaf of white bread from the Dollar Store. Why hadn't they been instructed to purchase it from Walmart? If I weren't so tired, I would have given their parents a what-were-you-thinking lecture. Attitudes like this could cost it for all of us free campers. Didn't your parents teach you about gratitude? Apparently they skipped over the chapter covering karma also, numbnuts...

Snap Quiz! (Not an open book test - you're on your own)

How fast does the wind blow near Shelby, Montana?
A. Faster than a speeding bullet
B. Faster than a dead parrot
C. Faster than vomit from a bus window
D. Extremely fast with _____king gusts
Answer: A bid llA

How many of you became perplexed when you tried to read the answer upside down and then spotted the A? Needless to say, many of you fell short with regards to your responses on this one. Don't let your morale take a plunge. I blame myself for much of what has taken place at this juncture. I should have given you more frequent quizzes to help you remain more vigilant. But instead of employing techniques to safeguard you against the expectant complacency, I squandered your keen sense of observation with verbiage that may have inadvertently overwhelmed your capacity to decipher, recall, and form your own conclusions regarding content and format. And for this, I am sorry.

One way to pick yourself up if you find yourself down in the doldrums is to hit the pavement running, increase your sales contacts, realize that you're a member of this unique but ever growing family of extraordinary people who have seen the light through these passages and know that it is their duty, their honor, their calling, to share this light with those few who have somehow missed it or have been overlooked by some time and space sequences, that you and only you have the power to unlock and bestow unto them. Surely by now you've felt it. Maybe you didn't recognize it for what it's worth. Let that little warm feeling down in the pit of your stomach arise up through your heart and hurtle itself from your lips with all knowing / all seeing assuredness that this book should be in every home. Stand and deliver! Do what is right! Don't do it for me! Do it for yourself! Do it for your mother! Do it for your future!

For those few of you who may be struggling with these sales tips, please feel free to send me a self addressed, stamped envelope, ten dollars (cash only) for shipping and handling for my personal "Additional Hints and Observations Regarding Time Proven Sales Techniques Over the Ages" pamphlet. You'll be glad you did. There are hidden riches here. All you have to do is mine them. Take a break from all this reading. Get out there and hit the pavement. If lethargy's got hold of you, just send me the $10 and lay low til your pamphlet reaches you (please allow 8-10 business days or more for delivery). If you're making a career move based on selling this book you may be able to write the $10 off as a business or educational expense. There I go again, inadvertently giving away more trade secrets and it looks like you're the sole beneficiary. Take advantage of me. I don't care. Remember, we're family. Those of you who've met your sales quotas can simply read on. Enjoy.

DAY #24, 7/24/2016

Got up at 7:20 AM, hot and muggy, and grabbed a cart and feigned some shopping techniques to throw off the employees but they knew. They always knew. Trying to pull one completely out of my hat in what may have been a futile attempt to throw them off, I approached a young stacker of shelves (sounds like one of Robin Hood's men). His shirt identified him as Stephen. So, he was Stephen, Stacker of Shelves. Do you catch the correlation here with Robin Hood now? Good. I asked Stephen if they had a bathroom. He immediately replied in current English that, "Yes, they have one for men and one for women." With a wide and happy smile he pointed to the sign that read "Rest Rooms" between the seafood and meat section. A great choice for aspiring Walmart management off-setting the need for non-cost effective air fresheners. No offense to Stephen, but the thought had crossed my mind that he may have ridden the little bus, missed few if any school days in all of his twelve years, and still managed to graduate with a special diploma. Don't read anything negative into this. I've found that folks like Stephen, Stacker of Shelves, are generally happier than the rest of us, worry less, have more friends, and make for the most loyal and trustworthy companions one can find. I had a lot of best friends and one of the best of the best was a Yupik Eskimo who'd have gone to school with Stephen, Stacker of Shelves, had he lived in these parts. Soon after we met, my Eskimo friend told me that he couldn't read or write, he could only see, speak, and hear. Think about that for a minute. What really constitutes genius? I still love you Wasile.

I achieved my goal in the bathroom and like you was simply delighted initially. It was my own fault for not surveying first, but I was in a hurry. There was no toilet paper. Fortunately, if I can utilize that adjective, they had that rough brown hand towel paper you must pull carefully from below while hoping it's not the last sheet.

To my dismay, it was 10-11 feet from the commode. I never really took the time for an actual measurement so let's just say it was a guesstimate. You don't even have to visualize the next few minutes there unless you're the type who's inclined to do so. Regardless, just accept that you're dealing with a resourceful traveler who got along just fine.

At least now, I could stand back up and wash my hands. Curses! There was no soap in the dispensers, neither #1 or #2. Desperate, I snuck quickly into the woman's bathroom and they had soap. I passed a lady coming in as I was going out. She said nothing but gave me a curious smile. I wasn't in the mood for explanations while departing with rapidity.

Doing my part for Walmart, I bought $4 worth of that same pollock from the fish department sensing it was becoming a real staple for me. Hey, it beats raw hot dogs by a long shot. So, to calculate it from yet another angle, my sleep over and morning BM cost me $4. How do you like those apples?

As I was leaving the store, a no-frills, middle-aged, management-looking lady with thick, black, rimmed glasses called out in a stern but encouraging grandmother-like voice, "Stephen, don't forget to clean and restock the restrooms." Stephen replied slowly with, "I already did."

Better safe than sorry, I found myself pulling into an oil change a few blocks from Walmart. Although it was just a few minutes before 9 AM, the man inside told me they didn't open until 9 AM. I parked directly in front of the nearest bay and busied myself inspecting the tie downs doing their job of securing the kayak since the winds of Shelby.

As has been their custom throughout this entire trip, a tall motley, pock faced Native American appeared from nowhere. As quick as it takes to print this, he shared the following to me: he needed $180 for parts for his broken down truck, he was Nez Perce, he was 200 miles from home, he had been in a coma for three months after a bad car wreck, and had broken his neck, back and pelvis. Following this disclosure, he showed me an impressive scar on the back of his neck to act as a qualifier guaranteeing his story. Although there was a slight detectable slur to his speech and just a faint roll to his gait, I was willing to give him the benefit of the doubt after concluding that his tale did not seem rehearsed and was worth $5 Canadian. He asked me if I had a drink then added, "Water or anything." I told him I only had water. Before I could get him some, he and the $5 Canadian vanished into the morning.

While unsuccessfully searching for the vanishing Nez Perce and reflecting how they had befriended and saved the Lewis and Clark expedition after abandoning their initial plan to kill the entire party following one of their females sharing that white people had once helped her, time and reality beckoned to me when the automatic bay door raised ever so slowly revealing the same gentleman who had revealed to me that they didn't open until 9AM approximately three minutes ago. Turns out, this guy was the manager or possibly the owner. To describe him as a drill sergeant would near bullseye him, but I would have to go as far as to depict his personality some-where between the Soup Nazi and Mail Call. I'm not going into great descriptive detail here. Let's just conclude that he probably doesn't get too many repeat customers. I will say this that I was glad that I hadn't bitched about the $77 I spent for the oil change in Canada when he gave me his bill for $80 (American). Back home, it would have been in the $40 range.

Photo #1 for this day was above Belt Creek. Note the holes in the cliff outcroppings to the right. The result of those manmade holes led to a great silver rush in the 1800's. The white speck on top of the mesa to your right is a ranch house. I'm assuming the thin brown line going up the right center of the valley is a road to the ranch. Hope they have a snowplow in the winter.

PH⊙T⊙ #1 - BELT CREEK SILVER MINES

This spot was so bright, sunny and silent except for a mild whispering warmed by the sun breeze that seemed to want to hug you, I decided, "What better place to have lunch." The van had a nice resting spot in a small pull off with natural orangish sandstone boulders whose silent duty was to keep the drunks and elderly from sailing their vehicles off this vertical faultscarp (cliff) and down into Belt Creek maybe a thousand or so feet below. If you find yourself sailing your vehicle in the directional selection made free for you by gravity, you're probably not going to become all that picky regarding the exact height as much as the exact halt to your sailing adventure.

After checking for rattlesnakes and things that go bump in the day, I selected one of those flat sandstone boulders that fit my butt and needs so well that it was as if it had been there just waiting for me for a millennium give or take a tad. While crunching on my first bite of dried veggies mixed in a half cup of warmish water, the warm light of the precious sun from behind me pointed out something shiny in the grass not two feet from where my feet were dangling lazily over my warm boulder seat.

I could give you a hundred guesses, but you nor I would want to waste our times on just such an effort in futility. No offense towards your abilities as a reader of the fine arts. I'll get you to it right away. What were the chances of finding a used syringe in such a majestic setting? Slim to none. Well, slim won out on this one.

Some SOB had sat on this very boulder and shot up. I was going to take a photo but why waste one on some trashed junkie's total disregard for all that's everything. I was afraid to touch it. So much for an all inspiring mystical location for having lunch. I did scoop it up with an empty plastic pop bottle securing the red lid, and determined to give it to the first game warden, park warden, state trooper I came across.

It was at this time, after prospects of an enjoyable lunch had vanished, that it dawned on me that this was part of the same Belt River drainage system to which I was the grateful recipient of the coldest bath I'd ever had in my life on my way north a handful of days past. Time is still flying! Don't waste one day!

PHOTO #2 - CASTLE MT. RANGE, HIGHWAY 89, MONTANA ABOVE RINGLING

Copious miles south above Ringling on Route 89, I came across a local officer of the law who was sitting along the highway scoping out the Castle Mountain Range with his binoculars. I gave him the syringe laden empty Coke bottle and told him my story and as good of a description of the spot I had found it as I could. He shook my hand, said thank you, and spun out doing a ubie that left visible Montana dust to that already clinging to the surface of the van. He wasn't Barney Fifish, but displayed a stare that seemed to read that he knew more about this syringe than I knew.

PHOTO #3 - NATURAL RAMP ROUTE 89 SOUTH

In keeping with my original log, it is warranted that I beg your pardon for an interesting omission that happenstance threw into my path earlier this morning in the southern outskirts of Great Falls.

Perplexed as to where to pick up Route 87/89 south, I sought directional assistance at the nearest quick stop. Attempting to kill two birds with one stone, refueling sounded like a good idea also. Left with my own devices, I pulled in next to the nearest available pump.

Climbing out of the van, I noticed two guys on foot cutting across the lot who looked to be locals. I said, "Hey guys" and they turned around in unison — baseball caps on backwards/muscle tee shirts….as soon as these ladies turned towards me, I became immediately aware of my mistake. I had inadvertently stumbled upon an alternative lifestyle times two."Hey guys", to my surprise, they took no offense, and, if anything, appeared delighted in my mistake. Like I said, they both sported macho outfits, but with a discretionary prudent approach without flaunting it which no doubt served them well given their chosen locale.

If anything, they were gracious and accommodating. They shared that they had no car but would gladly ask at the restaurant across the busy intersection where the larger of the two worked. Appreciating their kindness, but still muddled trying to find words to somehow retract "Hey guys," the best I could come up with was, "Thank you, that's OK, I'll just ask someone else."

They smiled, about faced and maneuvered their way through the busy morning traffic across the intersection towards the restaurant. Glad that I had not hurt their feelings and glad for their unwarranted warm reception, while pumping gas, I turned back in their direction and there they stood on the opposite corner in a lengthy full embrace without kissing as morning traffic raced by.

I was happy for whatever kind of love that they had as it was genuine and should be the envy of many so-called marriages I've stumbled into and upon. What's that saying, "Ain't love grand?"

Not to gawk, I hesitatingly looked away and busied myself with my refueling at $2.19/gallon, pushed "yes" for the receipt and scanned the grounds for other potential directioneers. Before making that calculated selection, for some reason, I took an additional peek towards the lovers embracing at the corner, but they were now just one, the smaller of the two now traipsing back over to me with big, brown, cow like eyes and perfect toothy smile, looking like she'd just had a good morning's bath and staring a giggle like hole through me upon eye contact. She had that Joan Jett look to her now as she pointed straight down the highway in front of the quick stop, and without detail or too much fanfare told me I couldn't miss it while still melting me with her giggling stare.

While the melting continued, she just stood there awaiting my next input. Looking back on it, she was a little thin. Maybe she was just trying to get a little breakfast out of me. My 70 year old chauvinist mind summoned thoughts that this 25 year wanted a brief morning's interlude of all the sex I could throw her way. I'll never know as the best I could come up with was, "I owe you one for that" while looking into those cow like eyes and trying to give her a complementary, "You're so cute and under different circumstances and decades of distance, I would enjoy plying your shores."

She gave me a departing giggling stare and off she skipped across the parking lot. Twenty miles down 87/89 I realized I had been mesmerized once again and missed an astounding photo opportunity. She was probably in their small apartment now thinking how much she missed her granddad back in Kansas. Anyway, regardless of their selections, I hope they both make it. Their gentle kindness and giggling eyes surely made my day.

Bounding back south ahead of the syringe in the Coke bottle down on Route 89, thanks to excellent directioneering at the hands of a demure femalien in a small apartment in Great Falls, I came upon this natural ramp in the landscape to the right of the highway just south of Clyde Park. It served to spark my geological curiosity for a few minutes and gave me a brief respite from thoughts of the cute persona and enchantress in the small apartment.

Two things learned on this trip: 1) absolute need and cherishment of warm positive human contact, and 2) the vast number of humans eager to fill that void. Can I hear a shout out for, "It is better to give than receive!" Another observation: don't wait for a stranger to "chat it up" with you. Initiate contact and more often than not, your target will be glad you did and will respond in kind much to your own pleasure. It's hard to tell who was the giver and who was the receiver in this scenario, but both seem to receive more than they gave. Can I hear a shout out for "win, win situation."

Not many miles from the natural ramp, I took a little sashay from Route 89 across a small bridge. I've always been fond of small bridges, but fonder still of what lays beneath them. In this case, a small meandering trout stream of the Montana variety. Unbeknownst to me, just a mere 1/4 mile further south, I was elated to find what the small stream noted above fed in to. I had rediscovered the mystical and history filled legendary Yellowstone River. I had discovered her in my youth back in the 70's and this was my second chance to gaze upon her power and magnificence. Oh, if she could only talk. It would probably be in Crow, or Pawnee, or Cheyenne, or Sioux, or many other hosts of Native American dialects she had picked up on her never ending journey through milleniums.

PHOTO #4 - TYPICAL MONTANA TROUT STREAM

She still displayed her green/blue raw power, but it was as if she were simply passing through silently, whispering on her own journey listening and carrying, but ever so determined and patient to reach her destination. Like so many others I'm sure, I once again became overwhelmed that I had been born too many centuries late as it would have been such a splendid adventure and honor to have lived here in peace with the Crow, with the Pawnees, with the Cheyenne, with the Sioux, with all the others, with the buffalo, and with the Yellowstone. Oh, for a time machine. Maybe if we are truly good in this life we may be allowed to select the time frame for the next. Guess where I may be? Where will you be?

Seeking bathing accommodations along the Yellowstone became an effort in futility. Those places you could get to the water were so crowded with other visitors, I opted out on the bathing quest for fear of an indecent exposure charge or just simply terrifying young children.

Photo #5 - Guide awaiting passengers with his back turned to the camera on the Yellowstone.

PHOTO #5

Photo #6 - Looking upstream from the Springdale Bridge towards pilings left from former bridge. Note a luckier guide with bikini clad babe as passenger - tough job....

Searching the map for potentially less populated locales, Route 78 south off of Route 90 looked promising. On the way south, I snapped a photo of some jagged distant mountains that reminded

PHOTO #6

me of Seneca Rocks near Franklin, West Virginia, not far from back home.

PHOTO #7

The road began to narrow as I came toward the Custer National Forest entrance to the west of Luther, Montana, but the map promised numerous campsites and further prospects for bathing site potential. To my chagrin, there was not one campsite not already occupied. It was OK, though. This area was so remote and desolate. It appeared to be an ideal spot for anyone seeking to be eaten by a grizzly or mountain lion, or mountain man for that matter. The hair on the back of my neck stood at high alert the whole time I was seeking a spot to bivouac here. Something or someone laid in wait for me. Maybe it would have been better had the sun shown up today.

PHOTO #8 - ENTERING CUSTER NATIONAL FOREST

So, without reluctance, a photo was taken just before leaving Custer National Forest just west of Luther, Montana. Note all of the traffic on this narrow road. If you look closely, the shining spot to the right lower center of the photo is a portion of the infamous Rosebud River of legend.

PHOTO #9 - LEAVING CUSTER NATIONAL FOREST

During my escape from Custer National Forest, I came upon a small roadhouse type of bar slightly larger than the fenced in electrical box directly across the highway that probably served the whole area. Though it was still early evening, I was hospitably greeted by a handful of locals who appeared to have already got a running start on the evening within and/or out of the confines of said bar. There were two staggering girls and I think three staggering guys. I wasn't sure on the count of the guys as it was more fun keeping track of the gals.

Fearing reprisal for air pollution, I stayed within the confines of the van. Confident in the power and hold my TV network cap had on sober folk, I couldn't help but to turn it loose on these unsuspecting inebriated celebrants.

All staggered somewhat closer to the van. I witnessed the magic of the cap and one of the ladies even asked, "Where are the cameras?" I feigned confusion which drunk folk seem to accept as a universal personality trait.

One of the three cowboys with a higher pitched voice than his tall/rugged stature led one to expect spouted, "Welcome to Nye." His Montana twang had a resonance and pitch that led one to think that he had made his way west from Mississippi.

I didn't care. All of the locals, transplanted or not, cheered me right up and made me feel that I had landed at the far end of a hospitality driven welcome committee. What made me feel even better about it was the fact that they threw out the welcome mat before they caught sight of the magic cap.

One of the male members in this troupe had a beard. He also had two short grossly distorted arms/hands like those unfortunates labeled thalidomide babies. Nothing held him or his spirit back. He performed an impromptu jig at my van door while cradling a beer in his arms without falling or spilling a drop. He jokingly said, "You almost hit me when you pulled in!" I shot back a retort, "I had you in my sights but let you go!" My own quick humor served to endear me a step further with he and his fellow troupers as they encouraged me to join them for the evening. With a dark history of being beat up in bars for having too good of a time, I elected to remain noncommittal. I've seen these most pleasant of times go south in an instant. So why take a chance at ruining the good thing we'd had already.

I asked if there were free accommodations for the van's boudoir here this evening. With their cumulative help, we all concluded that sound sleep would probably be run off should I elect to attempt to sleep in the small confines of the bar's parking lot. Their next suggestion was to pull the van across the highway and park along the fence surrounding the electrical box. It was easy to detect that my expression following suggestion #2 led them on to suggestion #3. Three or four of their number pointed back down the road less than a quarter mile away towards a bridge. For unknown reasons or perhaps because mileage this day had far exceeded 300 miles, I hadn't recalled crossing the bridge.

Anyway, to make a long story even longer, turns out that bridge in question just happened to pass over the legendary Rosebud River and there was a boat ramp with a few primitive campsites. Let me venture this challenge to the reader. The author, being a historian and enthusiastic history buff, was faced with a quandary of choices. Take your time now. Did he choose suggestion 1, 2, or 3? I commend your intuitiveness. Yes, he chose #3.

Not wanting to hurt their feelings, but still wanting to let them know how much I appreciated the free spirit that engulfed their troupe, I thanked them graciously for their hospitality and suggestions, told them how far I'd traveled this day, how hungry I was, that I would be camping at their suggestion #3, having supper, and if strength permitted, would consider joining them for further frivolity.

Knowing my own history of weakness for liquid spirit indulgence and it's potential for ruining a good thing, in my heart, I knew that I would probably choose the safer of these selections, and spare the troupe and the author any undue and regrettable recourses. To this day, I often ponder what more that evening could have had in store had I returned. If any of you Nye Montaniacs get hold of this piece of work, please contact me. I'm sure I could come up with 4 or 5 free copies and a promise to take you up on your initial offer.

You may not be able to find Nye, Montana on a map. But if you're as lucky as I was, you just might stumble upon it.

With the sunken sun telling me to move it, I claimed one of the two remaining primitive campsites along the Rosebud. I sat between this medium sized liquid freeway and listened to her rippling heartbeat pushing me towards sleep. Hunger lingered, though, nipping at my heels and I hastily fired up the Coleman and knocked off three knockwurst weiners on rye and yet another dried vegetable delight. Oh joy!

Still within shouting distance of the drunken troupe who had given me such delight, I swore I could hear one or two of them howling into the darkness that had silently captured us all. Feeling that it was not only a social courtesy, but a good way to thank them once again, and to let them know I was about to succumb to the bedroll, I hailed them with my own howl. We exchanged howls two or three times or more until we were all satisfied that all was well with old and new friends in Nye.

Noticing bits and pieces of corn on the cob left in the fire pit by thoughtless predecessor free campers, I was left with one last chore before lights out. Note: it is advisable to any thoughtful camper free or not to utilize this time tested safety measure corn cobs or not. Build up and save in a container preferably one with a tight sealing lid (size may vary but one cannot appreciate enough the necessity of that tight sealing lid) what will become over a short period of time rancid urine. Sprinkle around the exterior of your tent or vehicle liberally. The author did so in combination with the bleach/mothball containers previously utilized as we were still in high bear country. Any bear in his or her right mind will think twice before breaking that barrier and the odor will mask the scent of leftovers dropped by predecessors of the careless kind. I believe this was not the first time I shared this recipe with you. Bear with me. I'm old.

A gentle rolling thunderstorm with vague distant lightning tried to sneak by in the night, and would have passed unnoticed had the next door free campers young shepherd slept through it with the rest of us. I suppose he was doing sentry training barking at every vague distant lightning flash. Why had he not responded to my earlier howling? He eventually gave up as none of us responded to his warning or possibly he was hit by vague distant lightning.

DAY #25, 7/25/2016

Arose at 8 AM after a much welcomed sleep. I wrote another piece once way back and recalled a line in it that went something like this,

"Couldn't sleep last night — too dirty."

Facing up wind, I paced slowly over to my neighbor free campers who had secured the third and last of available primitive campsites at this pristine rendezvous and were just stirring up themselves. I was offered and accepted a steaming cup of strong black coffee, and was invited to breakfast with them by the head and friendly patriarch. I thanked him but declined as I had already breakfasted. I wish that my shyness, and not wanting to intrude would have allowed a full acceptance as the spitting bacon's aroma was beckoning so temptingly.

While others of this extended three generational family continued to emerge from a cluster of small tents huddled up to quite a large camper, I held court with the patriarch while the matriarch turned bacon in a large wrought iron skillet and assisted lesser matriarchs in preparing their yawning/babbling third generations for another day somewhat oblivious yet curious minds some of which now focused on this stranger in camp.

Between slurps on that delicious steaming black coffee and enjoying the emerging generations, I shared some of my back trail with the patriarch and what appeared as a friendly, but silent older son of the patriarch, no doubt responsible in part for some if not all of the emerging third generations.

I can't recall exchanging names as there was no real necessity for doing so. My patriarch friend confirmed my beliefs regarding three generations, and shared that they camp here as often as time and life would allow and had permanent residences not too distant. He asked if I'd heard the wolves howling last evening and said, "It nearly scared the wits out of the shepherd." I had no response beyond a smile and, "That was a welcome storm last night." Just noticing the shepherd peering out from behind the son's blue jean clad legs, trying its best not to make eye contact with me, but nevertheless remaining acutely vigil.

After a fond farewell to my neighboring Montana free campers, a hike to find a suitable bathing area downstream on the Rosebud was cut short and deemed futile at my first opportunity to test the water temperature with my hands. Recalling a former bathing experience on the Belt River some days prior, I was more than willing to forego duplicating that experience in the Rosebud. Options remaining: remain reekingly debased or attempt another portable shower.

Digging out the patched up portable shower and finding she still held sufficient and luke (who was this Luke?) warm water, she was strapped to the van's roof rack supports. Accompanied by my bathing suit, step stool for sitting, wash rag, and Ivory soap (biodegradable), an enjoyable shower was taken on the far side of the van away from my neighboring free campers and absolutely free of ice crystals.

A guy named Levi got real rich selling the first blue jeans to the cow punchers. That time machine could make the author rich as a grand scheme would have been to sell the portable shower to the cowboys, the Native Americans, and anyone else who preferred bathing without screaming. I'm surprised the Mormons hadn't come up with this idea...

PHOTO #1 - SNOW CAPPED MOUNTAINS ABOVE NYE

Refreshed and feeling like a new man, exploration of Nye became my morning's calling. The bar I'd met the memorable troupe at last evening was locked down, and appeared to have survived the night with but minor scratches and bruises. One broken whiskey bottle in the parking lot with complicity of several beer cans in differing degrees of crushation scattered on the portico and across the lot, each no doubt with it's own silent recollection of events best forgotten.

Taking a little dirt road off of the main highway I could not pass up this shot of the opposing topography all living under the same big sky. It's a foregone conclusion of why Montana is called "Big Sky Country." Oh yea, those are snow capped mountains reaching up to that big sky. They help to keep the Rosebud and others, shall we say, fresh and cool.

PHOTO #2 - NYE SCHOOL

Looking down my back trail, I snapped a shot of Nye School. Yea, that's it, the little thing with the green roof right center. It doesn't have to be big. Population in Nye keeps it small. The tree line outlines the course of the Rosebud.

PH⊙T⊙ #3 - SUNDANCE TRAIL

Saw a sign that read "Cemetery Road." Curiosity pulled me along the ruts and I came across another sign at a gate that read, "Sundance Trail." A third sign there read, "Keep Gate Closed." I could see cattle in the distance eyeing the gate, so I closed it. Say thank you, Robert Redford.

Serenaded between ruts by fine pebbles crackling in unison with the van's tires, we crept up a rolling grassy hill where a wrought iron gate designated our destination at the very well-kept and maintained cemetery of Nye. Should in the future, you too, pursue a quest to the cemetery of Nye, do so prior to nightfall or do so only at your own peril. Study the photo at your leisure but in detail. Suppose you had sought the cemetery of Nye after sundown only to be greeted in the night by the same greeters who welcomed the author by day. Your mind would run amuck conjuring visions of marauding banshies, with shadows, and sounds that would scare the bejesus out of you. Unfortunately that child's mortal terror still lingers in many adults to this day. There are indeed way too many ogres and mon-

PHOTO #4 - NYE CEMETERY

sters waiting to pounce on you just like when your parents doused the light and closed the door, leaving you to fend for yourself in the dark against unsurmountable odds, from all those horrific beasts living under your bed. So, go by day.

With the security of the lighted day and a host of black companions who seemed to be deliberating in unison, "You don't look like the guy who feeds us but you'll do in a pinch," I made my way to the gate they were protecting and enjoyed myself as much as one could while visiting dead strangers in the cemetery of Nye. There were no remarkable headstones. Serene and peaceful would be good descriptive narratives with a view to die for (no pun or disrespect intended).

Engulfed with a feeling of utter neutrality, I headed back to the van. I had my first optical illusion for the day. I could see a cow's head in the back of the van. Hastening my pace through his companions, not as cool as John Wayne in "Red River" but just as fast, I came upon my illusion. He was aggressively licking, but not chomping, on my red rear bungee. Don't know what was on it but he sure took a liking to it. I think he was the third one from the right in the photo but I can't be sure. With a minimum of verbal persuasion from me, he relinquished his brunch, bawled out a muffled bovine obscenity back at me and loped back to his buds.

After leaving the burgers to be, a quick brunch of pumpkin snack bars, cheerios, dried bananas, gulped down with a cup of cold java was ingested atop a hill on Route 78 looking south toward Red Lodge just past Luther.

Again, dramatic scenery abounds, but beyond the capacity of my throw away camera to render it justice. A constant companion since the winds of Shelby warrants written record at this point in our ride. The companion is one of sound, though its origin has never been found during this trip or after. A ventured guess would lead one to the kayak, the tie downs, the bungees, the luggage racks or God only knows what else. This sound, if it could be called that, would fall somewhere between a shovel scrapping a wheelbarrow and a spoiled, heavy, two year old female who is not getting her accustomed way. The sound was intermittent, but was a companion for days and then some, causing the author to pull over on more than several occasions to ensure that the kayak remained at her moorings, and that no foreign objects were punching holes in the roof of the van.

Turning the volume up on the radio did help some. Screaming didn't. But just when the author was considering a purchase of some heavy duty hearing protection, the sound left or we left the sound, no more shovel, no more two year old. It remains and shall remain a mystery. No source was found, no scratches, no dents, no nothing! Could this have been an audio mirage? Were there unworldly spirits at work here? Don't know, don't care, just so glad it or they are gone, like a person who thinks you like them dropping by for the weekend.

That's a statue of "Plenty Coupe," a Crow chief of renown courage, wisdom, etc., sitting atop his horse (no name given) at the Visitor Center in downtown Red Lodge.

PH⊙T⊙ #5

Fantasizing about "Plenty Coupe's" life and scanning my map parked along side his noble statue, I realized that I was within striking distance of Cody, Wyoming. I'd never been there, but free camper chatter had always been positive. It was only about two inches on the map. The map's scale delineated one inch to be about 30 miles. So 60 miles, give or take, and I would meet what was left of Buffalo Bill's West.

I followed 212 south out of Red Lodge after a brief stop for a greatly needed large Tastee Freeze zebra. A lot of places call them zebras now. You know, the vanilla/chocolate swirl. Not to toot my own horn but I feel I inadvertently played a major role in the renaming of this soft serve delight. I'll give you the short version. Years ago, while traveling across Idaho and standing in a short line outside a Tastee Freeze, I overheard a little boy ask for a zebra. It was perfectly logical to him and I for one applauded his poetic license at such a young age. Frequenting Tastee Freeze and/or Dairy Queen almost daily, especially when traveling, I made it a point to request a large zebra. It seemed to stick and after a few years, the Tastee Freeze folks didn't even look at me funny. So folks, we owe this pleasant distortion of linguistics to a little boy in Idaho. Step right up sonny, there's a free book in it for you. He probably has little zebra lovers of his own by now.

PHOTO #6 - ENTRANCE, BEAR TOOTH MOUNTAINS

Not long on 212, I entered the Bear Tooth Mountains. As there was no safe pullover to allow a photo, I stopped as soon as I could and snapped this shot looking back north towards the entrance. Not very formidable or foreboding. But wait, there's more.

Just up the highway was a welcoming sign hailing to travelers that they have entered the Bear Tooth Scenic Byway in Custer National Forest. Don't be fooled, we're not close at all to the legendary Last Stand. Custer's name appears in a lot of parks and places out here. In his day he was lauded a hero, which I think he was in the Civil War. But, a study of his exploits out here reveals a narcissistic, egotist with his target on the White House, willing to sacrifice the lives of women, children, and elderly Native Americans as well as his own men, to help him achieve his goal. I think the Native Americans missed the boat when they made him a martyr. I think their purposes would have better been met had they captured him and just gave him a good spanking.

Things started to get a little hairy as we ascended up the scenic byway — hairpin turns along this narrow two lane road brought fear akin to an old time roller coaster ride. But greater so, as you can recall, there were no roller coasters coming from the opposite direction and hogging more than their share of this narrow winding pathway. The few pullovers were extremely crowded with lots of folks on cell phones calling loved ones back home in case things got worse.

Some say primal like fear makes for a stronger person. I'll be glad to let you know if you can somehow get me off this God awful mountain. Photo #7 gives you some idea. If you look closely at the photo, you can see the road behind me left center. How do you like the dried sticks and twigs in the foreground that will prevent your plummet? Awe inspiring beauty. Awe inspiring fear. I found no petrified forest but numerous petrified travelers.

PHOTO #7 - BEAR TOOTH MOUNTAINS

To think that Native Americans traversed these mountains only increases the admiration I hold for them. They needed no forts. They had the Bear Tooth Mountains.

What was thought to be the summit held the largest pullover with much needed restrooms. Adrenaline boosting passages only served to increase urine production. God help those who had been constipated this morning. There was a slight scent of vomit the nearer one came to the restrooms. It was strangely silent in the restroom, except for an occasional, "How much further to the bottom?" Note: the author can only attest to communion in the men's restroom. Speculation would be our only consult as to chitchat in the ladies restroom, but it surely does peak one's curiosity. Could you imagine what a hidden microphone would pick up?

I suppose the state of Montana provides volunteer drivers to assist people too terrified to drive on. My dear old state of Maryland provides this free service for folks whose fear will not allow them to traverse the Chesapeake Bay Bridge. I'm not exaggerating. The fear was real and I was only driving a minivan. There were lots of much larger motor coaches, etc. probably looking forward to getting back to Iowa, Nebraska, or Kansas.

PHOTO #8

The restroomed pull over was like an oasis, but you couldn't stay there forever. Many folks had that 1,000 yard stare as if this was as far west as they were going to go and may just try to settle in here. Time didn't seem to erase expectation. Just after snapping a photo of a guy feeding a carrot to a chipmunk (note size of chipmunk), I looked up and behind us to find that this was at best a false summit as one could make out vehicle after vehicle winding their way up, and away from us ever so cautiously while others rode their brakes hoping they wouldn't fail trudging down towards this oasis.

It was monumental decision time. Should we retreat and return back down the trail we had just escaped death on and find an alternate route circumventing the Bear Tooth? Or, should we man up and climb even farther up into these fearfully exhilarating lofty crags? Just as Custer had decided so many years ago, we will push on with determination and courage knowing that our course had already been preset by a higher power, or something along those lines.

Begrudgingly we left the oasis behind and once again rejoined the meandering cautious string of all sorts of vehicles occupied by folks who shared common themes; was this a bad decision? Will we ever make the top? What's going down the other side have in store for us? If I would only have known the kid would have been throwing up that much I would have brought a second bucket?

Slowly grinding out foot by foot, inch by intrepid inch, the summit was reached. No real fanfare. No jubilation. Just a gravel pull over. How folks on foot or horseback must have felt reaching this majestic crown covering vistas of visual pleasure as far as one could stretch sight. Just maybe, the white knuckled fear accompanying our ascent proved worth it. Folks I spoke with at this point seem to share similar rationals.

Take for instance the photo of Ron and his daughter from the northeast corner of Connecticut. Ron shared that he drove a truck most of his life but was glad to have his daughter in the driver seat coming up. She openly admitted that she was near tears with fear coming up especially on all those "S" bends. I think I asked Ron if his hair was that white at the bottom and he was noncommittal. A

PHOTO #9 - TWO OF THE FINEST PEOPLE ON EARTH

PHOTO #10

brief but a great time was spent with these two while the two Ron's tried unsuccessfully to out joke the other. Maybe it was relief or high mountain hysteria. We were around 12,000 feet vertical. I'm sure thinner oxygen also played its part predictably, but well. We parted as friends after she snapped this photo of their new friend found along the highway of life.

Note: Study both of these photos. It's still July and yet we are above the snow line. Maybe the white from the snow made my hair appear whiter, but maybe it didn't. This was no place for those suffering from faint of height. I'd like to hold a party for everyone I met on this trip. Someday I may. You can bet Ron and his daughter will get an invitation. If only I had gotten their full names or addresses! And that's the only reason we had to zap their faces. Damned high mountain hysteria! We intentionally left the smiles for you. Hopefully, they'll read the book and get a hold of me and I'll make the appropriate changes.

That's another reason to read this book. What if I had run into you on this trip and you didn't even know it?

PHOTO #11 - MOUNTAIN LAKE

I can only accuse the oxygen deprivation or high mountain hysteria as the culprits that caused your author's negligence in not swapping full names, addresses, and phone numbers with two of the finest people on Earth. Maybe, they were mountain angels sent to caress my soul reminding me of the goodness of mankind leaving me with one of the fondest memories on the road to somewhere and it only took them but a few seconds — yep, there's a good chance that they were angels. I never saw them leave and, poof! We were all gone.

How's that for a mountain lake? Took this shot near pull over where I met Ron and his daughter. Two guys in their late teens pulled up here, took one look at each other, jumped from their Jeep, and ran headlong rapidly down towards the lake until they were lost from my sight. Was it drugs? Was it oxygen deprivation? Was it high mountain hysteria? Don't know, but they were sure having fun when I last saw them. I didn't wait around, I had a mountain range to descend.

PHOTO #12

Going down the south side of the Bear Tooth's was not near as horrendous as coming up the north side. Sure, there were places prayers were offered regarding the van's brakes, but the Dodge manufacturer had done his homework. Afterthought: maybe Dodge would like to sponsor this trip or future ones....

Notice how softer and inviting the mountain range gestures to those traversing down the south end of the pass. Quite a contrast or just more oxygen.

Near the bottom of the south pass the blue of this nameless lake stopped the van so I could snap this shot. I watched a guy, his wife, and son catching one trout after another using flies under bobbers from this same lake.

PH⊙T⊙ #13

I stand corrected. I just now noticed on my map that the elevation of Bear Tooth Pass is 10,994 feet, not the 12,000 noted above. However, my map is very old and elevation could have decreased some since the time my map was printed. In the meantime, I am left to stand before you with this most sincere apology.

The oxygen deprivation may have also been the primary culprit in causing me to forget telling you about a guy on a red Honda cruising bike. Still far from the bottom of the south pass while cruising through more "S" bends (Note: Precious calls them kiss-your-ass-turns) at a moderate, but comfortable speed allowing our driver to take periodic gawks while still maintaining safe maneuverability of the vehicle, a dangerous occurrence caught up to us. The dangerous occurrence was bestowed freely upon us by the gentleman on the red Honda cruising bike. Before I could even pick up sight of him in my rearview mirror, he took the opportunity to pass us briskly on a double lined blind bend with no true regard for his own safety, let alone anyone coming up the pass in the opposite direction. He made it safely but it wasn't of his own doing.

Maybe oxygen deprivation played no part in my forgetting this potential for fatality. I suppose it is easy to forget mentioning (I'll call him a person) of that mindset. I guess that's one of the reasons they're like they are. Had anyone been coming in the opposite direction, memory of him would have long outlived him. If anything, he did help me to meet my quota of at least one bonafide asshole per day. No book for you. Suffer asshole!

PHOTO #14 - CLARK'S FORK

Before any of us knew it (note: the subtle reference to multiple personality disorder — I can assure you that I don't have it and none of the rest of us do either). Anyway, before any of us knew it, we were entering Shoshone National Forest in Wyoming still on our quest to see Cody. Sounds a bit like a dime store novel, doesn't it? Take the first left onto Route 296 and welcome to Chief Joseph Scenic Highway. The Nez Perce fled all the way here being pursued by Uncle

Sam since leaving their lands in Oregon. They fled through here just trying to reach Canada.

That's the Clark's Fork of the Yellowstone. Didn't the Nez Perce save and assist Lewis and Clark when their expedition was starving itself to death trying to get across Oregon in the early 1800's? Yes. It's been 200+ years since then and this is how we thank a peoples who rendered a great service in the making of our country's history. Remember: when we did it, we called it "Manifest Destiny." When other countries do likewise, we call it "Genocide." Shame on us! Forgive us Great Spirit.

Look closely at the photo. Two of the dots in the river are fly fishing, that's their white truck with Virginia tags seeming to creep into the photo. The landscape here was of the rugged, yet pristine variety, little if much P.P.P. (permanent people population).

Chief Joseph allowed his worn out band to rest for a day or so and this rest was their undoing. Uncle Sam's well fed, well outfitted warriors forced the Nez Perce to finally surrender on October 5, 1877, just 30 or so miles from the Canadian border. God, I wish they would have made it. They were forced on to reservations. I think in flat Oklahoma. For the rest of his life, Chief Joseph begged our government to allow him to return to die in his homeland in Oregon, but they wouldn't let him. Which came first, greed or inhumanity? It's a toss up.

Crossed over a small feeder stream that feeds into Clark's Fork of the Yellowstone. Good luck loping leisurely along this stream. You'd get kilt on the rocks (no reference to Scottish men).

Closely related to Photo #15, the author and the rest of us piled out of the van and ran back to the small bridge that crossed feeder stream highlighted in Photo #15. Turning around to return to the van, the author couldn't pass up a shot of the mountains - see high things beyond the van. Clark had passed right through here after briefly separating from Lewis seeking the best trail to follow homeward. One wonders if he was taken aback the same way the author

PHOTO #15

was by the absolute splendor these mountains throw at you. I wish that I could talk to him and Chief Joseph. Some day, maybe.

Unfortunately for all of us, the author ran completely out of film here. Spellbound once again, this time by the streams and mountains, he unknowingly took his last shot. The unfortunate part here had to do with the driveway (gravel) you should be able to make out just to the right and behind the van. There lay on a knoll the most beautiful rustic ancient cabin looking to be still in use, but sealed off with an iron gate with the feeder stream gurgling past. It was small

PHOTO #16

but sturdy, unpainted wood that dated it's many years. Some painted trim around the windows, faded green, but holding its own. If there would have been a for sale sign on her, I would have gone all in, pending monetary shortcomings.

The author had estimated that he would use 3-4 rolls of film on this endeavor. We just passed 7. The author had no plan or intentions of writing a book outlining this journey, but here we are over 300 pages in. The original intent was a simple journal and a few photos. Travel plays a great game with the mind. Better than me chalking up another 300 words in a failed effort to describe this symbiotic relationship, why don't you get your ass up off that couch and do some traveling for yourself today. You don't have to go far. Find a trail to hike you've never trampled. Take the car, the bike, or canoe down any path you've yet to traverse. I can guarantee you contentment, happiness, wonder, excitement, intrigue, and the like. If you go there and these passions don't assault your senses, I have a number for a doctor who will see you. I feel sorry for people trapped on that couch. You probably know one. Push him or her off that couch. Steal the couch if you have to.

Chief Joseph Scenic Route 296 was aptly named. So much beauty, so little film. Lots of mountains. Not like the Bear Tooth, but still imposing. Whole mountains of red ochre. The spectacle and contrast of varied assortments of other hues from the trees, the land, and the sky thrown in all together as if to say, "Pick me, pick me for your favorite" were enough to convince me to run back out here if I can find a camera in Cody. I've got nothing to do. I'm retired!

After taking a right onto Route 120 coming off of Chief Joseph's route, it wasn't long before we coasted into Cody at what looked to be rush hour. Actually there wasn't all that much rushing but seeing more than 10 cars in the same spot at the same time constituted a rush after the topography we had covered already this day, save for the one big parking lot back up in the Bear Tooths.

Cody is a small town, a mingling of the old and new west. I saw no sky scrapers but lots of older stone buildings epitomizing the old west waking up one morning, looking out a second story window, and realizing that change had already come.

The old wooden buildings most of which had already burnt, collapsed, or were torn down had made way for a grand conglomerate of turn of the century unique structures that confidently called out, "If you think my exterior's a pleasure to the imagination, you should come inside where most of the players were busy making history long before your grandfathers were toddlers."

Pretty much exhausted and hungry enough to eat anything/everything that didn't have a pulse, and the tedium of dried vegetables in lukewarm water dominated my quest for a substantial eatery.

Yea, by now you got me figured out. Strategically situated in the heart of town on Main Street, with a few vacant parking spots left beckoning to the van, we cozied on up to the Chinatown Chinese Buffet. The van even seemed to cherish this time of rest and revitalization. She had carried me without so much as a whimper again this day as she had on all those days preceding.

Before dashing in and succumbing to the empty echos ruminating from my belly, I collected myself (what a great phrase) and put in a call to Precious, updating her on highlights since my last call. Not as enchanted as I assumed she'd be, her response seemed more focused on what my previous Asian buffet had cost me. Damned the torpedos, full steamed vegetables ahead! I was willing to gamble. Isn't that what helped make our West great, men who were willing to gamble in hopes of a brighter future? They put it all on the line. I strode up the steps to the front door willing to make my own personal sacrifice and put it all on the line. Granted, this time "the line" was the buffet line and gamble it was. But I remained steadfastly confident in my gastronomic ability to consume and conquer.

I walked gingerly up to the hostess. She looked confused. She said, "Is that you Charlie?" My reply was a thudding, "No." She said, "Oh Charlie, where you wife?" I assumed she realized her mistake, when I countered with, "Who is Charlie?" She said that, "He was a local sheriff who dines here frequently, usually with his wife in tow."

I got a table. Everything I sampled (and I sampled near everything) was of the finest quality with some accent towards western spices cause we're out West, I guess. The barbecue pork was to die for. Unfortunately no frog legs but I'll survive. The price tag would be $12.50. That represented a steal when compared to the quality of the cuisine and host of selections.

The hostess ambled up to my table and with a very warm grin said, "Is everything satisfactory, Charlie?" My answer to her was, "Absolutely" through a hardy laugh. I really wish Charlie and his wife would come in. I want to see the resemblance.

I returned to the buffet line knowing that seconds were no immediate threat, other than potential for clogged arteries, water retention from the salt, etc. You only live once. Who knows, this could be my last meal. May as well make the most of it.

By the time I returned to my table, it had been cleared and four fresh plate settings were looking up at me. Everyone became very apologetic to the point of embarrassment. Maybe it was a ploy to encourage grazers like the author to move on. Don't know. Didn't care. In a blink of an eye, three place settings were gone and the fourth awaited my second arrival. The busboy was a new female employee probably still in cultural shock as she witnessed single American patrons putting away enough food in one setting to feed her large family back in Nanking for a week.

Full to the brim, I gladly accepted my fortune cookie and bill. If you ever find yourself in Cody, go there. As I approached the register there was my hostess doing double duty as my cashier now. I calmly told her to, "Put it on Charlie's tab." We shared a big laugh together once more.

I told her I would like to meet Charlie and may look him up tomorrow. She seemed to want to change the subject. She informed me that she owned this restaurant with her husband Xiren Zhang (sounds like a Chinese warlord that you wouldn't want to mess with, doesn't he).

I asked her what her name was. She said "Lu." She also taught me that in China, the woman doesn't take the husband's last name but she had to, here in the U.S. Her first name is Yi pronounced Ye, but she enjoys being called Lu.

I told her about my trip and that I would like very much to include her in the journal and/or any subsequent writings. She was delighted and gave me her approval. She gave me her card. I asked if I could take her photo for the journal, etc. She seemed excited and pleased and gave me a second nod. Remembering now that I had no film, I sequestered directions to the nearest Walmart from one of her male waiters. He was spot on. Twenty minutes later and I was back with my green Fuji throwaway anxious to enter her world one more time. She spotted the camera and before I could snap her photo, she suggested, "Let's take our picture together." Actually it sounded more like "togezzor" but I didn't care. She brought a height of warmth and friendliness that matched many if not all contacts I'd made on this journey. Maybe it was the spices but I think it was just her honest demeanor.

CHINATOWN
Chinese Buffet

金 廚

(307) 586-9798

YiLu Zhang
Xiren Zhang

937 Sheridan Ave.
Cody, Wyoming 82414

She gave my Fuji to the male waiter, who had helped me earlier with directions, and he made our friendship immortal. She said she wanted to be in my book and that she hoped I would use the photo in the book. I told her that this photo may make my girlfriend (Precious) jealous, but that I was sure, if they met, they would become fast friends as she and I had.

Determined to retrace my steps back to those red ochre mountains to share a shot or two for you, I realized that I had made a wrong turn out of Cody and ended up 18 miles in the wrong direction at a primitive quick stop in Ralston. I limped back to the Walmart Hilton in Cody to spend the night there full of Lu's great provender and full of fond memories of a vastly rewarding day.

PHOTO #17 - "LU"

DAY #26, 7/26/2016

It was 63 degrees Fahrenheit at 7 AM. I had slept well. I found myself in the men's room of the Waldorf, whoops, make that Walmart. I was at peace with myself having taken a local free real estate flyer in with me for comfort/toilet literature.

As I entered my chosen stall, in pops two Russian mafia looking gents. They spoke broken English with heavy accents. The first line that I could make out from the smaller of the two who was larger than me was an encouragement, "Now, don't get angry." The one that was between my size and his larger angry partner took the one remaining stall and plopped down immediately with no forethought to clean any debris left by predecessors. You can learn a lesson the hard way like that.

As I reached quietly from my perch to secure the lock on the door, it became immediately evident that half of the lock was missing. The screw holes were still there but the much needed other latching counterpart was with Elvis. Visions of getting to meet Elvis rumbled through my brainpan now as the larger of the two began an escalating rant in Russian or some other Middle European gruff diction with no English inserts. I knew I should have taken Russian back in cowage when I had the chance. I took economic geography instead after learning that the guy who taught Russian counted spelling.

I discarded my literature and held the bottom of my stall's door closed with my left hand freeing my right hand up to perform point pressure on any possible holes stuck, shot, or carved into me by the ranting Russian, all the while sensing that economic geography is not going to help get me out of this situation.

You become vividly aware of how adrenaline kicks in at a time like this. Albeit, most of you haven't feared for your life at the black hairy hands of a large, ranting Russian in a Walmart restroom stall at 7 AM. But I'm sure you can sympathize. After thought: just think what Stephen King could do with this scenario.

Anyway, everything seemed to go into slow motion. Even the escalating ranting seemed at a greater distance now. The smaller of the two had taken the one stall to my left. I could see cheap looking bright white flip flops (had to be European) with red velvety silk-like sweat pants dangling down over them and the exposed black hairy toes protruding above the fake marble flooring.

Let's label his stall #1 regular stall. I had taken the only other stall. Let's label it #2 large deluxe handicapped stall. I prefer the extra space. I know what you're thinking. Although the van's tags don't confirm it, I consider myself handicapped with all the infirmities that accompany age, football, motorcycle wrecks, getting beat up in Alaska two straight Christmas, etc. And besides, what's the chances of a truly handicapped person with tags to prove it coming in here at 7 in the morning? I'm not ashamed to admit that I wished for one to come in here now so I could at least have a potential witness to my murder. Or, maybe, this was karma catching up to me as this was not the first time I had utilized a handicapped stall.

What kind of cruel person designs these restrooms? Correct me if I'm wrong. Why is the handicapped stall always down farthest from the door? Shouldn't it be closest to the door? Maybe it's paybacks as they do get all of the best parking spots outside. I know most troopers will fine you $250 for parking in a handicapped parking spot. Let me know if you've ever heard of a fine for illegally using a handicap stall in a restroom. I'm assuming the fine would be the same in a male or female restroom. Please let me know. I'd like to hear from you.

The stall neighbor just inches from my left foot seemed to take on the role of animal trainer. Though it was impossible to decipher his words, cause I had chosen economic geography. He seemed to have a way with the ranting one as he spoke infrequently between rants in a firm but soft melodic chant that one might employ to calm an angry junkyard pit bull who had broken free of his chain. I felt it was working as the rants were receding into angry mumblings with less volume. There was an occasional rant but shorter with less intensity. I felt like giving the trainer a high five but the positions we were squatting in rendered that impossible. How do you say gratitude in Russian?

White European flip flops and red silky sweat pants beat me to the finish line. Like, was there ever a contest going on? I was too busy wishing I had an escape route or an Uzi. Hell, I could be constipated for a couple of days after this. Fear had thwarted my original mission here.

Anyway, the ranting one had straddled the seat in #1 regular stall seemingly before his trainer had cleared the door. Now the angry pit bull was just inches from my feet. Thinking I had better chances with the trainer, I feigned an unnecessary flush and hastened with a put on limp out from the deluxe stall. A man will stoop to any level to save his hide. Red silky sweat pants was still out in the sink area. I nodded to him with a primeval bathroom courtesy gesture. My gesture was returned with a deadpan stare, not so much an aggressive one but one that had, "I bet he took economic geography" written all over it.

With some renewed sense of command of the situation and knowing that any good trainer would sense fear, I casually strolled over to sink #3 of 3 and began my shaving regimen. White flip flops now exited with a more favorable nod to me upon leaving.

Not knowing his partner had vacated, the Russian remaining in #1 regular stall began and continued a conversation with him in Russian for some time until he realized there was no response. I intentionally made enough noise while shaving to make him aware that he wasn't alone and/or to confuse him. I found in the past when dealing with an angry animal, if you can confuse it, it might just give you the upper hand or bite the living shit out of you in which case your initial strategy was negated.

Before I was finished, he was finished and this hulk of a Russian emerged from the #1 regular. How he fit in there, I'm not sure. It was plenty tall enough for him but from my viewpoint did not appear wide enough for him. Just maybe, I'd stumbled onto the source for his anger. But think of it this way, I may have saved him from getting a hefty fine for using the handicap stall. Not to sound cold or indifferent, but I wonder when they'll start calling them people with challenges stalls. I suppose that could become misleading though.

Feigning nonchalance but scrutinizing his every move, I soon became aware that I stood between him washing his hands and the paper towel dispenser. Without so much as touching me or bumping me out of the way, he gracefully reached that big fury paw around me and tore off a few sheets to dry his paws with. He said a few words in my direction still in Russian, still sounding a little gruff but who knows. If I'd had taken that class in Russian, I could have said something nice to him in Russian like, "I know the feeling" or "Been there, done that."

Never saw the two of them again, but recalled later that they did use one word a lot that sounded a lot like the English slang word, "_uck." Good for them. The Russian Mafia here in the States encourages their members to speak as fluent in English as possible I'm sure. What a sense of relief. In my book, constipation is always preferable to death.

PHOTO #1 - MT. GAP, CODY, WYOMING

Drove a few miles west towards Yellowstone on Route 14/16. Near the Cody city limits, I stopped at this park for a quick breakfast after making sure the Russians weren't following me. Snapped a photo of this gap in the mountains. A sign there informed that Native Americans buried their dead on platforms up in those mountains. Good luck getting the plus size ones up there.

Feeling an obligation had not been met, I returned to the Walmart Waldorf, scrounged enough U.S. coinage from crevices in the van, and bought a 7 pound bag of ice for $1.75 American. Again, not a bad exchange for sleeping and toileting facilities.

Ending up at a Blank Blank Bank as two others couldn't convert my Canadians for greenbacks, I was greeted warmly by a teller and a mid management older female. Both were extremely cordial. I had over $20 in Canadian change. They couldn't exchange the change. They could exchange the paper. I was given $350.41 U.S. for my investment of $485 Canadian. So much for making money when I was heading north.

PHOTO #2 - BUFFALO BILL CENTER

The elder management type lady now put on her sales person hat and did everything in her power short of twisting my arm to get me to open up a checking or savings account with them. She went so far as to pursue me out to the door. I told her that Blank Blank had no bank near to my home or I would open an account with them if anything just to shut her up. She was still leaning out the door as I raced for the van yelling counterproposals for why it would still be somehow to my advantage to have a Blank Blank account. Close call, not long after getting home, Blank Blank took a nose dive after being exposed for unscrupulous banking practices. I didn't realize it, but I had made two escapes today. One from the Russian Mafia and one from Blank Blank.

I took my new greenbacks to Buffalo Bill Center of the West. It was off the scale on a scale of 10 to the plus side. See photo of two teepees, flowers, etc. welcoming all who chose this trail. I was greeted inside by a lone, tiny lady running the ticket booth. Though looking old enough to have dated Buffalo Bill, she was a delight to the eye, kind, witty, and sported a great sense of humor. I bet they were glad when they found her for this position. She fit the role like an old comfortable sock. She was a fox long before they coined that phrase.

Possibly sizing me up as a frugal free camper, she softened the blow of the $16 admission fee by assuring my look of having second thoughts that the fee was good for two days as there was so much to see here, one could not do it justice over the course of a day. My senses returned with the color in my cheeks. $16 seemed like a good deal now plus I got a stamp of a buffalo from this precious heirloom's own hand onto the back of my left hand. She promised it would remain with me even through washings for two days. I would be reluctant to wash my hands afterwards as I wanted the touch of her hand to remain on my own for as long as I could hold off washing. Her touch was captivating. If only one could live the life that she no doubt has, and looked upon the scenes captured by her yet sparkling black onyx eyes. What a perfect setting for her. I had touched history itself already and hadn't made it past the ticket booth. I'm 70 and she called me "Sonny."

She would have been a great photo op but the line was multiplying and growing louder behind me. Sometimes, you get a sense that some folks don't really relish having their picture shot or just grow tired of it. With her, I was on the fence, but caved in giving her the most sincerest of thanks and as warm of a smile as I could work up, moving on, pretty sure that I'd made the wrong choice not shooting. Life is so full of, "wish I'd have done thats."

You'll find five sections in this museum: Buffalo Bill, firearms, art, natural history, and Native Americans. Actually, you could probably spend a day in each section. I never saw so many vintage guns (displays, photos, etc.) in one place. This place could make the Smithsonian a little envious.

I spent a good part of the day in there and enjoyed every second. You'll find a well-stocked food court. Hats off to the designer. There are plenty of restrooms and places to just sit, rest, enjoy, contemplate, you name it. It's also handicapped friendly.

By chance, I came across a live raptor program in an outdoor courtyard. I'd seen Peregrin falcons before, but learned this day that they reach speeds of 100 mph when swooping down on their prey. The screeching elongated scream easily discerned when they are attacking doesn't come from their voice boxes but from wind whistling through nose holes in their beaks. It may be more respectful to call them beak holes. I think the Germans tried to copy this in their Stuka Dive Bombers.

Up next was something I've seen in film but never imagined the luck I had in seeing one up close and personal - a golden eagle. This live one was average size. His wingspan was seven feet. No wonder Native Americans paid so much homage to these magnificent creatures of pure flight. I'm glad that Buffalo Bill didn't have a TV or computer. He would have missed so much.

Except for a few exhibit areas and numerous stuffed animals, most of the displays were under glass. I took numerous photos. Some turned out good, some didn't. I'll share a few with you:

A. Bow covered in rattle-snake skin. A word to the wise - don't piss off the owner.

B. Wild Bill Hickok's Model 1851 Navy Colt with ivory handles and holster. A word to the wise - don't piss off the owner.

C. Sitting Bull's tomahawk. Check the length of the handle. He could really reach out and touch someone with that. A word to the wise - don't piss off the owner.

D. I'm not sure about it but

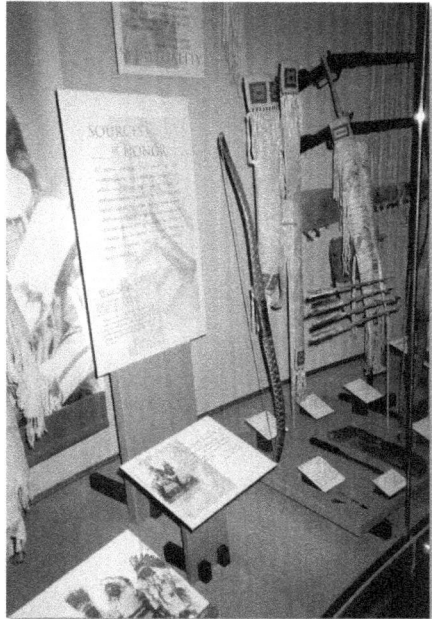

PHOTO #3 - BOW COVERED IN RATTLESNAKE SKIN

the double exposure occurred by accident. I think he's a Pawnee. Notice his necklace of grizzly claws. He didn't buy those at Cabela's. A word to the wise - ditto. He will be my monument to the romantic notion of the fading Indian. Fade hell! We killed most all of them.

I took numerous other photos depicting Buffalo Bill, Annie Oakley, Sitting Bull, and the like. Unfortunately, glare from the glass casings, etc. inadvertently ruined my attempts to bring them to you. I would hope that this may inspire you to get up, get your butt in high gear and go see them in person for yourself. I don't care where you live in the continental USA including much of Alaska, you're less

PHOTO #4 - WILD BILL'S PISTOL

than four days of hard driving from Cody. Remember, it's a small world. Our Earth is an itty bitty sized place when compared to other celestial locales. Anyway if you do get there, send me a thank you card for the push.

PHOTO #5 - SITTING BULL'S TOMAHAWK

PHOTO #6 - FADING INDIAN

On the way out, I stopped at a range cook display for some free samples of homemade (range made) biscuits and beans - excellent fare. Our cook's name was Ron Reed (believed to be no relation to the Reeds who played significant roles in the Donner Party buffet). Ron told me he'd been cooking here for 7 years but had cooked over an open fire for 20+ years. He was a quiet fellow, but one could tell he'd earned his way to Cody's museum through the thick and thin of the range. Though quiet, he answered a host of questions thrown to him by our small impromptu audience. He, like the lady at the ticket booth, not only looked and played the part, no doubt because they were the part. They held you captive in time in their grasp and you loved it and begged for more. I recall one of his answers to a question hurled at him regarding the strength of coffee served up to his cowboys. Without hesitation, he had caught the question and lobbed his answer back to us in a low, slow cowboy drawl, "Cooks' recipe for cowboys was one fistful of coffee per cup."

Take another gander back at Mr. Ron Reed (photo #7). There's much more to this quiet, modest, honest and down to earth specimen of mankind than greets the eye. Subsequent enjoyable phone contact with him while putting finishing touches to this

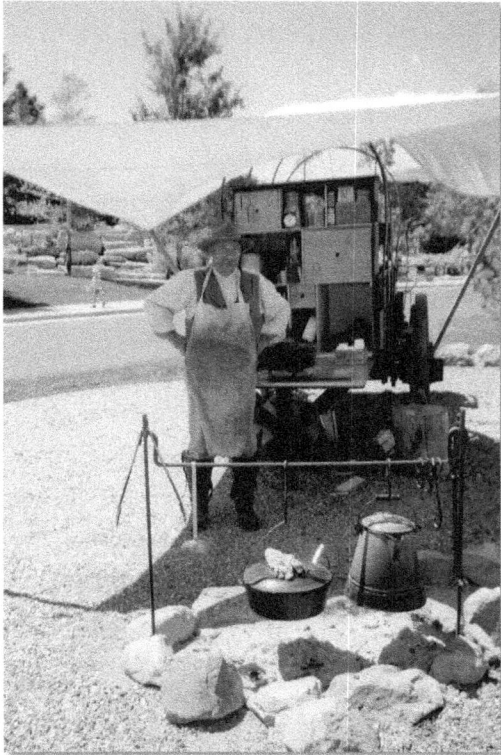

PHOTO #7 - RON REED RANGE COOK

book revealed that he also sports a history of success as a Cowboy Action Shooter galloping on a horse while shooting stationary targets, etc. Ron is also involved with more than one western-themed leather goods stores throughout the West. There's probably much more to him, but, like I said, he has a modest countenance. What a guy!

Determined to get photos of those red ochre mountains back up on Chief Joseph's scenic Route 120, I started my backtrack. Not too far out of Cody I came across Heart Mountain. It was shaped like an inverted heart. The original name had been conveyed by Native Americans as Heart of the Buffalo Mountain. But "whitey" had shortened it to Heart Mountain. Funny thing about "whitey." He had a tendency to shorten a lot of things especially the lives and lifestyles of the Native Americans.

Both times I passed by Heart Mountain I was slammed with what at the time seemed like unwarranted negative vibes, forebodings, and a sense of doom. I know you have probably experienced similar phenomenon out of the blue elsewhere and like myself were perplexed as to why. You may want to research the history of the locale where this happened to you. I did no research but later, by chance, found out that Heart Mountain had been one of those sites we interred Japanese Americans during WWII. Another piece of embarrassing / sad history we would like to but cannot sweep under the rug. I saw no trace of a camp having ever been there… Just under 14,000 Japanese <u>Americans</u> were interred there in 650 makeshift barracks.

Back to Bill Cody. He firmly believed that we had no right or justification to treat Native Americans like we did and absolutely no right to take their lands. He was a voice for the minority. He was also vehemently against the wholesale slaughter of the buffalo. Every one he killed was for eating. He wasted nothing and never got into robe sales, etc. He sold his buffalo meat to the Army by the pound. He was paid $500 per month as a scout for the Army which was rich man's wages back then. Oh, those government contractors. Myth has it that he killed 3,000 buffalo in one day. Who's this Myth guy?

PHOTO #8 - RED OCHRE MT.

Way back when as a U.S. history teacher, I would challenge my students to come up with one part of the buffalo that the Native Americans didn't eat or utilize. They had no success. So, today, I am challenging you, the reader, to come up with a part of the buffalo not applied to meet some need of the Native American. Good luck. Send me a self-addressed, stamped envelope and I shall reply. It took me a good 30 minutes to backtrack but captured the red ochre mountains for you while heading northwest.

I drove further northwest, jumped from the van and took a second photo of the same mountain looking southeast. To my delight and good fortune, an 18-wheeler was heading northwest when I snapped this photo. You may have to get your magnifying glass out but the dark line mid right center of this photo is the 18-wheeler barely discernible at the base of the mountain. I'm emphasizing this point to give you some perspective of the grand scale of these amazing mountains.

PHOTO #9 - RED OCHRE MT. WITH 18-WHEELER

PHOTO #10 - RED OCHRE MT.

Further up the road at a little pull over, I took another shot at yet another red ochre mountain. It looks like a ramp near the middle of the photo. Wish I had a docile horse. I'd like to ride cross country over to that one.

I would only hope that you readers appreciate the painstaking efforts made on your behalf by the author in an attempt to bring this land to life for you. Backtracking to these mountains is just one example of your author's commitment to you. The author only hopes that he doesn't come across more red ochre mountains on the remainder of this trip so as to make this monumental backtracking unnecessary.

Our next targeted destination was going to be Custer's commencement exercises on the Little Big Horn. In order to get there before they close today, I may have to buy some Depends like that crazy female astronaut did on her last mission in a car, not too many summers ago.

I was plenty big hungry on my way back so I stopped at a nice picnic spot adjacent to the Shoshone River on the outskirts of Cody. The Shoshone was green and gorgeous; and although it wasn't clear enough to see them, trout were probably in abundance.

PHOTO #11 - PICNIC GROUNDS / SHOSHONE RIVER

Once again, I thanked my lucky stars and You Know Who for giving me a life that has allowed me to be here. I also thanked Him for sending me the two blonde bikinied kayakers who put in below my perch, and waved at me before launching off down the Shoshone. I learned on this trip that without a drop car, friends, paid guides, or an indentured servant, the kayak could only serve me in lakes, etc. where I could put in and then paddle back to the van when I'd had enough.

I'd hit a few bumps getting back to Cody this morning and they awakened the noisy shovel and the spoiled two year old. They weren't alone this time. They were keeping company with a very aggressive mosquito about the size of a praying mantis that was relentless in his attempts to secure blood from me. He was careless one too many times, and I was left with just the shovel and the two year old to deal with. Their combined reverberations led me to believe that their source was coming from within the van. As quickly and meticulously as could be accomplished, contents were reconfigured with hopes of silencing them once again.

A hurried brunch of the remaining three bratwurst with ketchup on bread was devoured while plotting the course to Custer. Stale coffee seemed to wash it down thoroughly.

While pulling back onto the highway, conjuring thoughts of Custer and Sitting Bull's last meeting, a large, for these parts, brick complex came into view from the highway entrance. For the first time I caught sight of the sign. It read, "Park County Law Enforcement Center." Custer and Sitting Bull would have to wait. They were probably good with that as each of them had eternity to wait for your's truly. The hunt for "Charlie" had surpassed these historical persons.

Curiosity launched the van into the parking lot and then elbowed me down the cement path and through the front door. After the buzzer, I found myself peering through a very thick window that had what I will label a voice vent each configured to stop bullets or at least to alter their path to a nice plump lady in uniform.

I explained my quest for "Charlie." She told me, "No Charlie works here." I said, "How about a retired Charlie?" She replied that she didn't think so, looking at me as if she wanted an abrupt end to our 30 second conversation. Maybe she was trained not to assist inquirers seeking local constables in the event that said inquirer may be seeking some revenge earned or not by said constable of note. Not to be run off that easily, I stretched it for another 15 seconds telling this officer how convincing Lu had been. She cut me off with, "Well maybe Lu was mixed up or confused" with a tone that reared its ugly head letting the inquirer know that the inquiry stops now. I left abruptly perplexed, but thankful I wasn't paying taxes in Park County, Wyoming.

Well, a sad ending to an otherwise interesting tale. Regardless of the above officer's motivation, rest assured, my money's still on Lu. So, "Officer Charlie," if you read this and don't feel threatened or stalked, I'd love to hear from you in voice or print. It would be just grand if you could send a photo. I'm sorry I missed you. Tell Lu I said hello.

Our next pause came at a rest stop next to a flight museum with numerous old planes put out to pasture on Route 14 near Greybull, Wyoming. Of note, as I scanned the array of sleeping planes were the numerous red ochre mountains lined up wide awake behind them in the blistering heat. Thermometer in the van was reading a few notches over 90 degrees Fahrenheit.

Crossing the Big Horn River, not sure when the next gas station would come along, prudence whispered that we should stop for fuel just in case, as one can see vast distances here of nothing to some and everything to others. The very pleasant and friendly attendant told me that his thermometer had peaked at 100 degrees Fahrenheit so far today. Sensing it would not offend him, I asked, "Why are you wearing all black clothes in this heat?" Unoffended, he replied in his low slow cowboy drawl, "Stupid choice this morning." To icing the cake of unoffensiveness, I threw him a, "Been there, done that."

He shared that it had been 108 degrees Fahrenheit last week here in Greybull and that was not unusual for this time of year.

PHOTO #12 - OLD SCHOOLHOUSE

They need rain here badly. So bad, I found the author offering prayers to that effect on their behalf. Everything looked dried up even the nice kid wearing all black. The sun beat down so hot, it made you want to run away but where was there to run?

Heat or no heat, I couldn't pass up a shot at a very old stone schoolhouse on Route 14 northeast of Greybull. It was now private property and fenced off so this was as close as I could venture. Those are the Bighorn Mountains in the background. One would have to agree that this school came with a pretty fair sized playground.

For those of you not bored stiff from hearing about or seeing photos of red ochre mountains, here's another appearing to be guarding part of the Bighorn Mountains standing behind it.

Our baptism to the Bighorn Mountains started down low on Route 14 where she enters this beautiful, but foreboding gap leading up, up and away into these rugged majestic silent mountains. As

PHOTO #13 - RED OCHRE MT. IN FRONT OF BIGHORNS

you can see, there wasn't much traffic which assisted in my controlled gawking. Explore this photo. People lived and thrived in these mountains. Don't arm wrestle them.

PHOTO #14 - GAP INTO THE BIGHORNS

Entering the gap, visions and memories of fright back in the Bear Tooth Mountains reverberated in the author's psyche. How quickly we forget. Undaunted, but not without trepidation, we pressed on vertically, keeping a vigil on the van's heat gauge.

PHOTO #15 - PEAKS IN THE BIGHORNS

Maybe it was the lack of bumper to bumper traffic, or a somewhat wider, yet winding, road than that which helped the author to escape from the Bear Tooth. Prognosis remained guarded, but the fear factor, though still prevalent, never reached the crescendo it had in the Bear Tooths. Don't get me wrong, there were numerous sections of the Bighorns that reminded you that you still had hair on the back of your neck that would act as a silent, but very effective warning system. Anyway, I weren't as scared as afore.

There were small, but sufficient, pull overs for reflection, retreat, timeouts, photos, etc. Photos 15 and 16, hopefully, will give you some perspective of the views going up. We are going to be going up and over near those peaks you see in the far ground.

I saw no signs of wildlife other than a group of young revelers laughing and screaming their way down the mountain in a multi-colored van. The author will remain without judgement as the author had for many years considered himself a recovering hippie.

Nearing the summit at a pullover to ensure that the engine wasn't over heating, the unmistakeable resonance of water was heard cascading over granite and being crushed over and over again onto boulders waiting beneath to grapple with the water on numerous steps never admitting to inevitable defeat seeking their turn to the bottom miles and millenniums below.

PHOTO #16 - PEAKS IN THE BIGHORNS

I can attest that neither the water nor the boulders in this contest ever gave up or showed any signs of second thoughts or reluctance to do their duty while I was at ringside. If time would have permitted, I would have snuck back out there in the middle of the night to see if they took any breaks or if either one of them called for a truce at least until daylight.

There was a movie or a book entitled "Cast a Giant Shadow." I was not aware until after this photo was developed that I had "cast

PHOⵔO #17 - SHELL FALLS

a giant shadow" at a place in the Bighorn Mountains called Shell Falls. Question? This is not a test but you're long overdue for one. Is your shadow like a distant cousin of your spirit? Don't know, would like to. If you think you may have the answer, please contact me. I will not promise you a free book as I feel that your response would be one based on speculation more so than fact. However, I would applaud your effort with the enthusiasm it merits wholeheartedly.

Shell Falls was another of those oasis' in, on first appearance, what seemed to be a desolate landscape as we continued our struggle toward whichever summit in the Bighorn Mountains the meandering Route 14 would graciously carry us across. Review of the map left us with the realization that our only course here was to ride 14 out to Route 90 above Sheridan as there wasn't an abundance of other courses to choose from save for backtracking a long way south and taking Route 16 east to Buffalo.

All was well though, as either choice to cross the Bighorns was a designated scenic highway. Please refer to the dots on your map designating scenic highways. It's worth the extra time and effort to plot your course, follow the dots, and you'll be glad you did. Our freeways are nice if you're in a hurry to get from point A to point B. Mother Nature and Uncle Sam have joined in this effort to bring you visual and historic pleasures that have no measure other than the impact on your souls appreciation for a land you were born into. Take a break, find the state you reside in, look for the dotted highways. You'll be surprised how close you live to one. If you haven't already, take/ make the time to check it out. Let me know how it went.

As desolate as the ascent was, the crown made the ascent well worth the journey. Other than the blue sky, green dominated the rest of nature's canvas. I suppose they call them high mountain meadows. We owe a lot of thanks to the creator who plopped a couple of beaver down up here some years back knowing the beaver's assets and what he would do up here for us. There were small meandering streams with a myriad of beaver dams and dens slowing the water down before it ran out and leapt down Shell Falls and I'm sure many others I hadn't come across. There were numerous pockets of evergreens 50-100 feet tall making up the darkest of the myriad of greens stretching out on this rolling flat canvas for as far as the eye could gather. Without the beaver, this lush greenery would resemble moonscape.

One could only imagine what winter would be like up here, but the warmer months would bring much grasses to fatten our ponies and sacred beasts we could catch to fatten our women and children.

PHOTO #18 - MOOSE IN THE GREEN

My first encounter with a sacred beast not long after leaving the vertical ascent for the horizontal green was a bull moose standing in one of those many meandering streams chewing away on some aquatic vegetation that could only serve to brighten his day. He looked directly at me as if to say, "If you see those beaver, give them a big moose at-a-boy for me."

My throw away camera did this big moose no justice. That's him, the dark spot in the upper middle. I was going to discard this photo but after realizing that it shed some light on the different shades of green mentioned earlier that converge on the visual delights, I decided to include it just for you.

About a half an hour from the moose, the road became extremely congested with sheep. There were hundreds of them blocking the road and kind of melting off onto the shoulder then slipping off into the serene meadows bordering both sides of the road for maybe a quarter of a mile. Forgive me for not getting a photo here as I was too busy laughing and dodging sheep. It is a Dodge van you know.

Are sheep stupid or just in deep thought? Blowing the horn got a few of their attentions, but did not get them to move from my path. It was getting toward evening and I was already sleepy. I avoided trying to count the sheep for fear I would fall asleep at the wheel. Amidst severe hazardous yawning, I crept the van ever so slowly through their cud chewing midst. It took awhile, it was a challenge. Looking back on it, I enjoyed moving at their pace and got in a lot of gawking that would have otherwise escaped me had it not been for these free rangers.

Are sheep cute and cuddly or just oblivious to anything nearing a thought pattern? I suppose if you hung out with them long enough, you'd probably start feeling as if you were brilliant. I felt no carnal desire for any of them but two had beautiful eyes and well rounded buttocks. The author took complete poetic license with that last emission and will be surprised if the editor does not think we should strike it altogether.

Not too far from the future mutton chops, a sign appeared that read 3 miles to Tie Flume, a designated national campsite. I had been traversing a gravelly macadam road winding through these high mountain meadows pretty sure I was still in Wyoming. Getting increasingly fatigued but with less yawning since leaving the sheep behind, a right off of Route 14 onto a dirt road with only 3 miles to go was invitation enough.

Then another sign popped up and it read 5 miles to Dead Swede Campground. Dead Swede sounded, for some unknown reason, more romantic than Tie Flume. So, we sped past Tie Flume with only 2 miles to go to Dead Swede.

A recent but now forgotten rain helped to keep the road dust at bay. Taking the left into Dead Swede, a third sign appeared simply stating "Full" meaning you're out of luck free camper and you better get your weary carcass back to Tie Flume.

Good old campsite #5 was the only one left there out of many. To give you some idea of the size of this campground, there was more than one restroom facility. If you needed a rest, it fit the bill. But, if you needed a bath, you might want to try Dead Swede.

I had underestimated the popularity of these national campgrounds. I could only stay at good ole #5 for tonight as a notice on the #5 registration clip as you pull into the site let me know that another camper or camper family had already secured it (online) starting on the upcoming tomorrow. I felt the need for a two day layover but would gladly settle for one.

Good ole #6 was occupied by a very large family or a couple who brought most of their neighborhood with them. They were really roughing it in a very large camper. At 8 PM, he cranked up the Honda generator and two of the mid to late teen boys tried to out riff one another on their guitars. Some yelling by the ringmaster silenced the guitars. Good ole #5 and #6 campsites were not real close but close enough for #5 to hear the mutterings slung back at the ringmaster once he was out of earshot inside the trailer by the mid to late teens.

I could hear at least two TV programs being played simultaneously from within the trailer. One sounded faintly like an adult quiz show and the other sounded like cartoons, which should serve to keep you from second guessing the age ranges in this extended family. One female member age range 8-10 walked by my campsite as if on a scouting mission to gain as much knowledge as she could with regards to the free camper who had just taken up lodging in ole #5 for a reasonable fee of $8.00. She did return my neighborly greeting appropriately, but hastened on to good ole #6.

Not caring that the grinding hum of the Honda generator might challenge my sleep through the rest of the night, I pretended it was "white noise," unfolded my old green hunting chair, broke out the teriyaki jerky, onion chips, dried veggies, oatmeal, raisins, and some dried bananas, with 2 beers and a cigar for dessert and settled into my chair with feet propped up on the cement seat of the park provided picnic table as snug as a bug in a rug.

Midway through that second lukewarm beer, I noticed movement in good old campsite #4. There had been campers there but all that remained was their pop up trailer as they were obviously out and about in whatever vehicle that had gotten them here. I never did see any trace of them. What I did see was a female elk keeping a motherly eye on me as she and her single fawn strolled leisurely around campsite #4 with the fawn displaying expected childlike curiosity on every item including the pop up left in camp. Mom being the pro she was gifted with allowed the fawn full run of the camp while she diligently and patiently observed and protected.

Once the fawn's curiosity had been quenched, mom whispered something in elk baby talk which the fawn alerted to and they sauntered slowly out nearer to the gravel road to feed on some green tastees. I suppose the fawn was not weaned yet as it seemed only to mimic mom's crunching of the green.

Not knowing how many children were watching cartoons in good ole #6, I figured that getting a chance to see this elk family might be more beneficial to them than the cartoons, especially since they could probably put the cartoons on hold.

Hurrying in a way as to not spook the elk, I made my way up to good ole #6. It was at this time that I learned the family in good ole #6 kept at least one bull mastiff whose instincts were to maul and murder any intruder entering good old #6. Behind the bull were a handful of lesser, tiny yippers whose courage was magnified as long as they howled, yipped, and barked behind the bull mastiff whose growl/bark seemed much more guttural. I suppose the secondary function of the lesser canines with the shriller voices was to eat the smaller pieces of the intruder left behind by the bull.

Fortunately for the intruder, the bull mastiff had a well-trained master who sprang from behind one of their trailers and seized the bull by a convenient harness. And though being drug towards said intruder by the bull and close enough for the intruder to see the accumulation of white slobber dribbling over teeth that looked too big for a dog was able with a repetition of commands that probably meant "don't kill" to calm the bull to a somewhat more controlled frenzy finally getting it to sit with a fixed glare still holding the intruder at bay accompanied by a profusion of slobber. So much for being a good samaritan.

Knowing that the slobbering bull awaited it's next command, the intruder felt that it would be in his best interest to identify his mission and did a controlled blurt out to the well-trained master that his kids may want to see the elk family that the intruder lapsed to grasp were now long gone and still galloping away from the guttural warning they no doubt had picked up on coming from the intrusion. Two kids, a young boy and the female scout who had surveilled me earlier, emerged to investigate but never did see the elk.

Feigning confidence in the well-trained master's ability to keep his dog from certain injury to me, I slowly returned in reverse to the relative safety of good ole #5 all the while under the glare of a dog who either could see through my trumped up, "you don't scare me," or who just didn't give a rat's ass. He had a job to do.

Regaining a semblance of composure, I returned to my old green hunting chair and sipped on what remained of the second luker warm beer, thankful that I still had the same number of holes in my body that I had awoken with this morning. The temperature was still in the 90s and pre-shadows alerting campers that darkness was about to take over crept as still as a mouse through the pine filled campground. Being too tired to build a fire, I was still able to enjoy wood burning smells from fellow campers that pleasantly engulfed me as I fantasized life as it may have been on this green filled plateau thousands of journeys preceding.

While lost somewhere in the above consuming fantasy, I felt the approach of another. It was Shawn from Sheridan who just recently prevented a dog mauling by a canine that was just a tad smaller or just a tad larger than Shawn was. Shawn was the ringmaster noted earlier from good ole #6.

Once we got past the apologies regarding the bull mastiff and the thank you's regarding the bull mastiff, he settled onto the picnic table beside me, declined a lukewarm beer offer, but gravitated abruptly to an offered cigar. He had three choices. He chose to join the author in king sized "Parodi" — ironically made in Dunmore, PA. The "Parodi" is a short, black, hard cigar with an aroma making one contemplate about the ingredients that put off a distinct odor, not unlike melted down used tires. Disclaimer: the above description in no way should or could be utilized to defame the makers of the infamous "Parodi" cigar, a choice blend that your author has returned to over decades of puffing that to any intelligent beings could be characterized as slow suicide. You may have seen them or similar smokes made famous by Clint Eastwood in some of his early westerns.

After the usual campsite banter about where you from, where you going, I inquired as to his profession. Shawn replied, "I'm a fabricator." I couldn't hold back, "Are you a professional liar?" He replied, "I get that a lot." His feelings were not hurt as we shared a two guy chuckle between puffs.

Near dark and the wind died down signaling to the mosquitos about two guys in a good ole #5 ripe for the picking if they could fly through our Parodi smoke screen. They were persistent but no match for a well-placed exhale of Parodi. With complete darkness now giving them the advantage, Shawn and the author lost visual target recognition and stooped to another demention of exhaling toward any telltale buzzing. If those mosquitos had evolved a while longer, they would have figured out that if they turned off the buzzing, Shawn and the author would have been theirs for the taking. Thank God for making the wheels of evolution turn so slowly.

With our 4 1/2 inch Parodi's smoked down to about an inch and starting to burn our fingers, Shawn and the author, amid the buzzing, agreed to call it a night. He declined a Parodi for the road. Kids, don't try this at home. Note: former Parodi packaging informed your author that they were rolled in Scranton, PA, more recent packaging indicates Dunmore, PA. Go figure.

Welcomed sleep came fast this night as the author murmured his thank you to the Great Creator, thanking Him for all of His usual help this day from His placement of shear joy and wonderment laid out in our path to His protection and assistance when trouble came bounding with harmful intent. What a day! And as sleep rolled us away from reality, one last, "Thank you for my life."

DAY #27, 7/27/2016

Up at 8:15, 63 degrees Fahrenheit, no one stirring in good ole #'s 6 or 4. Realizing we hadn't made it to Custer's Folly (no disrespect to the poor young men under his command) as planned yesterday, breakfast was hurried. Gobbled down a health bar bought back in Canada called President's Choice / Le Choix du President, rich and chewy chocolate chip / riche et tendre brisures de chocolat (no "e" on the end in French), made in a peanut-free facility. This last part was also repeated in French but writing in French seems to tax the author even more so. This will probably be your last chance to witness the author's ability to write in French. We also plunged into and devoured a six pack of Ritz snackwiches with cheese. Old/cold coffee helped to wash all of the above down.

At home, eating seems to dominate the day. One often finds one contemplating what will make up the next meal many times prior to the close of the previous. On the other hand, eating takes a backseat when traveling and at times can seem more like an obstacle than a delight. The author lost approximately 18 pounds on this trip. Yet another perk granted via wanderlust.

Sorry, dear reader, for that sashay off of our intended route. A quick stop at one of the abundant restrooms provided at Tie Flume, a successful rest, and we're off back up that dirt road towards Route 14. Out on 14 I caught myself thinking of those two cute sheep I saw yesterday, wondered how their day was going, and hoping I'd come across some others back out on Route 14. There must have been an invisible dividing line. I saw hundreds of sheep yesterday. Today, I had to be on the alert for Black Angus cows dotting the landscape across this lush green garden that served to fatten them up. Had they been aware of their destiny, their appetites may not have been so paramount in their choice of activities.

All thoughts took an abrupt change of course as I rounded a bend and was flagged down by a biker in extreme panic who had been coming in the opposite direction on Route 14. He remained astride his Harley but had stopped in mid lane opposite mine. Something apparently had him mortified. He wasn't catatonic, but was nearing that zone of fright. Turning the Pink Floyd tape off and rolling down my window, I came to a drifting controlled halt in my adjoining lane. Close enough to touch him.

Remaining calm when others are not is a technique that has served me and others well over a lifetime of vocational and volunteer pursuits requiring relaxation techniques and other like methods to return a semblance of composure to the distressed. It's easy. If you can't do it, fake it. The terrified person won't know you're faking it but your display of calmness will be a catalyst to help the afflicted get a grip or at the least follow your lead.

Once the biker stopped flailing his arms and picked up on the author's calm demeanor, the flailing slowed down dramatically and pointing with just the one hand now, leaving the other to help steady the bike, ensued. Next came a better grasp on his speech patterns and volume. Before long and with more control of his gasping, the author was able to discern words or repeated word thrust from the diaphragm up through his vocal cords on its route into the crisp morning air. Finally, the author could make out the word "bear" being repeated loud and rapid at first and then slower with less volume as his hyperventilation prevented him from pushing the word out again. His pointing hand kept pace along with his vocalizations as both seemed to fade into his lap with his face and chin finally collapsing down now resting on his upper chest.

The author, once assured that the biker was still breathing on his own, scanned the green covered hill whose occupant had given the biker such panic and dread and found the source not a hundred American yards from where we sat.

Continuing to resonate a demeanor of calmness while silent, the catalyst was doing its magic as the biker began to stir as if coming out of a deep and lengthy trance.

Your author assessed the biker's level of consciousness. Breathing patterns, heart rate, etc. and found him fit to proceed on his own. It was at this time that the author felt that the biker deserved to discover the true culprit belying his mortal terror. The author calmly shared with him in a voice not much above a whisper that it was a Black Angus cow.

His mortal terror turned to near mortal embarrassment. Your author's past training once again kicked in to prevent him from kicking himself too much. I told him that maybe he just needed glasses. And, since we were the only known living souls here and now on Route 14, it would be our secret. I did warn him about the sheep he was likely to encounter. We shook hands and parted ways, with him I'm sure considering an appointment with an optometrist and me free to laugh my ass off recalling the expression on his face when he leaned towards the whisper and heard that it was just a Black Angus cow. Priceless. It was one of the gems of this trip. Thank you fellow traveler. I would hope that our paths would meet again. I was not laughing at your expense. But let it be known that I will forever be in your debt for the gift of humor you gave freely to me this day. There's a free book in it for you.

PHOTO #1 - BIGHORN MOUNTAINS ABOVE DAYTON, WYOMING

Once again, resuming our trek to meet up with what's left of Custer and his command (no offense, George. You should have stayed east. You were a genuine hero/legend back in the Civil War.), we find ourselves over the hump of the Bighorns and descending on 14 towards Dayton. Couldn't pass up a photo of these grandiose mountains guarding a valley between them. What really caught my eye though was the vast plains stretching beyond these mountains to the horizon. It resembles the ocean to me and once again invites all of us to appreciate vastness. A road sign here read, "40 mph for the next 9 miles due to elevation, gravity, brakes, etc."

Further along but not quite to Dayton, had to shoot a photo of this natural cathedral almost to the bottom, but still in the eastern foothills of the Bighorns. Pretty big feet if you ask me. The man-made wooden wall on the left is a snow barrier. One could only imagine as one does not want to be an eye witness to what winter must bring out here.

PHOTO #2 - NATURAL CATHEDRAL

I keep shooting with my throwaway camera as mentioned before, not knowing if the camera will do justice to what my eyes welcome and take in. I kept hoping so for your sake. Remember, the author had no intention of writing a book at the onset. I guess that's proof in the pudding of how inspiring travel invades our spirits. God, I feel sorry for people who can't travel. But, I feel beyond sorrow for those who won't travel. You don't have to take an epic journey. Thanks, again, Dad and Mom for those Sunday drives you treated and entreated us to.

PHOTO #3 - TONGUE RIVER POOL

Feeling a bit slimy, I had planned on bathing in the Little Big Horn River to help rinse Custer's and my own sins away. Reconnaissance up a lane hugging the Tongue River convinced me that this pool would provide the author with more opportunity for privacy so we took a leap of faith. This pool wasn't more than a few miles out of Dayton and turned out to be the best choice. Guess what? It wasn't freezing cold but just cool enough to be absolutely refreshing. I took my good ole time washing with the Ivory soap (biodegradable) and letting the slow current in this pool tongue it away from me (pun intended).

Ever on the alert for what may be behind me, I rolled over at half rinse and looked up to the sky and was treated to the view of this mountain watching over me. Dashing to the car and returning to my private salon with camera in tow, the author caught this view for you while partially submerged in the Tongue. Could you imagine seeing a handful of Sioux, Crow, or Cheyennes up there peering down from their ponies and wondering if they should dispatch you before or after they had their lunch? I think they were up there. I just couldn't see them. I cleared out some time before lunch. What a nice clear blue sky though.

PHOTO #4 - MT. BEHIND TONGUE RIVER POOL

14 carried us to 90. I chose to seek more film in Sheridan as names of towns the map showed me that I would pass through towards the last stand didn't sound like I could put all bets on finding film there, i.e., Wyola, Lodgegrass, Garry Owen, etc. And so, a southerly route to Sheridan made for a sure bet and it was only a few miles.

I was also interested in seeing a town named after General Phil Sheridan of Civil War fame, a bit Napoleon-complexed and so short you could say he also suffered from altitudinal challenges. "Little Phil" also gave us such diplomatic and caring phrases as, "The only good Indian, is a dead Indian." Many historians were disappointed when "Little Phil" had chosen not to accompany Custer to the Little Big Horn.

No offense to the good people of Sheridan, Wyoming. I can't help but loathe the namesake. Sheridan is known for dinosaur finds. It seemed so dry here that the dinosaur finds may be the result of dryness not supporting rot and decay.

The cashier at Walmart where more film was secured gave me the good news that the Pizza Hut I'd passed entering town offered a lunch buffet. I felt I was on a roll. I hadn't had a buffet since Lu's a couple of days ago and I supposed my stomach was primed.

My new waitress at Pizza Hut was a cute and tiny waif like girl with sad eyes. Finding myself alone in the Hut, I thought I had arrived too late for the buffet but she assured me that I had got there under the bell. She walked me to the yet steaming oasis that still had 5 different pizzas, mostly untouched, along with the usual salad bar accouterments. She looked toward my belly and said, "Do you think that will be enough for you?" Picking up on and trying to match her jovial ways, I replied, "It's a start."

I stuffed down at least ten pieces plus a couple of visits to the salad bar and all the fountain Coke I could suck down. Somewhere around the 7th or 8th piece, she stopped over to ensure that everything was satisfactory and probably to see who was most likely to win the pool they had on me back in the kitchen.

Feeling slightly embarrassed as my gluttony had been exposed, I was reluctant to fill the carry out box up with pieces she had offered me for the road. After she told me that they have to throw any left over pieces away anyway, I was convinced that filling the carry out box up to the hilt was the humane thing to do.

I gave her a hefty tip. Although she did not allow a photo, she would allow me to include her kindheartedness in this book. I told her that she would forever be known as the Sheridan, Wyoming Pizza Hut Girl.

I left with a smile, some pizza sauce on my face, and a solid grip on that carry out box. Thanks again, there's a free book in it for her. Whoever won the pool can put that money towards a purchase of the book.

Traveling north on Interstate 90 I was still perplexed about the contradictions between her jovial sparkle and countenance in contrast with that obvious sadness festering in her eyes. At times like this, I always wish for a magic wand to fix whatever has descended on folks like her. She's had a loss that meant a great deal to her somewhere recently. It won't hurt to say a little prayer when you come across a fellow traveler like her through these times of ours.

A fight up the highway in Montana resulted in everybody losing. Sometime before our arrival, a large elk had taken on an 18-wheeler. The elk lost the most but apparently disabled the 18-wheeler as it sat at the end of an antifreeze leak in a radiator taken out by the elk. It must have happened last night or this morning. Dear God, please take that elk to those clover fields in the sky. There was no driver in or around the truck which he was able to limp off to the shoulder after the fight.

A few miles north of the fight, signs started popping up announcing a museum of Custer's last hurrah. I'd been to the battlefield back in the 70's and sure didn't remember it being down here off of Route 90. I started to fill up on petrol at the pumps right there until I read they were charging us $2.99/gallon. I stopped pumping at $12 and some change. This wasn't my first rodeo and I smelled a potential rip off.

Inside the museum, my request to use a restroom was met with a curt reply from a bulbous middle-aged female who appeared to hate working here almost as much as she hated greeting customers with a warm and friendly smile. Don't you just hate people you can't slug in the chops as it is socially unacceptable plus it would cost you an aggravated assault conviction and magnified medical restitution. Maybe this was her attempt at getting a paid vacation. Anyway, with a glare, she growled her response to my request, "We only have one in here and it's for women and children." She pointed a heavy arm back towards the door and snarled, "Two portopotties for men at the far end of the parking lot." Without a thank you, I was out the door. Lots of don't signs and keep off the grass signs greeted me on my way to the end of the parking lot. I chose the left of the two as it had a makeshift cardboard hand torn sign stating, "For Urine Only."

I made my way inside only to find the reason for the sign. This toilet was full of everything, but mostly excrement, to the very top of the commode rim. It actually discouraged me from investigating the second green portopottie as it didn't come with cardboard directives duct taped to the door. Fortunately, I was able to urinate via the trough you see in the newer deluxe models while turning my back on the toilet with my left foot propping the door ajar so that I might breath in the outside air without throwing up pizza all over the parking lot.

As I don't know for sure where to lay blame on who neglected to pay the portopottie bill, I'll make no accusations. But with the thermometer cresting to 94 degrees Fahrenheit outside, one could hasten to a reasonable conclusion that someone should be held accountable at leastwise from where I stood.

Not many miles ahead, we landed at Custer's Battlefield. History is most often a chronicle written by the winners. Maybe this place should be called Sitting Bull's or Crazy Horse's Battlefield. My lifetime senior pass scored again saving me the $8-$10 entrance fee. Even if you don't have a pass, the fee is far less than what you'll walk away from here with.

The temperature that greeted and stayed with us throughout the day here hung at 95 degrees Fahrenheit. Oddly enough, that was the same temperature that I'm sure helped wear out both sides in this decisive struggle on that decisive day. Custer's men were wearing wool, buckskin, long pants, and boots. Your author was wearing a tee shirt, shorts, and rubber clogs and feeling completely drained by a relentless sun. Also, let it be known that the author was not running or fighting for his life in a contest whose end result was evident at the onset.

PHOTO #5 - CUSTER'S LAST STAND

Custer had divided his command into three separate forces after his scouts told him they were grossly out numbered. Had he had a sunstroke? Did he need hearing aides? Was he just off today? Had he been overtaken by karma?

The first photo taken there shows the last view of this country that Custer probably didn't have time to appreciate. Where he fell lies a headstone with a brownish plaque attached. Those plain headstones around him mark the sites where others were cut down, I'm sure, with some still adoring him and some still loathing him. Custer left his men one last time when his remains were eventually removed to West Point.

PHOTO #6 - HARRY ARMSTRONG REED

Two of Custer's brothers died with him on this ground on 6/25/76 (possibly a Sunday). Thomas died near to Custer — Thomas was so mutilated, the only recognizable piece of him was an arm sporting his tattooed initials. Thomas was awarded not one but two Medal of Honors during the Civil War. Brother Boston was killed further down the hill to Custer's left. Unfortunately for a very young nephew, Harry Armstrong Reed (age 18), the West did not live up to his expectations. He had joined his uncle's entourage by coming out West to improve his health. The marker in the middle of Photo #6 designates his last place on this Earth. Sending him off from back East, his parents remained confident that he would be safe under the watchful eye of his famous Uncle. But alas, he died no doubt confused and terrified with his protectors on that dust choking, blistering day.

I was glad to see other markers honoring some of the few Native Americans who fell that same day. One was Wasecu Sapa (Black White Man). I could not recall any such markers honoring the land-

PHOTO #7 - NATIVE AMERICAN
DEATH MARKER

owners who died that day on my first visit back in the 70's. Wasecu Sapa's death site marker is of brown marble and still appears to be trying to make his way up to those trespassers so eager to have his land.

Hiking down a gravel pathway, I turned for the next photo. Upper left, below the sky, is the Visitor Center. Upper right, below the sky, is the monument at the top of the hill honoring the fallen. Fallen hell, they were killed, lacerated, and butchered — rightly so. Please don't get the author's last insert wrong. But what would you do to people who stopped by your place, demanded to have it, insisted on you moving to a place of their choosing, that if you didn't die en route, you'd surely die there. In fact, they felt gracious in their swap for your land full of riches for their places they wouldn't consider habitable. Oh yes, and by the way, if you were reluctant to accommodate their wishes, they would visit another day with Howitzers and kill your women, your children, your ponies, your elderly, etc. Don't be timid! Get real! What would you do?

I'm also sure that the poor soldiers under Custer's command were brainwashed into a constant fear of the red man and bombarded with tales of massacres he brought down on defenseless white culture and soldiers while they slept. Most people will leave the boogeyman alone until you brainwash them into thinking that you must kill the boogeyman cause he's surely out to get you first.

PHOT⊙ #8 - PATH THROUGH THE DEAD

Do the numbers. Taking into account the history of white settlement across the U.S., make two columns, one for Native American dead and one for white dead. Which side has the longer list? You'll need extra paper for the first column. It got to a point in California, for example, where people went on hunting trips for pleasure like we might go out to deer camp or to scare up a few pheasant. But, these Christian-based Californians were hunting primitive natives most of whom had no modern weapons to even resist with. What was the rationale? They were in our way and they had the rich lands. Once again, when other countries do it, we call it genocide. When we did it, it was called Manifest Destiny. That phrase had to come straight from a devil's mouth.

Back on the path below the Visitor's Center and Custer's monument, you'll also see a handful of white death site markers. I'd seen them before but had assumed that they were killed trying to make their way up the hill to Custer. Wrong! Actually they are markers of about 40 men, they think were led by a Lt. Sturgis. They had made it up the hill with Custer, but made a futile attack into the midst of thousands of warriors intent on protecting their land, women, children, ponies, elderly, etc. It was said that the Native Americans held these guys in high esteem as although this attack was futile, it was brave.

See the guy in the upper middle of this same photo. I had passed him on my way down. He was of obvious Native American heritage. We did not speak or talk but gave each other an approving nod, maybe both in appreciation that we weren't here on that hot day in June of 1876 facing one and other.

40% of Custer's men were Scotch, Irish, and German immigrants. That leaves 60% who weren't by my calculations. Note: no photos were taken inside the Visitor Center as they were having electrical problems and it was very dark in there.

The coup de grace that finished Custer was a head wound. There were no powder burns proving that the wound was not self-inflicted. Different Native Americans claimed to have killed Custer. They reported that they killed a soldier wearing buckskin which Custer had chose to wear. However, just like nowadays, you'll have admirers or wanna be's who will get decked out emulating their hero. Custer was not the only soldier wearing buckskin that fateful day.

Most, if not all, of Custer's fallen comrades were hacked up and apart by the squaws present after the battle. Again, what would you do? It is also believed that if you left this world without all of your parts, you'd never be able to harm anyone else again now or in whatever future you were heading for. I suppose the squaws saw it as life insurance. Again, what would you sisters, you mothers, you wives, you daughters, and you grandmothers do? I'd like to hear your responses and how long it took you female relatives to reach your conclusions.

The women, for some reason, did not hack Custer up. They did thrust sewing awls deep into his ears to open them up as he had failed to listen to their chiefs who had basically and simply requested to be left alone long, long before the sun came up on this unforgiving hot day that June. My grandfather and father used to have this saying, "If you don't listen, you're going to have to feel." Immediately after hearing this, I had a tendency to listen intently.

A ranger gave an honest interpretation mingled with known facts and scholarly speculation on this conflict at a small outdoor amphitheater adjacent to the Visitor Center with a view from every seat of much of the entire battlefield. He was one of the best speakers that I have been lucky enough to witness. He pulled no punches for either side. His enthusiasm was captivating. He put you back there. You could all but taste the dust and the gun powder, the anger and the terror.

You may be one up on me on this. I learned something new this day from the Ranger's presentation. I was baked to the point that I did not want to climb back up that hill to the monument just above where Custer got his come up ins. I took the van on a narrow macadam road open to John Q. Public. It paralleled the cement walkway up and around behind the monument. Note: that monument marks the spot where 250 or so of Custer's men were finally laid to rest in a mass grave. Initially, they had been buried where they fell in shallow temporary graves. The memorial monument stands above it all listing all of the white fallen in perpetuity.

There's also a memorial shrine for the Native Americans very near the one for the whites. It can best be described as a semi-circle of stones lining a deep pit inside of a mound facing down the hill. You can taste the solemnity that seems to invade each visitor's soul at each of these shrines. Today, red, white, black, brown, and yellow visitors were all of one nation.

Returning to our quest up that road behind the white's marble shrine. Before learning it from the ranger today, your author was unaware that some of Benteen's or Reno's men (survivors from the other two columns) made an attempt to either huddle with or come to Custer's aid as they could hear the commotion of battle resonating through the ravines, hills and coulees. Lakota and Cheyennes lead by a student of Sitting Bull by the name of Gall stopped all of

PHOTO #9 - CALHOUN HILL

them in their tracks on the hill behind and below Custer. The white dots in the photo show where this melee played itself out. One ponders how many of these troopers were thinking, if we can just get to Custer, we'll be safe and he'll be forever in our debt for getting him out of this mess. One was Lt. James Calhoun, Custer's brother-in-law. I elected not to walk down through the thick dry grass for a closer look see. Not only because of the heat, but because of helpful signs and verbal warnings from the Ranger staff that this hallowed ground was fiercely protected by enumerable rattlesnakes. Peering down at my shorts and my rubber clogs, the debate was curtailed abruptly in favor of heeding the warnings. Too bad Custer had not done likewise.

Plum wore out and finding no Walmart, the author took refuge at a rest stop full of truckers east of Broadus, Montana. I parked the van in the farthest space left of the washroom to negate being awaken by the comings and goings of folks who stopped briefly for relief only.

Sleep came quickly as I continued to ponder Custer's command choices. Aroused around 10:30 PM by a female beating her gums like an AK-47 on full auto and nearly as loud. There were at least 10 empty parking spaces between our van and the restrooms, but she and her companions chose the space up against the van. The unknown number of companions' speech patterns and volumes were measurably less bombastic than hers. Initially there was a good deal of glass against glass and aluminum against aluminum clanging. So, my guess was this was a rolling party that except for one loud one was winding down.

Against better judgement, a peek out my side window couldn't be contained. It was a medium dark sedan showing a minimum of four heads inside with one continuing to do her AK-47 impersonation. As our vehicles were facing east, it was noted that they, too, had made attempts to block the sunrise with a well-placed dark wool blanket thrown over the outside of their windshield. So, it was assumed that we would be bunkmates for the duration.

I never did see Lady AK-47 but wanted to. The author owes a debt of gratitude to the very deep voiced male companion who interrupted her haranguing with just a few well placed low guttural words that I, for the life of me, couldn't make out but immediately silenced her. She never made so much as a peep the rest of the night. I know, I was that close. I would have heard her. I approached sleep once again forgetting all about Custer, but with a plan to introduce myself in the morning to that deep voiced male and offer him some sort of trade or even money if he would let me in on those well placed words.

DAY #28, 7/28/2016

But alas, it was not to be. I was up at 6:30 AM and they were long gone. Those words must be all powerful with lasting effort or she would have woke me up before 6:30 AM this morning. It had become so quiet, so fast, last night that I looked for blood where they had parked and for body parts in two nearby trash cans. That stranger with the deep voice is a mystical hero figure to me now. Who was that masked man? I'm thinking possible shaman.

All of the 18-wheelers must have similar sleep patterns to my own. As I listened to them crunch, then shimmy through the low gears as they sluggishly rolled back out onto Highway 212. Those on my side were heading southeast towards Belle Fourche, South Dakota, with me. I have no fetish about visiting places where white legends met their ends, but, the next bucket list target planned in advance was going to be a fateful card game in Deadwood, South Dakota.

But first, a breakfast of champions, Cheerios, dried milk, and dried bananas. One of my favorites if you remember to mix water with the dried milk which on most such mornings was a given. A lone enormous Black Angus bull with a hump standing on a hill behind us seemed to be bidding adios to each trucker as they rolled out. I guess he was lonely, too. Maybe he thought they were cattle trucks. Don't know, never will.

I felt the need to check in on the well being of an older guy in a Chrysler van that looked to have more miles on it than it could carry. I spotted the van last night when I pulled in but had not seen it's dark bronze, wrinkled, emaciated occupant with a white, long-handled mustache that appeared too big for his head until I was about to leave this morning. I inquired if he was broke down and he replied that he was not and that he was just hanging out, "my friend." I peered through his open side door. I could see no bed or platform but the seats had been pulled out many, many miles behind him. I offered him the box lunch pizza the pizza girl from Sheridan had given to me yesterday. He chuckled and declined. I told him to, "Have a good day my friend," as he turned and rooted for some unknown within the confines of his van. He reminded me of Gandalf in Lord of the Rings.

As I pulled away, it dawned on me that this guy had a very deep voice. Could I have just met the shaman from last night who shut the AK-47 girl down? Yet another unanswered mystery that accompanies travel and leaves one perplexed. There's a lot of that going around out there on the road. Be on the lookout for it. If you can pull your butt off the couch and get yourself out there.

Spotted two scrawny looking antelope not long after the possible shaman. They're the only "lopes" I've seen on this whole trip except for two unfortunates hit on the road. Other than the elk that took out the 18-wheeler, I've seen not one more fortunate elk in all these miles so far.

Pulled into Belle Fourche, South Dakota, pronounced "Fūshe" at 9:45 AM, still on Route 212, also known as the Warrior Trail. I'd always felt some sort of passionate, romantic connotation every time I'd read or heard the name Belle Fourche. Reality was somewhat of a letdown. Belle Fourche was a city on the move much of it living/ expanding, much of it old/dying. Lots of trailer parks. Many trailers had rust taking over where paint had long since vamoosed. A sign read, "Belle Fourche - City of the Year" but you couldn't make out the year.

I stopped at a large gas station / truck stop / casino close to the Belle's heart. I took a hike inside and discovered they had showers for rent. I told the middle aged cashier with the "I've heard it all too many times before so don't give me that one" look that, "I wouldn't need a shower for a few weeks yet, but how much are they?" Living up to her chosen expression, "$5.00."

By what I'd taken in in that brief period of surveillance, unless the cleaning lady had run off with some trucker, I couldn't be positive if I would or wouldn't come out of the showers dirtier than when I went in. I selected option #2 and retreated to the van wondering what untold substances now lodged on the bottoms of my rubber clogs.

I found reason to rejoice while gathering my wits in the van.

We've had a (medium, not full grown) common housefly inside the van since our stay in Cody, Wyoming a few days back. Spending that much time with any insect, studying it's mannerisms, interests, etc. you come to know them. I never knew the name but the coyness, the shyness, the devil may care attitude, just the way she carried herself, led me to conclude that she was indeed female. Had I been guessing, I would have had a 50/50 chance but there wasn't a hint of guessing going on here.

She loved it in here. I don't for the life of me know what attracted her here. But it was pretty evident, she was bent on staying. I tried to shoo her away on several occasions. Once I tricked her into flying out the driver's side window only to find her coming back in the passenger side. Had we bonded?

They say that travel is the best education. That she fly has seen a lot in her time and has been a long way to many places of interest. So, I no longer considered her a common housefly, but due to her own youthful wit, motivation, and stick-to-itness, she had become an uncommon housefly. It may not sound like much to the reader, but if you're a common housefly, it's a prestigious leap. What percentage of common houseflies make that leap to uncommon is unknown. Studies, though warranted, are at present non-existent. I could detect a change come over her on that second day in the van when she also realized it. She was much more confident and her composure resembled that of older, more sophisticated fly. She had grown up under my watchful eye. I had been there for her just at the right time in her life.

If you love them, let them go. She now resides in Belle Fourche. I had quietly but sadly opened just the driver's side window only a tad and gently coaxed her up to freedom with trepidation in a quandary over her true fate. Once she gained her freedom, I quickly, but with a degree of remorse, pushed the up button for the window.

I left this enterprise with mixed emotions. But, there, on the outside of my windshield holding on with all fours to the wiper blade, she sat pleading to go to the Black Hills with me.

I knew the Black Hills were no place for an uncommon single female housefly. She stood far better chances here in Belle Fourche. You could say this town was made for her. My lamenting almost got the best of me. I considered opening that window and welcoming her back into my life. It tugged at my heartstrings. But, alas, I had to base my decision on what was best for her.

Intentionally speeding up, I could see her grips on the wiper blade wavering. I could swear I heard a weak, shrill voice calling out, "Help me, help me." I was starting to ease up on the throttle recalling how she'd played in here all day as I drove, but never once bothering me at night while I slept. I've had much worse companions.

But, I needed to stick to my guns, not for me, but for her. I pushed that throttle down and watched one by one of those cute little fly legs lose their grip until the strongest of all could hold her fast no longer and she was gone. Mixed emotions crowded my brainpan once again. I hoped that she wouldn't hook up with some down and out gambler. I'm hoping she finds a nice horse or cattle trailer with many of her own welcoming her with open wings. She'll have plenty to eat and drink, fresher air than inside the van, and many new interesting friends. Given her luck, she might just run into a male uncommon housefly, one that's traveled and well-versed who can meet all of her needs that an old free camper just couldn't.

Spearfish was a clean, small, but bustling town straight south from Belle Fourche on Route 85. I stopped just long enough to get some postcards out to friends back home and to satisfy a craving I'd had for days. Total but friendly strangers whipped up an egg McMuffin with sausage for me. I'll let you guess where.

I spent not much more time in Spearfish than it took me to write it down above. No offense to the folks in Spearfish, but the town was my gateway to that card game in Deadwood and I felt full of piss, vinegar, and that egg McMuffin.

Before I knew it, I found myself in downtown Deadwood. Deadwood lies in a pit at the base of a collection of very steep converging mountains. No wonder they found gold here, it had nowhere else to go. It was booming with folks from all points on the globe. In fact, I felt fortunate in finding the last remaining remote space in a parking garage right off Main Street, which was not named after Jack McCall. Tell you why later. There was also a big time rodeo going on to fatten the crowd even more. Horses and giant cowboys everywhere. I snapped no photos of them for fear of spooking the horses.

Luck ran with me once again. She had stood by me much of my life and today looked to be no exception. Without a map or a guide, I turned a corner or two, looked up and found another of my bucket list. I stood on the wooden sidewalk outside Saloon #10 where Wild Bill met his end. Not a very romantic name for such a place of infamy. I suppose the owner was not a fan of prose as much as he was a fan of gold dust. Don't know, don't care. The original #10 burnt down long ago. Oddly enough, let me bring something to your attention, I wonder how many times the #10 popped up in Wild Bill's life? The author's birthday is 10/10. Do you ever get that number that keeps popping up? It is #27 for Precious.

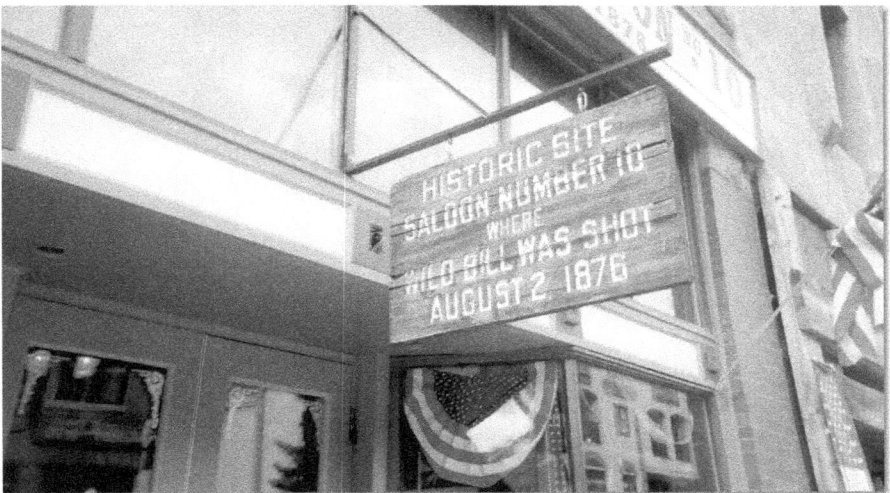

PHOTO #1 - WILD BILL'S END - SALOON #10

I can't read your mind but I know what you're thinking. Many of you readers just thought, "Oh God, here he goes again on some uninteresting tangent when all we wanted to do was to read about Wild Bill's demise."

OK! OK! If that's all you want me for, it's time to snap you back to your senses with a pop quiz. I've tried my damndest to be the best author I can be for you and this is the sophomoric appreciation that you sling back at me.

I might just stop this book right here, right now and suggest that you take that plunge out on a limb and find out by your own volition just what did happen to Wild Bill. Without me, most of you wouldn't even know that Hickok is spelled Hickok!

I must apologize to you loyal appreciative readers. My last outburst was surely not directed at you. Had it not been for the attitude of a minority of other readers, I had been considering forgoing any further testing. A truism that rears its ugly head throughout history time and time again, "The many must suffer due to actions of but few."

So, to you loyal, understanding, appreciative readers out there, should you have difficulty with or score below your expectations on this or any previous test, I implore you to write, call, or come see me and I'll see what I can do for you personally. This call goes out twofold to those of you who have sold in excess of 200 copies of this manuscript. You're the ones I'm hoping will come visit. I'm so looking forward to meeting with you. Maybe, if there's room, we could all fly up together to the convention. I'm also putting out the call to those of you who may want to give testimonials at the convention. Don't procrastinate. Let's get moving on this. Forgive my oversight. Had you been a procrastinator, you would never have hit those sales heights of over 200 copies. Somebody's got to be #1 in sales. Is it going to be you? I'm planning a surprise monetary package for #1 at the convention. I hadn't intended to let this slip out but you know once ink is put to paper, and so on and so on.

Anyway, we'll call this the Deadwood quiz:

T	F	1	Writing in French can tire you out more than writing in English
T	F	2	A Black Angus cow could be mistaken for a bear
T	F	3	Shamans are more powerful than an AK-47
T	F	4	Common houseflies should not be jealous or envious of uncommon houseflies
T	F	5	Readers should be loyal, understanding, and appreciative of their author

Answers: 1. T, 2. T, 3. T, 4. T, 5. F

I feel an obligation, now, to render unto you, the circumstances surrounding the death of Hickok. So, here goes: Wild Bill had moved on to Deadwood after learning of gold strikes in that locale. He may have convinced himself that he could find gold in them there hills but he was better and more inclined to find gold in them there pockets of gold miners at a game of chance. The night before he got it, he had bested another by the name of Jack McCall at the tables. The sum exchanged was unreported.

Your author stopped at #10, sauntered up to the bar and ordered a draft beer from a female barkeep in period dress with lovely features and cleavage. The rest of her, including her attitude, led one to believe that perhaps she had been rode hard and put back into the barn wet on one or more recent occasions. The beer was good and should have been considering the price.

Also sitting at the bar were two male and one female friendly bikers who had come all the way here from some parish in Louisiana for Sturgis Days. The female was unresponsive initially until she spotted my ever-present TV logo cap at which time she seemed to warm up, and slid herself to the bar stool adjacent to mine which

I had initially utilized as a buffer between myself and the other patrons. Once her attitude had warmed up, her significant biker grew increasingly interested in our conversation.

I did not want to spoil such a good day by being bludgeoned by bikers in Saloon #10. I intentionally limited myself to one slow beer and swapped a few tales regarding our journeys leading us all to here. I learned from these good folks, once the males realized I was no threat to their manhoods, that the original #10 had burned to the ground, but that there was an accurate facsimile on the actual site which lay below where we all sat sipping down our suds. I also learned from my newfound friends that one could obtain a walking tour for a pittance. The lovely but haggard barkeep keeping an ear on our conversations, informed yours truly that the pittance would be $10 (American).

I assumed that my Louisiana beer mates were waiting for the next tour. You know what they say about assuming. The bikers were not waiting for the next tour, they were waiting for the next pour. Note: have you ever met anyone from Louisiana who was not likable? Me neither.

Not seconds after the barmaid had enlightened me regarding the tour rates, I felt a soft pecking on my left shoulder. "Got a ten spot, stranger?" While half-beckoning to and half beckoning not to my Louisiana biker friends to join "The Stranger" for the $10 tour, I felt myself drifting aimlessly down the raw cut board steps to the actual site

PHOTO #2 - PROSTITUTE

where the cowardly deed was accomplished, with my tour guide steering from behind with one hand on each of my shoulders.

No, that's not her. That's a manikin that greets you near the base of the stairs plowing her wares.

That's her, smiling from behind the rebuilt bar, 3 bar stools, with two whitetails standing guard from above. The walls were of local stone easy to access down in this deep gorge called Deadwood. The floor was of untreated rough hewn lumber having it's own distinct low decibelled screech crying out to each stride landing across her.

Maybe my tour guide was as uncomfortable being alone with me as I was with her, but we proceeded with her extremely short presentation. Just to stand there where it happened warranted the $10.00 fee. If prostitution was currently legal in South Dakota, I had no inclination for pursuit.

PHOTO #3 - TOUR GUIDE WILD BILL'S

She allowed me another photo. This one is of the card table where Wild Bill was interrupted playing out his final hand. There was no way Wild Bill could have taken his preferred position with his back to the wall as the card table sat in the middle of the room.

I had numerous other questions for my tour guide about the scene I'd just witnessed in my fantasy. Either she didn't have the answers or she wanted to push on to her next $10.00. That was when it dawned on me that prostitution is legal in

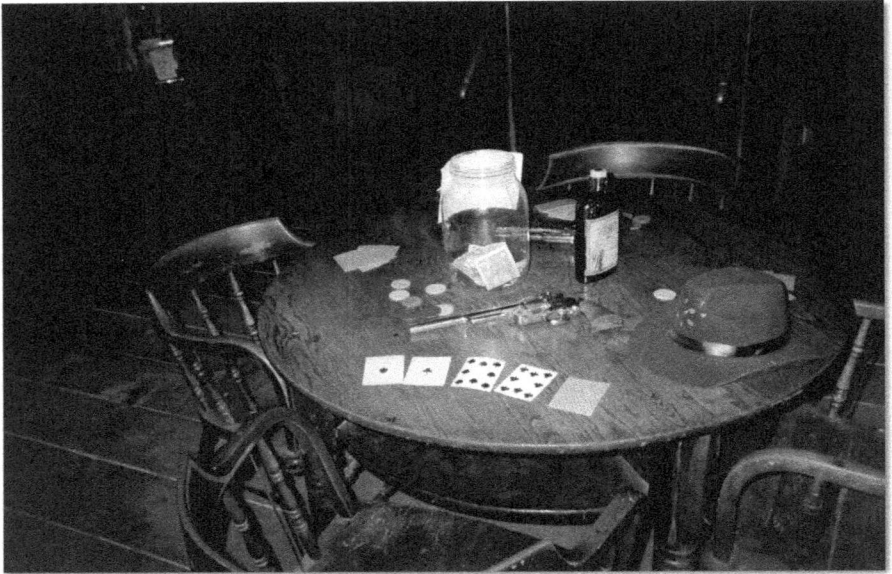

PHOTO #4 - WILD BILL'S TABLE

South Dakota. It just doesn't have anything remotely to do with sex. But, again, the $10 was worth standing at the scene. If the floor boards sang out then as each did today, I concluded that Wild Bill had to hear Jack McCall maneuvering back behind him. There were just too many unanswered questions. I would seek further professional help. No, let me put that another way. I would enlist input from a professional source for the answers.

Finding myself alone at the top of the stairs back in the street level bar I had had that slow beer in, I found that my tour guide had vanished as had my biker friends out of Louisiana. Per approval of my original barkeep, I took a handful of other photos inside this ever so interesting bar. Unfortunately, the light inside was way too dim, so I am only able to favor you with two.

Can you imagine lonely, half drunk, horny cowboys peering at the reclining brunette lady hanging behind the bar. I can assure you they weren't thinking about motherhood, the flag, or apple pie at the time of their gawking. It was a great management gimmick resulting/encouraging those cowpokes to order another one and another and another until oblivion took charge of them.

PHOTO #5 - BAR PAINTING

PHOTO #6 - BAR WALLS

Photo #6 is a good example of what meets the eye from every wall in this bar. Lots of old photos. If you look close two are of Wild Bill. There's a menagerie of stuffed animals, fish, etc. of all sizes and species. I know the animals and fish would have preferred a far differing outcome, but I enjoyed it.

I stumbled upon a gun dealer attached to the bar. He wasn't attached to the bar, but his place of business was. Maybe I'd found someone to help me with this plight of unanswered questions.

Though he didn't look the part, he played it exceedingly well. From him I learned that Jack McCall was a drifter. Yes, he did lose a pot to Wild Bill the night before. How substantial? Do the numbers. Any loss to a drifter would be considered substantial. McCall walked in with a pistol concealed under a small brown hat held in his hand. He and Wild Bill acknowledged each other. Yes, Wild Bill was holding aces and eights x2 which would be a good hand to bet on in draw poker with a more than fair chance of winning the pot. Maybe this hand and its chances caused Wild Bill's usual cautious persona to lapse as the snake slid round behind him and fired once into the back of his head.

I asked my newfound expert what kind of a gun it was? He looked down to the floor as if not wanting to recall the specifics, and then look me straight in the eye with a tear in his eye as if he was a personal friend of Wild Bill and through grit teeth snarled, "He shot him with a Saturday Night Special cause that's all the son of a bitch could afford." My expert turned and abruptly walked away from me as if his own manhood would have suffered, had I been witness to a cavalcade of angry tears. I busied myself looking under glass at a vast and enviable collection of ancient firearms, knives, arrows, coupe sticks and like relics of a century long gone past. Never once did I question the manhood of my expert. Real men can and do cry over a loss and it takes more courage to let those emotions surface in public than it does to hide behind a false sense of bravado.

He must have sensed my position on the above for as soon as he regained his composure, there he was in front of me, without being asked, with the rest of the story. McCall pleaded in court that he had shot Hickok because Hickok had shot and killed his brother. This was not the case. It did not happen. But, the jury believed it and found him not guilty. Makes me think of the O.J. Simpson trial.

Anyway, McCall slithered out of Deadwood and ended up somewhere in the Wyoming territory. The sheriff at the time in

PHOTO #7 - BULLOCK
MOTEL, DEADWOOD

Deadwood, by the name of Bullock, learned that Mr. McCall was bragging everywhere he landed in Wyoming about his brave feat back in Deadwood.

Incensed, Sheriff Bullock left his jurisdiction (illegal), captured/arrested McCall in Wyoming, (illegal), had him tried (illegal), convicted (illegal), and hung (illegal). All of my notations overdone above stem from the fact that: Sheriff Bullock was out of his jurisdiction, Wyoming was still a territory, and the alleged murder took place in South Dakota, and Mr. McCall had been found not guilty by a jury of his peers back in Deadwood.

Mr. McCall was allowed to remain in Wyoming six or probably less feet down in an unmarked grave with the noose still around that "son of a bitch's" neck. Hats off and kudos to Sheriff Bullock. I'm not sure if he built it or it was just named in his honor, but it suggests that Sheriff Bullock had many more admirers in Deadwood than that "son of a bitch" McCall. Please refer to the photo of Bullock Motel in present day downtown Deadwood, a far cry from the hole in the wall where Wild Bill didn't get to collect on his last winning hand.

Telling me the end of the story sure seemed to pick up the spirits of my expert. His tears had left and dried and were replaced with a twinkle and a hint of pride. I didn't intentionally try to rhyme this.

That's, for the most part, how it came down. We parted ways after a firm and understanding handshake.

For those of you keeping a timeline (not a requirement but a nifty idea), Wild Bill left the planet on August 2, 1876. Do the numbers. It had only been about 38 days since Custer had left for points unknown. Try to imagine the mood the country was in.

Learning that Wild Bill's final resting place sat high above the town in the Mount Moriah Cemetery, I took the short but nosebleed drive up Mount Moriah, just one of those steep mountains surrounding as if protecting Deadwood laid out far below. I left the van in the parking lot after checking the emergency brake twice. Photo #8 gives you a ground level view of the walking pathway entrance.

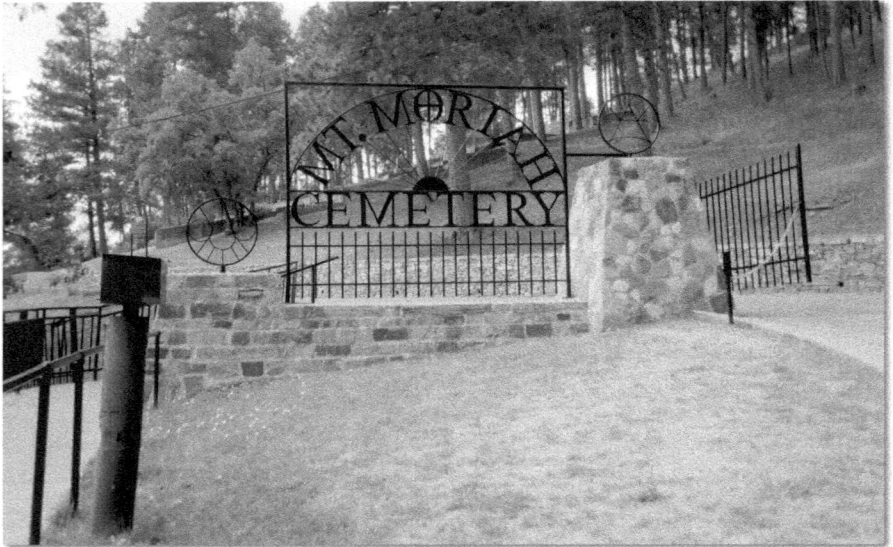

PHOTO #8 - MT. MORIAH CEMETERY

If you're careful with your footing, there's some great views of Deadwood from these heights. Don't try it in flip flops. It's a long way down and the last thing people will remember you for would be the screaming and bouncing.

There were hundreds of graves scattered all over this mountain. There's probably more graves than current full time residents way down there in Deadwood. Many headstones were of noteworthy interest.

PH⊙T⊙ #9 - KENNETH

The one that stirred me the most was Kenneth (no last name), died May 9, 1906, aged 4 years, 7 months, and 13 days. Kenneth gets many visitors. Some leave stones, wood, and coins, but his constant companion is a lamb that sleeps with him night and day. I left him something also but that's strictly between me and Kenneth.

One could spend days in this cemetery just reading headstones, but I was on a mission. I said a prayer for Kenneth, left him there with his lamb, and continued on with my search for Wild Bill. You'll find a labyrinth of cart paths and foot trails weaving you throughout the silent headstones. I saw a few folks who brought basket lunches. I for one have never favored dining with the dead, but to each his own. It was not the least bit crowded.

All of a sudden, there he was! Well, there his headstone was. It was Wild Bill. He was fenced off but you can walk right up to the fence and touch his dark brown headstone. Curiously, he faces away from Deadwood. But, after all he'd been through down there, can you blame him? I'm pretty sure he's facing south, maybe looking for Jack McCall.

As you can see in the photo, folks leave stones, etc. at the base of his headstone as well. I left a lucky penny I'd been carrying on this whole journey. I know he can't do much with a penny. It was the luck I was trying to send his way. I lingered there caught up in private reflection not too long, not too brief, said a prayer for Wild Bill, bid him adieu, and wandered slowly back in the direction of the van, somehow feeling his approving smile on the back of my neck. I reason that him and I would have gotten along just fine. I know I would have tried my darnedest.

PHOTO #10 - WILD BILL'S GRAVE

Calamity Jane lived until 1903, spouting off to anyone she thought was listening, that she and Wild Bill had been secretly married. They buried her there near his grave but not side by side which was probably more representative of their true relationship.

I sat in the van for a few minutes pondering my options. There would be only one way off of this high mountain cemetery and that way was down via aptly named Cemetery Street. After another prayer that my brakes would not fail me because the only thing that would stop your rapid descent would be the town of Deadwood itself and I was not one to seek fame at any cost, I dropped down into the lowest gear. How, in God's name, did they ever get the dead, their coffins, etc. up that hill without losing horses in the attempt is beyond this author. Maybe they used pulleys. Forget it if there was snow or ice. If you did make it up, you'd die on the slide back down. If you get there, you'll have a better appreciation for what I'm talking about.

I'd like to meet the folks who were on the site selection committee for the Mount Moriah Cemetery. I'm guessing their reasoning went something like this. "We better bury them all up high as the gold will be found down low, and we won't have to start digging them up if we bury them down here and some lucky miner comes along and finds gold close to them." I'm not sure that's the most likely explanation but from where I'm sitting, it could be. Give it some thought. Give me a call.

I hyperventilated my way to the base of the straight shot Cemetery Street where she returns the frightened back into downtown Deadwood. Now, there were throngs of folks lining up on both sides of Main Street. Mine was the last vehicle they let come through as they were setting the stage for a reenactment of a gun battle on the street. I could not stop for the gun battle, but intentionally slowed to a crawl, made sure my TV network hat was adjusted the way I liked it, opened the two front windows and proceeded to wave at the hundreds of folks lining up for the duel in the sun. To my delight, numerous spectators waved back at me. It was yet one more fifteen minutes of fame and I loved it.

I left Deadwood with a mixture of emotions. It was a grand city and I would like to return. Regarding Wild Bill, my jury is still out.

I don't know if he was a good guy or bad. He was probably open for speculation and perplexed on this same issue himself. But what an interesting tale and trail he left behind for us. Like most icons, he probably didn't see his life as we see it, looking in from the outside, for he was stuck with seeing it from looking out from the inside and that, dear reader, makes a whirlwind of difference. Let's let him rest. He's probably long since caught up with Jack McCall and settled it.

Feeling the need to leave all these ghosts behind, yet jubilant about the throngs of folks who turned out for my departure, I took the first road out of Deadwood. We were now rolling south on Highway 385 towards Rapid City.

I stopped long enough at Pactola Reservoir to fire up the Coleman, have a warm, but less than memorable meal, and to make another stash of coffee. Pactola is gorgeous and is a gateway into the Black Hills. That's just one arm of Pactola serving as a grand view for me near my picnic table. There's a beach up the road from here. Great place for family outings.

We bypassed Mount Rushmore. I elected not to go there. I'd been there twice in the past and had learned that the faces there still remain. I wonder what Washington, Jefferson, Lincoln, and Roosevelt feel when they go there? Not far away is the workings of an unfinished statue of Crazy Horse. It is taking decades to complete this work. What gives? We are still reluctant to give Native American their due. Could it be our conscience at work here backfiring on us when we realize what we handed these peoples?

I could have shot a whole roll of film or more going through the Black Hills. I selected three for this book and for you. See the gravel road descending down the hill in Photo #13. We almost got stuck at the bottom in a bit of a quagmire created by rain, gravity, man and beasts. See Photo #14 - parking the van off of the shoulder, I walked back to snap this shot of a formidable rock outcropping. Returning to the van, I thought I'd run into my first flat tire of the trip. However, the hissing sound was not coming from a puncture in a tire but from my first sited, in the flesh, rattlesnake laying in front of my back left tire doing his job of letting me know where he was so our two worlds wouldn't collide. In appreciation of his signaling me instead of ruining a perfectly good day for him, I backed up and pulled onto the highway without sending him to Custer. He was approximately three feet long and light brown in color verging on yellow, and full of death. I'm sure he and the rest of them don't appreciate what those fangs can deliver. Hell, he doesn't even know he's a rattlesnake. A penny for his thoughts. I didn't press him for a photo.

PHOTO #11 - PACTOLA LAKE

From here still on Highway 385, we glided through Wind Cave National Park. I had the place virtually to myself. I guess most tourists are more attracted to Mount Rushmore. When I passed the road taking you to Rushmore, it was bumper to bumper traffic. Don't let me discourage you from visiting Rushmore if you haven't already. The first time for me was the charm.

PHOTO #12 - BLACK HILLS

PHOTO #13 - BLACK HILLS

The solitude and lack of traffic in Wind Cave was medicine to me. I, like most others, traveling through the Black Hills can easily understand why the Indians felt it was sacred ground. You can feel it. It's palpable. If you can't feel it, you need your karma realigned or you should check your kerosene heater for leaks or something.

PHOTO #14 - BLACK HILLS RATTLESNAKE

We found ourselves virtually alone on rolling high hills of mostly buffalo grass as green as green can green speckled with alcoves of tall pines swaying like a chorus with the flowing grass seemingly enjoying the pushes and shoving from an invisible wind. Wind Cave was the right on nomenclature for this vast and mystical national park. Thanks Uncle Sam for saving this land. You know, it wouldn't have been the same had it been dotted with condos and beer joints.

Another gift from above this day was a lone buffalo bull who wasn't sure whether he wanted to stay on Highway 385 with me and the van or hike up Wind Ridge before darkness set in. I took this shot of him through the passenger side window just as he made up his mind. He was much closer than the photo depicts. He was so close, the only thing I could do was whisper, "Thank you" to him. He acknowledged my thank you with a nod of his great shaggy head peering directly into the van with eyes larger and softer than a cow's and trudged off up Wind Ridge alone yet content.

PHOTO #15 - BUFFALO BULL

It was trying harder to get dark on me as we pulled into Hot Springs, South Dakota. I had time for one more photo. That's a waterfall coming down over a cliff 60 feet more or less, tumbling in trickles over, around, and through green algae clinging to the rough surfaces of the cliff for dear life and winning. It empties into a small stream that meanders through much of the town.

Any free camper will tell you that we certainly welcome seeing anything on our maps that indicates a hot spring and we'll make a beeline for it with visions of a hot, free bath dancing in our heads. I'll admit that this was, if not the main reason, then certainly close to it for selecting this route. Plus, the route was a dotted scenic route on my atlas. How could I resist? It would also get me closer to my next bucket list destination - Wounded Knee.

Cruising through town, I could find not one area of that hot spring stream that was secluded enough to match my level of mod-

PHOT⊙ #16 - H⊙T SPRING

esty rendering me a degree of comfort commensurate with total bathing bliss. Curses, foiled again!

To add salt to the injury, there was no Walmart. Dark had now plunged into its total glory. I could feel panic knocking to come in. I fought that demon off and called on luck to find me once again. Would she come or was she going to let me down for the first time? She found me lickety split and pushed us up a dual lane highway leaving town towards a large lit up parking lot cradling a local supermarket as it's only occupant. Thank you lady luck. Nice to see you again.

I now targeted this local supermarket as a potential B&T (bed and toilet). All I had to do now was some discreet surveillance quickly as this was no Walmart and we were no doubt closing in on closing time. It was a nice clean market with reasonable prices. I bought some chips to throw the remaining two cashiers off regarding my true purpose for being here. I could sense this wasn't their first rodeo and that they could identify a free camper at their leisure, especially at this time of evening. It was somewhere in the vicinity of 9 PM. This was not my usual mode of operation, but I was trapped and was feeling the pressure. "Free Camper" was written all over me. And knowing I hadn't had a bath since the Tongue River, there was no use in deception. They knew.

There was only one other shopper in the market. He and I had spoke rounding a corner into each other earlier. He ended up in line in front of me to check out. Thinking Lady Luck may have abandoned me to the elements, feeling desperate, and too tired to drive on, I approached him by driving the van opposite his in the parking lot, driver's door to driver's door.

Sensing that since this market was not open 24-7, they probably didn't tolerate free campers with the same degree that the Walmart Astorias do. According to my new friend and his white dog "Lucky," my surveillance conclusions were correct. The dog's name alone is a staunch indicator how Lady or Mr. Luck has embraced the author for much of a lifetime. Don't rule out guardian angels at work also. He did tell me about a park downtown that did allow free campers to do their thing as long as they were discreet, didn't party, didn't litter, etc. I indicated that I could meet all those criterias with ease. I thanked him and asked for one more favor - directions.

After a couple of lefts and a couple of rights, he concluded that it might be better for me to follow Lucky and him to that park. I was too tired to object and followed him faithfully to my lodgings for the night. We B.S.'d briefly there and exchanged names. He was Charlie McCoy and I still knew who I was. I thanked him wholeheartedly and he left. He returned in a few minutes and said that he and his wife had room and that I could bunk there for the night. I gave him all the appreciation I could muster, but declined letting him know that he had done plenty for me already. We shook hands again and he and Lucky rolled off.

I parked opposite a public restroom and watched a local elderly police officer locking a steel grated door blocking all access to the restroom. No rest for the weary tonight, at least wise not in that restroom. A quick oatmeal, raisins, and the usual, and yours truly was more than ready to call it a day. Except for a couple of teenagers out catting around probably without the knowledge of their parents, the night passed uneventful, until a lone drunk woke me briefly by shaking and rattling that barrier locking up access to the restroom. He was a reasonably quiet drunk or he had passed out without my knowledge on the far side of the cinder block outhouse between it and the Hot Spring stream shining in the glow of numerous street lights. It didn't matter, I caught back up with sleep near on to immediately.

During the brief encounter last night with Charlie and Lucky, Charlie revealed that he was a transplant from Jackson, Mississippi. He loves it here as the humidity is much nicer than Old Miss'. He's been married to current missus for 12 years. He recently retired from the post office as a delivery/counterman. His resume also includes stand up comic in small comedy shops and Former Marine. Lucky is 12 years old.

DAY #29, 7/29/2016

Morninged up at 6:30 AM. Had not heard the unbolting of the steel grated access blocker to the restroom in Centennial Park, but greatly appreciated it. All morning rituals were met save for a more than a much needed bath. Some good samaritan had donated the remnants of a bar of what looked to be Dial soap in the sink. I opted out and washed upper extremities with biodegradable Ivory.

Still feeling quite squalid even after my spot bath and bailing out on counting on baby wipes to redistribute and reconstitute sloven areas remaining untouched, I considered attempting to kick myself in the "arse" for not taking Charlie up on his offer of lodging and a shower.

Exiting the Centennial Park's near perfect restroom, up pulls Charlie and Lucky both with the same grins they had on their departure last evening. Charlie didn't have to "sweeten the pot" but did so with an offer of not only shower, but much needed shave.

PHOTO #1 - CHARLIE & LUCKY

Reluctance took a hike while the van and I followed Lucky and Charlie to their basement man cave. Let it be known that your author agreed to accept this present, but only if your author could take them to breakfast of their choosing.

Much refreshed and feeling that life had reentered my body, I requested to take this photo of Lucky and Charlie down in the man cave. To my relief, Charlie wasn't gay nor was he a serial killer. He was just a good ole boy originally from Jackson, Mississippi. Although invited, Lucky did not accompany us to the restaurant that was situated downtown, almost directly across from the diminutive waterfall snapped two photos back. Lucky may have needed some down time.

It was like walking into "Cheers" with Norm. Nearly everyone hailed Charlie and the place was bustling. Charlie introduced me to the owner, a miniature but overworked beauty, another transplant from State College, Pennsylvania. We ordered then devoured two humongous western omelettes. Adding even more interesting limbs to his resume tree, Charlie shared that he loves woodworking, he's good and plays blackjack and Texas Hold'em locally, and he's currently 55 years old after 34 years with the Post Office.

Charlie is in the early phase of contemplation about pursuing his own bucket list. I encouraged him to not procrastinate, as the degree to which this trip has worn on me physically, tends to make me believe that I may have started too late in life for the quest of my own bucket list. Hope not, but the frame is aching.

As was becoming my custom, Charlie was invited to the cigar stash. He was tickled with two. He chose a Parodi and a Filipino. He could have had more, but didn't.

Charlie, upon learning that my next bucket list was Wounded Knee, warned me that there wasn't much there beyond a graveyard and that I may not receive a warm reception. This he left open ended without explanation.

Feeling I'd short changed Charlie for his hospitality, I decided to give him "the shirt off my back." He was initially reluctant, but accepted it. It was still clean and was from some yacht club in Georgia. I hadn't worn it yet since acquiring it at a Goodwill store in Florida. Hell, one of the few things Charlie hadn't been yet was a yacht owner, but potential remained high.

In parting, I reiterated my stance on not procrastinating, exchanged addresses/phone numbers, asked him to send me a post

PHOTO #2 - HORSES, PINE RIDGE

card or note when he knocks off that first bucket list, welcomed him to my home anytime, and asked him to give Lucky a "so long" from me. Unfortunately, recent contact with Charlie revealed that Lucky had passed after living 18 happy years.

Although holding onto an uneasy feeling about Charlie's open ended warning, I volunteered to drive south out of Hot Springs still on Route 385 crossing the Cheyenne River, giving it my best to connect with Wounded Knee. We took a left onto Route 87 in the direction of Pine Ridge.

Near to Pine Ridge, I stole away with two photos of horses. I don't know if they were part of the reservation or not. I hoped that they were. Another study on the concept of wild and free.

Photo #3 was taken in a full blown attempt to show you the most perfect horse I'd ever seen. I've seen the Lipizzan stallions up close and personal once. They were extremely impressive in form, beauty, temperament, motion, etc., but if someone would give me that little gray colt standing with his Pinto mother near the middle of Photo #3, I'll be more than glad to take him off your hands. I'm not a professional judge of horse flesh, but I know rare and priceless beauty when I see it.

Remember several pages back when your author was going on and on about how whitey had one way or another removed the noble Native American from his prime ancestral lands and offered in exchange lands, that for lack of better terminology, were somewhat less desirable. Please review Photo #4. This is what they got for the swap. This photo as well as photos #5 and #6 were taken on the Pine Ridge Indian Reservation. Let me know if you can see any lakes, rivers, timber, etc., essential for even the barest fundamentals of life. I challenge you to go there and eke out a living for yourself and your family.

There was no explanation for the unmarked white cross stuck in the sand in Photo #4 other than someone had died there. How prophetic! I really felt lonely here. Other than the two lane asphalt

PHOTO #3 - HORSES, PINE RIDGE

PHOTO #4 - TYPICAL LAND, PINE RIDGE RESERVATION

belching up an infrequent vehicle once in a great while, it was as if nothing was alive here. Now would be a good time to take a break from reading and skip back through this work and re-enjoy the numerous photos showing magnificent geographic beauty that once belonged to the red man. He didn't buy or sell it. He simply lived there. Keep in mind, some of our earlier photos were taken in the Great Lakes area. That's where the Sioux once lived.

PHOTO #5 - TYPICAL LAND, PINE RIDGE RESERVATION

No photos were taken of the occasional worn out houses and rusty trailers with landscaping via piles of junk, broken down cars, broken down refrigerators, broken down peoples staring out into nowhere as if exhausted in their faith that God would pluck them away and return them to their former lands and lives of abundance.

It was difficult to even make eye contact with them while driving by. I had never killed a Native American. I had never removed their buffalo. I had never stolen their lands. However, upon reflection, I do own a house and property on a place called Opessa Street. I've told you this before. The street was named after a great and respected Indian leader once called King Opessa. I have half or more of a mind to research the Great Opessa, find out if any of his kind remain and will my land back to them.

PHOTO #6 - TYPICAL LAND, PINE RIDGE RESERVATION

I would be remiss not to ask, did the mighty Opessa take this land by forcing other peoples out or did he just wander on to it and found no other occupants and then decided to set up shop? We know that some Native Americans were ruthless deceivers who took full advantage of their own weaker neighbors. Is mankind doomed to this scenario repeating itself over and over again where the strongest stomp the weaker into submission? I hope not, but history is a chronicler.

About the time I was losing all hope for these people and mankind's indifference to greed and suffering, a message for renewed hope galloped into my world. Hope this time, sent by chance or a guardian angel took the form of a 20's something Native American young man astride a magnificent Palomino horse. The tall/lanky Sioux was decked out in blue jeans, cowboy boots, western shirt and cowboy hat. They went flying by as if on the wind, splendid beast and rider as one.

By the time I did an immediate ubie for a photo op, they were gone from all sight, having crossed the highway and into the rolling sandy grass hills. It was that Native American magic thing again being able to disappear at will, and this time a horse was part of the magic show. I wish I could learn how to do that.

The simple sight of this guy's skill, courage and mastery of the saddle restored me as if finding an island of hope in a sea of misery. You go boy! Could be, there is light at the end of their tunnel.

There was very little if any roadside signs to guide the free camper to Wounded Knee. It was as if Uncle Sam's conscience had bothered him so much, and in an attempt to hide his shame and guilt for what was perpetrated there, he wanted to discourage visitation there for fear that the truth might surface giving him a black eye. What does it say on the Statue of Liberty — give us your poor, your hungry, your downtrodden, and so on.

It's easy to miss the cutoff to Wounded Knee. My atlas didn't even have a route number for it. As was stated, it was so easy, we ended up on the outskirts of the Bad Lands. For all intents and purposes, the Bad Lands adjoin the Pine Ridge Indian Reservation.

PHOTO #7 - BADLANDS

If you think lands traveled on the reservation were bleak, check out the two photos I'm submitting for the Badlands. Sorry, it's so dark. The sky was doing it's best to cough down some rain. These photos were taken in midday. Don't know who the portly fellow is in #7. He carried the look of a guy who wished he hadn't gone down there once he reached my parking lot pull over.

Realizing the ere of my ways, I did a ubie and headed back south on Route 40, returned to Oglala, and learned that Route 18E was the route I had inadvertently missed about 40 miles ago. About 7 miles on 18E and I was in Wounded Knee (a light sprinkling of framed small houses and trailers that had long lost their luster).

A heavily rutted dirt road will lead you up to the cemetery sitting atop a high knoll with commanding views down toward the unseen stream hidden in the bushes below called Wounded Knee, a creek. Before I made it to the top of that knoll, a beat up red Chevy truck slid to a stop beside me. It came from out of nowhere and threw dust every which way that hadn't settled yet as the driver brought her to a halt.

PHOTO #8 - BADLANDS

A young, large Sioux buck leaped from the shotgun seat and walked briskly to my door. He didn't have to walk that far as the Chevy settled in the dust three feet from the frightened van. This guy didn't mince words and got right to the point, "Could you help us out with some gas money?" He sported intermittent teeth with a gap between each one he still carried. He didn't seem to care one iota about the missing teeth. Like the missing teeth, there was no trace of self consciousness. I would have to describe his demeanor as unthreatening bravado.

I had wound my window down upon his approach trying to show no fear or intimidation. Quick thinking on my feet, though I was actually still seated, led me to the Canadian coins I couldn't exchange back in Cody. I asked, "Could you use some Canadian money?" He replied, "I guess so." I handed him $4-$5 in Canadian coins. He looked them over intently for a few seconds, rolled them in his hand, and handed them back to me just that quick saying, "We can't use them." I was really hoping they could.

Concern grew for the $180 American I had in cash in my wallet. I usually never carry that much cash and had forgotten to stash it, or most of it, far from my wallet in the confines of my other particulars inside the still quivering van. I still had bucu warm Millers in my cooler which it was far too late to regret now. Either one I figured might spark the interest of this gentleman or his three shadowy companions sitting silent and motionless inside the Chevy. They could have been martians or worse yet, Klingons, for all I knew. I never caught a good look at any of them. More magic. God, they're full of it.

There was a very brief period of uneasy silence and then he quipped, "How about the Pringles?" I said, "What?" He reiterated, "Can we have your Pringles? The boys are hungry." I was never so happy to share food in all my life. He had spotted the Pringles (vinegar and salt) that I had purchased back in Canada before crossing the line. I knew that there was less than half of them left to be split between four hungry growing bucks. Wondering what he might up the ante to but not being in any position to question or challenge, I said, "Sure" with as much pleasantry and camaraderie I had left in me. He snatched the green canister rapidly from my hand, jumped back into the Chevy and they were off and gone in a cloud of reddish/orangish dust. Had he not been so quick on his feet, I had already contemplated volunteering to give them much more of my provender as I calculated I had much more fodder than I needed as my journey was nearing the end. The van seemed to take this encounter much harder than your author. She just seemed to sit there spent. I could have sworn I heard a sigh of relief coming from somewhere under her hood.

I for one was wishing that I was sitting down outside after the dust settled providing the boys with a decent lunch and swapping tales. That was not in the stars today as I had just received another gift of the vanishing phenomena God had extended to native peoples. Whitey held most of the technological advantages, but never in this realm. How I envy them for this power. I'm sure they're aware of it and no doubt appreciate it.

Sensing some apprehension on the part of the van, I nudged her gently towards the summit of this small knoll. The ruts got ruttier and the holes got holier, as I sought to let the van rest and graze in a clean but unkempt reddish/orangish dirt parking lot. Go slow if you value the undercarriage or oil pan of your vehicle.

Out of nowhere from my blind side, I was greeted before the van had come to a complete stop by a very enterprising young boy of 7 or so on a bicycle I was glad I hadn't run over. He put his hand out and through my open window, shook mine heartily and said, "Welcome to Wounded Knee." I could feel the apprehension rising again from the van. I felt non-threatened but remained guarded. His small hand gave mine a firm and confident shake. This was not his first day as a greeter.

Maybe too proud or ashamed to ask, he handed me a well worn

yellow slip of paper and there printed in large penciled words in somewhat haphazard alignment revealing his request, "Can you help me with a donation for my school clothes?"

I was immediately touched by his gesture and to subdue the tears I felt welling up inside me reached for the nearest humor I thought might reach him. I told him, "I don't think my clothes will fit you." For 7, he was savvy and with a little grin replied, "No, a donation of money."

Feeling and seeing the presence of other children cautiously or shyly appearing in my left side mirror, I felt it best to ask him how much do people usually give as it appeared that all of these hapless waifs might also be in need of some new school duds. He hesitated and weighed his response while sizing me up. Like I said, this wasn't his first day as a greeter and he was keenly savvy. His response gave away his length of tenure and experience. Sounding more like a question than a declaration, he half whispered "20?" As the rest of the waifs leaned in closer as if they were judging his performance while working as a team. I inquired, "How about $5?" He snatched it up like it was a green Pringles can and he was gone.

In a jiffy, up pops a second Sioux lad of 10 or so presenting more of a lingering hesitation, much more awkward than the 7 year old. His strength came in his sincerity. Almost under his own breath, he confided, "Could you please help me? My mother is on oxygen and we need the money." This wasn't your author's first rodeo either. These kids could have been conning me. I didn't care. The beyond dismal condition of the living quarters and landscape I'd seen on the way in ensured me that these kids needed all the help they could get. So, if they told me they needed money because the sky was falling, I would have helped them. I don't know the origin, but I adhere to the following. "The best way to find out if you can trust someone is to trust them." The 10 year old got another of my vanishing $5's. I wasn't being stingy. I just didn't know how many more would be in need and the van only gets 23 miles/gallon. The 10 year old looked at the $5 and back at me and through sad/sincere eyes as if this was his only score in a long time said, "This is greatly appreciated."

Keep in mind, these two 5's were gone before I had shut the engine off. My 10 year old was also on a bike but chose not to vanish. He sat off on his steed observing the action, his once forlorn expression erased and replaced with a joyous beam recognizable at a great distance. He glowed.

Before I could exit the car, from nowhere appeared a middle aged Sioux male whose name I did not catch. He said he would gladly give me a tour for $10. I balked. I was already out $10 and hadn't got out of the van yet. I could sense the van was totally against this and really wanted to just "haul ass." I fought off her proposal and without showing my cards gave this guide, who by the way was for all intents and purposes drunk, my undivided attention. I will give him this. Though he reeked of liquor, he and his clothing were clean, not immaculate but acceptably clean. The ground in the parking lot was so uneven and full of ruts we will give him the benefit of the doubt and describe his gait as one of light on his feet. This man was not overbearing or pushy. He was kind and polite.

I tried to be honest with my new inebriated friend. I told him I was already out $10 and hadn't left the van yet. He sensed my reluctance and produced a pair of earrings that I knew Precious might not wear, but would cherish. I sensed he had dismissed completing the tour and had hung his lot on the earrings. I thought this was an ideal setting to attempt a "bundle." Thank you Frank. I made the offer. $10 Canadian coins for the tour and the earrings. He said, "Let me help you out of the car." While assuring him that I was not an invalid, I could make out some disdainful murmurings coming up from under the hood.

My new friend told me that he was an Afghanistan veteran and had been wounded by a shell fragment. This info preempted my question of why he was wearing a back brace outside of his white dress shirt. He also wore black dress pants matching the brace and

414 | U.R. McFarland

reddish/orangish dust over black dress shoes. He also revealed that he was homeless except for the tent he lives in near the creek. He assured me he could cash in the Canadian coins.

I shared that I had passed by a veteran's hospital yesterday in Hot Springs. He quipped that they closed that one and the closest one he could count on was back up in Sturgis. I exclaimed that that was even beyond Deadwood and at best a two day drive. He said, "Yea, if you have a car."

As my guide tripped the light fantastic with me through the white painted cement block and exposed red brick columns supporting a metal arch topped off with a simple white cross guarding the cement path into the cemetery, a pretty and seemingly very shy Sioux princess not beyond 14 appeared from nowhere. She wore blue jeans and a dark tee shirt. And though gorgeous, clung to what seemed to be that tomboy stage that holds many a rare beauty of her age captive and probably for a very good reason.

I had to ask her twice to speak up as she spoke in a half whisper so faint even those with good hearing easily surpassing what's left of mine would be forced to request repetition from her as well. She presented like she was a person who had been abused and/or was extremely timid or shy.

I found myself leaning my best ear closer towards her just to make out her words. She was selling dream catchers. I put my hands up as if I was being robbed. She backed off but without a smile. I instantly hoped that I had not hurt her sensitivities while my reluctantly hired tour guide gently tugged at my arm to proceed with the tour.

I told my guide that I had studied what the whites labeled a battle, but had the truth been known was a choreographed massacre. The Seventh Cavalry (438 troopers and 22 artillery men) surrounded the Native Americans, demanded their weapons, the unknown shot rang out, and the Seventh opened up with everything they had including Hotchkiss Mountain Cannon x4 on peoples who were simply trying to make their way to the Pine Ridge Reservation. Many believe the handful of soldiers killed occurred as a result of friendly fire. Uncle Sam lost 25 that cold day.

I told my thoughtful but tipsy guide that I thought that the soldiers fired down on the Sioux from an elevated position as he and I stood looking over the fenced in cemetery ringed with rectangular lines of cement maybe six inches wide enclosing an area guessed to be about 25 or so feet long and 10 or so feet wide. Don't know how deep but it became the final resting place for about 90 warriors and 200 or so women and children. Wounded Knee was unfortunately the end of the road for these innocent nobles.

Uncle Sam paid some white guys $2 a head to bury the frozen corpses a few days later. One can only speculate if this burial party came up with the lowest bid. It all came down for these cold, hungry people with ranks filled by many sick on 12/29/1890. I now recalled the chilled feeling that crept over me back in Deadwood's Saloon #10 as I studied a small photo of a white guy standing by a bunch of Native American things labeled "Relics from Wounded Knee." The SOB had stripped them of some of their remaining possessions and dignity.

I was taken aback and immediately felt light headed and sick on my stomach when my trusted guide told me, "Yes, the soldiers were firing from here where we are standing now." Why the grave diggers chose this spot remains a mystery. Maybe the ground was less frozen and easier to dig in than below where the corpses ended up. They found women and their children killed nearly 2 miles away as a result of pursuit by brave soldiers. My trusted guide and companion told me one woman ran with about 25 kids in tow to the left of where we were looking, but the soldiers cut them all down. Another account from witnesses recalled a group of small younger boys who were told if they surrendered would be treated well. They were all dispatched while trying to surrender.

No less than 20 soldiers received Congressional Medals of Honor for their heroism that day against this multitude of hostiles. What a ___ king disgrace! Sounds like camouflage for a cover up to me. To call this a battle was a mockery of history and justice.

Thank God and the Great Spirit for allowing 44 of the 51 wounded captive belligerents to survive their wounds to become living witnesses. Their accounts of the action seems to have been somewhat suppressed. Some did say a deaf Sioux who didn't understand English anyway refused to surrender his weapon, was wrestling with soldiers intent on taking it from him when young Sioux warriors threw the first rounds. Other accounts disclaim this and swore that the first shot rang out from the hill where the soldiers looked down.

Either way, if you come into my house and demand the only means I have of feeding or protecting my loved ones, I guarantee you that shots will ring out. I have a sneaky suspicion that Colonel Forsyth had the foresight to figure chances of this happening were a done deal long before he ordered his men to demand the Sioux weapons while he stood at the ready, no doubt in close proximity to his four Hotchkiss Cannons. I tried to find if Colonel Forsyth was one of the Medal of Honor recipients from this catastrophe which he commanded. My short search ended in vain as I figured, "What the hell." For the rest of his career, he remained in the service of his country moving up the ladder in rank, prestige, and honor. He may have lost all control of his men at Wounded Knee, but it was his decision to surround and disarm these so-called ruthless savages.

As I stood there above the dust left as a result of the wholesale slaughter of nearly 300, I thought of the irony of this book's title, "The End of the Road." Yellowknife, Northwest Territories, was your author's original intent for the name of this book. But, that plan took a backseat in the van when compared to where these fine, innocent, naive people stumbled upon their end of the road. I couldn't hear their screams but I could feel them.

I remained nauseated and light headed. Though standing beside my host and tour guide, his voice sounded far off. I heard him say that only survivors of survivors could be buried on this hill outside of the fence. He pointed out the graves of his parents. He said, "I will be buried next to them someday." It's hard to fathom survivors of survivors of Wounded Knee going off to fight for their country. I'm not sure I could do it.

I told my companion that I felt the need to apologize to him and all Native Americans for what had happened here as well as all such atrocities that took place in this conquest of sea to shining sea. Standing here as an absentee witness, it felt to me that Uncle Sam was still punishing these descendants for what we had perpetrated on their ancestors. Is that twisted or what? Was this the tail end of the cover up?

The guide replied after a prolonged silence that he blames nobody now for what happened here, but that he used to. To my utter shock, he then spilled his guts out to me and said that he had killed women and children in Afghanistan. If this was true, had what happened here well over a century ago been a spark for the taking of innocents in another distant land in the present?

Before I had recovered from the broadside hurled into me, he shook my hand, and disappeared down that hill after telling me that it was time for him to take some more medicine for his wounds.

Left alone, I said a prayer for all these people lying below my feet. I prayed that their death had come swift and whisked them away to a land of freedom, abundance, and peace as they had once shared briefly so long ago.

I had attempted to make this book light and jovial throughout my wanderings, but that became impossible to do with Wounded Knee. It's an abscess on our collective psyches that we cannot lance. It was a result of misguided hate, greed, revenge, and ignorance. Unfortunately, Wounded Knee would not be the first or the last annihilation of innocents on both sides of gun barrels. It would be an interesting study to research the lives of these soldiers as they made their way through life living with the images they couldn't erase that happened on that December day. It was way too late for second guesses.

With feelings of wanting to escape this place as soon as possible, I turned to make a beeline for the van. I found that I had not been alone. Standing on that hill with me were the two boys I'd given 5's to and the shy girl I'd initially brushed off. They had a fourth companion now. Not necessarily much older but a much taller boy wearing all black with a tee shirt emblazoned with a large number "6" in white.

Immediately embarrassed for my uncalled brushing off of the young shy princess who had tried to sell me a dream catcher, I hastily strode directly to her with renewed interest regarding her wares. With the same whisper like voice, but projected an octave or two higher while I gave her my undivided attention, she said her dream catchers were rare and not made by machines. Her aunt makes them one at a time and uses sage brush for the outer oval which she gathers locally. With the three boys creeping non-threateningly closer, I asked her, "How much?" She said in a flat whisper, "$20." I grabbed my chest feigning a heart attack and stumbled back a few steps while the three onlookers howled in merriment. She didn't break a smile.

I wanted at least to get a little smile or chuckle out of her, but she remained steadfast in her deadpan. Asking to examine them, I let her know that a sale was imminent. Her expression didn't change but she leaned in closer as if examining my examination. All three or four were well made, unique, and lovely. I asked her

PHOTO #9 - MY INSPIRATION - THE FOUR AMBASSADORS

which one she liked best. She shrugged her shoulders. I chose the one I liked best and it catches dreams in my home today, but mostly at night. I gave her a $20 bill without dickering or haggling. I could swear I heard a faint whispered, "Thank you" but it was difficult as the three witnesses were giving soft clapping in unison. To this day, I'm not sure what they were applauding; me, her, or the guarantee of four decent meals. I could now feel their gratitude and warmth. I was only after the warmth.

I ran back to them after heading to the van and requested their permissions to take their photo. One of the boys yelled, "OK." They lined up at their posts like silent child guardian protectors of an ugly truth that robbed their ancestors of life, liberty, and the pursuit of happiness.

Looking back on today, it all just came at me so fast. The guys in the old Chevy truck, the kids, my tipsy tour guide, my remorse for these people living and dead, and my feelings of guilt and sorrow. I was caught in a whirlwind being buffeted by emotions I did not want to carry. These emotions and feelings seemed to chase me and the van back out onto the highway. It was then that it dawned on me that I had not taken a photo of my cherished tour guide and had never asked the kids their names, and I never made the princess smile. But there was no way I could turn around and go back. The targets in this so called battle must have been struggling with similar feelings, fear, confusion, and anger before they were scooped up by death.

I did recall then that just before speeding back down through the same ruts and holes I had dodged coming up, I stopped by #6 and asked him what the "6" stood for. He quickly worked up a tremendous grin and shrugged his shoulders before I left, yet to realize that of the four, he was the only one who had asked for nothing.

It is high time for me to drift this long journey of 10,060 miles to an abrupt stop. Nothing of major note happened on the rest of my flight (in the van) home. If it did, it was grossly overshadowed by everything that grabbed me at Wounded Knee. I didn't realize it at the time but it dawned on me later, that I had run all the way home from Wounded Knee. It became a race to get home to Precious where I knew I would find goodness after losing it to Wounded Knee. That's Precious greeting me the instant I arrived back at her home. Now, I realize, this was the end of the road for me and with it came a happy ending.

Don't let this be the end of the road for you. I hope that it is only the beginning. Don't delay your bucket list. You're getting older every day. Go out with a bang or better still a bunch of bangs.

Since getting home, I did look up King Opessa's family tree. The best I could come up with was that he was probably Shawnee. Still considering willing my place back to the Shawnee, I searched for Shawnees in the state of Maryland. They're all gone. If I want to find Shawnees, I'll have to go out to Oklahoma. That's where their remnants were driven or removed to. Way back, the Shawnees lived in the Ohio Valley, Illinois, Pennsylvania, Maryland, and Georgia. Hopefully, the descendants in Oklahoma struck oil. I have their tribal address. I will pursue this further.

PHOTO #10 - PRECIOUS

Also since getting back home, I realized and welcomed that #6, the shy princess, and my two "5's" have become four of my new inspirational heroes and unwitting ambassadors, helping me to spread the word regarding the needs of scores of other kids like them trapped in poverty and need.

I want you to know that my four ambassadors live within the boundaries of the Pine Ridge Indian Reservation located in the poorest county in the United States. Of the six poorest counties in America, you'll find three in South Dakota - all homes to kids on Indian reservations. Come on people, Custer was the aggressor and none of these ambassadors or their families killed him. Did you know that Haiti has the lowest life expectancy in the Western Hemisphere with some Indian reservations posting a close second place. Men - 48; Women - 52.

Your author must come clean with you now and let the cat out of the bag. The entire reason for this work was to generate help from the fortunate to the less fortunate. I'm in no way rich but I'm filthy rich compared to these kids. Not just these kids. There are less fortunates for one reason or another everywhere you look if you're not wearing blinders.

Don't just go to the Washington Monument, Mt. Rushmore, Disneyland, Daytona, or Sturgis. Have your bucket list take you to a reservation or any place where there is need far beyond your own. If you possess a compassionate conscience, you will be moved to help. If you can't give monetarily, then give of your time. Try to make life easier for someone who has never had it as easy as you. There's more to rewards than rewards. Give it a try. Ambassador #6 never asked for anything but he needs all of us. He's earned it.

Please allow me to share with you one more unexplained happenstance just recently discovered. Karma continued to zip in and out of this work at will. A calendar recently arrived from Red Cloud Indian School smack dab on the Pine Ridge Indian Reservation. I wanted to see what day of the week my birthday would be falling on. Unbeknownst prior to the calendar's arrival, Indigenous Peoples' Day, since 1977, has been designated as the second Monday of October. We will be submitting this book for publication in 2022 and in that very year, Indigenous Peoples' Day just happens to fall on your author's date of birth. Tell me there's not some mysterious phenomena going on here working it's way through this pen. I felt its presence from the start. Could this be why Sitting Bull gently pushed and pulled and chose me for this journey from a litany of better and worthier potential souls. My hope is that he keeps on nudging me and when the time is right, nudges you too.

I must take leave of you now. You will be pleased to know that as a reward for finishing this book, those of you who scored low on any of the quizzes will be given blanket "C's." Should you buy the book, convince anyone else to buy the book, or make a donation to relieve any oppressed peoples or people with needs, we'll change your overall grade point average on your quizzes to A+.

As God (the Great Spirit) is my witness: I (the author) take this double dog dare pledge that 40% of the profits of this monumental work will go to Pine Ridge Indian Reservation with the Lion's Share going to needs in Wounded Knee, and that 40% of these same profits will go to St. Jude Children's Research Hospital in Tennessee. I think my four ambassadors would like that. The remaining 20% will go to any "Ends of the Roads" left in me or to some other cause I may have the privilege to champion.

See you, or better still, see you on the road or at the convention….

Huggs,

Ron

Yea, I know it's spelled wrong. I did it on purpose because I feel hugs are so important, they deserve two g's.

P.S. Find something to sink your heart into.

ACKNOWLEDGEMENTS

Without the assistance, patience, input, encouragement, drive, push, enlightenment, etc., by the following folks we wouldn't have gotten here. "Thank you" is almost too shallow but thank you.

- ◆ "Precious" — Bonnie Boswell — Mate of Mates, proof-reader, innate encourager, suggestions, my rock.
- ◆ Annie Hrezo — Initial editor, dear friend, buddy, Dead Bob's ex, and great cook.
- ◆ Alyssa Rowland — Quiet angel, seller of dreamcatchers, ambassador.
- ◆ Patric Rowland — #6, ambassador, go-to man.
- ◆ Note: Our two mystery ambassadors from Wounded Knee for some unknown reason, known but to them, elected not to be identified in this work. Hence, you now know the reason behind their faces being concealed. Should they change their minds in the future, I would welcome this and advocate for adjustments/updates in text and photo. You've found other faces blotted out in the text for similar reasons. The author felt that these folks' roles were of such significance and a gift to this work, they remain a part of it with name designations distorted also to ensure their anonymity.

- Laura Kaye — Post Mistress (retired), Wounded Knee, S.D. Help with names, addresses, guardians, etc.
- Shawna Browning — Post Mistress, Canada Post, Fort Resolution, N.W.T., Canada.
- Roberta Hazelton — Lead Hand, Canada Post, Yellowknife, N.W.T., Canada, people finder.
- Nathan McFarland — Nephew, suggestions, a positive force to be reckoned with, a great catch for Meredith.
- Meredith McFarland — Niece-in-law, suggestions, supreme transcriber, photo enhancer, a great catch for Nathan. To date, I still owe Mere some money. So, buy this book to help me pay her off if nothing else.
- Alix Locke — Cover design and artist.
- Sheredith Boore Heitzenrater — Steerage.
- Quinton Crowshoe — Head-Smashed-In Buffalo Jump marketing and events, Fort MacLeod, Alberta, Canada, people finder.
- Natasha Lee-Kaglik — Post Mistress, Canada Post, Fort Simpson, N.W.T., Canada, people finder.
- To the ghost Canada Post female employee in Yellowknife who was also a classic and unselfish people finder.
- Robert Piper (Living Bobbie) — Step stool breaker, tie-down instructor.
- Dead Bobbie

And lastly, Lord, let me never forget just what was given to me by all those creatures, human and otherwise, alive and not, who by happenstance bumped into a life on this path.

APPENDIX: PREP FOR CANADA TRIP

- ☑ Don't forget inner ear blue pills
- ☑ Rig up pop cans on front and back doors
- ☑ Get "Thief" sign up on doors
- ☑ Aluminum foil
- ☑ Stink pretty's for mosquitos
- ☑ Window cleaner
- ☑ Take big rat trap to catch small game
- ☑ Take rechargeable crank radio
- ☑ Bleach for bears
- ☑ Moth balls for bears
- ☑ St. Mary's River - Michigan and Sault Ste. Marie in Ontario - Hemingway said it's the best trout fishing in the world
- ☑ Peroxide/alcohol/crotch powder
- ☑ Little handsaw
- ☑ Swiss Army saw
- ☑ Gloves for mosquitoes
- ☑ Mosquito repellent
- ☑ 15-17 lb. test line for fishing
- ☑ Mosquito net for shitting

- ☑ Folding green camp chair
- ☑ Spare watch
- ☑ Oatmeal/raisins/cinnamon/almond meal/sweetener
- ☑ Powdered milk
- ☑ Clothespins/clothesline
- ☑ Camera x2 or +
- ☑ Extra vitamins
- ☑ Wire fishing leaders
- ☑ All Canada fishing lures
- ☑ Flies and fly rod
- ☑ Hard boiled eggs
- ☑ Take all extra bungees/rope in case of problems with tie downs
- ☑ Hide a key
- ☑ Folding shovel
- ☑ Epoxy
- ☑ Sylocone
- ☑ Extra belts
- ☑ Twistys
- ☑ Spare hose clamp
- ☑ Tire repair kit
- ☑ Tire pump
- ☑ Toolkit bag/flares
- ☑ Tailbone pillow
- ☑ Yellow Armageddon backpack
- ☑ Boomerang
- ☑ Brown overnight bag/nail clippers/tweezers
- ☑ Lubricated eye drops
- ☑ All medications

- ☑ Salt/pepper/ginger
- ☑ Nathan's surf reel
- ☑ Zebco
- ☑ Heavy reels
- ☑ Gum bands
- ☑ Rope
- ☑ Get Bonnie's email if phone can't reach her
- ☑ Magnifying glass
- ☑ Extra toilette paper
- ☑ Paper towels
- ☑ Plastic garbage bags
- ☑ Lint for fire starting
- ☑ Fire starting striker
- ☑ Wire
- ☑ Duct tape
- ☑ Toilette plunger for cleaning clothes
- ☑ Shitter bucket, lid, plastic bags
- ☑ 5 gallon bucket washing machine
- ☑ Hand towels
- ☑ Bath towels
- ☑ Bathing suit
- ☑ Funnels
- ☑ Little magnifying glasses above microwave
- ☑ Never take my real glasses in kayak without hooks on glasses
- ☑ Sunscreen
- ☑ Pipe for leverage to take lug nuts off
- ☑ Flip flops
- ☑ Don't forget meds in refrigerator

- ☑ Fillet knife
- ☑ Stink pretty's (dryer towels) for mosquitos
- ☑ Big clear plastic bags
- ☑ Clothes in basement
- ☑ Mushroom to Bonnie's
- ☑ Take onions out of fridge
- ☑ Socks (long and short)
- ☑ Calendar
- ☑ Breath mints
- ☑ Make sure fridge doors are closed
- ☑ Passport
- ☑ Big "JB" hatchet
- ☑ Snorkel and goggles
- ☑ Extra batteries, AA, AAA, etc.
- ☑ Ketchup/mustard/mayo
- ☑ Coffee
- ☑ Tequila
- ☑ Clean out veggies in fridge and take with me
- ☑ Cat food to Dianna
- ☑ Cat food to Dennis and Sandie
- ☑ Sun blind for van
- ☑ Crotch meds applicator from Mom or Bonnie
- ☑ Ivory soap
- ☑ Pee jugs
- ☑ Buttermilk ranch
- ☑ Aluminum foil
- ☑ Fishing boots
- ☑ Fishing shoes

- ☑ Water flowers before I go
- ☑ Don't forget maps
- ☑ Magnifying glass
- ☑ Blue flashlight off fridge
- ☑ Handheld lights from firehall
- ☑ Shut down H2O in basement
- ☑ Clothes in basement
- ☑ Make sure all windows are closed
- ☑ Cube steaks in fridge
- ☑ Dried veggie
- ☑ Beef jerky
- ☑ Soups
- ☑ Cereal
- ☑ Bug suit for mosquitos
- ☑ Cell phone
- ☑ Extra coffee
- ☑ Coca Cola / Tums
- ☑ Take my sign down in P.O.
- ☑ Locktite for bolts on car
- ☑ Pick up hydrochlorate
- ☑ Hot dogs
- ☑ Carrots
- ☑ Hi Bonnie - If you read this and I'm dead, I still love you. We had a good run.